MW00814946

RAILWAY STEAMSHIPS OF ONTARIO

RAILWAY STEAMSHIPS OF ONTARIO

Dana Ashdown

THE BOSTON MILLS PRESS

Passenger services were seldom scheduled for the late navigation season due to the unpredictable weather encountered, especially storms. This photograph is a case in point, showing *Algoma*, completely covered in ice, arriving at Port Arthur (Thunder Bay) on 24 November 1884. — *OA S13202*

Canadian Cataloguing in Publication Data

Ashdown, Dana William
Railway steamships of Ontario, 1850-1950

Includes index.

Bibliography: p.
ISBN 0-919783-80-5

1. Ship-railroads - Ontario - History. 2. Steamboat-lines - Ontario - History.
3. Shipping - Ontario - History. I. Title.

HE635.Z706 1988 385'.77'09713 C88-090403-8

Dedicated
to
B.M.A. & S.W.A.

Published by:
THE BOSTON MILLS PRESS
132 Main Street
Erin, Ontario N0B 1T0
(519) 833-2407 Fax: (519) 833-2195

American Association for State and Local History Award of Merit

Winners of the Heritage Canada Communications Award

Design by John Denison
Cover by Gill Stead
Edited by Noel Hudson, Guelph
Typography by Lexigraf, Tottenham
Printed by Ampersand, Guelph

The publisher wishes to acknowledge the financial assistance and encouragement of The Canada Council, the Ontario Arts Council and the Office of the Secretary of State.

CONTENTS

7 Preface

9 Acknowledgements

11 CHAPTER ONE
Before the Railways and Beyond

27 CHAPTER TWO
The Transit Trade

61 CHAPTER THREE
The Portage Railways

87 CHAPTER FOUR
The River Ferries

127 CHAPTER FIVE
The Iron Ore Carriers

151 CHAPTER SIX
The Coal Boats

177 CHAPTER SEVEN
Navigation Companies Large & Small

211 CHAPTER EIGHT
The Lake Superior Routes

263 List of Railway Shipping

279 Bibliography

283 Index

Keewatin as seen around 1930. — *OA Acc. 9254*
S14294

PREFACE

While much has been written on the history of Ontario's railways, the story behind their involvement with steamships and lake shipping has gone relatively untold. This volume attempts to correct this oversight by identifying and briefly documenting the various shipping enterprises carried on during the first century of steam railway operations (1850 to 1950) within the province. Not overlooked are some of the major steamship routes run in connection with the railway companies, as well as references to more recent developments and the American railway steamship lines.

In the pages that follow, the story of Ontario's railway shipping activities is related, with each chapter covering a particular aspect of steamer operation. For example, in the fourth chapter, the railway ferry operations across the St. Lawrence, Niagara, Detroit and St. Clair rivers are highlighted, while the eighth chapter covers the passenger steamers operated between southern Ontario and Lake Superior. Within this framework, the steamer operations are individually described following a loose chronological and/or geographical order as befits the situation.

In avoiding repetition of ship dimensions within the text, and for the sake of providing a quick reference, key vessel statistics have been placed at the rear, with only gross tonnages used regularly within the text as a basis upon which to compare the overall size of the individual vessels. The three principal dimensions reported are gross tonnage, length and beam. *Gross tonnage* is a measurement of the total volume of space contained within a ship as expressed in tons. This volume includes non-revenue-earning space such as crew quarters, engine rooms and boiler rooms. *Length* refers to the overall hull length, while *beam* refers to the actual width of the hull, as opposed to the overall width of the ship. This is an important fact to remember, particularly with regard to side-paddlewheelers, whose total width over the paddle boxes and guards could be almost double that of the hull! Two dimensions (among the many) not used are depth of hull and draught, since these terms can sometimes be misleading. Please also note that all dimensions given are imperial; thus, length and beam are in feet (fractions of a foot have been rounded up or down) and tonnages, unless otherwise specified, are in short tons (one short ton equalling 2,000 pounds).

As a general point regarding illustrations, the author has attempted to present at least one photograph or drawing of every pre-1950 railway-owned ship identified, along with a selection of photographs representing related shipping, shipping facilities, docks, etc. In many cases, however, either no photographs were ever taken of a vessel (especially the early ships) or no photographs have yet come to light. Photographic quality also presented some problems. Ideally, only the sharpest and clearest pictures should be used in a book, since these illustrations are easily reproduced and readily understood. If that were the rule, though, many rare and interesting photographs would have to be omitted. Therefore, the author has chosen to include a number of "marginal" photographs, if for no other reason than they represent the only picture available at the time of writing.

This volume is not, nor should it be considered to be, a definitive history of railway shipping in Ontario. Rather, it is hoped that through the identification of individual vessels, shipping facilities and companies, a greater degree of awareness will be achieved and, as a result, encourage others to carry on with further, more detailed research.

D.W.A.
June 1986

The *Père Marquette 12* passing under the Ambassador Bridge, seen from the Detroit side, in the late 1940s, heading for Windsor. — *UBL No. 8798*

ACKNOWLEDGEMENTS

Without the many individuals and organizations who provided information and photographs, this volume would not have been possible. The author would like to express his appreciation and thanks to the following:

Archives of Ontario, Toronto; Charles A. Armour, Dalhousie University Library, Halifax, Nova Scotia; Bruce J. Beacock, Simcoe County Archives, Minesing, Ontario; J.G. Beldham, Toronto, Hamilton & Buffalo Railway, Hamilton; Arthur M. Bixby, Sr., Roanoke Chapter, National Railway Historical Society, Roanoke, Virginia; R.W. Brooks, Ontario Northland Transportation Commission, North Bay; Margaret Campbell, Public Archives of Nova Scotia, Halifax; Patricia Carter, Huron County Pioneer Museum, Goderich, Ontario; Alice C. Dalligan, Burton Historical Collection, Detroit Public Library, Detroit, Michigan; R.R. Firestone, Bessemer & Lake Erie Railroad Company, Monroeville, Pennsylvania; Jane Foster, Lennox & Addington County Museum, Napanee, Ontario; Louise Frechette and Elizabeth Krug, National Photography Collection, Public Archives of Canada, Ottawa; Betty Fudge, Hamilton Public Library; Susan Gallant, Canadian National Railways, Winnipeg, Manitoba; Gail Herman, Deseronto Public Library, Deseronto, Ontario; Jamie Hunter, Huronia Museum, Midland, Ontario; Dave Jones, Canadian Pacific Archives, Montreal; Lori Komus, Cargill Limited, Winnipeg, Manitoba; Nora Logan, Lakehead Harbour Commission, Thunder Bay, Ontario; John H. Lutman, D.B. Weldon Library, University of Western Ontario, London, Ontario; Mary E. Maclean, Cobourg Public Library, Cobourg, Ontario; Nada Martel-Warner, Ontario Hydro Archives, Etobicoke, Ontario; Sharon McDonald, Peterborough Museum & Archives, Peterborough, Ontario; Metropolitan Toronto Library; Art Millien, Chesapeake & Ohio Historical Society, Grand Haven, Michigan; Ontario Arts Council, Toronto; G.G. Parsons, Goderich Elevators Limited, Goderich, Ontario; Marcia Poirier, St. Catharines Historical Museum, St. Catharines, Ontario; Connie Romani, Canadian National Photographic Library, Montreal; Herman Sass, Ph.D., Buffalo & Erie County Historical Society, Buffalo, New York; J.J. Sjoblom, Steamship Historical Society of America Collection, University of Baltimore Library, Baltimore, Maryland; Stanley G. Triggs, Notman Photographic Archives, Montreal; T.J. Tronrud, Thunder Bay Historical Museum Society, Thunder Bay, Ontario; James Wilson, Steamship Historical Society of America, Staten Island, New York.

To the many others who aided with comments and suggestions, thank you.

Lastly, the author would like to thank The Boston Mills Press for publishing this work, and his parents for putting up with the mess.

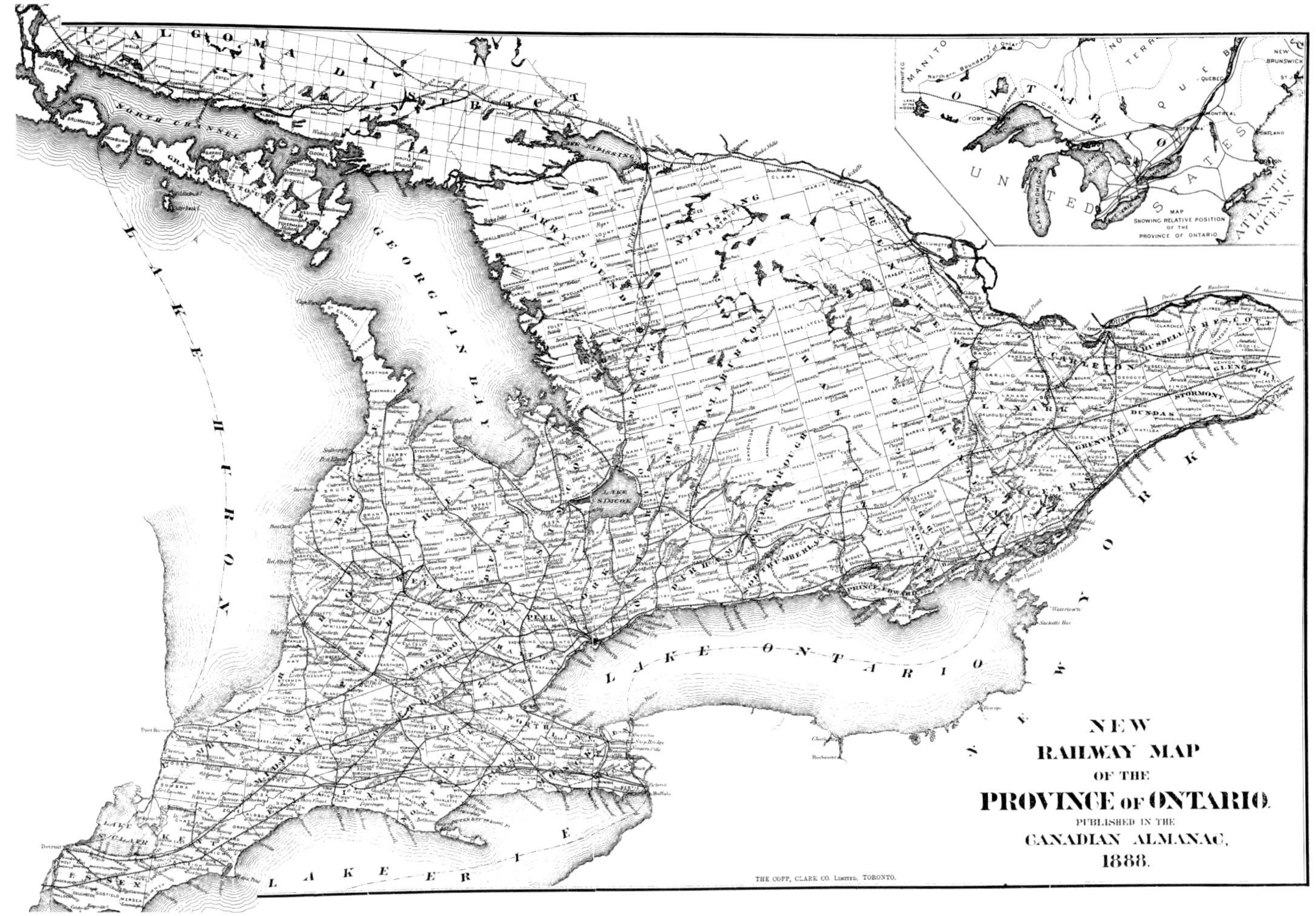
NEW
RAILWAY MAP
OF THE
PROVINCE OF ONTARIO
PUBLISHED IN THE
CANADIAN ALMANAC,
1888.
THE COPP, CLARK CO. LIMITED, TORONTO.
LAKE ONTARIO
LAKE ERIE
LAKE HURON
GEORGIAN BAY
LAKE SIMCOE
ALGOMA DISTRICT
NORTH CHANNEL
NEW YORK
MAP SHOWING RELATIVE POSITION OF THE PROVINCE OF ONTARIO
ATLANTIC OCEAN
UNITED STATES
NEW BRUNSWICK

— OA

I

BEFORE THE RAILWAYS AND BEYOND

Early Navigation on the Great Lakes

In the beginning, the Indian canoe was the only vessel to venture out onto the waters of the Great Lakes. That was before European settlement, when life was simpler and the birchbark canoe was the only means of long-distance travel. Then came the French and the fur traders, who quickly adopted the canoe as their own. Extending their influence far into the continent, the legend of the *courier du bois* was born.

It was the French explorer LaSalle who changed the future of shipping on the Great Lakes. Under a commission to explore the far reaches of North America, he built the first sailing vessel to ply the lakes. Christened the *Frontenac,* she was a ten-ton schooner constructed in 1678 near the present site of Kingston. In November of that year, LaSalle set sail, only to be stopped by the mighty Niagara Falls. Undaunted, he wintered there until the following spring, when he built his second ship, in which he would explore the reaches above the cataract. This was the ill-fated *Griffin,* launched in May 1679. At 60 tons she was much larger than the *Frontenac* and, armed and loaded with supplies, headed west, eventually to reach the head of Lake Huron. In September 1679 *Griffin* headed back to Niagara with her hold filled with furs. She never reached her destination. *Griffin* disappeared without a trace.

While it would be some years before sail returned to the upper lakes, shipping continued on the St. Lawrence River and Lake Ontario.

On the St. Lawrence, a long, pointed, flat-bottomed boat called a "bateau" was popular. Able to pass through the small locks and canals built around the treacherous rapids, the bateaux relied on the brawn and skill of the boatmen to pilot them along. Later the bateau would be superseded by the "Durham" boat, capable of carrying ten times the load of the bateau but still reliant on manpower, although animals were often employed to pull the boats through the stiff currents around the rapids.

Following the American Revolution, shipping on the Great Lakes began to pick up, especially on Lake Ontario, along whose shores grew the farms and settlements of the Loyalists, from Kingston to Niagara. For most of the year, the lake was the only way to travel; roads were few and far between, and most of the time, mud, potholes and fallen trees made them impassable. Only in winter, when snow covered the roads, could any speed or comfort be attained. To the early traveller, those early sailing vessels must have appeared luxurious in comparison with the hazards and crude vehicles of the road.

Let us not forget the shipment of goods and produce. The first real merchant ship on Lake Ontario, the *York,* was built at Niagara in 1792. (It would only be a matter of time until this type of ship would be seen throughout the Great Lakes.)

It was 1797 before the sailing ship appeared on any of the lakes above Lake Ontario. That first ship, the schooner *Washington,* was built at the present-day city of Erie, Pennsylvania, on Lake

Frontenac, shown here from a sketch drawn in 1827, was typical of most early steamships in that she was essentially a steam-powered sailing ship. She holds the distinction of being the first Canadian steamship to operate on the Great Lakes. — *Ontario Archives S13031*

Ploughboy, seen here at the Northern Railway dock at Collingwood in the late 1860s, was but one of many ships displaced by the railways. Built at Chatham in 1851, *Ploughboy* originally linked Chatham with the communities of Amherstburg, Ontario, and Detroit, Michigan. With the opening of the Great Western Railway in 1854, her route became redundant and she was subsequently placed on Lake Huron, serving Canadian ports as far away as Owen Sound and Collingwood on Georgian Bay. *Ploughboy* burned at Detroit in 1876. — *OA Acc.14996-49*

Erie. By 1798, however, she was sold to Canadians, who hauled her down to Lake Ontario, where she sailed under the British flag as the *Lady Washington*.

Steam navigation in the region made its appearance in 1809 when the steamship *Dalhousie* was launched at Prescott for service on the St. Lawrence River. But it was not until the years following the War of 1812 that steamers were built for service on the Great Lakes. Whether it was Canada or the United States who built the first steamship on the lakes is a matter of some debate.

Between 1816 and 1817 both countries were engaged in the construction of steamships. At Kingston, the 170-foot, 700-ton *Frontenac* was launched in September 1816. After her maiden voyage the following June, she took up a weekly route between Prescott and Kingston in the east and York (Toronto) and Niagara at the west end of Lake Ontario. The *Frontenac* later burned at Niagara after 20 years of faithful service.

The Americans weren't standing still. At Sackett's Harbour, New York, the steamer *Ontario* was built. At 110 feet and 240 tons, she was much smaller than the *Frontenac*. Perhaps it was because of her size that on her first voyage, in April 1817, she suffered serious damage to her paddle wheels, bearings and paddle boxes when she encountered rough water on Lake Ontario. She was, however, very much an experiment, being built to a design of Robert Fulton, Hudson River steamboat builder, with a grant from Fulton's heirs. *Ontario* later operated regularly between Lewiston, on the Niagara River, and Ogdensburg, opposite Prescott on the St. Lawrence, calling in at ports along the American shore of Lake Ontario every ten days until 1832, when she was scrapped at Oswego, New York.

Following the successful introduction of steamships on Lake Ontario, the Americans launched the *Walk-in-the-Water* at Black Rock, New York, in May 1818. She was the first steamer on Lake Erie. In many ways comparable to her Lake Ontario contemporaries, she had a length of 135 feet and weighed in at 383 tons gross. But despite this, *Walk-in-the-Water* tended to be underpowered, especially against strong currents such as those encountered on the Niagara River. Her short career took her as far as Lake Huron, though her usual route was between Black Rock and Detroit. It was in regular service that she was wrecked off Buffalo, New York, in November 1821.

The screw propeller, designed by Swedish-born engineer John Ericson, came to the Great Lakes in 1841. Able to give ships the speed and handling that paddle wheels couldn't provide on open water, the first steamer to use it was the 140-ton *Vandalia*, built at Oswego, New York, on Lake Ontario. After her maiden voyage in the late fall, she travelled to Buffalo in the following spring of 1842 by way of the Welland Canal, making a great impression on the public. By the 1860s one half of all steamships on the Great Lakes would be "propellers." In terms of the number of vessels, steamships would overtake sail by the mid-1880s.

The Canal Age

Moving goods and people by water during the 1600s and 1700s was the most convenient method of shipping and travelling in an age without steam trains and without good roads. The one problem was that water transport was only available on natural waterways — oceans, lakes and rivers — that possessed a depth suited to the passage of vessels. If, however, shallow water prevented passage, an alternative had to be found. The earliest canals, therefore, usually involved little more than dredging a channel in an existing river deep enough to permit the passage of a canal boat. At rapids, dredging seldom solved the problem, and unless a portage around them was an acceptable solution, it then became necessary to dig a canal around the rapids wide enough and deep enough to float a boat in.

Other than the manual work of actually digging the canal, the engineering was relatively simple. Simple, that is, providing that the drop in land elevation that caused the rapids in the first place was minor. If not, the new canal would be unable to provide the depth of water necessary for the passage of any boat, and that is assuming that the drop was not so great as to cause the canal simply to become another rapid.

If the drop in land elevation became too great, it then became necessary to control the water levels in the canal itself, and that could only be accomplished through the use of a fixed dam or a lift lock — a section of the canal divided off with gates at either end, thus creating a chamber in which the water level could be altered without altering the canal level outside the lock. As opposed to the dam, which prevented passage, the lock, through its gates, formed a "movable" dam which permitted the passage of vessels. The most important asset of the canal lock was its ability to control water levels and permit passage without complicated technical means.

Once the technology of canal and lock construction had been established, it was a simple matter to build canals across areas where no natural water courses existed.

The development of the modern canal took place in England, spread quickly throughout Europe and eventually reached North America, where numerous canal projects, large and small, were proposed and/or undertaken.

One of the greatest canal projects undertaken in North America during the first half of the last century was the construction of the Erie Canal (also known as the New York State Barge Canal) between Buffalo, New York, on Lake Erie, and the Hudson River at Albany, which was navigable to New York City. The first proposals for the Erie Canal were made as early as 1768, but it was not until 1810 that anything concrete was formulated.

Actual work on the canal began in 1817, with the middle section of the canal between Utica and Montezuma being the first to be opened in July 1820, followed by the eastern section from Utica to Albany in October 1823, and finally the western section from Montezuma to Buffalo in October 1825, making a total length of 363 miles between Buffalo and Albany, or 513 miles including the length of the Hudson River to New York. Forming a new American route between the Atlantic and the Great Lakes, the canal incorporated 83 locks, 90 feet by 15 feet with a depth of 4 feet, allowing the passage of barges of up to 76 tons, carrying a maximum load of 100 tons of goods. Additional branches were later built to Oswego on Lake Ontario, to Lake Champlain, and to Seneca and Cayuga lakes.

It did not take long before traffic on the Erie began to exceed the capacity of the canal, and in 1836 the work of enlarging the waterway was started. Due to a lack of funds, construction was halted between 1843 and 1850, and it was not until 1862 that the work was completed. As a result, the length of the canal was reduced by 14 miles and the total number of locks, which now measured 110 feet by 18 feet by 7 feet deep, was decreased to 72. The end result was that 210-ton barges measuring 98 feet by 17½ feet, with a capacity of 240 tons (or approximately 8,000 bushels of grain), could now pass through the canal.

Though the barges were originally drawn by horses or mules, after the opening of the second canal in 1862, efforts at developing commercially successful self-propelled barges were made, culminating with the introduction of steam barges and tugs during the mid-1870s. A single tug was able to haul up to four barges at one time, with a total cargo of 900 tons. Until 1895, however, all freight to or from Lake Erie ports had to be transshipped at Buffalo. This problem was partially overcome in 1895 when the Cleveland Steel Canal Boat Company revolutionized transportation on the Erie Canal by building a flotilla of steel canal boats consisting of one steamer and five unpowered barges capable of plying the open waters of Lake Erie. The boats of that company formed a through line from Cleveland, Ohio, to New York.

In 1896 the Erie Canal carried 2,742,438 tons of freight, over twice that carried by the Welland Canal, but after the turn of the century, the Erie gradually lost its competitiveness to the railways and the Welland, a trend in regards to the railways that had its roots back in the canal reconstruction days of the 1850s, when the railways running east out of Buffalo were becoming established. Nevertheless, the Erie Canal did much to boost the prominence of Buffalo as a lake port.

The construction of the Welland Canal between Lakes Ontario and Erie (of which more will be said in chapter three) was undertaken between 1825 and 1829, and when completed between Port Dalhousie and Port Robinson on the Welland River, the canal contained 32 wooden locks measuring a minimum of 110 feet by 22 feet by 8 feet deep. Thus, lake-going ships of up to 100 feet in length and of up to 165 gross tons could pass through the canal carrying loads of up to 5,000 bushels of grain. This first canal was further extended between 1831 and 1833 to Port Colborne on Lake Erie, adding an additional eight locks and making the total length of the Welland 27½ miles.

As with the Erie Canal, traffic on the Welland soon outpaced its capacity. In 1841 the work of rebuilding the canal was commenced, and in 1851 the "second" Welland Canal was completed.

During those ten years, all of the original locks were replaced with 27 of stone, measuring a minimum of 150 feet by 26½ feet by 10 feet deep, thereby permitting the passage of ships up to 142½ feet long with a width no greater than 26¼ feet, carrying up to 400 tons or 20,000 to 23,000 bushels of grain.

By the late 1860s the canal was again too small and work on enlarging the Welland was carried out between 1871 and 1887, resulting in the elimination of one lock and a little over one mile of canal. When the "third" Welland Canal was finished, the minimum lock size was 270 feet by 45 feet by 14 feet deep. Now 262-foot ships grossing up to 1,800 tons (often called "canalers") could pass through the waterway with loads of 3,000 tons or 75,000 to 80,000 bushels of grain.

Following the completion of the Welland Canal reconstruction of the 1870s and 1880s, there was a significant change in the nature of shipping through the waterway. The following figures show the number of loaded ships that passed down through the Welland in 1870:[1]

		Number	Aggregate Gross Tonnage
Canadian Steamers		— 1,199	104,100
Canadian Sailing Vessels		— 2,657	487,474
	Total	— 3,856	591,574 tons
American Steamers		— 878	271,243
American Sailing Vessels		— 2,006	494,300
	Total	— 2,884	765,543 tons
Total Steamers		— 2,077	375,343
Total Sailing Vessels		— 4,663	981,774
	Grand Total	— 6,740	1,357,117 tons
Average Steamer Gross Tonnage			— 181 tons
Average Sailing Vessel Gross Tonnage			— 211 tons
Average Vessel Gross Tonnage			— 201 tons

The fact that sailing vessels passing down through the canal were on average larger than the steamers is a significant factor. Within two decades there was a considerable turnaround in these numbers due to the enlarging of the canal, as the following 1890 figures prove:[2]

		Number	Aggregate Gross Tonnage
Canadian Steamers		— 342	110,056
Canadian Sailing Vessels		— 443	117,400
	Total	— 785	227,456 tons
American Steamers		— 202	204,542
American Sailing Vessels		— 142	50,622
	Total	— 344	255,164 tons
Total Steamers		— 544	314,598
Total Sailing Vessels		— 585	168,022
	Grand Total	— 1,129	482,620 tons
Average Steamer Gross Tonnage			— 578 tons
Average Sailing Vessel Gross Tonnage			— 287 tons
Average Vessel Gross Tonnage			— 427 tons

Steamer tonnage rose 219 percent to an average of 578 gross tons, while sailing vessels rose only 36 percent to an average of 287 gross tons. Not only did the average size of vessels in the canal rise, but within two decades the size of the steamers rose to almost double that of sailing vessels, and in 1891 the actual number of loaded steamers surpassed that of sailing vessels.

Another interesting comparison can be made by examining the above figures in relation to table 1-1, which shows freight tonnages for the canal from 1872 to 1896. In 1872 it took 6,063 ships to carry 1.3 million tons of freight through the Welland. In 1890 only 2,885 vessels were required to move one million tons. It therefore took fewer than half the vessels in 1890 to move almost the same freight tonnage as it took in 1872, noting as well that not all of the ships were loaded.

Another point worth noting is not only the number of American vessels using the canal but their tonnage as well. The American ships tended to be fewer in number but larger than their Canadian counterparts. Furthermore, the American ships tended to carry a larger portion of the traffic through the canal. In 1892, for instance, of the 955,554 tons carried through, 685,348 tons consisted of eastbound through freight, with Canadian ships carrying 245,739 tons and American ships carrying 420,527 tons. Westbound, 270,206 tons were carried through, 22,267 tons by Canadian ships and 241,413 tons by American ships.

In 1913 work on enlarging the canal was again undertaken to accommodate the larger freighters being built on the upper lakes. Owing to the outbreak of World War I, completion of the project was delayed until 1932, when the 27½-mile "fourth" Welland Canal of today was opened. From the 26 locks of the third canal, hydraulic engineers eliminated all but eight, with these new locks measuring 820 feet by 80 feet by 30 feet deep, thus permitting passage of ships measuring up to 730 feet, with gross tonnages of up to 28,000 tons. Due to navigation difficulties on the section from Thorold through St. Catharines to Port Dalhousie on Lake Ontario, a new channel was dug to Port Weller, east of Port Dalhousie.

Throughout its history the Welland Canal has tended to soon become "undersized" in relation to the Great Lakes ships passing through it, though the present Welland system has fared better than its predecessors.

Another bottleneck in the Great Lakes system has been the St. Lawrence River canals between Prescott and Montreal. From the 1890s until the opening of the St. Lawrence Seaway in 1959, the locks on this system, built to the standards of the third Welland Canal, allowed only the small, canaler-type Great Lakes freighters to pass down to Montreal, with the resulting loss of Montreal-bound lake traffic (especially grain) to the railways at either Port Colborne or Prescott.

Of the other major canal systems on the Great Lakes, only the ship canals at Sault Ste. Marie have had as great an impact on lake shipping. The first attempt at building a ship canal around the St. Mary's Rapids was made by the Americans when a one-mile canal with two locks, 350 feet by 70 feet by 12 feet deep, was opened in 1855, thereby permitting vessels to pass up to Lake Superior. This important canal was further enlarged during the 1870s, and in 1881 a new lock, 515 feet by 80 feet by 16 feet deep, superseded the older locks. The increasing size of the ships using the lock resulted in the opening of an 800 foot by 100 foot by 21-foot-deep lock in 1896 on the site of the original 1855 locks. By 1919 two new locks were built, measuring 1,350 feet by 80 feet by 23 feet deep. The 1881 lock was replaced in 1943 by an 800 foot by 80 foot by 31-foot-deep lock, while the 1896 lock was replaced in 1968 by a 1,200-foot by 110-foot by 32-foot lock.

Due to congestion at the American locks in the late 1880s, the Canadian government built its own lock at Sault Ste. Marie, Ontario, to handle Canadian steamers (especially those of the Canadian Pacific Railway), as well as American ones, and to ensure the passage of Canadian ships to Lake Superior should a political crisis cause the Americans to refuse the passage of Canadian ships, as had happened during the first Canadian Northwest Rebellion.

The Canadian canal was opened in 1895 when the *Majestic* of the Great Northern Transit Company passed through on 7 September with 700 passengers on board. The Canadian lock measured 900 feet by 60 feet by 20 feet deep, and it is still in place. When it was built, up to three "large" ships could be handled at one time.

Linking Lakes Ontario and Erie, the Welland Canal was by its nature a busy waterway as this view of Port Dalhousie, its Lake Ontario terminal, attests. The original Welland Railway elevator is visible to the right, as is the steamer *Garden City* at the bottom right. The canal's Lake Ontario entrance can be seen at the centre-left along with the ship's coaling stage. Even though steamships abound in this early 1900s view, sail is still in evidence with the schooner tied up at the left of the Lake Ontario entry. — *OA Acc.12026-247*

The only other canals of any major importance in Ontario are the Murray Canal near Trenton, the Rideau Canal from Kingston to Ottawa, and the Trent-Severn System from Trenton to Georgian Bay by way of Peterborough and Lake Simcoe. With respect to the railways, these canals had little influence commercially, and today operate as waterways for pleasure craft and tourists, in which role they are probably more successful.

The Influence of the Railways

The coming of the railway had a deep impact on the development of shipping in the Great Lakes region, just as it encouraged the spread of population away from the waterways and made it possible for the vast inland areas to be settled and exploited. The railways forced the shipping companies into the rationalization of their fleets, such that rather than becoming weaker, the shipping lines became stronger as they gradually moved into areas in which they could successfully compete. As will be seen in the chapters that follow, once the railway companies and the ship owners agreed to co-operate and complement each other, there was more than enough business for all. This volume focuses on the railways' shipping ventures.

Railway Harbours

Dozens of Ontario harbours became "railway harbours" following the construction of the various railway lines to the water's edge and this volume would not be complete without at least a listing of these ports. Included in the following list are a few short notes to put the harbours into perspective, with the harbours listed by geographical location — i.e. according to the body of water on which they are situated — and including a short list of American railway harbours at the end of each section.

a) St. Lawrence River & Lake Ontario Ports

Coteau Landing, Quebec — Established as a railway harbour by the largely Ontario-based Canada Atlantic Railway in 1882, the car ferry *Canada Atlantic Transfer* linked the railway on either shore until a bridge was built. The Canada Atlantic later built a half-million-bushel grain elevator here for transferring grain from Depot Harbour into barges for Montreal.

Prescott, Ontario — First served by the Bytown & Prescott Railway (St. Lawrence & Ottawa Railway) in the 1850s, the port later saw the establishment of a car ferry service to Ogdensburg, New York, first for the Grand Trunk and later for the Canadian Pacific and New York Central lines. The harbour, because of its position above the St. Lawrence rapids, was also an important grain transfer point between the larger Great Lakes ships and the railways and smaller canal-type ships and barges. Lumber was also transferred from Prescott to Ogdensburg.

Brockville, Ontario — The Brockville & Ottawa Railway reached Brockville harbour by way of a tunnel under the town, opened in 1860. A car ferry service operated to Morristown, New York, during the 1870s and 1880s, but it was largely replaced by the Prescott car ferries.

Gananoque, Ontario — The Thousand Islands Railway linked the Grand Trunk Railway with the town of Gananoque and with the St. Lawrence River steamers.

Kingston, Ontario — A busy lakeport from the early days of lake shipping, Kingston was first served by the Grand Trunk on a branch opened in the early 1860s and later on by the Kingston & Pembroke Railway.

Deseronto, Ontario — Deseronto was controlled by the Rathbun family, who owned several lumber-related industries there in the late 1800s and early 1900s. The Rathbuns built the Bay of Quinte Railway in 1881 to provide a link with the Grand Trunk Railway at Deseronto Junction, and later built the Kingston, Napanee & Western Railway. Through the Rathbuns' Deseronto Navigation Company, freight and passenger connections were made with a number of ports on the Bay of Quinte, Lake Ontario, and the St. Lawrence River.

Belleville, Ontario — This harbour was first served by the Grand Junction Railway, but it was not an important railway port.

Trenton, Ontario — The Central Ontario Railway perhaps had the greatest influence of the railways which passed through Trenton, but by and large there was little interaction between the railway and shipping interests at the harbour.

Weller's Bay, Ontario — The Central Ontario Railway built an ore dock on this Lake Ontario natural harbour in the 1880s. A planned railway coal dock was never constructed.

Cobourg, Ontario — During the 1860s and 1870s, the Cobourg, Peterborough & Marmora Railway shipped iron ore through this harbour. From 1907 until 1950, the car ferries *Ontario No. 1* and *Ontario No. 2* linked the Grand Trunk and Canadian National railways with Charlotte (Rochester), New York.

Port Hope, Ontario — First served by the Port Hope, Lindsay & Beaverton Railway, later reincorporated as the Midland Railway, the harbour was controlled by the Port Hope Harbour & Wharf Company, founded in 1829. The company was purchased by the town in 1852, and in 1864 control of the harbour was acquired by the railway.

Whitby (or Port Whitby), Ontario — The Port Whitby & Port Perry Railway was built north from Whitby to Port Perry and was completed by 1873. The railway was later extended to Lindsay.

Toronto, Ontario — Possibly the most important harbour in Ontario from about 1850 until World War I, every railway that has been built into or out of Toronto has tried to gain access to the harbour. The Northern Railway was probably the most important of the early railways serving the harbour, followed by the Grand Trunk.

Hamilton, Ontario — The status of Hamilton harbour was greatly improved by the Great Western Railway, who established headquarters in the city. The Hamilton & Northwestern Railway, built later, also helped boost tonnage through the port, although not to the extent of the Great Western. Hamilton's current harbour tonnage, however, is the product of the steel mills, a trend started in the early years of this century.

Port Dalhousie, Ontario — The northern terminus of the original Welland Canal until superseded by Port Weller in 1932, Port Dalhousie was also the northern terminus of the Welland Railway and the electric Niagara, St. Catharines & Toronto Railway. For years, Port Dalhousie and Toronto were connected by passenger steamers.

Niagara, Ontario — One of the oldest and most historic towns in the province, Niagara (or Niagara-on-the-Lake) was the Lake Ontario terminus of the Erie & Niagara Railway and for years was served by the Niagara Navigation Company's steamers for Toronto.

American Harbours — American harbours served by rail along the St. Lawrence River and Lake Ontario have included Ogdensburg, Morristown, Clayton, Cape Vincent, Oswego, Sodus Point, Fair Haven, Charlotte (Port of Rochester) and Lewiston. All are in New York State.

b) Niagara River & Lake Erie Ports

Chippawa, Ontario — Now part of the town of Niagara Falls, this Niagara River port was once the transfer point for goods from Lake Erie bound for Lake Ontario by way of the early horse-powered Erie & Ontario Railway.

The design of the modern Great Lakes freighter dates back to the end of the last century when the need to carry bulk cargoes such as grain, coal and iron ore cheaply and efficiently became paramount. The *City of London* shown here is representative of the early freighters, of which many were constructed of wood as in the case with *City of London,* and even more of steel or iron. Despite the fact that freighters on the upper lakes grew rapidly in length, smaller steamers such as the *City of London* often found years of useful employment running through the Welland and St. Lawrence Canals where only the smaller ships were able to pass. — *Public Archives of Canada PA-144696*

Fort Erie, Ontario — Transfer ferries once linked the Buffalo & Lake Huron Railway here with Buffalo, New York, across the water, until the Grand Trunk opened the International Bridge between Bridgeburg (Fort Erie) and Black Rock (Buffalo) in 1871.

Port Colborne, Ontario — Technically the second (or even third) southern terminus of the Welland Canal, Port Colborne was first served by the Welland Railway.

Port Maitland, Ontario — As a railway harbour, Port Maitland owes its development to the Toronto, Hamilton & Buffalo Railway. The company once operated the car ferry *Maitland No. 1* from this port to Ashtabula, Ohio.

Port Dover, Ontario — The Hamilton & Port Dover and the Port Dover & Lake Huron railways reached Port Dover in 1878 and 1875 respectively, and as Grand Trunk constituents, gave that railway control of the harbour. Port Dover was the original Canadian car ferry terminal of the United States & Ontario Steam Navigation Company of Conneaut, Ohio.

Port Burwell, Ontario — Reached by a branch of the Canadian Pacific early in this century, the car ferry *Ashtabula* of the Pennsylvania-Ontario Transportation Company provided a link with Ashtabula, Ohio, until the 1950s.

Port Stanley, Ontario — Served by the London & Port Stanley Railway from the 1850s, control of the harbour was transferred to the railway on 1 September 1859. During the first three decades of the century, the ferries of the Marquette & Bessemer Dock & Navigation Company ran from here to Conneaut, Ohio.

Erieau, Ontario — First served by the Erie & Huron Railway, this harbour became another terminus for the Marquette & Bessemer car ferries in 1899.

American Harbours — Black Rock (Buffalo), Buffalo and Dunkirk, New York; Erie, Pennsylvania; Conneaut, Ashtabula, Fairport, Cleveland, Lorain, Sandusky and Toledo, Ohio.

c) Detroit River & St. Clair River Harbours

Amherstburg, Ontario — This was the original terminus for Canada Southern Railway and Michigan Central Railroad car ferries between Ontario and Grosse Isle, Michigan.

Windsor, Ontario — First reached by the Great Western Railway in 1854, for many years it was a focal point for railway car ferries crossing to Detroit.

Courtright, Ontario — Named for the president of the Canada Southern, this was the railway's other western Ontario terminus. Work on car ferry slips was begun here but was not fully completed. At St. Clair, Michigan, on the opposite shore, a short section of the Canada Southern ran westerly to Ridgeway, but no further construction was carried out.

Sarnia, Ontario — The Grand Trunk reached Sarnia in 1856, followed two years later by the Great Western in December 1858. The Grand Trunk ran transfer ferries from here to Port Huron. The Sarnia or St. Clair Tunnel ran from Sarnia to Port Huron, Michigan, and was opened in 1891, thereby replacing the ferry operations here and at Point Edward.

Point Edward, Ontario — Located immediately north of Sarnia, Point Edward was reached by the Grand Trunk in 1856 and was the site later chosen for the Grand Trunk's car ferry terminal due to better ice conditions on the St. Clair River here during the winter. The ferries operated between Point Edward and Fort Gratiot, Michigan, north of Port Huron.

American Harbours — Grosse Isle, Detroit, St. Clair, Port Huron and Fort Gratiot, Michigan.

d) Lake Huron & Georgian Bay (including the St. Mary's River)

Goderich, Ontario — The Buffalo & Lake Huron Railway arrived at Goderich in 1858 but its tracks did not reach the harbour until 1860. The harbour became a grain-receiving terminal after the railway built an elevator in 1866. The Canadian Pacific built into Goderich early in this century.

Kincardine, Ontario — A minor harbour at the end of a Grand Trunk branch line.

Southampton, Ontario — A minor harbour at the end of a Grand Trunk branch line.

Wiarton, Ontario — This was the Grand Trunk's northern terminus in western Ontario until largely superseded by Owen Sound when the railway rerouted its main branch line to there in 1894.

Owen Sound, Ontario — For years dominated by the Canadian Pacific as the home port for its Great Lakes steamers, the Grand Trunk reached the harbour in 1894. An interchange between the two railways, which were separated by the Sydenham River, was not built until 1924.

Meaford, Ontario — A minor harbour at the western end of a Northern Railway branch from Collingwood.

Collingwood, Ontario — Established by the Northern Railway in the early 1850s as its northern terminus, the locality was originally called the Hens and Chickens, after a nearby group of islands. Collingwood was an important grain and lumber harbour, as well as a shipbuilding centre.

Penetanguishene, Ontario — Located at the end of a Northern Railway branch, Penetanguishene was primarily used to ship lumber.

Midland, Ontario — The Midland Railway built into Midland around 1880, and in 1881 the company erected a grain elevator.

Port McNicoll, Ontario — Situated near Midland, Port McNicoll was laid out by the Canadian Pacific in the first decade of this century as its new southern grain terminal and steamer port instead of Owen Sound.

Rose Point, Ontario — Located near Parry Sound and Depot Harbour, steamers linked the Canada Atlantic Railway with Parry Sound from this station.

Parry Sound, Ontario — In the early 1900s Parry Sound was reached by the Canadian Pacific Railway and the Canadian Northern Railway, each of whom built spurs down to the water.

Depot Harbour, Ontario — Established by the Canada Atlantic Railway at the end of the last century, Depot Harbour was a major grain-receiving terminal until the 1930s. The ships of the Canada Atlantic Transit Company provided a link between Depot Harbour and Lake Michigan and Lake Superior until the Second World War. Depot Harbour was located close to Parry Sound, but its harbour was vastly superior in regards to lake shipping.

Pointe au Baril (Station), Ontario — Steamers ran between Canadian Pacific's Pointe (sometimes spelled Point) au Baril station and a handful of local communities on Georgian Bay.

Key Harbour, Ontario — Established by the Canadian Northern Railway, some ore was shipped through this port, but it was later abandoned by Canadian National.

Little Current, Ontario — This small Manitoulin Island community was joined to the mainland early in this century by the Algoma Eastern Railway. The Algoma Eastern built a large coal dock here to supply the Sudbury mines and surrounding communities.

Algoma Mills, Ontario — Originally located at the end of the Canadian Pacific branch from Sudbury, Algoma Mills was to be the southern terminus for Canadian Pacific

Canadian Pacific's steel steamship *Algoma* represented a significant advancement in Great Lakes steamship technology when introduced in 1884; nevertheless, supplementary sails were still carried on each mast. *Algoma* is seen here at the Horne Elevator at Port Arthur (now Thunder Bay), the first grain elevator to be erected there. *Algoma* was wrecked in 1885. — *OA S13200*

The Great Lakes were also home to numerous ocean going ships such as the *Turret Chief* of Newcastle. While some ships were purchased used, especially by Canadian lines on the Great Lakes, for lake duty, others were merely summertime visitors. *Turret Chief* represents an unusual design developed by the shipbuilding firm of William Doxford & Sons of Sunderland, England, in the early 1890s. The narrow "turret" deck provided two advantages over other contemporary designs, namely lower weight resulting in higher cargo capacities, and lower harbour tolls because of the smaller top deck area. The Great Lakes also had their own unusual designs such as the "whalebacks" which featured a rounded deck. The *Turret Chief* is pictured here at Midland in 1901. — *OA Acc.2375 S5279*

lake steamers operating to the Lakehead, but the railway's acquisition of the Toronto, Grey & Bruce Railway between Toronto and Owen Sound put an end to any plans for Algoma Mills and the harbour became little more than a supply depot. By 1887 the Algoma Mills branch had been extended to Sault Ste. Marie.

Sault Ste. Marie, Ontario — Situated on the St. Mary's River, Sault Ste. Marie was an early trading post. The ship canals, the Canadian Pacific (rail line and steamers), and the Algoma Central Railway became important factors in the city's development.

American Harbours — Bay City and Cheboygen, Michigan.

c) Lake Michigan

American Harbours — Mackinaw City, St. Ignace, Frankfort, Ludington, Muskegon, Grand Haven, St. Joseph, Michigan City, Escanaba and Menominee, Michigan; Chicago, Illinois; Kenosha, Racine, Milwaukee, Sheboygan, Manitowoc, Green Bay and Marinette, Wisonsin.

f) Lake Superior

Michipicoten, Ontario — Michipicoten Harbour was a supply depot during the construction of the Canadian Pacific around Lake Superior because of its natural harbour qualities. These same reasons attracted the Algoma Central's engineers, and it was from Michipicoten Harbour that the first section of railway to be opened on the Algoma Central was built. The Algoma Central shipped iron ore out of the harbour during the first three decades of this century and switched to receiving coal at the end of the 1920s. Around 1940 the shipment of iron ore from Michipicoten was resumed.

Port Arthur and Fort William, Ontario — These two adjacent harbours located at the Lakehead are now the primary components of the city of Thunder Bay. The Canadian Pacific had the monopoly on railway movements from these two towns until the Grand Trunk Pacific and the Canadian Northern systems were built early this century. Most of the tonnage shipped from Port Arthur and Fort William did and still does consist of western Canadian grain, the result of which has been the construction of numerous massive grain elevators which dominate the harbours. While Port Arthur was located on Thunder Bay, Fort William was situated on the Kaminstiquia River.

American Harbours — Marquette, L'Anse and Ontonagon, Michigan; Ashland and Superior City, Wisconsin; Duluth, Superior and Two Harbors, Minnesota.

g) Inland Ontario Harbours

Sand Point — This small Ottawa River community was reached by the Brockville & Ottawa Railway in 1867, and until the railway was completed to Pembroke in 1876, it acted as a transfer point for the Ottawa River steamers.

Ottawa — The Canada Atlantic Railway's station and yards were located beside the Rideau Canal in the heart of Ottawa, and it is probable that at least some traffic was exchanged between the canal steamers and barges and the railway.

Trent River Bridge — This small village on the Trent River was the southern terminus of the Cobourg, Peterborough & Marmora Railway branch to the Blairton iron mines, and it was here that the ore was transferred to scows for shipment to Harwood.

Harwood — Located on the south shore of Rice Lake, Harwood was the receiving terminal for the Blairton iron ore, and it was here that the ore was transshipped from the scows to the rail cars for Cobourg; connections were also made here for steamers to Peterborough and points on Rice Lake.

Lakefield — Transfer point between Stoney Lake steamers and Midland, Grand Trunk, and Canadian National trains from the 1880s until the 1940s.

Chemong — During the 1890s this station on Lake Chemong, west of Peterborough, was a transfer point for passengers between the lake steamers and the trains of the Peterborough & Lake Chemong Railway, a Grand Trunk-owned branch line.

Lindsay— A transfer point for passengers between Kawartha Lakes steamers and the Midland, Grand Trunk, and Canadian National railways.

Bobcaygeon — A transfer point for passengers between steamers on the Kawartha Lakes and trains of the Canadian Pacific Railway.

Peterborough — A transfer point between the railways and Otonabee River steamers, although probably not as important as Lakefield with regards to railway-steamer transfers.

Port Perry — During the 1870s and 1880s Port Perry was a transfer point for steamers connecting the Whitby & Port Perry Railway with Lindsay and Lake Scugog points.

Beaverton — A steamer transfer point for Midland and Grand Trunk trains, for points on Lake Simcoe.

Jackson's Point — A southern Lake Simcoe community near Sutton and transfer point for Toronto & Nipissing and Grand Trunk passengers for Lake Simcoe steamers.

Bradford — From 1853 to 1854 Bradford, located on the Holland River, was the transfer point for trains and Lake Simcoe steamers of the Northern Railway until replaced by Belle Ewart.

Belle Ewart — This Lake Simcoe port was opened by the Northern Railway in 1854 as the company's principal Lake Simcoe port.

Allandale — Before the Northern Railway was extended to Barrie, passengers had to board ferries for Barrie at Allandale (the station itself was first called Barrie and renamed Barrie again in the 1960s following the closure of the downtown Barrie station by Canadian National).

Barrie — After the Barrie station was built by the Northern Railway, the waterfront station became a transfer point for Lake Simcoe steamers.

Orillia — A steamer transfer point for Midland, Northern and Grand Trunk Railway trains.

Sparrow Lake — Following the completion of the Canadian Northern Railway through this small community on Sparrow Lake, small steamers were introduced to connect the station with other points on the lake.

Muskoka Wharf — Built by the Northern Railway in the 1870s, Muskoka Wharf was an important transfer station for Muskoka steamers; Muskoka Wharf was just south of Gravenhurst station.

Huntsville Dock — Located at Huntsville, this transfer point came into its own under the Grand Trunk following the turn of the century, particularly in connection with the steamers of the Huntsville & Lake of Bays Navigation Company.

Burk's Falls — Primarily a Grand Trunk-Canadian National transfer point for Magnetawan River steamers until 1934, when the last steamer was withdrawn from service.

Bala — The main Canadian Pacific transfer point for Muskoka Lakes steamers.

Bala Park — A Canadian Northern-Canadian National transfer point for Muskoka Lakes steamers.

Lake Joseph Wharf — Another Canadian Northern-Canadian National transfer point for Muskoka Lakes steamers.

North Bay — Terminal for the *Chief Commanda* of Ontario Northland and other Lake Nipissing steamers.

Temagami — Transfer point between Lake Temagami steamers and the Temiskaming & Northern Ontario Railway.

Mattawa — A small town on the upper Ottawa River where transfers were made between steamers for Lake Temiskaming and the Canadian Pacific Railway.

Haileybury — Temiskaming & Northern Ontario Railway station and minor transfer point for Lake Temiskaming steamers.

Kenora — Located on the shore of the Lake of the Woods, near the Ontario-Manitoba border, this Canadian Pacific station was linked with the Devil's Gap Lodge, also owned by Canadian Pacific, by a small fleet of motor launches owned by the lodge.

Others— There were other stations at which passengers and freight were transferred between inland lake and river steamers and trains, but in most cases these connections were relatively minor. In general, wherever the railways touched a navigable body of water, there was bound to be some sort of transfer arrangements between the ships and trains, even if the arrangement was only temporary in nature.

Table 1-1
TONNAGES OF FREIGHT PASSED THROUGH THE WELLAND CANAL 1872-1896

Year	Total Vessels[1]	Grain	Fruits & Veg.	Coal	Ore	Tonnage[2]	Total Between U.S. Ports
1872	6,063	535,402	2,745	186,932	98,605	1,333,104	606,627
1874	5,814	638,720	8,677	323,503	56,825	1,389,173	748,557
1876	4,789	406,590	3,198	288,211	81,654	1,099,810	488,815
1878	4,429	401,101	2,302	295,318	15,229	968,758	373,738
1880	4,104	440,702	1,480	109,986	34,139	819,934	179,605
1882	3,334	306,079	403	237,559	23,700	790,643	282,806
1884	3,138	296,556	9,168	274,471	53,205	837,811	407,079
1886	3,589	400,155	14,657	271,356	27,447	980,135	464,478
1888	2,647	406,178	13,608	223,871	16,872	878,800	434,753
1890	2,885	498,425	20,876	202,384	8,138	1,016,165	533,957
1892	2,615	494,611	32,815	211,616	355	955,554	541,065
1894	2,412	530,736	60,673	203,608	.....	1,008,221	592,267
1896	2,766	832,427	56,591	223,445	1,158	1,279,987	653,213

Notes: 1) Includes empty vessels.
2) Includes miscellaneous freight.

Source: *Saga of the Great Lakes*, Coles Publishing Company Limited, Toronto, 1980 (first published, Chicago, 1899), pp. 228-9.

CHAPTER ONE — NOTES

1) **J.B. Mansfield,** *The Saga of the Great Lakes* (Toronto, 1980/Chicago, 1899), p. 224. The figures cited are for the fiscal year ending 30 June 1870.

2) Ibid., p. 228. Figures cited are for the 1890 navigation year.

II

THE TRANSIT TRADE

The years approaching 1855 were among the most prosperous for lake shipping. The areas surrounding the Great Lakes were being settled at unprecedented rates and the navigation companies had a virtual monopoly on long-distance and heavy goods transportation. The only railways then in existence in the region were in the United States, and of those, none could be in any way thought of as a true system. Differences in track gauge, management and construction practices meant that interchange of equipment between the railways was often impossible.

Many companies, especially those in the United States, established their own steamship lines in order to extend themselves into new territories. Table 2-1 lists several such enterprises founded by various American railways on the Great Lakes in the latter half of the last century. The termination of many of the steamship operations by the railways in 1916 was brought about due to the American anti-trust laws.

Table 2-1
EARLY AMERICAN RAILWAY STEAMSHIP LINES ON THE GREAT LAKES 1849-1916

Line	Period	Operator or Affiliate*
Michigan Central Line	1849-1862	Michigan Central Railroad
New York & Lake Erie Line	1851-1869	New York, Lake Erie & Western Railroad
Michigan Southern Line	1852-1857	Michigan Southern Railroad
Western Transit Company	1855-1916	New York Central & Hudson River Railroad*
Erie & Western Transportation Company	1865-1916	Pennsylvania Railroad
Union Steamboat Company	1869-1916	New York, Lake Erie & Western Railroad
Lake Erie Transportation Company	1876-1916	Wabash Railroad
Flint & Pere Marquette Transportation Company	—	Flint & Pere Marquette Railroad
Lehigh Valley Transportation Company	1881-1916	Lehigh Valley Railroad
Lackawanna Transportation Company	-1916	Delaware, Lackawanna & Western Railroad
Northern Steamship Company	1888-1916	Great Northern Railway
Clover Leaf Steamboat Line	1890-	Toledo, St. Louis & Kansas City Railroad

The *Mississippi* was built for the Michigan Central in 1853 but her career was foreshortened by the opening of the Great Western Railway in 1854. In 1857, *Mississippi* and her sisterships *Western World* and *Plymouth Rock* were laid up, only to be sold in 1862 for dismantling. Owing to their comparatively large size, their hulls were rebuilt as dry docks.
— Coles Publishing Company

Western World and her identical sister *Plymouth Rock* were the last steamers built for the Michigan Central's Lake Erie service. Large steamers for their day, the above ships and their sister *Mississippi* were not unlike the steamships *Canada* and *America* introduced on Lake Ontario by the Great Western Railway in 1854. It should be noted that this *Western World* is not the same ship as that chartered by the Great Western for Lake Ontario duty. *— Coles Publishing Company*

Minneapolis, St. Paul & Buffalo Steamship Company	1890-	Minneapolis, St. Paul & Sault Ste. Marie Railroad
Union Transit Company	1892-	New York, Lake Erie & Western R.R.; Delaware, Lackawanna & Western R.R.; Eastern Minneapolis R.R.; Chicago, St. Paul, Minneapolis & Omaha R.R.; Northern Pacific R.R.; Eastern Minnesota R.R.; Great Northern Ry.; St. Paul & Duluth R.R.; Lehigh Valley R.R.* (all affiliates)
Great Lakes Steamship Company	1896-	Wisconsin Central Railroad*
Ontario Transportation Company	—	Central Vermont Railway*

N.B. — The above table also includes affiliated steamship lines not necessarily owned by their respective connecting railway line, these railway lines being marked with an asterisk (*).

The Michigan Central Railroad was typical of many American railways. It formed its own line on Lake Erie in 1849, linking its eastern terminus at Detroit, Michigan, with Cleveland, Ohio, and Buffalo, New York, where connection was made with the New York Central Railroad for the east. A list of ships which ran under the Michigan Central flag is outlined in table 2-2. Of these ships, however, only four ships were actually owned, these being *Mayflower*, *Plymouth Rock*, *Western World* and *Mississippi*; the others were chartered.

In 1855 the Michigan Central Line offered the following sailings between Buffalo and Detroit with its "new and magnificent low pressure steamers" *Western World*, *Plymouth Rock* and *May Flower* (alternate spelling of *Mayflower*):

1855 SAILINGS[1]

Leave Buffalo		Leave Detroit
Mondays, Thursdays	WESTERN WORLD	Wednesdays, Saturdays
Tuesdays, Fridays	PLYMOUTH ROCK	Mondays, Tuesdays
Wednesdays, Saturdays	MAY FLOWER	Tuesdays, Fridays

Table 2-2
STEAMSHIPS OF THE MICHIGAN CENTRAL LINE
1849-1862

Ship	Built	Period Owned/Operated
Mayflower*	1849	1849-1855
Atlantic	1848	1849-1852
Southerner		1850-1851
Baltimore		1850-1851
Forest City	1852	1852
May Queen	1852	1852
Buckeye State		1852-
Ocean		1853
Plymouth Rock*	1854	1854-1862
Western World*	1854	1854-1862
Mississippi*	1853	1855-1862

* denotes ship owned by the Michigan Central Line/Michigan Central Railroad.

The iron steamer *Philadelphia* was built at Buffalo in 1886 for the Erie & Western Transportation Company owned by the Pennsylvania Railroad. The Erie & Western was known as the "Anchor Line" with the slogan and anchor featured prominently at *Philadelphia*'s bow. The ship is shown here at Chicago in 1889. The grain elevator at the right is the Rock Island B, (capacity 800,000 bushels) operated by C. Counselman & Company. The *Philadelphia* was lost in a collision with the *Albany* of the Western Transit Company on Lake Huron in 1893 in heavy fog.
— *OA S13092*

Western Transit's *Buffalo* was built in 1878 by Thomas Quayle & Sons at Cleveland. The arch-truss bearing the inscription "New York Central & Hudson River R.R. Line" was a common feature of large wooden steamers in North America.
— *OA S15949*

Western Transit's *Harlem*, built by Detroit Dry Dock in 1888, is seen here at Midland in 1901 with the Grand Trunk Railway elevator behind. — *OA S5290*

The steel freighter *Owego*, along with her twin *Chemung*, was built at Buffalo in 1888 by Union Dry Dock for the Union Steamboat Company. The Union Steamboat Line was a subsidiary of the New York, Lake Erie & Western Railroad, more commonly known as the Erie Railroad, and it is the name *Erie* that is proudly worn on *Owego*'s stack on the white rings. *Owego* could carry up to 2,600 tons of freight and is pictured here leaving South Chicago. — *OA S13060*

The *F.H. Prince* of the Ontario Transportation Company, operating as the "Central Vermont Line", is seen here at Port Dalhousie sometime around the turn of the century. Ships such as the *F.H. Prince* gave the Central Vermont Railway access to mid-western American markets by way of the Great Lakes through Ogdensburg, New York. The former Welland Railway grain elevator can be seen above the stern of the vessel while crew members are making themselves busy by doing some paint work at the ship's bow.
— *OA Acc. 12026-139*

The Northern Steamship Company was formed in 1888 as a subsidiary of the Great Northern Railway, thereby forming a link between the railway's eastern terminus at Duluth on Lake Superior, and the railways at Buffalo. In 1889, six freighters, built by the Globe Iron Works at Cleveland and grossing 2,500 tons each, were introduced by the company, named: *North Star, North Wind, Northern King, Northern Light, Northern Queen,* and *Northern Wave.* It was not however, until 1894 that the company placed two passenger steamers into service. Built by Globe Iron Works, the new 4,200-ton steamers *North Land* (pictured) and *North West* were among the finest on the lakes with each carrying up to 540 passengers. The ships each measured 383 feet in length with a beam of 44 feet. — *OA S17572*

The Great Western Railway of Canada

It was during this period that the Great Western Railway was conceived north of the border. With a line projected from Windsor, opposite Detroit, to Niagara Falls by way of Hamilton, the railway roughly parallelled the water route of the Michigan Central Line, and compared to railway routes south of Lake Erie, the Great Western was significantly shorter. Completed in 1854, the Great Western Railway formed a land link between the Michigan Central and the New York Central superior to anything the steamship line could provide. That was despite the fact that the gauge of the Great Western was the "Provincial" gauge of 5 feet 6 inches, as opposed to the standard gauge of 4 feet 8½ inches utilized by the two American lines, thus necessitating the transshipment of freight at either end.

This through traffic, bound mainly for the East, was commonly referred to as the transit trade and became an important source of revenue for the young Great Western. The shift in traffic also made the Michigan Central Line redundant, and in 1857 the fleet was laid up permanently. The ships were sold for scrap value in 1862. But the shift also limited the Great Western's ability to develop links with other railways without sharing the profitable transit trade with the New York Central and the Michigan Central railroads. At the time, the Great Western had no other alternatives in the area. The Grand Trunk was still under construction, as were most of Canada's other railways, and there was little hope for any change in the near future. To the Great Western's management, the establishment of a line of steamers to be run out of Hamilton seemed to be the only solution.

Preparations for the new service began in 1854, and in 1855 the company announced that it would begin steamer operations on Lake Ontario, linking Hamilton with Oswego, New York, in order to improve the flow of New England traffic. As Col. G.R. Stevens noted, the decision was "bound to lead to rate-cutting by the existing lines," not to mention problems with the New York Central and other American railways with whom the Great Western exchanged traffic at Niagara Falls. Company president Harris, however, justified the action on the premise that the additional traffic would come from railways without direct access to the Great Western.[2]

Daily service was inaugurated on 25 June 1855 with the railway's two new steamers, the *Canada* and the *America*, built at Niagara in 1854 at a combined cost of $380,699, along with an additional two chartered steamers, the *Europa* of the A.P. Brown Company of Hamilton and the *Western World* (not to be confused with the *Western World* owned by the Michigan Central on Lake Erie). The results of the service were disappointing, to say the least, with the line losing $60,000 in that first season alone. The company's directors placed the blame on competing steamers owned by the Huron & Ontario Railway, a company chartered as early as 1836 to build a railway from Burlington Bay to Goderich. Although the Huron & Ontario never built its railway, it did apparently use its charter's authority to operate steamers on Lake Ontario during the 1850s.[3]

For the 1856 season, the Great Western opted for a new daily route, operating from Hamilton to Cape Vincent, New York, Brockville and Prescott, Ontario, and Ogdensburg, New York.[4] Although this new strategy was an improvement over the previous year, the steamship line still lost a further $25,000. Disappointed, the directors decided to withdraw the ships from the route on August 23 rather than to continue and sustain further losses. Besides, by this time the Grand Trunk was almost completed, offering that additional outlet the railway needed without the expense of operating ships.

In 1857 the *Canada* and the *America* were "sold to parties connected with the Detroit & Milwaukee Railway" in return for "shares of that line bearing 7 percent interest." As for the other two ships, the *Europa* was sold by its owners in 1857 and was eventually scrapped in 1873 after spending its remaining years on the St. Lawrence River. No hard evidence concerning the *Western World*'s fate has come to light, but there is a possibility that she was purchased by the United States Navy, since a ship of that name served in the early 1860s, when the American government purchased many Great Lakes vessels for service during the Civil War.[5] The Great Western's

The Great Western's *Canada*. Both *Canada* and her sister *America* were large vessels not unlike those operated by the Michigan Central Railroad on Lake Erie. — *MTL T-16159*

After being sold by her original owners, the *Europa* was taken down to the St. Lawrence where she spent her remaining days. The ship is seen here at Montreal only a few years before scrapping. — *PAC PA-43035*

The fact that the Great Western's *Canada* and *America* were sold to "parties connected with the Detroit & Milwaukee Railway" is noteworthy since the Detroit & Milwaukee itself, through charters if not ownership, was an operator of steamships. These vessels were primarily employed to connect the railway's terminal at Grand Haven, Michigan, with Milwaukee, Wisconsin, on the opposite shore of Lake Michigan. The 1,123-ton propeller *Ironsides*, built at Cleveland in 1864, was one of these ships. Originally constructed for the American Lake Superior Line, she was later transferred to Lake Michigan, eventually coming into the hands of the Engelmann Transportation Company for the Detroit & Milwaukee R.R. Line. *Ironsides* was lost in a storm near Grand Haven on 15 September 1873, taking with her 28 lives. Typically, only one trip each way was offered by the railway between Grand Haven and Milwaukee, each day, in connection with the railway's Detroit trains. In 1870, for example, a steamer left Grand Haven for Milwaukee at approximately 7:00 p.m., arriving at 5:00 a.m. the next morning. On return, the steamer departed Milwaukee at 9:00 p.m., reaching Grand Haven the following morning in time for the 8:00 a.m. train for Detroit. *— OA Acc. 14996-14*

Successor to the railway-owned steamship lines was the Great Lakes Transit Corporation of Buffalo, New York. Great Lakes Transit's package freighter *North Lake* came to the company when it acquired the assets of the Northern Steamship Company (subsidiary of the Great Northern Railway). This 1917 view shows the *North Lake* at Sault Ste. Marie, Michigan. Note the hand-carts for handling cargo grouped on the *North Lake*'s deck. — *PAC PA-145142*

Seen here at Sault Ste. Marie, Michigan, in 1924, the package freighter *Boston* came to Great Lakes Transit by way of the Western Transit Company. The 1,669-net-ton iron ship was built in 1880 by Detroit Dry Dock at Wyandotte, Michigan. The enclosed upper pilot-house and the large, three-doored deck-house were added to the vessel around 1920. — *PAC PA-145715*

America and *Canada* were acquired by New York interests in 1858 and taken to the Atlantic after the Detroit & Milwaukee discovered (assuming they didn't know) that it was impossible for the ships to pass up the Welland Canal — the *Canada* and the *America* were each registered at 1,100 tons (gross) and were almost 300 feet long, twice the length of the Welland Canal locks. After varied careers, the *America* was burned in 1869, while the *Canada* lasted only until 1862, when it sank.[6]

While the Great Western Railway may have rendered the steamships of the Michigan Central obsolete by taking over their functions, it in no way had any drastic effect on lake shipping. Indeed, most of the other railway-owned steamship companies in the United States thrived until around 1916, when a government order forced the railways into selling off their package freighters, putting an end to cut-throat competition and rate-fixing among the lines. Many of the ships were acquired by a new company, the Great Lakes Transit Corporation, formed by W.J. Conners of Buffalo on 22 February 1916.

The Great Western's attempt at forming a Lake Ontario steamship line, and subsequent failure, can only be put down to bad judgement on the part of its directors at a time when economic depression was just around the corner and competition from vessels already threatened by another rival, the Grand Trunk Railway, was beginning to reach a peak.

The Grand Trunk Railway of Canada

The Grand Trunk wreaked havoc among shipping interests on the lakes, especially on Lake Ontario, when it opened in the mid-1850s. The ship owners lost much of their passenger trade to the railway, along with a significant volume of freight, since speed and efficiency were not their strong points. As a further blow, the financial crash at the end of the 1850s forced many a vessel off the lakes for good.

Oddly enough, the Grand Trunk did not take the lake traffic seriously, especially in light of the fact that it was supposedly built to aid lake navigation, not compete with it. Many of the harbour communities along the north shore of Lake Ontario, for example, were by-passed entirely, forcing shippers to continue sending and receiving goods by ship. Where the railway did touch harbours, facilities were poor to non-existent. In 1858 E.T. Blackwell, Managing Director of the railway, reported on the state of the line following his personal inspection: "The line was left incomplete in many important points of detail . . . . The traffic has not yet had adequate opportunities of development . . . . The stations at Kingston, Cobourg and Port Hope were so located that access to the watercraft at these ports without branch lines was an impossibility. The line at Toronto was so inconveniently arranged . . . that up to the present time, two distinct locomotive and station establishments have had to be maintained. The terminus at Sarnia, as located according to the Company's charter, was on the bare shore of the lake, without any means whatsoever of intercepting any of the western traffic passing down Lake St. Clair."[7]

This was a sad commentary made even worse by the railway's freight rate policies, by which little was done to win the favour of the now disgruntled populace. Most shippers, as G.R. Stevens noted, found that despite the slowness of the lake vessels, most general merchandise could be sent at a rate half that charged by the Grand Trunk, and when it came to bulky goods such as timber and grain, the railway's rates were so high that it could not compete at all. The railway introduced seasonal rates on which it hoped to regain in winter what it had lost in the summer, but rather than pay the high winter rates, shippers withheld as much freight as possible from the Grand Trunk until spring came and navigation reopened.[8]

Only after a government enquiry in 1861 would any improvements be made.

When it came to introducing its own line of steamers, the Grand Trunk opted for a more conservative approach than that of its contemporaries. After all, the company's problem was not so much that of reaching out into new regions — it was going to be Canada's "trunk line" extending from Sarnia in the west all the way to Portland, Maine, on the Atlantic — but rather it was getting its own lines built. Since a good part of the route from Toronto to Montreal followed the Lake Ontario and St. Lawrence River shorelines, and since its western terminus was to be at Sarnia on the

Algerian, viewed here running the Lachine Rapids on the St. Lawrence River, was built in 1854 as the *Kingston* and may have first been operated by the Grand Trunk before passing into the hands of the Royal Mail Line. *Kingston* burned in 1872 and was rebuilt as the *Bavarian*. She was again rebuilt following a fire a year later, coming out as the *Algerian*. She was renamed *Cornwall* in 1904 and was scrapped in 1930. *— OA S13306*

St. Clair River, carrying supplies to isolated construction sites by ship would appear to be far more practical and economical than hauling heavy material overland.

To that end, the railway took delivery of two new paddle-steamers between 1854 and 1855. One was the 344-ton *Kingston*, built in 1854 by the Montreal shipyard of Bartley & Gilbert, featuring an iron hull with a wooden superstructure. Teamed up with six barges of 100 tons each, built at Kingston that same year, she would have provided an excellent transport for the many heavy materials needed during the railway construction, not to mention the movement of passengers and employees around the uncompleted sections of track.

After the main line was completed between Montreal and Toronto in October 1856, the *Kingston* became surplus and was soon after sold to the Royal Mail Line of steamers, who placed her on the Montreal to Toronto route. Under her new owners, the *Kingston* went on to have a colourful career, to say the least. In 1860 she carried the Prince of Wales on several excursions on Lake Ontario and the St. Lawrence. Twelve years later, *Kingston* caught fire on the St. Lawrence and burnt, taking one life with her when she later capsized. The hull was salvaged and came out later that year as the *Bavarian*, only to catch fire again in 1873 off Oshawa, with the resulting death toll of 14. Her sturdy hull was rebuilt once again, and between 1874 and 1904 ran between Toronto and Montreal as the *Algerian*. From 1904 until her final scrapping at Hamilton in 1930, she operated under the name of *Cornwall*.[9]

The *Canadian* was also built in 1854 for the Grand Trunk, this time for service on the upper lakes. Launched by Jenkins's Shipyard at Chatham, the 339-ton wooden steamer probably served as the supply ship for the western end of the Grand Trunk main line by feeding materials into the terminus at Sarnia. It is interesting to note that throughout its entire career, the *Canadian* was registered at Goderich, a port that was not to be served by the Grand Trunk until that railway's acquisition of the Buffalo & Lake Huron Railway in 1869. Unlike the *Kingston*, the *Canadian* was retained by the Grand Trunk after the railway opened to Sarnia, serving there as a ferry between Sarnia and Port Huron, Michigan, until finally being scrapped in the early 1870s.

The Northern Railway of Canada

Most venturesome of the early Ontario railways was the Northern Railway of Canada, known as the Ontario, Simcoe & Huron Railway from its formative years until 1858.

Constructed in the early 1850s to promote development in the regions north of Toronto, the Northern became an important link in the American transit trade, much to the credit of its chief engineer, Frederick William Cumberland, appointed in 1852. Bringing to the railway his working knowledge of dock construction and railway-building gained in Great Britain, Cumberland was responsible for the establishment of Collingwood harbour on Georgian Bay as the railway's northern terminus, and through his efforts he persuaded the Northern's directors to establish steamship services on the Great Lakes.

In 1854 Cumberland took note of the advantages offered by the Northern's route in relation to the American transit trade with a view to increasing traffic on the line. By combining the short rail link the line provided with the economies of water transportation, "he estimated that he could deliver New York freight to Chicago for $9.50 a ton less than any United States' railway, $8.45 less than the Great Western and $4.80 less than the Grand Trunk."[10] Furthermore, passengers bound for the American West would be attracted by the savings in time over other water routes and by the scenic wonders.

These were substantial claims, and yet, with such advantages over the competition, how could a steamship service possibly fail? With the completion of the railway to Collingwood in June 1855, Cumberland's claims were about to be put to the test, and the railway could certainly use the additional traffic.

Early that year the Northern chartered five steamships, probably from the United States' Lake Superior Line, at a cost of £21,750, to operate a tri-weekly service between Collingwood and Chicago, Illinois, and a weekly service between Collingwood and Green Bay, Wisconsin. These ships included the *Lady Elgin* and the *Niagara*, and later the *Hunter*, the *Montgomery* and the *Ontonagon*. At the same time, complementary services were established on Lake Ontario, linking Toronto with Oswego, New York, where connections were made with the Oswego & Syracuse Railroad and the Oswego Canal.

Despite all the Northern's advantages, the company was unable to generate sufficient traffic to even cover its costs. The 1856 navigation season did not fare any better. Of 63 round trips to Chicago, few made a profit; the nature of the rates set by the railway were such that profits could only be had with full cargoes. The situation was further complicated when the *Niagara* burned off Port Washington on Lake Michigan on September 24 with the loss of 60 lives and a full cargo.

Faced with severe financial losses not only on the steamship line but also on the railway, the Northern's management gave serious consideration to the abandonment of the lake service, but Cumberland, now a director, still had faith in the service and argued for its retention. The other directors gave in, and fortunately for Cumberland the route turned a profit of more than $10,000 for the railway after all costs were found. Its success may have been due in part to the reduction of the Lake Michigan route to four vessels as a result of the *Niagara* tragedy in 1857. Yet, as happy as the directors may have been, they "resolved to entertain no proposition for future connections with the Upper Lakes which would involve any subsidy or guarantee."[11] Service to Lake Michigan ports continued until 1860.

Frederick Cumberland became general manager of the railway after the government placed the company into receivership in 1859 due to outstanding debts. By 1861 the company was faced with an extensive rebuilding program for its lines which had fallen into a bad state of repair. There was no money for steamship lines and the Great Lakes services were terminated with only a minor loss in traffic for the railway, amounting to no more than $2,000. Private shipping companies were more than happy to take up the slack.

By 1862 the railway was once again in a position to charter steamers for the lakes, and by the end of the first month of navigation, it brought "four first-class propellers" under contract to operate between Collingwood and Chicago. On Lake Ontario, however, the railway had difficulty in obtaining charters due to the scarcity of ships on the lake; many ships on Lake Ontario were purchased by either the United States government or by blockade runners during the American Civil War and were taken down the St. Lawrence to the Atlantic. As a result, the Northern incurred substantial liabilities due to delays in shipping at the Toronto end. Fortunately the company was able to obtain the services of two steamers later in the season, thus averting any further costs.

Northern chartered steamships on the Great Lakes for the last time in 1862. The company found the American transit trade far too risky to merit special and usually costly provisions. As a replacement, Cumberland negotiated traffic agreements with the Grand Trunk Railway to carry all freight east of Toronto and with an American shipping line to handle the Collingwood to Chicago trade.

It would be easy to write off the Northern's attempt at operating steamships on the Great Lakes as bad judgement or even mere folly. Yet Cumberland's faith in the service was justified in many ways and showed foresight. At a time when railway companies and steamship lines were often at odds while competing for the same traffic, Cumberland saw how co-operation could be of benefit to all. The steamer service attracted freight and passenger traffic to the Northern that it might not have otherwise carried.

While statistics on the Northern's early years are obscure, Trout's *Railways of Canada* does provide an excellent breakdown of general costs and revenues for the railway after the government reorganization in 1859 to 1870. It clearly shows that during 1862, when steamer services were provided, overall tonnage and revenue for through freight was up a significant amount over the years preceding and following, as table 2-3 shows. However, it should also be noted that increases in revenue from local traffic after 1862 more than made up for any revenues lost on the transit trade after the steamship charters were suspended by the railway.

Given other circumstances, the Northern's Great Lakes services may have been the envy of the Grand Trunk and the Great Western, but given the odds, the Northern did remarkably well,

Built at Buffalo in 1851, the 1,038-ton steamer *Lady Elgin* was one of the vessels chartered by the Northern in order to form a line of steamers with which the company connected Collingwood with ports on Lake Michigan. This engraving was based on a photograph taken of the *Lady Elgin* while at Chicago in 1860 a day before she was lost in a collision on Lake Michigan with the schooner *Augusta.* 300 lives were lost, many of them excursionists from Canada. The *Lady Elgin* was owned by the Ontonagon Lake Superior Line at the time.
— *University of Baltimore Library No. 8210*

This view of Collingwood Harbour, taken around 1870, shows the original Northern Railway grain elevator and wharf. The railway's warehouse is located at the far end of the dock. The steamship is the *Ploughboy.* — *OA S1628*

By the 1890s, Collingwood Harbour had changed considerably as this circa 1900 view attests. The elevator was erected by the Northern Railway in 1871 with a capacity of 250,000 bushels of grain. Except for a handful of small pleasure craft and a derelict schooner, sail has been replaced entirely by steam. *— OA Acc. 14996-39*

thanks to Frederick Cumberland. A brilliant organizer, he was one of the most admired and respected figures of his time.

Table 2-3
NORTHERN RAILWAY
FREIGHT REVENUE
1859-1870

Year	Freight Tonnage (tons)	Local Freight Revenue	Through Freight Revenue	Total Freight Revenue
1859*	—	$50,763 (70)	$21,906 (30)	$72,669
1860	125,345	186,086 (79)	50,367 (21)	236,453
1861	145,754	260,435 (84)	48,432 (16)	308,867
1862	174,345	209,066 (69)	92,693 (31)	301,759
1863	145,994	275,463 (94)	18,206 (06)	293,669
1864	189,100	333,207 (96)	14,884 (04)	348,091
1865	118,871	340,912 (93)	26,388 (07)	367,300
1866	174,816	340,114 (87)	24,364 (13)	388,842
1867	200,668	376,824 (95)	21,551 (05)	398,375
1868	194,583	364,206 (97)	12,691 (03)	376,897
1869	270,922	479,292 (98)	8,584 (02)	487,876
1870	296,045	505,180 (95)	28,328 (05)	533,508

* six months only

N.B.: Figures in parentheses ( ) show percentage of total freight revenue.

Source of figures: J.M. & Edw. Trout, *The Railways of Canada*, The Monetary Times, Toronto, 1871. pp. 112-113.

The Canada Atlantic Railway
The Canada Atlantic Transit Company

Born in 1826, John Rudolphus Booth was a native of Quebec, and from humble beginnings as a carpenter, he grew to become the lumber king of the Ottawa Valley. His empire included vast tracts of timber, sawmills, and the Canada Atlantic Railway, a line formed out of several smaller eastern Ontario railways.

For Booth, the Canada Atlantic was a necessary adjunct to his lumber interests. By the 1870s, demand for his lumber in the United States put a great strain on the traditional water route down the Ottawa River, and a railway running from his Ottawa mills to the American border could provide the most efficient alternative. By 1882 the railway was opened to the St. Lawrence River and the Grand Trunk. Within 15 years the Canada Atlantic was in direct contact with the Central Vermont Railway, running into the heart of eastern America.

The railway was an instant success, and not just as a lumber carrier. Passenger and general freight traffic also became important sources of revenue. But Booth was a dynamic individual and was not content with just one victory. To the west lay more timber for his mills, and ultimately Georgian Bay and the lakeborn traffic. In 1888 Booth obtained the necessary charters and began construction of the Canada Atlantic's western extension, and in 1896 the railway was completed to Depot Harbour on Georgian Bay, not far from the town of Parry Sound.

As part of Parry Sound, Depot Harbour was one of the last harbours on Georgian Bay not reached by railway. The Grand Trunk and the Canadian Pacific systems had long recognized the value of harbour terminals as traffic generators, and this point was not overlooked by J.R. Booth. If his western extension was to be successful, it would have to be more than just a lumber carrier; it

The Canada Atlantic's Depot Harbour elevator is seen in this view shortly after its completion. The elevator's power house in the foreground is still having its roof applied. As built in 1896, the elevator had a capacity of one million bushels, but this was doubled in 1907 when a second storage annex was completed, all construction being of iron and concrete. In terms of overall size, some general dimensions of the original elevator are as follows: workhouse (the tallest section at the rear) 92 ft. deep, 80 ft. wide, 149 ft. high; marine tower (right) 25 ft. deep, 17 ft. wide, 139 ft. high; storage annex (behind the power house) 80 ft. deep, 196 ft. wide. — *OA Acc. 13098-51*

This 1908 view of Depot Harbour was taken shortly after the Grand Trunk completed its addition onto the original grain elevator. The ship at the base of the elevator's marine tower is the *Ottawa;* the other ship is unidentified, but it is seen here unloading coal. Note the Grand Trunk steam engine at the head of a freight train. — *OA S2542*

needed to diversify if it was to succeed, and capturing lake traffic from the West, especially grain, was just the ticket.

Nothing in this world is guaranteed, however, a fact Booth was well aware of. The new port needed a grain elevator, a dredged harbour, railway and docking facilities, a new town for employees, and a regular line of steamers to keep the elevator supplied. With Booth's financial resources, nothing was beyond the limits of his organization, and soon the harbour was completed, along with the formation of his own steamship line, the Canada Atlantic Transit Company.

The Canada Atlantic Transit Company was among the last of the railway-owned steamship companies formed for Great Lakes service, and it was the last organized for the American transit trade. Incorporated in two segments, the Canadian operation received its charter on 13 June 1898 "to construct, acquire and navigate steam and other vessels, for the conveyance of passengers, goods and merchandise, between ports of Canada, and to and from any port of Canada to any port of any other country."[12] In October the Canada Atlantic Transit Company of the U.S. was incorporated under American law to handle traffic to and from the United States.

Much of the traffic anticipated for the transit company was to be grain from the West, to be delivered to the railway's elevator at Depot Harbour, from whence it would be moved by the railway to the company's elevator at Coteau Landing on the St. Lawrence River, at which point the grain would be transferred to barges (many of them railway owned) for the final leg of the journey to Montreal. In short, the route was offered as the fastest, the shortest and the cheapest lake-and-rail grain route to the East. It was therefore logical that the company's first vessel acquisitions were three bulk carriers purchased by the end of 1899. Built at Chicago, the 2,745-ton *Arthur Orr*, the *George Orr*, and the 3,092-ton *Kearsarge* were all modern steel lake freighters and none were older than six years.

Canada Atlantic Transit's performance was impressive. Within the first full year of operation, 1899, it was serving routes to Chicago, Duluth and the Lakehead. With the aid of other steamship lines running into Depot Harbour, the company was responsible for delivering over 260,000 tons of grain to the Canada Atlantic Railway, clearly one-third of all the freight handled by the railway, closely rivalling the lumber traffic for which the Canada Atlantic was constructed.

The 1900 navigation season was even better. Total traffic for the railway was up by 50 percent. Of the 320,000 tons of freight carried east by the railway to Montreal, grain comprised 303,000 tons.[13] The Canada Atlantic Railway was now carrying more grain to the East than both the Grand Trunk and the Canadian Pacific railways combined. Depot Harbour had become the principal grain port on Georgian Bay, and all because of the Canada Atlantic Transit Company.

Throughout 1900 prospects for the steamship line were looking better and better. So much so that the Canada Atlantic took delivery of its first new steamship, the 2,431-ton *Ottawa*, built at Toronto. But the nature of the traffic was also changing. In 1901 the railway carried 321,000 tons of freight to Montreal from Depot Harbour, of which grain comprised 278,000 tons, down by approximately eight percent from the previous year.[14] Package freight was becoming an increasingly more important commodity for the line.

In the next few years the Booth organization reconsidered its involvement in the railway industry. Times were changing and railway ownership in Canada was gradually being concentrated into three big systems: the Grand Trunk/Grand Trunk Pacific, the Canadian Pacific, and the Canadian Northern. The Canada Atlantic could not begin to meet such competition. It was small by comparison and any extension of the line would involve such large expenditures as to make expansion out of the question. Even the government was unwilling to help, despite its support for the transcontinental lines. When in 1899 Booth requested federal aid for the improvement of elevator and dock facilities at Depot Harbour and Coteau Landing, Prime Minister Sir Wilfrid Laurier turned him down for political reasons.[15]

In 1903 J.R. Booth had had enough and put the Canada Atlantic Railway and its subsidiary, the Canada Atlantic Transit Company, up for sale. While many eyed the railway with great interest, it was the Grand Trunk Railway who came out victorious in September 1904 after paying $14 million.[16] The Grand Trunk needed the additional capacity to handle the increasing volumes of grain coming from the Canadian West, but instead of buying a major grain carrier, it wound up with a run-down railway which needed large sums of money invested just to bring it up to Grand Trunk standards — money the railway would never recover. The Canada Atlantic Railway would never be the same.

For the Canada Atlantic Transit Company, operations continued much as they had before, carrying western grain to Depot Harbour and returning loaded with packaged goods. Improvements made at Depot Harbour in 1907 by the Grand Trunk, including an addition to the grain elevator which doubled its capacity, allowed freight to be handled more expeditiously. It was the kind of capital input that only a large system such as the Grand Trunk could muster. Without it, revenues could have been lost as delays forced shippers to switch to alternative routes or file for compensation.

Disaster struck the line in 1909 when the *Ottawa* sank on Lake Superior. The loss of the *Ottawa* meant that the other three ships would have to work harder or else have business chipped away by competing lines. It was not long before a replacement was found in the British-built 2,179-ton *Newona*, constructed in 1909 and probably purchased new. Judging by the number of ships operated by the Canada Atlantic Transit Company for any given period, it would appear that company policy required a complement of four ships. And no wonder. In 1910 westbound package-freight traffic alone moved through Depot Harbour averaged 125 carloads a day, much of which was shipped by way of the Canada Atlantic Transit Company.[17]

The outbreak of war in 1914 put added pressure on the line. The war effort required all ships to work to the limit. Backlogs at Depot Harbour were commonplace as workers rushed to transfer cargo; no sooner had one ship been taken care of than another arrived at the dock. Then in 1917, after the Americans entered the conflict, the United States government requisitioned the *George Orr* for war service. The war in Europe was at its height and the steamship line could little afford to lose a ship, but it had no choice, as the *George Orr* was registered in the United States (under the Canada Atlantic Transit Company of the U.S.) and therefore was subject to American law. At this time it was impossible to obtain a replacement. History tells us that the Americans should have left the *George Orr* alone, for in January 1918, not long after being brought down the St. Lawrence, the *George Orr* was wrecked off Prince Edward Island.

Finally the Great War was over and business returned to normal. With the coming of the "Roaring Twenties," new prosperity was just around the corner, and so was a new master. World War I had taken its toll on Canada's railways, especially the Canadian Northern and the Grand Trunk, whose rapid expansion earlier placed them into deep debt. The First War made recovery impossible, and the federal government formed Canadian National Railways, begun in 1917 with the Canadian Northern and completed in 1923 with the amalgamation of the Grand Trunk, including Canada Atlantic Transit.

Under the control of Canadian National, the Canada Atlantic Transit Company concentrated its steamers on the Depot Harbour to Chicago and Milwaukee trade, a route reminiscent of Northern Railway days. The line was advertised in Canadian National timetables as the "Canada Atlantic Transit Company of the U.S. Lake and Rail Freight Route (via Depot Harbour) . . . Between New York, New England and all Eastern points, and Milwaukee, Chicago and all points West." Offered were "Frequent Sailings. Lowest differential rates. Special Care in Handling Traffic. Rates from all Agents."

While this is not a discussion of rates and tariffs, the reader may be wondering what was meant by "differential rates." Briefly, differential rates were freight rates dating back to 1857 when the Grand Trunk formulated special rates for oceanbound import and export traffic. Substantially lower than rates charged on domestic traffic, hence the differential, the special rate was used to attract ocean shipping to the Grand Trunk at Montreal and Portland, Maine, and allowed the

The *Arthur Orr* is captured in this early 1900s photograph with the Depot Harbour elevator in behind. In later years the *Arthur Orr*'s forecastle was rebuilt, during which the walkway between the bridge and the forecastle was eliminated. The Depot Harbour coal dock is evident astern of the *Arthur Orr*. — *PAC PA-8561*

A stern-end view of the *George N. Orr* (centre) taken while she was passing through the American locks at Sault Ste. Marie. The ship was requisitioned by the American government in 1917 for war service and sunk a year later off Prince Edward Island.

— *UBL PB No.8864*

The *Ottawa* early in her career. — *PAC PA-144694*

The *Newona* was acquired as a replacement for the *Ottawa*. In this picture, the British-built *Newona* is seen either before her purchase by Canada Atlantic Transit or after her sale in 1927; the existence of Plimsol marks on her hull (lower hull, centre) suggest the former, since few Great Lakes freighters carried these British-developed loading marks at that time.
— *PAC PA-144695*

In this early 1900s scene, *Kearsarge* is leaving Depot Harbour for Lake Michigan, evidence for which is the full load of fuel coal ahead of her stack. Two of *Kearsarge*'s cargo loading doors, just visible along the hull, are open in this view. The Depot Harbour coal dock is at the right. — *PAC PA-8560*

Photographed here at Sault Ste. Marie, Michigan, in 1924, the *Kearsarge* exhibits several modifications made to her since she was first acquired by Canada Atlantic Transit, among them being: a raised forecastle; an altered and rebuilt wheelhouse; shortened masts; and a new funnel. The *Arthur Orr* underwent similar alterations as well. — *PAC PA-145716*

railway to grant shippers through billing to foreign ports. It was not long before the practice spread to the American trunk lines, resulting in rate wars among the railways until traffic agreements in the 1880s finally put an end to the cut-throat pricing. This form of differential was known as a "port differential rate." Similar "domestic differentials" were later developed on the same formula, allowing circuitous rail routes such as the Grand Trunk, or rail-and-water routes such as the Canada Atlantic Transit Company, to compete with the through trunk lines like the New York Central for traffic between New England and Chicago.[18]

Like the Grand Trunk before it, Canadian National could attract cargo from a number of New England and eastern ports: from Portland, Maine, via the Grand Trunk; from Boston, Massachusetts, via the Boston & Maine Railroad and the Central Vermont; and from New York City and New London, Connecticut, via the Central Vermont. All traffic, including that from Montreal, could then be funnelled through Depot Harbour and carried economically by Canada Atlantic Transit to Chicago and Milwaukee for all points west, despite the length of the route and the extra time needed over other all rail routes.

In 1926 Canada Atlantic Transit was finally in a position to purchase a replacement for the *George Orr*. Not only that, but it was decided to replace the *Newona* as well. The vessels purchased were two bulk carriers built following the war to a standard design, probably for government service. The first was the 2,415-ton *Canadian Gunner*, constructed at Collingwood in 1919, and the second ship was the 2,394-ton *Canadian Harvester*, launched at Port Arthur in 1921. Upon acquisition, the company renamed them *Canatco* (for Canada Atlantic Transit Company) and *Delwarnic* respectively, and sent them off to Collingwood for rebuilding as package freighters in 1927. Some years before, the *Arthur Orr* and *Kearsarge* underwent similar conversions.

When the new ships were ready, the *Newona* was sold and the line returned to its standard complement of four ships, this time the *Arthur Orr*, the *Canatco*, the *Dalwarnic* and the *Kearsarge*. No further alterations to the fleet would be made.

The prosperity of the 1920s was swiftly followed by the Depression years of the 1930s. Freight traffic began to dry up, an ailment to which Canada Atlantic Transit was not immune. In 1929 the company carried a total of 322,311 tons of freight between Depot Harbour and the ports of Chicago and Milwaukee, of which 82,447 tons of package freight were carried to the United States, while 239,864 tons were carried back. By 1934 tonnage had fallen drastically to 187,175 tons, with 60,991 tons of package freight taken west, while eastbound traffic dropped by almost 50 percent to 126,184 tons.[19]

By the 1930s westbound traffic was principally package freight, including coffee, sugar and crude rubber, while eastbound shipments were largely made up of bulk grain, bagged grain products and wool.

It was not just a lack of traffic, however, that hurt the transit company. In 1933 a bridge washout on the former Canada Atlantic main line through Algonquin Park put an end to through trains to New England, as well as most of the grain traffic through Depot Harbour.

The steamship line was in desperate straits. No longer able to provide a through route to New England, it was only the backing of its parent company, Canadian National, that kept the line going through the depths of the Depression. In all likelihood, Canadian National would have sold Canada Atlantic Transit had it not been for the outbreak of World War II in September 1939.

The war gave Canada Atlantic Transit a temporary reprieve, but by this time traffic was so low that in 1940 the government requisitioned the *Canatco* for duty as a supply ship, operating out of the St. Lawrence to remote Newfoundland ports. Of the three ships remaining, only the *Dalwarnic* was really fit for service, but it too was requisitioned, this time by the United States Coast Guard for service on the Atlantic coast. The *Kearsarge* was in such poor condition that it was sold for scrap in 1943. Somehow, though, it managed to escape the breakers' yard and in 1948 it was rebuilt as a barge.

The year 1945 was the last in which the company operated any of the remaining ships, the fleet, including the *Canatco* and the *Dalwarnic*, which were returned by 1946, subsequently being laid up. In 1947 the *Canatco* and the *Dalwarnic* were sold and the *Arthur Orr*, now 54, was

The *Canatco,* photographed here at South Chicago in the 1930s, joined Canada Atlantic Transit in 1927. Both *Canatco* and her identical sister *Dalwarnic,* represented a class of small ocean-going freighters built to replace heavy shipping losses experienced during the First World War. Built to standard government designs, hundreds of similar vessels were built for the Canadian and British governments, the majority of which were later sold to private owners. The *Canatco* (which stood for CANada ATlantic Transit COmpany) was lettered for the Canada Atlantic Transit Company of the U.S. This was indicative of an apparent legal manoeuvre on the part of Canadian National Railways in order for it to continue to carry American transit goods. All of Canada Atlantic Transit's ships carried the "of the U.S." as part of the company's name after the 1920s. — *OA Acc. 14508-2*

The *Dalwarnic,* photographed off New York in 1942, while serving in the United States Coast Guard on the Atlantic coast. — *UBL PB No.8863*

scrapped. After the directors failed to file an annual report for the Canada Atlantic Transit Company, the company was officially dissolved in December 1950.

Thus ended the lakebound transit trade in Ontario. Had it not been for the Depression of the 1930s, the Canada Atlantic Transit Company may have still been operating today, even if not in the same role. Yet times change and so do traffic patterns. As a final point, it is worth noting that unlike its predecessors, Canada Atlantic Transit never carried passengers, even though it was provided for in the charter. By the time the company was formed, train travel was much faster, better appointed and even cheaper than those ships of the 1850s and 1860s.

Early Railway Grain Elevators

Much of the early transit trade was based upon the shipment of grain, as well as barrelled flour and other products. But while grain could be manhandled in bags, it was far more economical to ship it loosely in bulk. To handle these bulk shipments of grain the railways constructed grain elevators at major ports, the sole function of which was the transfer, weighing, cleaning, grading and storage of grain shipments.

In Ontario the railways were most responsible for the construction of these terminal elevators before 1900. It was only when private grain brokers and elevator companies came into being, not to mention farmers' co-operative organizations, that the railways withdrew from elevator operation.

What follows is a brief review of railway elevator construction in Ontario according to railway ownership (subsequent railway affiliations appear in parentheses) and location. For each elevator, the year(s) of construction and/or completion, the principal construction materials used, and the storage capacity are given along with other pertinent details. In addition, elevator names used by the railways are given where applicable.

a) BROCKVILLE & OTTAWA RAILWAY (CPR)

Brockville: built 1876, wood, 25,000 bushels.

b) BUFFALO & LAKE HURON RAILWAY (GTR)

Goderich: built 1866, wood, 60,000 bushels, burned 1897.

c) CANADA ATLANTIC RAILWAY (GTR/CNR)

Coteau Landing, Quebec: built 1896, iron and concrete (assumed), 500,000 bushels.

Depot Harbour: built 1896-1907, iron and concrete, 2,000,000 bushels, closed 1930s, destroyed 1945.

d) CANADIAN NORTHERN RAILWAY (CNR)

Port Arthur (Thunder Bay): Canadian Northern Elevator A built 1902, wood and tile, 3,244,700 bushels, workhouse burned 1920; Canadian Northern Elevator B built 1902-1904, wood and tile, 3,244,700 bushels, workhouse burned 1920; Canadian Northern Elevator A-B built 1902/1912/1920, wood and tile, 7,334,100 bushels, included storage sections of elevators A and B plus a 1912 storage annex and a new 600,000-bushel workhouse, sold 1957; N.B.; these elevators built by Canadian Northern subsidiary Canadian Northern Terminal Elevators.

e) CANADIAN PACIFIC RAILWAY

Fort William (Thunder Bay): Elevator A built 1885, wood, 1,039,880 bushels; Elevator B built 1889, tile, 482,000 bushels, supplemented Elevator A; Elevator C built 1890, wood, 1,195,000 bushels; Elevator D built 1902, steel, 1,976,000 bushels.

Owen Sound: Elevator A built 1885, wood, 250,000 bushels, burned 1911; Elevator B built 1897, wood, burned 1911.

Port McNicoll: built 1910-1936, concrete, 6,500,000 bushels.

The Grand Trunk's Toronto grain elevator, is seen here about 1865. The railway's yards are located at the left. This elevator survived into the early 1900s. — *MTL T-10353*

The Buffalo & Lake Huron Railway built this 60,000-bushel grain elevator at Goderich in 1866. In 1869, the railway and the elevator passed into the hands of the Grand Trunk which continued to operate the elevator until it burned in 1897. The Grand Trunk invested the insurance proceeds into a new replacement elevator built in 1898 by the Goderich Elevator & Transit Company. Named Elevator No. 1, the new 500,000-bushel structure burned seven years later. Both structures were built of wood. — *Huron County Pioneer Museum*

f) GRAND TRUNK RAILWAY (CNR)

Buffalo, New York: International Elevator built 1886, construction unknown, 650,000 bushels, possibly owned by Grand Trunk Railway.

Midland (Tiffin): Tiffin Number 2 built 1908, concrete, 4,650,000 bushels, offered for sale 1986.

Owen Sound: built 1897, wood, 500,000 bushels, Grand Trunk Railway part owner, demolished about 1924.

Point Edward: Elevator A built circa 1860, wood, 120,000 bushels; Elevator B built 1880, wood, 300,000 bushels, both elevators burned in 1901 and were replaced in 1903 by a new fireproof structure.

Toronto: built 1862-63, wood, 200,000 bushels, owned and operated by Messrs. Shedden & Company on behalf of Grand Trunk Railway.

g) GRAND TRUNK PACIFIC RAILWAY (CNR)

Fort William (Thunder Bay): *Grand Trunk Pacific Elevator*, built 1909-1912, concrete, 5,750,000 bushels.

h) GREAT WESTERN RAILWAY (GTR)

Hamilton: built 1854, wood, capacity unknown.

Sarnia: built 1858 or 1859, wood, 56,000 bushels.

i) MIDLAND RAILWAY (GTR)

Midland: built 1881, wood, 150,000 bushels.

Port Hope: built late 1860s, wood, capacity unknown.

j) NORTHERN RAILWAY (GTR)

Collingwood: first elevator, built circa 1865, wood, capacity unknown, replaced 1871; second elevator built 1871, wood, 250,000 bushels.

Penetanguishene: built circa 1880, wood, capacity unknown.

Toronto: first elevator built circa 1865, wood, capacity unknown, burned 1870; second elevator built 1871, wood, 275,000 bushels, burned 1903.

k) ST. LAWRENCE & OTTAWA RAILWAY (CPR)

Prescott: built 1870s, wood, 20,000 bushels; also a floating transfer elevator at this location.

l) WELLAND RAILWAY (GWR/GTR)

Port Colborne: built 1859, wood, capacity unknown.

Port Dalhousie: built 1859, wood, capacity unknown.

m) WHITBY & PORT PERRY RAILWAY (GTR)

Whitby: built 1872, wood, capacity unknown.

The Midland Railway built this 150,000-bushel elevator at Midland in 1881, not long before being acquired by the Grand Trunk. Although considered a small elevator by the turn of the century, through this elevator and the old Midland mainline, the Grand Trunk was able to give the Canadian Pacific some stiff competition in the grain trade. The steamer in the foreground is the *Rosedale* of the Hagarty & Crangle line, astern of which is the schooner *F.L. Danforth.*

— OA Acc. 12026-69

Canadian Pacific built its first elevator at Owen Sound, Elevator A, in 1885 of wood with a capacity of 250,000 bushels. In 1897, the railway erected a second elevator, Elevator B, directly behind Elevator A, and with it added an additional 800,000 bushels of capacity. Both elevators burned in 1911 but by this time, they had been displaced by Canadian Pacific's new elevator at Port McNicoll. This view shows the elevator in 1885, still only partially painted, with the steamer *Algoma* of Canadian Pacific's steamship line tied up in front.

— OA S16001

Viewed from the railway yards in this late 1890s photograph, Canadian Pacific's first three Fort William grain elevators can be seen. From left to right are: Elevator B, built in 1889 to supplement Elevator A; Elevator A, built in 1885; and Elevator C, built in 1890. These elevators were replaced later by modern, privately owned concrete structures.

— *OA S4741*

Elevator D, built in 1902, was Canadian Pacific's last elevator to be built at Fort William. Constructed of fire-proof steel, the elevator held 1,976,000 bushels of grain. All of the railway's elevators at Fort William fronted on the Kaminstiquia River.

— *Thunder Bay Historical Museum Society 983.29.65*

The concrete Grand Trunk Pacific grain elevator, operated by the railway's subsidiary the Grand Trunk Pacific Terminal Elevator Company, was opened in 1909 with a total capacity of 3,250,000 bushels. In 1912, capacity was further enhanced with the construction of a two-and-a-half-million-bushel storage annex. In this postcard view, the original workhouse is at the dock face at the right, with its storage annex connected to it by overhead bridges to the rear. The 1912 addition is behind the box cars (lettered for the Grand Trunk Pacific) at the left. To give some idea of the structure's overall size, the workhouse alone measured 240 feet in length, 68 feet in width and 182 feet in height. The storage annexes were approximately 100 feet in height. In 1909 the elevator cost 1.25 million dollars to build. It was later sold by Canadian National to the National Grain Company. — *TBHMS 974.135.2*

In 1902, the Canadian Northern Railway erected this elevator at Port Arthur with two wooden workhouses, designated A and B, and tile storage annexes. With each workhouse holding a million bushels and the storage annexes 5 million bushels, the total capacity of the complex was 7 million bushels. The choice of wood in the construction of the workhouses may have been made for financial considerations but if there were any savings to be made, they could not have been great in light of the risk of fire. Elevator B burned in 1919 and was replaced in 1920 by a concrete structure. Elevator A was subsequently demolished although the storage annexes are still in use. Canadian National Railways inherited the elevator from Canadian Northern, but the company sold the structure in 1960 after leasing it for a number of years. Today, the elevator is known as Saskatchewan Pool No. 6. — *TBHMS 984.42.8*

One of the last railway grain elevators to be built in Ontario was Canadian Pacific's two-million-bushel elevator at Port McNicoll. Constructed of concrete by the Montreal-based John S. Metcalfe Company and opened in 1910, the elevator was enlarged further until by 1936 it had reached a total capacity of 6.5 million bushels of grain (some 5.5 million bushels short of the elevator's original maximum projected size). In this view, which includes Canada Steamship Lines' freighter *W. Grant Morden*, two of the elevators' movable marine unloading towers can be seen, each with a handling capacity of 20,000 bushels of grain per hour. The advantage of using movable towers was that the towers could move along the length of the ship, unloading each hold consecutively without having to move the entire ship, thereby reducing the length of the elevator dock face and saving a great deal of time. — *OA Acc. 2375 S5380*

CHAPTER TWO - NOTES

1) Lance Phillips, *Yonder Comes the Train* (New York, 1965), p. 103. From New York Central Railroad advertisement.
2) G.R. Stevens, *Canadian National Railways, Vol. 1* (Toronto, 1960), p. 108.
3) J.M. & Edw. Trout, *The Railways of Canada* (Toronto, 1970/1871), p. 55 and p. 95.
4) Erik Heyl, *Early American Steamers, Vol. 6* (Buffalo, n.d.), p. 135. Erik Heyl indicates that *Europa* took up a regular route between Hamilton and Ogdensburg in June 1855, stating that *Europa* left Hamilton "every Monday and Thursday at 7:00 a.m., arriving at Kingston, Ont., at 11:00 p.m. and then continuing to Ogdensburg . . . *Europa* left Ogdensburg every Tuesday and Friday at about 2:00 p.m. after the mail train from Montreal had arrived; she called at Kingston at 8:00 p.m." While the date coincides with her commencement of service under charter to the Great Western, the route seems to be more in keeping with the 1856 schedules, during which time the steamer routes were extended to Ogdensburg. However, due to a lack of information on the railway's steamer services, the above may indeed be correct.
5) United States Navy logbooks do exist for an *America* for the periods 28 July — 2 September 1866 and for 1 October 1866 — 30 October 1868; as well as for a *Western World* for the periods 3 January 1862 — 17 November 1863 and for 14 November 1864 — 26 May 1865. Due to the common use of names such as *America* and *Western World* during the last century, any direct relationship between the above vessels and those of the Great Western's line would be difficult to prove. The logbooks mentioned are now on deposit with the National Archives in Washington, D.C. See also note 6.
6) Erik Heyl, op. cit., p. 19 and p. 69. *America* operated as *Coatzacoalcos* from 1859 to 1862 and is listed by Mr. Heyl with the following owners after leaving the Detroit & Milwaukee interests: Peter A. Hargous, New York, 1858-60; Marshall O. Roberts, 1860-62; Peoples Line, 1862-64; Central American Transit Company, 1864-66; North American Steamship Company, 1866-68; Pacific Mail Steamship Company, 1868-69. *Canada*, renamed *Mississippi* in 1859, similarly had the following owners: Peter A. Hargous, New York, 1858-60; N.P. Stewart & Company, and George Savary, New York, 1861-62.
7) G.R. Stevens, op. cit., pp. 282-283.
8) G.R. Stevens, op. cit., p. 283.
9) Based on information available.
10) G.R. Stevens, op. cit., p. 398.
11) J.M. & Edw. Trout, op. cit., p. 107.
12) John O. Greenwood, *Namesakes 1930-11955* (Cleveland, n.d.)
13) John P. Heisler, *The Canals of Canada* (Ottawa, 1973), p. 143.
14) Ibid.
15) G.R. Stevens, *Canadian National Railways, Vol. 2* (Toronto, 1962), p. 369.
16) Ibid., p. 244.
17) Niall MacKay, *Over the Hills to Georgian Bay* (Erin, 1981), p. 76.
18) William John Wilgus, *The Railway Interrelations of the United States and Canada* (Toronto, 1937), pp. 199-201.
19) Ibid., p. 112.

The southern entrance to the Welland Canal at Port Colborne, looking north towards the canal. The Welland Railway's elevator is on the right. A comparison between the Welland's two elevators will show how they differed, most notably in the provision of an unloading arm and integral marine tower with the Port Colborne elevator (the tall structure on the left side).
— OA Acc. 13967-19

III

THE PORTAGE RAILWAYS

As related in chapter one, much of Ontario's early development was linked to the province's waterways and particularly to the Great Lakes. But like all waterways, there were many obstacles to navigation: rapids, waterfalls, reefs, rocks, etc. Aids to navigation such as canals and lighthouses alleviated many hindrances, yet they seldom provided permanent solutions. While lighthouses could be remodelled with limited expense, canals were extremely expensive undertakings and governments usually resisted reconstruction until absolutely necessary, by which time the canals had become outdated. Such was the plight of the Welland Canal, one of the earliest and probably the most ambitious undertakings of its kind in early Ontario.

The First Welland Canal

The Niagara Peninsula had long been a barrier to early travellers, and as lake commerce evolved it became increasingly apparent that the laborious and costly portage of goods around Niagara Falls was strangling trade between Lakes Erie and Ontario. Although the idea of a canal to carry ships around Niagara Falls had long been proposed, it was not until 1821 that the government of Upper Canada (as Ontario was then known) made provision for a new waterway under "An Act to make provision for the Improvement of the Internal Navigation of the Province," by which a board of commissioners was appointed to investigate the most viable navigation routes between Lakes Erie and Ontario and to the border with Quebec. When they made their final report in 1823, the commission proposed that a canal running from the mouth of the Grand River on Lake Erie all the way to Burlington Bay on Lake Ontario be constructed, at an estimated cost of £206,554[1]. A tidy sum to be sure, and the government could little afford to pay out on such a project (which was later deemed to be unfeasible).

In 1824 private enterprise came to the rescue in the form of the Welland Canal Company, formed in that year to construct a canal system to link Lake Erie with Lake Ontario. Led by William Hamilton Merritt, a Niagara Peninsula merchant, with noted civil engineer George Keefer as president, the company first proposed to link the two bodies of water by combining a canal from the Welland River (Lake Erie would be reached via the Welland River and the Niagara River) to the crest of the Niagara Escarpment, where a marine railway would carry boats down to Twelve Mile Creek and thence to Lake Ontario. Work began in November 1824, but with little public support, since the scheme limited the size of vessels able to pass through, such that many felt that there was limited to no benefit to be gained from the enterprise.

The company soon gave in to public opinion, and by the spring of 1825 a new plan was unveiled, this time allowing schooners, then the principal lake vessels in service, to pass through. The marine railway was eliminated with the intention now to bring the canal down from the Welland River at Port Robinson, all the way to Lake Ontario, terminating at Port Dalhousie. Construction started in earnest, and finally on 29 November 1829 the Welland Canal was opened, with the Lake Ontario schooners *Ann and Jane* of Toronto and *R.H. Boughton* of Youngstown, New

York, becoming the first ships to pass through the canal. The ships reached Black Rock (Buffalo), New York, on Lake Erie on December 2 and returned to Lake Ontario on the following day, thereby completing the first round trip through the Welland; the upper and lower lakes were now united.

By the end of the following season, it was determined that the route along the Welland and Niagara rivers was unsuitable due to the currents, and the canal was subsequently extended directly to Lake Erie at Port Colborne.

The Erie & Ontario Railroad

It was not long before it was realized that the capacity of the canal was inadequate. Larger ships were being built, capable of handling larger cargoes, while the steamships which were then being introduced were totally incapable of passing through the narrow locks. In an attempt to resolve this problem as well as compete with the Welland Canal, a group of businessmen from the Niagara River area obtained a charter in 1835 for the Erie & Ontario Railroad Company. It proposed to build a portage railway from Chippawa, where the Welland River and Canal intersected the Niagara River upstream of the falls, down the escarpment to Queenston on the lower Niagara River. Steamers would connect either end of the railway with Toronto and Buffalo, and it was hoped that traffic from the Welland Canal could be diverted its way.

The line was finally completed in 1839, but not as a steam railway as proposed. The route up the escarpment face was too steep for the small steam locomotives of the day, and horse-drawn wagons guided by iron-capped wooden rails were substituted. While it proved a success with tourists, the Erie & Ontario could barely compete with the Welland Canal.

The Second Welland Canal

During the early 1840s the Welland Canal underwent its first major rebuilding, now under the auspices of the government of Upper Canada, which had assumed control of the canal company as a result of financial problems in 1841. The old wooden locks were replaced with fewer stone locks of greater capacity. When the work was done and the "second canal" opened in 1845, much of the transshipment of cargo that had taken place earlier was eliminated and, with it, the need for the Erie & Ontario Railroad. The railway could not survive on tourist traffic alone, and by the end of the decade it had faded into oblivion.

The Welland Canal, however, was not out of the woods yet. The ships being launched were increasingly larger, especially the steamships.

Sometimes the larger ships were able to lighten their cargoes, thereby reducing their draught and enabling them to pass through the shallow locks. That was often a costly proposition, but if the amount to be transshipped was small, or if it could be transferred to another ship passing through in the same direction, the procedure was economical. When the hull dimensions surpassed those of the locks, real difficulties arose. It was then necessary to unload the entire contents of the ship and either transfer the freight to smaller vessels to complete the journey (if a ship or ships were available) or else team the entire cargo over the Niagara Peninsula by horse and wagon, to be reloaded onto another ship at the opposite end of the canal. This was a very expensive process, particularly when teaming the freight by horse and wagon. Often, many ship owners preferred to send their cargo east through the Erie Canal by way of Buffalo rather than the Welland Canal.

Attempts were made by the government in 1853 to relieve the situation by deepening the locks, but to no avail. Though a few more ships with deeper draughts were able to pass through the canal, the basic problems remained. With the millions of dollars already invested by the government, any further reconstruction was out of the question.

The Port Dalhousie & Thorold Railway
The Welland Railway

Meanwhile, William Hamilton Merritt, the original promoter of the Welland Canal Company, returned to the scene in May 1853 and with other investors incorporated the Port Dalhousie & Thorold Railway. Projected to run from Thorold on the Great Western Railway's main line to Port Dalhousie on Lake Ontario, terminus of the Welland Canal, the line was to serve as a branch of the Great Western by providing it with additional access to Lake Ontario shipping. It was a dubious venture, to say the least. Even though the railway would provide the Great Western with an additional port on Lake Ontario, the Great Western's own home port was only a short distance to the west at Hamilton, and it is doubtful that the railway's proximity to the canal would have been able to draw any extra traffic for the Great Western. The scheme's only saving grace was the provision under the railway's charter allowing the company to "construct, own, or employ . . . a steamboat or steamboats for the transportation of passengers and freight from the terminus of their railway at Port Dalhousie to any point on Lake Ontario."[2] While typical of many such railway charters granted during those early years, the influence of Merritt on the railway is clearly in evidence.

Industrialist Merritt had for years been a staunch proponent for canals, opposing any and all railway proposals. It was his belief that all efforts at establishing a transportation network in Upper Canada should be directed towards the development of the most economical and efficient system possible, or, in other words, canals. He was not anti-railway, he simply believed that canals had top priority. By the 1850s the canal systems in the province had become firmly entrenched and William Hamilton Merritt could turn his attention to the railway boom. In his view, railways could supplement the canals, carrying valuable freight not suited to shipment by water and providing a transportation alternative during the winter months.

The steamship provision of the charter allowed Merritt and his company to keep a foot in both camps, railway and water, and if a line of steamers was established it would guarantee a steady flow of traffic for the Port Dalhousie & Thorold Railway, even if only for the season of navigation. But would this be enough to support the enterprise?

The answer was no. As it stood, the railway could serve no useful purpose for the Great Western, nor would its proximity to the Welland Canal alone provide any benefit. If, however, the railway could be extended south following the canal to Port Colborne, the railway could then attain real purpose as a portage railway. As the company's "Prospectus" of June 1856 stated: "Immediately on the arrival of steamers at either end of the Welland Canal, light and valuable freight will be transferred by Railway from one Steamer to another in the same line, having previously passed through the Canal, and ready to proceed to her port of destination on the opposite lake. By this arrangement heavy freight will not be subject to transshipment, while light freight will secure speed and certainty."[3]

The type of freight the railway hoped to carry was further defined in its "Prospectus" of September 1856: "Passengers, livestock, butter, cheese and valuable merchandise will be transferred to the Railway, while timber, lumber, grain, iron, salt and cheap bulky articles will go through the Canal, and each will add to the business of the other."[4]

These "Prospectus' " served to attract new capital to the railway, particularly British. With it, the company received new life and vitality, and in June 1857 was renamed the Welland Railway Company, reflecting its new goals.

One aim of the new Welland Railway was to develop a competitive grain route to the eastern seaboard, singling out the Erie Canal, which terminated at Buffalo, as its primary target. Just as Frederick Cumberland estimated the comparative freight costs for the Northern Railway, the Welland's management, too, made comparisons, estimating that on a cost per ton-mile basis the Welland could deliver grain to New York via the Oswego Canal at $5.41, as opposed to the Erie Canal at $6.01, and Montreal via the Grand Trunk Railway at $11.46.[5] These were impressive savings indeed, based on the premise that the railway would be in possession of a Lake Ontario fleet of steamers when it opened, and that the Erie Canal would continue to lose its competitiveness — the Erie had been losing traffic to the Welland Canal and the various railways radiating from Buffalo since the early 1850s.

But the railway had yet to purchase any steamships, and as for the Erie Canal, while it was losing some business to the railways, the New York Central in particular, the volume of freight carried by the Erie far exceeded that carried by the Welland Canal. In 1856, for example, the Erie moved 4,022,617 tons of freight, as opposed to only 976,656 tons shipped through the Welland.[6] Much of the grain and flour traffic from the American West continued to be sent east via the Erie Canal mainly because of the inability of the Welland to handle large steamers. Most shippers felt that if cargoes had to be transshipped, they may as well send them through the Erie rather than the more round-about Welland route.

Coal traffic from Pennsylvania was also looked upon with promise, eventually taking second place to grain as one of the Welland Canal's major commodities. The railway hoped that an increased demand for coal in Canada would bring additional revenue for the company.

By the autumn of 1858 all the track for the Welland Railway had been laid and was ready for use. The only hurdle left was the construction of the necessary stations and buildings, of which none were even started, despite the planned opening in the following April! But by the next spring all was nearing completion, and in June 1859 regular operations commenced.

The first steamship for the Welland Railway had been purchased in time for the railway's opening on 27 June 1859 (identity of the ship has not been determined), and at Port Colborne and Port Dalhousie, grain elevators capable of handling 4,000 bushels of grain per hour were ready to transfer the grain between the ships and trains. The future was bright and rosy for the Welland, and for a time the management's expectations of handling ten million bushels of grain each year seemed to be within grasp.

In the following year the railway "received cargoes of 230 vessels at Port Colborne, 150 of which were of such dimensions as admitted their passing through the Canal."[7] In terms of grain carried, the railway moved a total of 86,004 tons, of which 81,243 tons were destined for American ports, most probably going to New York City by way of the Oswego Canal.[8] Yet this represented less than one-fifth of the railway's capacity to move grain. The elevators at Port Colborne and Port Dalhousie were each designed to transfer 500,000 tons of grain each year.

Something was wrong, and it soon became apparent that unless the railway could secure a sufficient number of ships to carry the grain on Lake Ontario between Port Dalhousie and Oswego, it could lose the grain traffic entirely to Buffalo and possibly go bankrupt in the process. The shortage of ships on Lake Ontario was the same problem faced by the Northern Railway at Toronto, and to a large degree was responsible for the demise of that company's operations on the Great Lakes after 1862. The Welland could not afford to get itself into that predicament and needed the ships even if it had to buy them itself.

In 1864 the Welland Railway took delivery of two new steamships from the Shickluna Shipyards at St. Catharines. The first was the 564-ton *Perseverance*, launched in early July, followed by the 600-ton *Enterprise* in late October. Similar in size and probably in appearance, they were capable of carrying both passengers and freight, including up to 37,000 bushels of grain each.[9] Together they would maintain the route between Port Dalhousie and Oswego for the railway until 1868, when tragedy struck the line.

In October 1868, while heading for Oswego, the *Perseverance* burned on Lake Ontario, taking with it 14 lives. This may not have been the first such disaster for the company and it certainly would not be the last. There is no record of the first ship owned by the company — a ship whose name is not even known — but it may have been possible that it was destroyed in a similar incident.

To replace the *Perseverance*, the railway commissioned a new ship from Shickluna Shipyards, the 353-ton *Dalhousie*, delivered in 1869. Significantly smaller than the *Perseverance* and the *Enterprise*, *Dalhousie* was able to pass through the Welland Canal, allowing it to operate independently of the railway whenever it wasn't needed for Lake Ontario service. That was the case in 1872. While carrying a load of pig iron and general merchandise from Chicago to Montreal, the *Dalhousie* caught fire and burned on Lake Ontario off Charlotte, New York. The date was September

The 564-ton *Perseverance* is seen here shortly after completion. Features of the vessel to note are the twin, side-by-side stacks, the clerestoried passenger cabins on top, and the octagonal wheelhouse. Most of the main deck's space was reserved for freight.
— *St. Catharines Historical Museum N 3953*

Here is Port Dalhousie station as it appeared around 1890, during the days of the Grand Trunk. While the station house seems to be of Grand Trunk origin, the other buildings, including the grain elevator at the left, are probably Welland Railway structures. It is very possible that this view was taken shortly before the departure of the *Empress of India* for Toronto, as evidenced by the passenger trains and what looks like crates of fruit stacked near the box car at the right (which, incidently, is a Grand Trunk car lettered for the Welland Railway). The entrance to the Welland Canal can be seen above the stern of the *Empress of India*, at the left of her paddle box. — *SCHM N 1586*

26, but this time no lives were lost, as the steamship *City of Concord* came to the rescue. There would be no replacement for the *Dalhousie.*

Increases in grain traffic failed to materialize and the railway was in no position to gamble on any further ships. They would have to make do with the *Enterprise* and local railway freight traffic. Fortunately for the railway, some relief was gained when the Canadian government decided to rebuild the Welland Canal, beginning in 1871 and finishing in 1887, allowing ships of up to 262 feet in length to pass through. The transport of materials to the construction site was almost exclusively handled by the Welland Railway, amounting to thousands of carloads of stone, cement and timber.

In 1873 the Great Western Railway obtained running rights over a portion of the Welland and, as a result, the Welland's broad-gauge track was changed to standard gauge. For the next few years the Welland would maintain close connections with the Great Western.

During this period the *Enterprise* made its final runs, and by 1881 it had been sold to private interests. The *Enterprise* survived several rebuildings and changes in ownership, including a change in name, before it was scuttled in 1912.

By 1882 the Grand Trunk Railway was in control of the Great Western as it made its bid to control the railway network in southern Ontario. In 1884 the Welland Railway became part of the Grand Trunk and was relegated to a branch line.

Other steamer links with the Welland Railway remained however. As early as 1859, the year the railway opened, the steamship *Peerless* was running twice daily between Toronto and Port Dalhousie, where it connected with the Welland's regular passenger trains. The *Peerless* served on the run until 1860. In 1861 she was sold to the United States government for its blockade of southern ports during the American Civil War.

The paddle-steamer *Empress of India* was introduced onto the Toronto run in 1884 after the Grand Trunk assumed control of the Welland. Brought under contract to run between Toronto and Port Dalhousie, she connected with a fast train to Niagara Falls and Buffalo as an alternative to the Grand Trunk's regular rail service. The following extract from the Grand Trunk timetable of 22 September 1887 illustrates the service:

Read Down		Read Up
3:40 p.m. Lv.	Toronto (via EMPRESS OF INDIA)	Ar. 12:45 p.m.
6:20 p.m.	Port Dalhousie	10:15 a.m.
7:05 p.m.	Niagara Falls	9:30 a.m.
7:15 p.m.	Suspension Bridge (N.Y.C.)	9:20 a.m.
8:17 p.m.	Buffalo (N.Y.L.E. & W.)	8:15 a.m.
9:00 p.m. Ar.	Buffalo (N.Y.C. & W.S.)	Lv. —

(N.Y.C.) - New York Central Railroad
(N.Y.L.E. & W.) - New York, Lake Erie & Western Railroad
(N.Y.C. & W.S.) - New York Central & West Shore Railroad

It must have been a pleasant diversion for tourists and business travellers alike, but the route was never able to compete with services offered through the Canada Southern Railway over the old Erie & Niagara line. In part it was probably the scenic value of the Niagara River that gave the Canada Southern its advantage over the Grand Trunk, especially for excursionists, but it was also frequency that was to blame. The Grand Trunk only offered one trip per day each way via the *Empress of India;* Canada Southern provided two trips each way, enabling passengers to make a one-day excursion trip to Buffalo or Toronto without the need for an overnight stay. It was no wonder that the *Empress of India* service only managed to draw local traffic from the Niagara Peninsula, but it was sufficient to keep her on the route well into the 1890s. When the *Empress of India* left, she took with her the Welland's last real vestige of steamer service.

Photographed during the late 1890s, the *Empress of India* is seen here arriving at Port Dalhousie with a full load of summertime excursionists. In 1899, *Empress of India* was rebuilt as the *Argyle* and subsequently moved on to other steamer routes. As the *Frontier*, she sank on the Detroit River in 1918. The structure at the right of the picture is the steamship coaling dock.

— *OA Acc. 12026-138*

In the years preceding the First World War, militia units from the western Lake Ontario region traditionally headed for the military training grounds at Niagara-on-the-Lake for summer exercises; part of that tradition included the steamer trip to Niagara. In this view, members of one of the militia regiments, including many family members, are seen boarding the *Lakeside* at Niagara for the return journey, possibly to Toronto or Port Hope. At the time this photograph was taken, the *Lakeside* was still probably under the ownership of the Lakeside Navigation Company, operating here under charter. *— OA Acc. 13098-93*

The *Garden City*, the second steamer acquired by Lakeside Navigation, was considerably larger than her sistership *Lakeside*. Whereas *Lakeside* acquired its name from the Lakeside Navigation Company, *Garden City* was named for the City of St. Catharines, known as the "Garden City". *— OA Acc. 12026-104*

The Niagara, St. Catharines & Toronto Railway
The Niagara, St. Catharines & Toronto Navigation Company

Successor to the Welland Railway, at least in terms of passenger service, was the Niagara, St. Catharines & Toronto Railway, an electric interurban operation strongly influenced by the steam railways around it. Its roots dated back to 1881, when the St. Catharines & Niagara Central Railway was formed to construct a series of lines throughout the Niagara region. It was a steam operation with great expectations, but in the end it only managed to construct 12 miles of railway between St. Catharines and Niagara Falls. It was those 12 miles, built to very high standards, which were to form the backbone of a new enterprise.

When the company ran into financial difficulties in 1899, it was sold to a group of American businessmen with large interests in an electric interurban railway based out of Saratoga Springs, New York. Under their control the steam railway was reincorporated as the Niagara, St. Catharines & Toronto Railway, and by 1900 they had completely electrified the line. Between 1900 and 1902 other local electric railways were added, including the street railways at Niagara Falls and St. Catharines.

The year 1901 was one of diversification. An extension was built from St. Catharines to Port Dalhousie, where docking facilities and an amusement park were developed opposite the old Welland Railway terminal. Most importantly, they established the Niagara, St. Catharines & Toronto Navigation Company following the purchase of the Lakeside Navigation Company.

Through Lakeside Navigation the new navigation company obtained its first two steamships, the 348-ton *Lakeside* and the 637-ton *Garden City.* They allowed the company to move into the Toronto market, providing tourists for the amusement park and passengers for the railway, many of whom were no doubt bound for Niagara Falls.

Meanwhile, back in the United States, the company's owners were fighting for control of their American lines and were forced to sell the Niagara, St. Catharines & Toronto in 1907 to raise capital. They sold to William Mackenzie and Donald Mann, owners of the Canadian Northern Railway.

The new owners of the Niagara, St. Catharines & Toronto Railway and its steamship subsidiary immediately embarked on an expansion program aimed at the establishment of a new line from St. Catharines to Port Colborne. With the new line, the railway hoped to capture a portion of the passenger and freight traffic between Lakes Ontario and Erie, which had been controlled for so long by the Grand Trunk and earlier by the Welland Railway. The extension was opened to traffic in 1911. In 1913 a line was built from St. Catharines to Niagara-on-the-Lake.

By 1911 passenger traffic on Lake Ontario had increased so much that the small *Lakeside* was hardly able to keep up with demand. She was replaced by the 1,256-ton *Dalhousie City,* launched earlier that year by Collingwood Shipbuilding. Well equipped to handle the route to Toronto, *Dalhousie City* was even able to take over the duties of the *Garden City* in 1916.

When the Canadian Northern fell into financial despair during the First World War, the Canadian government had no choice other than to take over the assets of the railway in 1917, including the Niagara, St. Catharines & Toronto Railway and Navigation Companies, and in 1923 they came under the control of the newly formed Crown Corporation, Canadian National Railways.

Government backing brought with it many advantages for the companies. During the post-war period, passenger traffic experienced an upturn and for the Niagara, St. Catharines & Toronto Navigation Company, the volumes were too great for the *Dalhousie City* to handle alone. Fortunately the steamship *Northumberland,* which since 1894 had provided a ferry service for the government across the Northumberland Strait between Prince Edward Island and the mainland, had become surplus and in 1920 was transferred to the navigation company for duty on Lake Ontario. While ownership of the 1,255-ton, British-built *Northumberland* remained with the federal government through the Minister of Transport, she was in all other respects a part of the navigation company's fleet.

For the next three decades the *Dalhousie City* and the *Northumberland* carried thousands of excursionists between Toronto and Port Dalhousie, keeping the interurban line supplied with passengers and Canadian National supplied with needed revenue. Table 3-1 outlines the steamer

In a race for Toronto Harbour's Eastern Gap, and hence Lake Ontario, the *Garden City* is seen running flat-out with the *Cayuga* of the Niagara Navigation Company in hot pursuit. Within the confines of the harbour, the paddle driven *Garden City* could hold its own, especially over the short distance to the gap, but on the open lake, she was no match for the powerful propeller *Cayuga*. Fortunately for the *Garden City*, the two would go their separate ways once on the lake. *— OA S17375*

Named in honour of Port Dalhousie, the *Dalhousie City*, built in 1911, was the only ship to be built expressly for the Niagara, St. Catharines & Toronto. Built at Collingwood, the 1,256-ton ship replaced the *Lakeside* in 1911 and assumed responsibility for the company's entire lake business in 1916 when the *Garden City* was withdrawn. Shown here entering Port Dalhousie, the *Dalhousie City* appears in her original configuration. *— Canadian National X45427*

Built in England in 1894 for service on the Northumberland Strait between Prince Edward Island and the mainland, *Northumberland* was transferred by the government in 1920 to Lake Ontario to bolster the service offered by the Niagara, St. Catharines & Toronto Navigation Company. This early 1920s photo shows *Northumberland* arriving at Toronto in her original condition. *— OA Acc. 12026-153*

In the late 1920s or the early 1930s the *Northumberland* (left) and the *Dalhousie City* (right) were given roofed enclosures above their top after decks as additional weather protection for passengers. In this stern view, taken at the Niagara, St. Catharines & Toronto dock at Port Dalhousie, these alterations are plainly visible, as is the new stairway to *Northumberland*'s upper deck at the stern. The lettering on *Northumberland*'s ornamented stern reads "Northumberland" along the top and "Charlottetown" (P.E.I.) — her port of registry — below. *— OA Acc. 12026-107*

This is how *Northumberland* appeared in the late 1930s and the 1940s following the extension of her top deck over her upper deck to provide her passengers with maximum protection from rain. *Northumberland* is seen here leaving Toronto Harbour by way of the Western Gap. — *OA Acc. 12026-174*

Here is *Dalhousie City* in the late 1940s leaving Toronto through the Western Gap. The lettering at her bow reads "Canadian National Steamers", below which is written, in small letters, "Operated by N., St.C. & T. Ry.". Note that the lower half of the hull is painted in a darker colour, not white. — *OA 9-F-189*

schedule for the busy summer of 1943 and was typical of these years. By the end of the 1940s, though, it was becoming evident that many former patrons had abandoned the railway and steamships in favour of the automobile; the days of the navigation company were coming to a close.

The end for the *Northumberland* came quite by accident in June 1949. While docked at Port Dalhousie, the aging *Northumberland* caught fire and burned beyond the point of reasonable repair. She was later towed to Port Weller and scrapped. The *Dalhousie City* was sold in the 1950s, only to catch fire and burn in 1960 at Lachine, Quebec, thus ending the saga of the Niagara, St. Catharines & Toronto Navigation Company. The railway would only survive for a few more years.

Table 3-1
NIAGARA, ST. CATHARINES & TORONTO NAVIGATION COMPANY STEAMSHIP SERVICE TORONTO - PORT DALHOUSIE

Summer 1943

29 May to 8 June

Southbound	Toronto Leave	Port Dalhousie Arrive
Daily	8:30 a.m.	11:00 a.m.
Saturday & Sunday Only	2:30 p.m.	5:00 p.m.
Daily	6:00 p.m.	8:30 p.m.
Saturday & Sunday Only	9:30 p.m.	12:00

Northbound	Port Dalhousie Leave	Toronto Arrive
Daily except Sunday	8:30 a.m.	11:00 a.m.
Sunday Only	10:30 a.m.	1:00 p.m.
Saturday & Sunday Only	2:30 p.m.	5:00 p.m.
Daily	6:30 p.m.	9:00 p.m.
Saturday & Sunday Only	8:30 p.m.	11:00 p.m.

9 June to 6 September

Southbound	Toronto Leave	Port Dalhousie Arrive
Daily	8:30 a.m.	11:00 a.m.
Holidays & Sunday Only	9:30 a.m.	12:00
Daily	2:30 p.m.	5:00 p.m.
Daily except Friday	A6:00 p.m.	8:30 p.m.
Wednesday, Saturday, Sunday & Holidays	9:30 p.m.	12:00

A - Fridays only leave 6:30 p.m.

Northbound	Port Dalhousie Leave	Toronto Arrive
Daily	11:00 a.m.	1:30 p.m.
Wednesday, Saturday, Sunday & Holidays	2:30 p.m.	5:00 p.m.
Daily	6:30 p.m.	9:00 p.m.
Daily except Friday	B8:30 p.m.	11:00 p.m.
Saturday & Holidays	12:00	2:30 a.m.

B - Fridays only leave 10:00 p.m.

The *Clifton* was constructed to carry Erie & Ontario Railway passengers between Chippawa, above Niagara Falls, and Buffalo, New York, along the Niagara River. Once the railway was extended to Fort Erie, opposite Buffalo, as the Erie & Niagara Railway, *Clifton's* services were no longer required and she was subsequently sold to the Owen Sound Mail Line around 1865. Seen here at Owen Sound, *Clifton* was shortly after reduced to a barge. — *OA Acc. 19996-45*

The steamer *Peerless*, launched at Niagara in 1853 for Captain Dick and Andrew Heron. Sold to American interests in May 1861, the *Peerless* sank off of Cape Hatteras on the Atlantic coast the following November. — *MTL T-30729*

The *Samuel Zimmerman* was built in 1854 for Oliver T. Macklem. Macklem owned a large foundry at Chippawa, just south of Niagara Falls. — *MTL T-16153*

The Erie & Ontario Railway
The Erie & Niagara Railway

The Erie & Ontario Railway was a reincarnation of the extinct Erie & Ontario Railroad first chartered in 1835. Promoted by the American-born entrepreneur Samuel Zimmerman, known for his dubious business transactions, the company used the charter of the original line, as amended in 1852, to build a new steam railway between Chippawa (Niagara Falls) and Niagara-on-the-Lake, roughly parallelling the old horse line along the Niagara River. Unlike the old company, the new Erie & Ontario Railway was built for the convenience of travellers, especially tourists and those making the trip between Toronto, Niagara Falls, and Buffalo, New York, and not as an adjunct to the Welland Canal.

It was therefore appropriate that the Erie & Ontario developed strong links with lake steamers operating on Lake Ontario between its terminus at Niagara and Toronto. After all, when the railway opened in 1854, there were only two other railways operating in the province, the first being the Ontario, Simcoe & Huron (later the Northern Railway) and the second being the Great Western Railway, both of which were still under construction. Long-distance travel was still very much the domain of the navigation companies in Canada, and for an isolated railway like the Erie & Ontario, steamers were the only means of receiving passengers, for which the company made ample provision.

Operations commenced on 28 June 1854 with the railway's lone steam engine, the *Clifton*, providing the motive power for the four daily trains. Initially only the paddle-steamer *Peerless*, built the previous year at Niagara from components prefabricated in Scotland, provided the needed link with Toronto, as shown in the following timetable based on an advertisement for the Erie & Ontario which appeared in the Toronto *Globe*:

Effective Wednesday 28 June 1854
Daily except Sundays

Read	Down	Read Up
6:25 a.m. 1:20 p.m. Lv.	Toronto (via steamer PEERLESS)	Ar. 11:15 a.m. 6:15 p.m.
9:00 a.m. 4:00 p.m.	Niagara	8:35 a.m. 3:35 p.m.
9:40 a.m. 4:40 p.m.	Suspension Bridge	8:00 a.m. 3:00 p.m.
9:55 a.m. 4:50 p.m.	Clifton House	7:45 a.m. 2:45 p.m.
10:05 a.m. 5:00 p.m. Ar.	Chippawa	Lv. 7:25 a.m. 2:25 p.m.

Within months of opening, the *Samuel Zimmerman*, newly built at Niagara and named in honour of the Erie & Ontario's promoter, was added to the Toronto run and shared the route with the *Peerless*. For the convenience of passengers travelling to Buffalo, the services of the steamer *Clifton* were secured to operate between Chippawa and Buffalo.

The steamships were able to provide service during ten months of the year on Lake Ontario, depending on winter ice conditions, and probably nine months on the Niagara River. It is interesting to note that none of the ships were ever owned by the railway. Their owners knew that a connection with the Erie & Ontario would give them a dependable source of passengers, thereby benefitting all parties concerned.

By the end of the decade the economy was looking bleak and passenger traffic had begun to dry up. Realizing that there was insufficient business for both ships, the owner of the *Samuel Zimmerman*, Oliver Macklem, decided to withdraw his ship from the Niagara River in 1860 in favour of the *Peerless*. Indeed, as early as at least 1859, the *Peerless* was also making a connection with the Welland Railway. But this arrangement did not last. In May 1861 the *Peerless* was sold to the American government, who took her down to New York. It was their intention to use *Peerless* in the blockade of Confederate ports during the Civil War, a demand that took many ships off the Great Lakes during those years. Fate intervened, however, and shortly after arriving on the Atlantic, she sunk off Cape Hatteras.

With the *Peerless* gone, the *Samuel Zimmerman* returned to the Toronto run, but it too was destined for a violent end. In August 1863 the steamer burned while docked at Niagara. Two crewmen were burned to death in the accident.

The year 1863 brought other changes to the Erie & Ontario as well. To the south the Fort Erie Railway, incorporated in 1857 to build a railway from Chippawa to Fort Erie, made the decision to purchase the Erie & Ontario and thereby create a through line all the way from Niagara-on-the-Lake to Fort Erie, opposite Buffalo. The two companies were merged and together formed the Erie & Niagara Railway Company.

The *Clifton* was out of work. Now passengers arriving at Niagara could travel all the way to Fort Erie by train, requiring only a short ferry trip across the Niagara River to reach Buffalo. The *Clifton* finished up in Owen Sound, where she was dismantled in 1866. What remained of *Clifton's* hull was converted into a barge the following year.

By 1867 the steamship *City of Toronto* was making connections with both the Erie & Niagara at Niagara and the New York Central at Queenston. An advertisement in the Toronto *Globe* of 1 July 1867 included the following information for the *City of Toronto*:

"The following timetable will take effect on and after Monday, the 1st July:-

Via New York Central Railway	—	Toronto to Buffalo
Leave Yonge Street Wharf	at	7:00 a.m. and 2:00 p.m.
Arrive at Queenston	at	9:45 a.m. and 4:45 p.m.
Arrive at Suspension Bridge	at	9:50 a.m. and 4:50 p.m.
Arrive at Niagara Falls	at	10:15 a.m. and 5:10 p.m.
Arrive at Erie St. Buffalo	at	11:35 a.m. and 7:10 p.m.
Via New York Central Railway	—	Buffalo to Toronto
Leave Erie St. Depot Buffalo	at	9:00 a.m. and 2:45 p.m.
Arrive at Niagara Falls	at	9:50 a.m. and 4:00 p.m.
Arrive at Suspension Bridge	at	9:55 a.m. and 4:05 p.m.
Arrive at Lewiston	at	10:15 a.m. and 4:25 p.m.
Arrive at Toronto	at	1:15 p.m. and 7:30 p.m.
Via Erie and Niagara Railway	—	Toronto to Buffalo
Leave Yonge Street Wharf Toronto	at	7:00 a.m. and 2:00 p.m.
Arrive at Niagara Town	at	9:15 a.m. and 4:15 p.m.
Arrive at Fort Erie	at	11:00 a.m. and 6:00 p.m.
Arrive at Buffalo	at	11:30 a.m. and 7:30 p.m.
Via Erie and Niagara Railway	—	Buffalo to Toronto
Leave Foot of Main St. Buffalo	at	8:30 a.m. and 3:00 p.m.
Arrive at Niagara Town	at	10:30 a.m. and 5:00 p.m.
Arrive at Toronto	at	1:15 p.m. and 7:30 p.m.

For Through Tickets, Railway Freight, and all necessary information, apply at the office, No. 9 Front St."

The reader will note that the New York Central route followed the American side of the Niagara River. A ferry transferred passengers from Queenston, Ontario, to Lewiston, New York, on the Buffalo-bound trip.

For a short period of time the Erie & Niagara was leased to the Great Western Railway, but the arrangement was terminated after the Great Western obtained running rights over the Welland Railway.

In 1875 the Erie & Niagara became a part of the Canada Southern Railway and thereafter became the Erie & Niagara branch of the Canada Southern.

For a short time a ship brought up from Halifax in 1867 also operated on the Toronto run, serving as the *Rothesay Castle*, although also known as the *Southern Belle*.

The *City of Toronto*, seen here at her wharf at Toronto, was built in 1864 for D. Milloy of Toronto and spent most of her career plying between the city and Niagara in connection with the Erie & Niagara Railway. She was destroyed by fire at Port Dalhousie in 1883.
— *MTL T-30155*

The small, 85-ton *Rothesay Castle* was perhaps the most unusual vessel to run to Niagara on account of her size and her history. Information provided by the Dalhousie University Archives indicates that she was built at Renfrew, Scotland and originally registered at Glasgow. Taken at some point to Halifax, Nova Scotia, she finally was brought to Toronto around 1867, probably by one Thomas Leach of Toronto, who maintained ownership until 1872 when the *Rothesay Castle* became the property of Mrs. Sarah Boomer of Yorkville (Toronto). Mr. Leach regained ownership of the vessel in 1877, at which time she was renamed *Southern Belle*. Leach only kept the vessel for two years for in 1879 the *Southern Belle* was sold for the last time to David S. Keith. It is not certain as to when the ship was taken back to Nova Scotia, if indeed she did return (her port of registry remained at Halifax despite spending a good portion of her career on Lake Ontario), since a ship by the name of *Southern Belle* and looking remarkably similar to the *Rothesay Castle/Southern Belle* was rebuilt by the Rathbun Company at Deseronto, Ontario, during the 1880s. Whichever the case, she was broken up in 1906. This view shows *Rothesay Castle* at the Yonge Street Wharf, Toronto, about 1867. Her lack of an enclosed wheelhouse (her wheel is located between the funnels) was unusual considering the climate. — *MTL T-30981*

By 1882 the *City of Toronto* was joined on the route by the *Chicora*, a ship of the recently founded Niagara Navigation Company. A newspaper advertisement of 20 May 1882, the day the *City of Toronto*'s season commenced, indicated that she would be: "Leaving Niagara on the arrival of the Canada Southern train 9:45; returning leave Toronto 3 p.m., connecting with Canada Southern at 5:30 p.m. Tickets from D. Milloy, Agent, 8 Front Street, East. Chicora 1882 season starts Mon. 22 May 1882 with usual trips from Toronto at 7 a.m. and 2 p.m. connecting at Niagara with Canada Southern and at Lewiston with New York Central Railway."

When the *City of Toronto* burned at Port Dalhousie in October 1883, the days of the private steamboat connections with the Erie & Niagara came to a close. The *Chicora*'s entry on 1 June 1878 brought in the era of the Niagara Navigation Company.

The Niagara Navigation Company

The Niagara Navigation Company was organized in April 1877 by a group of Toronto businessmen who observed that the service provided by the *Rothesay Castle* and the *City of Toronto* to Niagara was lacking. With connections available with both the Canada Southern at Niagara and the New York Central at Lewiston, a lucrative market lay open to those who knew how to exploit it.

Niagara Navigation's first ship was the *Chicora*, built in 1864 at Liverpool, England, as the *Letter "B"* for duty as a Civil War blockade runner. Arriving at Halifax too late for that service, she spent three seasons in the West Indies trade until 1868, when she was brought to the upper lakes. There, as the *Chicora* of the Lake Superior Royal Mail Line, she operated between Collingwood and Port Arthur until 1877, when she was purchased by Niagara Navigation and taken to Port Colborne for rebuilding before being brought through the Welland Canal to Lake Ontario.

To better serve the increasing number of passengers transferring between Niagara and Lewiston for the New York Central observation trains, the small ferry *Ongiara* was added in 1888. Constructed three years earlier as the *Queen City* for the Doty Ferry Company of Toronto, *Ongiara* spent her first years running to the Toronto Islands, becoming surplus after the Doty Ferry Company acquired a rival firm in 1887, and subsequently sold to Niagara Navigation.

The year 1888 also brought with it the brand-new $200,000 steamer *Cibola*, launched by the Rathbun Company at Deseronto on 21 November 1887. Incorporating a steel hull prefabricated in Scotland by the Dalzell Company of Glasgow, considered at that time to be superior to any other steel hull, *Cibola* was slightly larger than the *Chicora* and thus doubled the capacity of the Niagara Navigation Company.

Traffic levels continued to increase and so too the demand placed upon the *Cibola* and the *Chicora*. By 1892 it was clear that another ship was needed, resulting in the *Chippewa*. Launched at Hamilton in 1893, the *Chippewa* became the largest steamer in the fleet, carrying almost 2,000 passengers.

The 1890s marked the beginning of Niagara Navigation's golden years. At no time before in the history of the Niagara region had so many people taken excursion trips to the many attractions, and most of those people made part of the trip on one steamer or another. It was no wonder that in 1895 Niagara-on-the-Lake was, in terms of steamer traffic, the busiest Canadian port on Lake Ontario. In that year 3,198 steamship arrivals and departures were made at Niagara, amounting to a total ship tonnage of 1,581,643 net tons. Toronto came next with 3,844 arrivals and departures, with total tonnage at 1,569,123 net tons, followed by Kingston and Hamilton, coming in a distant third and fourth respectively. Niagara's rival, Port Dalhousie, ranked at number ten in terms of tonnage.[10]

While Niagara Navigation was not the only steamship line serving Niagara, it was probably the largest and most popular. In the June 1893 edition of the *Traveler's Official Guide*, the company advertised its steamers *Chicora*, *Cibola*, *Chippewa*, and mail steamer *Ongiara* as providing "the shortest and picturesque route between Buffalo, Niagara Falls and Toronto," stating that it was "the only line giving views of Falls, Rapids, Brock's Monument and all the romantic scenery of the Lower Niagara." Service was as follows: "Steamers leave Geddes Wharf, Toronto, 7:15, 9:00, 11:00 a.m., 2:00,

3:00, 4:45 p.m. Returning, leaves Lewiston on arrival of New York Central trains from Niagara Falls. Trip about two hours. Connections at foot of Rapids with New York Central R.R. on American side and Falls Electric road on Canada side, and with Michigan Central R.R. at Niagara at entrance of the 'Niagara' into Lake Ontario. Connections at Toronto with Grand Trunk Ry., Canadian Pacific Ry., and Richelieu & Ontario Navigation Co.'s steamers."[11]

By this time, Canada Southern had been absorbed by the Michigan Central Railroad, itself under the indirect control of the New York Central through railway tycoon Cornelius Vanderbilt of New York City; New York Central control became official in 1929.

For passengers arriving at Niagara, three trains each way were offered by the Michigan Central over its Niagara Division to Niagara Falls and Buffalo (see table 3-2). At Lewiston, New York, opposite Queenston, the New York Central provided one train in each direction for Niagara Falls and Buffalo in connection with Niagara Navigation (see table 3-3) along with several other trains. With the exception of New York Central's trains 208 and 203, connections tended to be somewhat informal, lacking direct co-ordination. Nevertheless, the steamers and the trains complemented one another, resulting in a profitable situation for all concerned.

Disaster hit Niagara Navigation in 1895. While docked at Lewiston on July 15, *Cibola* caught fire and burned, taking with her the third engineer. It was indeed fortunate that only one life was lost; had *Cibola* been out on Lake Ontario, many more might have perished.

Table 3-2
MICHIGAN CENTRAL RAILROAD
NIAGARA DIVISION SERVICE
Effective 28 May 1893
(daily except Sunday)

SOUTHBOUND

		Train 51	Train 53	Train 55
Toronto	Lv.	(via steamer)		
Niagara-on-the-Lake		8:20 a.m.	12:25 p.m.	6:00 p.m.
Queenston		8:35 a.m.	12:39 p.m.	6:15 p.m.
Clifton		8:53 a.m.	12:53 p.m.	6:33 p.m.
Niagara Falls		8:59 a.m.	12:59 p.m.	6:39 p.m.
Falls View		9:04 a.m.	1:06 p.m.	6:41 p.m.
Chippawa		9:11 a.m.	1:13 p.m.	6:48 p.m.
Black Creek		9:23 a.m.	1:23 p.m.	6:58 p.m.
Niagara Junction		9:31 a.m.	1:33 p.m.	7:05 p.m.
Fort Erie		9:37 a.m.	1:38 p.m.	7:10 p.m.
Black Rock, New York		9:45 a.m.	1:45 p.m.	7:20 p.m.
Buffalo, Exchange St.		10:00 a.m.	2:00 p.m.	7:35 p.m.

NORTHBOUND

		Train 50	Train 52	Train 54
Buffalo, Exchange St.		6:00 a.m.	10:40 a.m.	3:30 p.m.
Black Rock, New York		6:15 a.m.	10:55 a.m.	3:45 p.m.
Fort Erie		6:20 a.m.	11:00 a.m.	3:50 p.m.
Niagara Junction		6:27 a.m.	11:09 a.m.	3:57 p.m.
Black Creek		6:34 a.m.	11:16 a.m.	4:04 p.m.
Chippawa		6:44 a.m.	11:27 a.m.	4:14 p.m.
Falls View		6:52 a.m.	11:36 a.m.	4:22 p.m.
Niagara Falls		6:54 a.m.	11:39 a.m.	4:24 p.m.
Clifton		7:00 a.m.	1:45 a.m.	4:30 p.m.
Queenston		7:15 a.m.	12:02 p.m.	4:45 p.m.
Niagara-on-the-Lake		7:30 a.m.	12:15 p.m.	5:00 p.m.
Toronto	Ar.	(via steamer)		

Source: *Traveler's Official Guide*, June 1893, p. 198.

Built in England in 1864 as the *Letter B.* to run the American Civil War blockade of the south, she arrived on this side of the Atlantic too late for that service and she eventually wound up on the upper Great Lakes in the employ of the Lake Superior Royal Mail Line as the *Chicora. Chicora* was purchased by the newly formed Niagara Navigation Company in 1877 and rebuilt at Port Colborne for the Toronto-to-Niagara run. This view shows *Chicora* at Toronto early this century.

— *OA Acc. 12026-133*

Originally the Toronto Island ferry *Queen City, Ongiara* was acquired by the Niagara Navigation Company in 1888 to provide a ferry service on the Niagara River between the New York Central at Lewiston, New York, and the company's dock at Queenston. Though still registered as late as 1912, *Ongiara* was probably laid up around 1900.

— *OA Acc. 12026-63*

The *Cibola* was the first vessel to be built expressly for Niagara Navigation. Built in 1887, she was only nine years old when she caught fire and burned at Lewiston in 1895. Still in her prime, *Cibola* is seen backing out of her dock at Toronto about 1890. — *OA Acc. 14313-20*

When delivered in 1893, the Hamilton-built *Chippewa* was the largest ship in the Niagara Navigation fleet. With a capacity of 2,000 passengers, she was proof of the popularity of the Niagara River service. — *OA S1740*

The loss of the *Cibola* in 1895 severely hampered Niagara Navigation's service. Within a year, however, she was replaced by the even finer *Corona.* In this classic photograph from the early 1900s, *Corona* "shows her stuff" in a race out of Toronto Harbour with the *Macassa* of the Hamilton Steamboat Company close alongside. — *OA Acc. 12026-26*

The *Cayuga* was the only surviving Niagara Navigation steamer left when Canada declared war on Germany in 1939. She maintained the only regular service to Niagara throughout the years of World War II but during the post-war period, traffic levels dropped to such an extent that she became uneconomic to run and in 1953 she was sold. In an attempt to keep the last Lake Ontario passenger steamer operating, a group of Toronto citizens purchased the ship through the formation of the Cayuga Steamship Company, but this move only delayed the inevitable and she was scrapped in 1957. In this view, *Cayuga* is seen leaving Toronto in the 1940s. — *OA S17784*

Table 3-3
NEW YORK CENTRAL RAILROAD
LEWISTON BOAT TRAIN SERVICE
Effective 28 May 1893
(daily except Sunday)

Read Down Train 208				Read Up Train 203
7:00 a.m.	Lv.	Toronto (via steamer)	Ar.	1:30 p.m.
10:30 a.m.		Lewiston, New York		10:20 a.m.
10:55 a.m.		Suspension Bridge		10:00 a.m.
11:01 a.m.		Niagara Falls		9:53 a.m.
11:09 a.m.		LaSalle		9:42 a.m.
11:23 a.m.		Tonawanda		9:27 a.m.
11:35 a.m.		Black Rock		9:15 a.m.
11:46 a.m.		Terrace		9:04 a.m.
11:50 a.m.	Ar.	Buffalo, Exchange St.	Lv.	9:00 a.m.

Source: *Traveler's Official Guide*, June 1893, pp. 186, 187.

The loss of the eight-year-old *Cibola* was a blow to the company, but it was not long before work began on her replacement, the *Corona*. Launched in May 1896, *Corona* was, according to her owners, "a model of marine architecture, and one of the finest day-steamers in the world!" Though at 1,274 tons *Corona* was somewhat smaller than the *Chippewa*, built three years earlier, she was still able to carry almost 2,000 passengers.

With so many ships on the Niagara route, it must have been sometime around 1900 when Niagara Navigation withdrew the *Ongiara*. Too small to operate on Lake Ontario and with ships now calling at Queenston and Lewiston anyway, she would have been redundant.

The last addition to the fleet came in 1907, when passenger demand was still increasing. Built at Toronto and capable of carrying 2,500 passengers, the 2,196-ton *Cayuga* was the largest and most popular ship to be operated by Niagara Navigation. She was also the first and only propeller-driven steamer owned by the company, all the others being side-wheelers.

The year 1913 was one of mergers for the Great Lakes shipping lines when Canada Steamship Lines was formed on 4 December through the amalgamation of Niagara Navigation, Richelieu & Ontario Navigation, and the Hamilton Steamboat companies, to name a few. Many of these companies retained a certain amount of their identity for a number of years before becoming fully integrated within Canada Steamship Lines.

The First World War was the beginning of the end for most of the steamship excursion lines, and the Niagara Navigation Company was no exception. It was not that there was a sudden drop in traffic; indeed, the war stimulated traffic as the need to transport militia units to the army reserve at Niagara for training resulted in increasing revenues for the company. Even before the war, each and every summer the militia and their families made the trip from Toronto, but the war multiplied their numbers. When it was all over in 1918, that era finished and another began. The "flapper era" of the twenties was a time of relative prosperity and brought with it the automobile and the freedom that the car represented — freedom from railways and freedom from steamships.

The first casualty came in 1921 when the old *Chicora* was sold, afterwards being converted to a barge. Then, in 1929, the *Corona* was laid up, marking the end of the "Roaring Twenties" and the beginning of the Depression years.

The Depression ended the boom of the 1920s and further accelerated the decline of the steamship lines. Niagara Navigation managed to hang on with the *Cayuga* and the *Chippewa*, but no longer with the through connections to Buffalo at Niagara. During the 1920s Michigan Central removed most of its Niagara Division, leaving only the segment between Niagara-on-the-Lake and Niagara Falls, but without passenger service. Even the electric lines serving the area were being cut back.

In 1937 the mothballed *Corona* was scrapped, and then two years later, with traffic at rock bottom and with no hope for future growth, the decision was made to scrap the *Chippewa* as well.

Only the *Cayuga* was left to maintain the route between Toronto and Niagara throughout the Second World War and into the 1950s. In the post-war years, *Cayuga* was the last steamer to operate between Toronto and Niagara, as well as the last passenger steamer to make regular trips out of Toronto.

In 1953 the *Cayuga* was sold by Canada Steamship Lines to the Cayuga Steamship Company, who continued to operate the ship until 1957. But after losing $70,000 over those five years, *Cayuga* was withdrawn.[12] After carrying nearly 15 million passengers over a 50-year career, *Cayuga* was scrapped in 1957.

CHAPTER THREE - NOTES

1) (J.B. Mansfield), *The Saga of the Great Lakes* (Toronto, 1980/Chicago, 1899), p. 220.
2) John N. Jackson and John Burtniak, *Railways in the Niagara Peninsula* (Belleville, 1978), p. 67.
3) Ibid., p. 68.
4) Ibid., p. 69.
5) Ibid., p. 70.
6) John P. Heisler, *The Canals of Canada* (Ottawa, 1973), p. 115.
7) Ibid., p. 115.
8) Ibid., p. 115.
9) John N. Jackson and John Burtniak, op. cit., p. 198.
10) James Croil, *Steam Navigation* (Toronto, 1973/1898), p. 329.
11) National Railway Publications Company, *Travelers' Official Guide - June 1893* (New York, 1972/1893), p. 226.
12) Paul Dalby, "Metro - Niagara Cruises to be launched in June," Toronto Star, 31 March 1976.

The Brockville terminus of the Brockville & Ottawa Railway was located on Blockhouse Island in the St. Lawrence, but by the time the railway had finished filling in the harbour between the island and the shore, Blockhouse Island had become nothing more than a man-made peninsula, albeit a dominant one. In this view from about 1880, the yard appears to be covered with sawn lumber ready for shipment to the United States, while at the left, the domed roundhouse rises above the freight sheds and shops. The passenger station is hidden by the steamer which appears to be the *Passport* of the Richelieu & Ontario Navigation Company. The famed Brockville Tunnel is on the right. — *OA S1978*

IV

THE RIVER FERRIES

Despite being considered an inland territory, much of Ontario is surrounded by water of one form or another, from lakes and rivers to the salt water of Hudson and James bays. Of great help to the early explorers and travellers, these bodies of water could scuttle the plans of many a pioneer railway company which lacked the money and technology to cross them, since without some sort of bridge their proposals would be useless. This led many of the companies to establish transfer ferries and later car ferries on the St. Lawrence, Niagara, Detroit and St. Clair rivers. Sometimes these services were started by private firms who recognized the need to link railways on either side of the rivers. More commonly, it was the railways who introduced the ferries out of necessity.

The Wolfe Island, Kingston & Toronto Railway
The Wolfe Island Railway & Canal Company
John Counter & Company

In the decade preceding the incorporation of the Grand Trunk Railway, there was great interest in building a railway line linking Montreal, Kingston and Toronto. Capitalists large and small, shopkeepers and municipalities all looked to the railway as the key to future growth and prosperity. For many the culmination of their efforts came on 26 December 1846, when the Montreal & Kingston Railroad Company and the Wolfe Island, Kingston & Toronto Railway Company were chartered by act of Parliament. They had great expectations, yet despite the initial fervour, very little was accomplished. The incorporation of the Grand Trunk Railway in 1852, along with earlier legislation, put an end to their plans but ensured that the new railway would be given a firm footing with solid support from England and Canada.

Of the two early railway companies, only one would have the dubious distinction of placing one of its proposals into force. Among the provisions made under the charter of the Wolfe Island, Kingston & Toronto Railway was the construction of a branch line across the St. Lawrence River, connecting Kingston with Cape Vincent, New York, by way of Wolfe Island and a car ferry. Cape Vincent had been reached by the Rome & Watertown Railroad in 1846, giving it access to the markets the eastern United States, and for Kingston businessmen it created the potential for an export trade with the United States and Europe once the branch was in place.

When the Wolfe Island, Kingston & Toronto project fell through, so too did the initial plans to link Kingston with Cape Vincent. However, two prominent Kingstonians, Henry Gildersleeve and John Counter, were not about to give up without a fight. They still believed that Kingston needed a link with Cape Vincent and in 1851 obtained the backing of the Kingston city council in the organization of the Wolfe Island Railway & Canal Company. The fact that John Counter was mayor of Kingston at the time must have had a good part in persuading the city.

While the original plans called for the construction of bridges across all, or at least most, of the St. Lawrence, it was realized that, for the new company, such engineering works were beyond its means. Gildersleeve and Counter felt a better alternative would involve the construction of a 2½-mile canal across Wolfe Island which would allow the passage of a car ferry (or any vessel with a draught no greater than six feet) between Kingston and Cape Vincent. If at a later date the ferry was unable to keep up with demand, then the construction of a bridge would probably have to be reconsidered.

By 1853 construction on the canal had begun and attention was turned to the construction of the car ferry. Christened *John Counter,* the ferry was built by Counter's own Kingston Marine Railway Company. According to the 1854 *Great Lakes Insurance Register,* the 296-ton steamship was owned by John Counter & Company and remarked that the hull was too low.[1] It was no wonder. The *John Counter* was the first car ferry in the Great Lakes region and, to insurance investigators used to seeing ships built for the open water of the lakes, the appearance of the vessel must have seemed odd indeed.

Although little is known about the capacity of the *John Counter,* it is known that it was built to carry passengers as well as loaded freight cars, probably amounting to no more than a handful. Operationally, the freight cars were loaded on at Cape Vincent and carried across the river to Kingston where, while still on board, their cargo would be unloaded and transferred to warehouses or awaiting wagons. On the return trip the cars would be reloaded and carried back to Cape Vincent, where they would be rolled off and dispatched on the next train south.

The *John Counter* made its debut on 1 December 1853 under the command of Captain Creighton. An advertisement in the *Kingston News* described the service, stating that the steamship "will leave U.S. wharf, Kingston, every day (Sunday excepted) at 9 a.m. for Cape Vincent, New York and Boston via Rome & Waterdown Railroad."[2] A few weeks later, service was suspended for the winter but resumed on 11 April 1854 on the old schedule. On 9 May service was increased to two trips per day in each direction, possibly indicating a rise in traffic, but by this time it was apparent that the *John Counter* was not meeting the full expectations of its owners. Five days later the ferry was withdrawn and its route taken over by the steamship *Star.*

In many ways the project was doomed from the start, particularly when there was no rail connection at Kingston. It would still be another two years before the Grand Trunk was completed, and even if it had been finished, the differences in track gauge between the American and Canadian lines would have prevented interchange of equipment. As it turned out, the use of the simpler transfer ferry, such as the *Star,* right from the beginning would have made greater sense, especially when it is considered that, without the additional weight of the freight cars, increased capacity and efficiency would have been gained. But by far the biggest reason for the ferry's ultimate demise was the simple fact that the canal across Wolfe Island was not completed until 1857, forcing the *John Counter* to brave the open water of Lake Ontario on a much longer route than originally planned, thereby reducing the number of daily round trips and increasing operating costs.

As a consolation, the enterprise did provide one benefit. Up until the 1890s ferries travelling between Cape Vincent and Kingston were able to use the canal, which not only shortened the distance between the two points but also provided a sheltered waterway.

Soon after the *John Counter* was withdrawn, the ship was sold to Nelson McLaren Bockus, a Montrealer. In 1857 the vessel was scrapped.

The Northern Railroad of New York
The Ogdensburg Railroad
The Ogdensburg & Lake Champlain Railroad
The Vermont Central Railroad

The next attempt at bridging the St. Lawrence River between Ontario and the United States with a car ferry came in 1863 when the Ogdensburg Railroad placed the ferry *St. Lawrence* on the Prescott, Ontario, to Ogdensburg, New York, route.

The Ogdensburg Railroad was originally opened in 1850 as the Northern Railroad of New York with a line extending from Ogdensburg east to Rouse's Point, New York, on Lake Champlain, where it connected with the Vermont Central Railroad. At this time in its history, most of the Northern's business consisted of moving western lakebound freight from Chicago and other Lake Michigan ports to New England markets by way of Lake Champlain and the Vermont Central. Some of this lake traffic was handled by a small fleet of steamers operated by the Northern.

Unfortunately, the railway was just getting itself established when the Great Western Railway of Canada was opened up to the West, and soon a great deal of freight previously shipped by way of the Northern Railroad was finding its way east over the Great Western and the New York Central Railroad instead. Combined with the drop in the number of sailing ships on the Great Lakes which normally served the smaller harbours such as Ogdensburg, the Northern soon fell into hard times. In an effort to keep the company out of the red, the shareholders reorganized the company in 1857 as the Ogdensburg Railroad, but to no avail.

One saving grace came in the form of the Bytown & Prescott Railway, opened in 1854 between Prescott, Ontario, opposite Ogdensburg, and the lumbering centre of Bytown (now Ottawa) on the Ottawa River. The whole purpose of the Bytown & Prescott (or Ottawa & Prescott, as it became known in 1855) was to provide an outlet for Ottawa Valley lumber by feeding it into the Northern Railroad, which could then carry the lumber south into the rich American markets. In anticipation of the future addition of a car ferry across the St. Lawrence, the Bytown & Prescott was built to standard gauge, just as the Northern had been, as opposed to the wider provincial gauge adopted by all other railways in the province. In the meantime, any lumber destined for the Northern had to be transferred across the river by steamer.

The Bytown & Prescott, however, failed to locate its Bytown (Ottawa) terminus close to the major sawmills and, as a result, the projected lumber traffic failed to materialize. Within a few short years the railway found itself in financial difficulties, and in 1857 the company was placed into receivership. What traffic there was for the Ogdensburg Railroad, successor to the Northern, could be handled by that company's ferry *Boston*, a 334-ton side-wheeler built at Quebec City in 1852. Although the *Boston*'s career was relatively uneventful, she was involved in one serious incident in 1856, when she sank the steamship *Protection* in a collision on the river. The *Boston* survived, seemingly without major damage.

Once the Ogdensburg's management realized that there was little hope for any major business from the Ottawa & Prescott, they turned their attentions to the Grand Trunk, which held the promise of greater rewards. Negotiations between the two companies opened in the early 1860s, and by the fall of 1862 an agreement was finally signed for the interchange of freight cars by car ferry between Prescott and Ogdensburg. It was left to the Ogdensburg to provide the necessary car ferry and ferry docks, while the Grand Trunk put up any capital required to supplement the Ogdensburg's work.

This still left the problem of how the Grand Trunk would obtain access to the Prescott waterfront; the Ottawa & Prescott held the only suitable right-of-way to the St. Lawrence and it was doubtful that any other practical alternative could be found. Facing facts, the Grand Trunk's management approached the Ottawa & Prescott with the ultimate objective of obtaining trackage rights between the main line and the waterfront, five miles in all. In no financial position to refuse, the Ottawa & Prescott soon agreed, obtaining $7,000 from the Grand Trunk to assist with the reconstruction of the docks and the laying of a third rail to accommodate the Grand Trunk's broad-gauge cars, as well as an additional compensation of 35 cents for every ton of Grand Trunk freight handled and "fair allowance for passengers passing over this part of the line."[3]

With that settled, attentions were turned to the construction of the car ferry. The contract for the steamer was let to the Ogdensburg shipyard of Harrison C. Pearson, and by the summer of 1863 the 244-ton ship, appropriately christened *St. Lawrence*, was ready for service. Although a wooden vessel, her hull was sheathed with iron, thereby enabling winter operation in all but the thickest river ice. Equipped with two broad-gauge tracks, the *St. Lawrence* could carry up to six loaded freight cars at a time, more than likely belonging to the Grand Trunk, carrying them to

Ogdensburg, where the freight was transferred to standard-gauge cars. There is the possibility that the ferry was able to carry standard-gauge cars, for by 1871 the Ottawa & Prescott had installed a "change gauge car pit" at Prescott Junction, allowing specially equipped freight cars to be converted from broad gauge to standard gauge and vice versa, eliminating the need for transshipment.[4] While this was done largely for the benefit of Ottawa-bound freight, it may also have been used for cars crossing the river as well.

After the *St. Lawrence* was introduced, the *Boston* was sold and by 1864 was serving as a Bermuda-based Civil War blockade runner.

For ten years the *St. Lawrence* gave steady service, but in August 1873, during an inspection, the ship's hull was found to be badly rotted and she was subsequently withdrawn and abandoned. For the next four decades, private enterprise would take over from the railways in carrying freight cars across the river.

It is worth noting that the Ogdensburg Railroad was reorganized as the Ogdensburg & Lake Champlain Railroad in 1865, following several unprofitable years. In 1870 the line was acquired by the Vermont Central, which two years later became the Central Vermont Railroad Company. Before the close of the century, the railway would be in the firm control of the Grand Trunk. The Ottawa & Prescott Railway was forced into bankruptcy in 1865, and it was strongly suspected that the Grand Trunk was behind the bankruptcy, hoping to gain control. The attempt failed and in 1867 the railway was reorganized as the St. Lawrence & Ottawa Railway, maintaining its independence until the 1880s.

The Canadian Pacific Car & Passenger Transfer Company

When it became clear that the Vermont Central Railroad, Ogdensburg & Lake Champlain Division, was not going to replace its car ferry *St. Lawrence*, Isaac D. Purkis, a Prescott coal merchant, decided to start his own service. His motivations were twofold. First, most of his coal was probably imported from the United States through Ogdensburg, where it would have arrived by rail. Moving that coal across the St. Lawrence was a time-consuming and costly operation and, if it already required a steamer to make the transfer, why not make that steamer a car ferry and deliver those cars right to the coal yard. Second, since the *St. Lawrence* operated for ten years with moderate success, there was no reason for another car ferry not to succeed.

Owing to the time the *St. Lawrence* was withdrawn, Purkis was not in a position to introduce any ferry onto the route during the remaining months of 1873, but there was enough time to have a new vessel constructed for the following season.

In 1874 the 141-ton *Transit*, a product of the Clayton, New York, yard of Robert Davis and Z.W. Wright, was delivered to Purkis at Prescott, complete with a single standard-gauge track capable of holding three cars. Since the Grand Trunk had made the conversion to standard gauge in October 1873, there was no longer any need to provide accommodation for broad-gauge cars.

With only enough room for three cars, *Transit* was kept busy. On one day alone, in January 1877, she moved 50 freight cars across the river, translating into about nine round trips between Prescott and Ogdensburg.[5] Passenger trade was also brisk and, in addition to the *Transit*, Purkis began to acquire his own steamers to handle passengers and less-than-carload lots of freight. The first was probably the *Caribou*, built in 1868 by Augustin Cantin of Montreal. This small, 114-ton wooden steamship may even have been operated by Purkis before he ventured into the car ferry business, perhaps purchasing it new. In 1878 the 101-ton *City of Belleville* was launched by the Shickluna Shipyards at St. Catharines and added to Purkis's expanding fleet soon after. Two American ships were also added, these being the *Henry Plumb* and the *Outing*.

Further gains in business resulted in Isaac Purkis ordering a new car float in 1880 from a Sorel, Quebec, builder. Named after the famed elephant at the London Zoo, later to be brought to North America by P.T. Barnum, the 150-ton *Jumbo* could carry three freight cars, effectively doubling the line's transfer capacity. The *City of Belleville* or the *Henry Plumb* normally provided the motive power.

By now Purkis was serving four railway companies. On the New York side, the Utica & Black River Railroad had arrived at Ogdensburg, joining the Central Vermont. The Utica & Black River would later pass to the Rome, Watertown & Ogdensburg Railroad and, still later, both lines would come under the control of the New York Central Railroad. In Ontario, connections were made with the St. Lawrence & Ottawa Railway and the Grand Trunk, although by 1884 control of the St. Lawrence & Ottawa would be in the hands of the expanding Canadian Pacific Railway.

Upriver another entrepreneur was about to enter the car ferry business. In November 1876 the passenger steamer *William Armstrong* was launched by shipbuilders A. & J.W. Wood of Ogdensburg for Captain David H. Lyon of Brockville, Ontario, and soon after was placed into operation between that point and Morristown, New York, on the opposite shore.

Brockville at this time was served by the broad-gauge Brockville & Ottawa Railway, running from Brockville Harbour north, under the town hall by way of a tunnel, to the Grand Trunk junction, on to the Ottawa River at Pembroke, and via the Canada Central Railway to Ottawa. Within two years the two railway companies merged under the corporate name of the Canada Central Railway. Across the river at Morristown, the Utica & Black River Railroad was just being built into town, but until it was finished that town had to depend on the St. Lawrence River and Brockville for its main transportation links. It is therefore clear that at this stage there was no need for any car ferry and, indeed, the fact that the Canada Central remained a broad-gauge railway even into the early 1880s discouraged any rail ferry link with the standard-gauge Utica & Black River.

All that changed in 1881, for in that year the Canada Central was acquired by the fledgling Canadian Pacific Railway, serving as the nucleus of Canadian Pacific's line from Ottawa to North Bay on its long journey west. By this time most of the Canada Central had been converted to standard gauge, with the exception of the most northerly section, which remained in broad gauge until the end of the year for sake of convenience.

This activity soon piqued the interest of Captain Lyon who, after noting Purkis's success at Prescott, decided to convert his own ship to a car ferry in 1882 by cutting out the superstructure along the centre line of the ship and installing a single track with a three-car capacity. Lyon had little difficulty in attracting traffic for his ferry, not only maintaining the usual passenger trade, but also gaining a share of the Ottawa Valley lumber traffic destined for the American market, for much of the freight business built up by the Canada Central consisted of lumber. Coal from the United States also made up a sizable amount of traffic across the river.

In Canadian Pacific's timetable issued 9 September 1884, one of the company's earliest, particular emphasis was placed on the Brockville branch over that of the newly acquired St. Lawrence & Ottawa. Even more significant was the importance the railway placed on its connections with the Utica & Black River Railroad during this period, as shown in table 4-1, outlining the many American cities passengers could reach by this route and going as far as providing free omnibus and ferry transfers across the river. The Canadian Pacific proclaimed this as "The Quickest Route between Montreal and the cities of Central and Western New York," but as Brockville crossing's appeal waned and the railway obtained more direct and convenient connections elsewhere, such special mention soon disappeared.

Table 4-1
CANADIAN PACIFIC RAILWAY
CONDENSED TIMETABLE VIA BROCKVILLE
AND THE UTICA & BLACK RIVER RAILROAD
AND ITS CONNECTIONS

Effective 9 September 1884

			Morning Express	Night Express
Lv.	Montreal	CPR	8:45 a.m.	8:00 p.m.
Lv.	Ottawa	CPR	12:15 p.m.	1:35 p.m.
Lv.	Carleton Junction	CPR	1:25 p.m.	12:22 a.m.
Lv.	Smith's Falls	CPR	2:10 p.m.	1:00 a.m.
Ar.	Brockville	CPR	3:30 p.m.	2:20 a.m.

(Free Omnibus and Ferry Transfer)

Steamers Bohemian and Corsican at C.P.R. Dock,
Brockville Sept 10th, 1897.

The *William Armstrong* (left) at Brockville in the 1890s. At the right are the Richelieu & Ontario steamers *Bohemian* and *Corsican*. — *UBL PB No. 4943*

This is how the railway terminal at Prescott appeared at the turn of the century before fire destroyed the roundhouse and engine facilities in 1908 (top centre), as viewed from the grain elevator. Two ferry slips seem to have been in existence at that time, one beside the station at the right and the other located at the upper left of the station near the three passenger coaches. — *PAC PA-112556*

Lv.	Morristown, N.Y.	U & BR	3:59 p.m.	9:27 a.m.
Ar.	Theresa, N.Y.	U & BR	5:10 p.m.	10:42 a.m.
Ar.	Carthage, N.Y.	U & BR	6:00 p.m.	11:40 a.m.
Ar.	Watertown, N.Y.	U & BR	9:35 p.m.	12:40 p.m.
Ar.	Lowville, N.Y.	U & BR	7:00 p.m.	12:25 p.m.
Ar.	Lyons Falls, N.Y.	U & BR	7:30 p.m.	1:00 p.m.
Ar.	Boonville, N.Y.	U & BR	8:00 p.m.	1:25 p.m.
Ar.	Utica, N.Y.	U & BR	9:15 p.m.	2:50 p.m.
Lv.	Utica, N.Y.	NYC	9:45 p.m.	3:12 p.m.
Lv.	Little Falls, N.Y.	NYC	10:29 p.m.	3:45 p.m.
Lv.	Amsterdam, N.Y.	NYC	11:52 p.m.	4:50 p.m.
Lv.	Schenectady, N.Y.	NYC	12:25 a.m.	5:15 p.m.
Lv.	Albany, N.Y.	NYC	1:00 a.m.	5:50 p.m.
Lv.	Troy, N.Y.	NYC	. . .	6:40 p.m.
Lv.	New York, N.Y.	NYC	6:45 a.m.	10:00 p.m.
Lv.	Pittsfield, Mass.	B & A	4:32 a.m.	10:39 p.m.
Lv.	Springfield, Mass.	B & A	6:15 a.m.	12:40 a.m.
Lv.	Palmer, Mass.	B & A	6:56 a.m.	3:38 a.m.
Lv.	Worcester, Mass.	B & A	8:20 a.m.	5:00 a.m.
Lv.	So. Framingham, Mass.	B & A	9:01 a.m.	5:40 a.m.
Lv.	Boston, Mass.	B & A	9:40 a.m.	6:25 a.m.
Lv.	Utica, N.Y.	DL & W	7:00 a.m.	6:15 p.m.
Ar.	Binghampton, N.Y.	DL & W	10:55 a.m.	10:10 p.m.
Ar.	Scranton, Pa.	DL & W	1:20 p.m.	1:30 a.m.
Lv.	Utica, N.Y.	NYC	1:07 a.m.	4:40 p.m.
Ar.	Rome, N.Y.	NYC	. . .	5:09 p.m.
Ar.	Syracuse, N.Y.	NYC	2:35 a.m.	6:25 p.m.
Ar.	Rochester, N.Y.	NYC	4:55 a.m.	9:25 p.m.
Ar.	Buffalo, N.Y.	NYC	7:05 a.m.	12:15 a.m.
Lv.	Buffalo, N.Y.	LS & MS	7:40 a.m.	12:55 a.m.
Ar.	Erie, Pa.	LS & MS	9:20 a.m.	2:50 a.m.
Ar.	Ashtabula, Ohio	LS & MS	10:32 a.m.	4:14 a.m.
Ar.	Cleveland, Ohio	LS & MS	12:15 p.m.	6:05 a.m.

CPR - Canadian Pacific Railway
U & BR - Utica & Black River Railroad
NYC - New York Central Railroad
B & A - Boston & Albany Railroad
DL & W - Delaware, Lackawanna & Western Railroad
LS & MS - Lake Shore & Michigan Southern Railroad

Source: Canadian Pacific Railway Timetable, effective 9 September 1884

Evidence of the Brockville route's gradual decline came early, for even in the mid-1880s Lyon's *William Armstrong* came to the aid of Purkis's ferries at Prescott when freight cars waiting to make the river crossing began to back up. Though Purkis often reciprocated by sending *Transit* or *Jumbo* up to Brockville, the Prescott route, perhaps because of its earlier founding, was preferred by shippers as the more convenient.

It was this co-operation and interdependence that led to the final merger of the two operations in 1888, when on March 17 Captain Lyon incorporated the Canadian Pacific Car & Passenger Transfer Company. In adopting the name of Canadian Pacific, Lyon reflected the importance of that railway in the company's developing traffic pattern. By the beginning of the 1890s most of the freight cars being carried across the St. Lawrence were exchanged between the Canadian Pacific and the Rome, Watertown & Ogdensburg (successor to the Utica & Black River).

The first major accident to happen to the new company, or its predecessors for that matter, occurred on Sunday, 30 June 1889 while the *William Armstrong* was returning from Morristown to Brockville with a full load of coal hoppers and six passengers. The train crew that had loaded the ferry at Morristown had failed to place the freight cars correctly on deck, allowing too much weight to be located over the aft section. Consequently the stern sat so low in the water that water began to flow unnoticed into the engine room through a steam exhaust pipe. Not until the ship had reached mid-stream was it noticed by the engineer, who quickly ordered the crew out just in the nick of time. No sooner had they evacuated than water found its way through some open hatches and the ship went down in 83 feet of water. Fortunately only one person was lost, a passenger from Montreal who drowned.

The *William Armstrong* was not a total loss despite its sinking. Utilizing a salvage system never before used on the St. Lawrence River, pontoons were attached to the side of the sunken ship and slowly pumped full of air. Finally, after three weeks of hard work, the *William Armstrong* was raised — but it surfaced so rapidly that another smaller steamer being used in the salvage operation was sunk! Following several more weeks of repair, the *William Armstrong* was returned to its regular duties.

An accident similar to that of the *William Armstrong* almost happened to the *Transit* in 1892 while en route from Morristown to Brockville. A deckhand, believing that the ferry's load of coal cars was too far forward, attempted to move them back. But he lost control and the cars rolled back, hitting the rear bumpers and putting the ship's stern down into the water. The hull began to fill with water, but this time the captain saw what was happening and ran the *Transit* onto shore before she was able to sink. The ferry was ready for service within two days.

The Prescott crossing continued to gain in traffic volume during the late 1880s to the point that another car ferry was needed, and so on 14 April 1890 Captain Lyon purchased the 395-ton car ferry *South Eastern* from the Richelieu & Ontario Navigation Company.

South Eastern was originally built in 1881 by Augustin Cantin of Montreal for *La Compagnie du Traverse de chemin de fer d'Hochelaga à Longueuil*, a company jointly formed by the South Eastern Railway and the Quebec, Montreal, Ottawa & Occidental Railway in 1879. As the name implies, the company was organized to provide a summer car ferry service and, in winter, to lay tracks over the ice on the St. Lawrence between Longueuil on the south shore and Hochelaga on the north shore in order to provide a link between its two respective parents. As it was, the Quebec, Montreal, Ottawa & Occidental was faced with the serious problem of lacking any connection with any other railway, due to the concerted efforts of the Grand Trunk Railway. The South Eastern, on the other hand, owned a number of small lines in southern Quebec running from St. Lambert on the St. Lawrence to Newport, Vermont. While it had connections with the American railways at Newport to Portland and Boston, it possessed no such connections at St. Lambert, for it was separated from Montreal by the St. Lawrence. Normally the South Eastern closed down for the winter and lost money in the summer. The new company was the answer to their predicament, joining the two companies by car ferry from April to December and from January to March by railway over the frozen river. Since the crossing from Hochelaga and Longueuil was west of either company's terminus, extensions had to be built. Whether or not the *South Eastern*, named for the South Eastern Railway, was the first ferry purchased is not certain, although the company laid its first rails over the ice on the St. Lawrence in January 1880.

The relationship between the two parent railways collapsed in 1883 when the Canadian Pacific Railway foreclosed on the South Eastern's mortgage, assuming complete control by the following year, thus giving Canadian Pacific direct access to New England. *South Eastern* continued to operate on the route on behalf of the South Eastern Railway, during which time Canadian Pacific undertook the construction of a new railway bridge at Lachine, completed in late 1886. No longer needed, *South Eastern* was sold to the Richelieu & Ontario Navigation Company.

The *South Eastern* gave the Canadian Pacific Car & Passenger Transfer Company an additional capacity of five cars for the Prescott route and made it possible for the *Transit* to be shifted to Brockville whenever necessary without disrupting service at Prescott. Thus, *South Eastern* became the mainstay of the Prescott service, and as time went by *Transit* was only employed as required. Likewise, in 1892 the passenger steamer *Caribou*, rebuilt only four years earlier to 144 tons, was retired; she would not be scrapped, however, until 1901.

With most traffic by the middle of the decade being handled for the Canadian Pacific and the New York Central lines between Prescott and Ogdensburg, Captain Lyon moved his entire operation to Prescott in 1896. In that year river shipments received at Ogdensburg, or shipped from that port, totalled 307,827 tons, with 209,875 tons moving north and 97,952 tons going south. Of the northbound freight, coal made up 115,286 tons, while cereals comprised 69,880 tons. Southbound, lumber made up the lion's share with 81,606 tons.[6] If the transfer company was not responsible for the entire river tonnage handled at Ogdensburg, it is reasonable to assume that the company carried the majority of it.

In June 1897 the *South Eastern* caught fire and burned at Prescott. It was rebuilt soon after and renamed *International.*

By 1901 the *Transit* was retired, leaving the *William Armstrong*, the *International* and the barge *Jumbo* to maintain the railway transfer service. But these were wooden vessels prone to rot and sooner or later they would have to be replaced. Captain Lyon thought sooner would be for the better, especially in consideration of the age of the ferries, and in 1906 he decided to have a new ferry built.

The new ferry was ordered from the Polson Iron Works of Toronto and constructed of steel. At 1,658 tons, it was larger than all of the company's previous passenger and car ferries put together, enabling the new ship to carry up to 12 freight cars. The track arrangement on deck, however, was somewhat unusual in that, while three sets of tracks were installed, tight clearances required that either the two outside tracks be loaded, allowing the ferry to carry up to 12 cars, or the single track down the centre could be used, permitting up to six cars to be loaded, but not all three tracks at the same time. The track layout may sound illogical, but it was probably designed in that fashion so that when the ship only carried a few cars, they could be positioned along the centre of the ferry without affecting the vessel's balance, thereby avoiding any serious listing to one side or the other. Not only did the track arrangement differ from any other in the Great Lakes region, the general design of the ferry was also different. It was a double-ended ship, eliminating the need to back into or out of the ferry slips. Stranger yet was the ship's peculiar hump at the centre, causing the deck to slope down to either end. It was truly unique.

At first the new car ferry was to be named *Ogdensburg*, but Captain Lyon chose to name it after his father, and so when it was launched in December 1907 the ship was christened *Charles Lyon*. In the spring of 1908 the *Charles Lyon* entered regular service at Prescott, operating out of new ferry slips built by the Canadian Pacific and the New York Central to accommodate it.

With the *Charles Lyon* in operation, the old ferries were quickly displaced. First to go was the *International*, sold in 1909 and cut down to a sand barge. In 1914 she was broken up. The two remaining passenger steamers, *City of Belleville* and *Henry Plumb*. were also sold in 1909, going to the Prescott & Ogdensburg Ferry Company, newly organized to operate a passenger ferry service across the river. The *William Armstrong* was also sold to the new company, perhaps as a horse-carriage and automobile ferry, but it was soon after sold and converted to a barge. As the *Mons Meg*, the old ferry was abandoned in 1938.

For the next two decades Canadian Pacific Car & Passenger Transfer would make the crossing almost exclusively with the *Charles Lyon*, maintaining the car float *Jumbo* into the 1920s as a backup, although there is little evidence that it ever had to be used.

In 1929 Captain Lyon died and Canadian Pacific subsequently purchased the company from the estate on 1 September. This was a wise business move, for in 1929 alone 927,693 tons of freight were transferred across the river by the *Charles Lyon*, 350,325 tons of flour and forest products moving south and 577,368 tons of predominantly coal moving north.[7] In comparison to Canadian

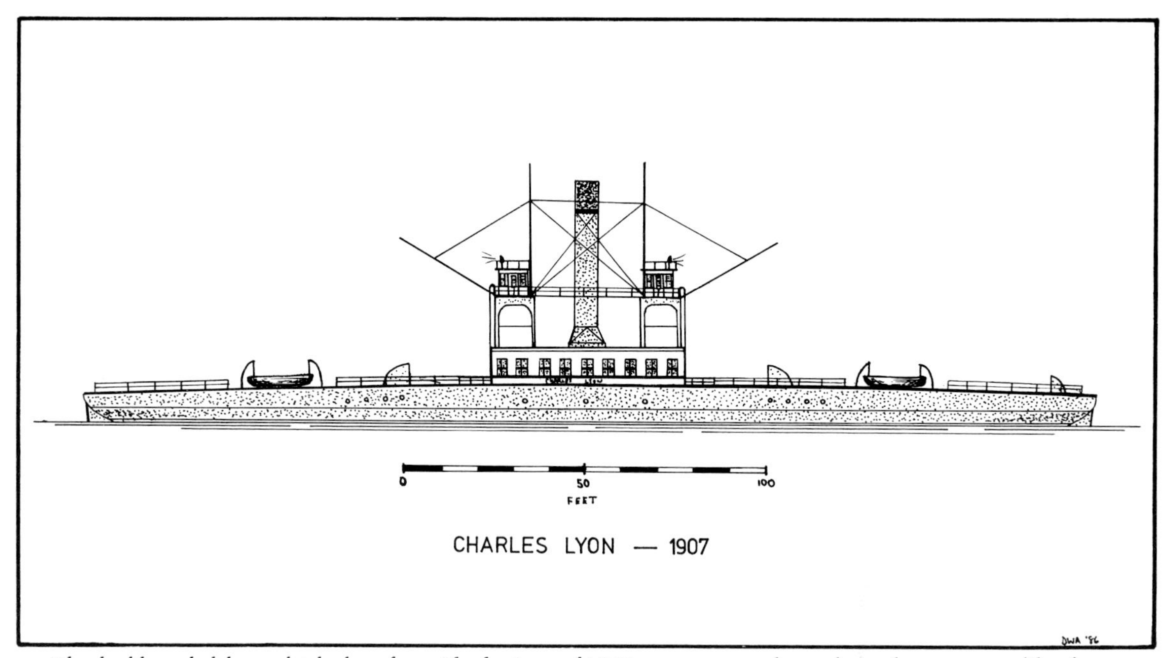

The double-ended, hump-backed car ferry *Charles Lyon* of 1907 was an unusual vessel, yet she was not unlike the car ferries at Windsor. Note that the ferry's two wheelhouses were located at the centre of the ship, where they were connected by an overhead walkway — a convenience for the captain but not entirely practical so far as visibility during docking was concerned. Had she followed a more conventional design, the wheelhouses would have been placed at each end. Note also that the *Charles Lyon* had two smoke stacks, located one per side above the passenger cabin. (N.B. — This drawing is approximately to scale but some features vary from the original ship as built.)

— *Author*

Fully completed, *Prescotont* undergoes her "sea" trials on the St. Lawrence near Lauzon in October 1930. Her colour scheme follows the Canadian Pacific pattern for tugs, namely: mustard yellow superstructure and funnel; white lifeboats and wheelhouse (although some Canadian Pacific tugs had mustard yellow wheelhouses); dark green trim and hull.

— *PAC PA-145139*

Pacific's other connections to the United States in Ontario, the Prescott route was second only to the Windsor-Detroit gateway.

Since most of the traffic was exchanged with the New York Central at Ogdensburg, Canadian Pacific managed to persuade that company into buying a 50-percent stake in the Canadian Pacific Car & Passenger Transfer Company, signing the agreement on 1 May 1930. With the new capital obtained, the company was able to order a replacement for the *Charles Lyon*, though not a conventional car ferry. Instead, a diesel-electric tug and car float combination was chosen.

The tug was ordered from the Lauzon, Quebec, based Davie Shipbuilding Company, who completed the 302-ton steel *Prescotont* by the fall of 1930. Fitted with firefighting equipment, *Prescotont* was able to double as a fireboat should the need arise. Her workmate was christened *Ogdensburg*, a large 1,405-ton steel car float built by the American Shipbuilding Company at Lorain, Ohio. Like the *Charles Lyon*, it also had three tracks installed on deck, but in the *Ogdensburg's* case, all three tracks could be used at the same time, permitting up to 18 freight cars to be carried.

In order to allow the duo the maximum amount of manoeuvrability possible, the *Ogdensburg* was equipped with rudders synchronized with those of the tug. Additionally, the car float's bridge incorporated controls identical to the tugs, enabling the captain to have complete control of the *Prescotont* from the *Ogdensburg*. No other car ferry operation in the world utilized such a system.

Regular year-round service with the *Prescotont* and *Ogdensburg* began on 2 November 1930, after which the *Charles Lyon* was seldom used; it was finally laid up in 1935. In 1937 the *Charles Lyon* was sold and served as a barge until it was scrapped at Hamilton in 1941.

Like so many companies, the Depression of the 1930s took a drastic toll on the Canadian Pacific Car & Passenger Transfer Company. From the 927,693 tons of freight carried in 1929, tonnage on the route dropped to 630,950 tons in 1931, and two years later fell to a record low of only 295,975 tons. The year 1934 brought a mild recovery with 320,761 tons, of which 119,597 tons of freight were carried to Ogdensburg, with 201,164 tons returned north.[8] It would not be until the outbreak of the Second World War, however, that any real recovery would be experienced.

Throughout the fifties and sixties, the *Prescotont* and *Ogdensburg* provided faithful service, but the volume of traffic handled was gradually declining. When the Ogdensburg ferry slip burned on 25 September 1970, the owners of the company decided against rebuilding the structure, effectively putting an end to the service. On 10 January 1972 the pair was sold to the Windsor Detroit Barge Line of Detroit, where they were put to use moving containers.

One question that remains is whether or not the ferry company ever transferred passenger cars across the St. Lawrence River. In George Musk's history of Canadian Pacific's shipping interests, *Canadian Pacific — The Story of the Famous Shipping Line*, he notes that railway passenger cars were carried across the river until 1958. According to timetables issued before that time, no regular Canadian Pacific passenger trains were ever ferried across the river. As a matter of fact, there appears to have been little or no attempt by Canadian Pacific and New York Central to even co-ordinate their passenger trains terminating at Prescott and Ogdensburg such that passengers could make convenient connections without prolonged waiting periods. Even in the 1890s, when Prescott took over from Brockville as the primary ferry crossing, no direct passenger connections existed between Canadian Pacific and the Rome, Watertown & Ogdensburg. Timetables only mentioned that a crossing existed and that trains of the Rome, Watertown & Ogdensburg Railroad to various points in New York could be reached at Ogdensburg.

As a final note on passenger connections between Prescott and Ogdensburg, the Canadian Pacific Eastern Lines timetable of 1 March 1930 gave this rare schedule, probably for the Prescott & Ogdensburg Ferry Company: "Ferry for Ogdensburg leaves Prescott 5:45 a.m. and daily on the hour from 7:00 a.m. to 10:00 p.m.; last boat 11:15 p.m.; returning leaves Ogdensburg for Prescott 6:00 a.m. and daily on the half hour from 7:30 a.m. to 11:30 p.m."

The paddle-driven ferry *Canada Atlantic Transfer* was little more than a floating, self-propelled wooden truss bridge, but she provided the Canada Atlantic with an important connection with the south shore of the St. Lawrence River before a permanent bridge could be built. A bow-loader, as were most river car ferries, the *Canada Atlantic Transfer* was a wood burner as evident by the spark arresters on the smoke stacks. Among the items worth noting are the approach ramps and counterweights and the box cars, both of which have link and pin couplers. The right hand car is Soo Line No. 3678.
— PAC C-29161

The Canada Atlantic Railway

Although technically not in Ontario, Canada Atlantic's brief car ferry service at Coteau Landing, Quebec, on the St. Lawrence River, nevertheless had an important influence on the province as well as this Ontario-based railway.

The Canada Atlantic Railway was built to exploit the vast timberlands of the Ottawa Valley and give the mills of J.R. Booth, the railway's builder, an outlet to the American lumber markets south of the border. The stumbling block came in the form of the St. Lawrence, which blocked the railway's free passage south to the United States. The St. Lawrence was first reached by the railway from Ottawa in 1882, but it was not until July 1884 that the line on the opposite side of the river was completed (it would still be quite a few years before a link up with the Central Vermont would be achieved) and that meant the railway needed a connection between the two.

Unsure of traffic requirements, Canada Atlantic's management opted for a car ferry instead of a bridge and in 1884 contracted John Dunbar to build the new ferry. Primarily of wood construction, the *Canada Atlantic Transfer* was built on site at Coteau Landing, and at 619 tons the side-wheeler could carry six passenger cars or about 12 freight cars on two tracks.

The success of the railway surprised even its owners, and between 1884 and 1888 passenger traffic grew 300 percent, while freight traffic grew an astonishing 800 percent.[9] The *Canada Atlantic Transfer* was not built for such heavy tonnages, and in 1889 the company conceded that a bridge was the only way to make the St. Lawrence River crossing in the future. Without dragging their heels, the railway started to erect the bridge soon after, and by February 1890 the bridge was completed. The *Canada Atlantic Transfer* was laid up and four years later was sold. In 1895 the ship was rebuilt as a barge and in her final days served as a lighter in the employ of the Montreal Lighterage Company.

The Brantford & Buffalo Joint Stock Railroad Company
The Buffalo, Brantford & Goderich Railway
The Buffalo & Lake Huron Railway

When it appeared that the town of Brantford was to be by-passed by the Great Western Railway, thereby seriously inhibiting the town's future business prospects, a group of local merchants joined together to organize their own railway link, but not with the Great Western. They proposed a new line which would link Brantford with Buffalo, New York, and in 1851 incorporated the Brantford & Buffalo Joint Stock Railroad Company. Support came from all sectors, including $100,000 from the Town of Brantford, chief beneficiary of the railway, and soon after incorporation, $70,000 from the City of Buffalo. Buffalo too realized the benefits of such a line, which could open up a new hinterland for exploitation by the city's business interests.

By the end of 1852 the company had set its sights on an extension to Goderich on Lake Huron and on 12 November received the official sanction from Parliament, as well as its permission to change the company's name to the Buffalo, Brantford & Goderich Railway in recognition of the new route.

In February 1854 the railway was completed between Brantford and Buffalo (actually Fort Erie, Ontario, opposite Buffalo) and regular trains had been introduced. Paris, on the Great Western main line, would be reached in March, although it would be some time before a direct connection with the Great Western would be made allowing for the interchange of cars. At the Buffalo end, an abandoned rail line running between Black Rock, opposite Fort Erie, and Exchange Street Station, Buffalo, was secured, encouraging the possibility of extending rail service directly into Buffalo's core. But for the meantime the railway would have to make do with ferries in making the connection with Buffalo.

The first company ferry, appropriately named *International*, was built in 1854 for the railway at Chippawa at a cost of $35,000, entering service early that year. Constructed of wood, the *International* was capable of carrying passengers and freight, but on account of the railway's lack of facilities on the American side and the difference between American and Canadian track gauges, no railway cars were carried. William Wallace, chief engineer of the Buffalo, Brantford & Goderich, wrote of her: "The steamer *International* gives great satisfaction. She crosses the river in four minutes, and the time occupied in conveying passengers from the Canadian side to the new depot of the Albany, Boston and New York Lines (in Buffalo) does not exceed twenty minutes."[10] Unfortunately before the *International* had completed its first season, fire broke out on board and spread quickly throughout the vessel. She was a complete loss. Until a new vessel could be obtained, two chartered vessels, the *Sandusky* and the *Troy*, were employed in completing the link between Fort Erie and Buffalo. In the meantime the railway continued its push for Goderich.

On 28 June 1858 the Buffalo & Lake Huron (the railway's name since 1856) reached Goderich on Lake Huron. Once the harbour was completed, the railway planned on receiving cargoes of grain from Chicago for transshipment to Buffalo, to be sent east by way of the Erie Canal or one of the railways running out of the city. This made direct connection by rail with Buffalo imperative, since the transfer ferries then in operation would require excessive cargo handling to be practical or economical. That is why, when a replacement for the old *International* was built in 1857, the company opted for a car ferry.

The new ship, also called the *International*, was built at the Buffalo shipyard of Bidwell & Banta. Over twice the size of its predecessor, she could carry 14 loaded freight cars on her two tracks and had the distinction of being the first successful railway car ferry in Ontario (the *John Counter* of Kingston, built four years earlier, was anything but successful). *International* also had the honour of carrying the Prince of Wales across to Buffalo during his Royal Tour of 1860.

But traffic was not immediately forthcoming, for delays in receiving government loans for the construction of new harbour facilities at Goderich forced back the opening of the port to lake shipping until the winter of 1861. In anticipation of the event, the Buffalo & Lake Huron had made agreements to receive and transport freight from Lake Michigan ports to Buffalo and points east. However, snags occurred in construction and for a month or so ships were diverted to the Grand Trunk at Sarnia. Though only temporary, the volumes of traffic carried by the Grand Trunk on behalf of the Buffalo & Lake Huron were enough to give the Grand Trunk cause to buy stock in the railway, eventually leading to the takeover of the line in 1869.

In 1866 traffic for the Buffalo & Lake Huron was further stimulated by the addition of a 60,000-bushel grain elevator at Goderich. Grain from Chicago could now be sent east to New England much faster, while at the same time giving the ships an opportunity to make extra trips during the navigation season by shortening their route.

Business for the company boomed and it became clear that the ferry across the Niagara River was no longer adequate to meet expected traffic demands. A bridge was the only answer, and in 1866 the Buffalo & Lake Huron and the Grand Trunk agreed to jointly undertake the construction of a single-track bridge between what became Bridgeburg (Fort Erie), Ontario, and Black Rock, New York. Following the acquisition of the Buffalo & Lake Huron in 1869 by the Grand Trunk, the project became strictly a Grand Trunk endeavour.

By the time work on the International Bridge began in 1870, the costs of operating the car ferry *International* had reached £16,000 each year.[11] The new bridge would not only save on the cost of operating the ferry, but give the Grand Trunk additional revenue through receipt of tolls from the Great Western, Canada Southern, and Erie railways, who were to be given trackage rights over the structure, not to mention the extra traffic for the Grand Trunk itself.

With the opening of the International Bridge to regular traffic on 3 November 1873, the days of usefulness for the *International* were over and the veteran of 16 years of faithful service was withdrawn, probably ending its days as a barge, a fate common to many car ferries.

The Great Western Railway of Canada

The Great Western was one of Ontario's pioneer railways, second only to the Northern Railway (Ontario, Simcoe & Huron Railway), the earliest steam railway to operate in the province. Yet it was not the intention of its promoters to build a railway to serve the interests of those early Upper Canadians alone. The owners of the Great Western recognized that the railway project could

The Buffalo & Lake Huron's second *International* was the first successful railway car ferry to operate in the Great Lakes region. This drawing shows how the *International* probably appeared, complete with passenger accommodations above the train deck. In this view, *International* is docked at her slip at Black Rock while her Fort Erie slip is just visible at the upper right corner. The wooden truss swing bridge spans the Erie Canal, separated from the Niagara River by the rocky breakwater; the New York Central train at the bottom of the picture is on the branch running from Lewiston and Niagara Falls, New York, to Buffalo. — *CN No. 85119*

This is a very early photograph of the *Great Western*, probably taken during the first half of the 1870s. A double-ended ferry (with her bow loading end at the right), the *Great Western* had wheelhouses fore and aft; note, however, that each wheelhouse has an octagonal rear section and a rectangular addition extending to the edge of the top deck, suggesting that the rectangular portion may have been a later modification to improve visibility while docking. Note also that the train enclosure extends vertically fully two decks, resulting in passenger cabins running length-wise along each side of the vessel. — *The Windsor Star*

provide a valuable link in the American transit trade, joining the eastern railways terminating at the Niagara River with those terminating at Detroit from Chicago and other western centres.

When the main line was opened between Niagara Falls and Windsor on 27 January 1854, the Great Western was ready to carry transit freight in all but two very important points. At both ends of the line, the railway was separated from its American counterparts by water. At Niagara Falls, the company was able to span the Niagara River and Gorge through the construction of a suspension bridge, a feat completed in May 1855, although passengers and goods were carried across the bridge well before then in horse-drawn wagons. The Detroit River was a different story. At almost half a mile wide and with a strong current, construction of any sort of bridge would have been difficult, to say the least, while shipping on the river demanded free passage. It was obvious to the Great Western that the erection of a bridge was out of the question, as was a tunnel.

Under these circumstances the railway had no other choice than to use steam ferries to make the crossing between Windsor and Detroit. Since the broad-gauge Great Western was unable to interchange equipment with the standard-gauge Michigan Central and Detroit & Milwaukee railroads across the river at Detroit, the first vessels employed were transfer ferries capable of carrying passengers and freight only. According to the early shipping registers, the first steamers purchased by the railway were the *Niagara* and the *Transit*, both constructed in 1854. While little is known about the *Niagara*, it was probably much like *Transit*, a 500-ton wooden side-paddle-steamer built at Newport, Michigan. Together, they served the Great Western during a period of remarkable traffic growth.

Between 1854 and 1856 the company's total revenue more than doubled, rising from £284,088 in 1854 to £616,135 in 1856. But even more astonishing than that was the rise in freight revenue from only £68,015 to £236,432 during those same years.[12] While income from passengers still exceeded freight, and bearing in mind that only a portion of the freight revenue came from the transit trade, it was enough to tax the ability of the railway and its ferries as they struggled to carry the American transit goods east. The ferries were especially susceptible. In the winter of 1856, for example, there was so much ice on the Detroit River that the *Niagara* and the *Transit* were unable to make the crossing. By February over 200,000 tons of freight destined for the Great Western were in storage at Detroit awaiting shipment, enough to fill 25,000 freight cars![13]

Although sleighs could fill the needs of passengers during the interim, the railway could not afford to be without the ferries when it came to freight. It was clearly evident that the railway needed a vessel capable of breaking through the ice if the company was to remain competitive.

The solution came in 1858, when the railway took delivery of the 1,190-ton transfer ferry *Union* from Jenkins' Shipyard at Windsor. Powerful enough to break through heavy ice and therefore guarantee an open passage year-round for the ferries, the *Union* could carry a trainload of passengers in its "spacious saloon." It would seem that the *Union* was designed to carry only passengers and their baggage, leaving the *Niagara* and the *Transit* to handle the freight.

There were of course other ferries operating between Windsor and Detroit by various firms which supplemented the Great Western's own service. In the spring of 1866, for instance, the Detroit & Milwaukee Railroad chartered the 233-ton ferry *Windsor*,, built in 1856, for the purpose of carrying passengers and freight between its wharf at Detroit and the Great Western's Windsor terminal. Not long after, on 23 April, the *Windsor* caught fire and burned with the loss of 30 lives. The steamer was so badly damaged that the hull was only suitable for use as a barge.

No sooner had the *Union* arrived than an economic depression forced revenues down, but by 1860 freight traffic had made sufficient gains to turn the Great Western's profit picture around while exceeding passenger receipts for the first time. As the volumes of American freight carried by the railway rose, so too did the cost of transshipping goods. The company could not afford to leave freight waiting on the docks at Detroit for transferal to Windsor for any length of time, but on the other hand labour costs prohibited the hiring of more men. Between 1864 and 1866 the Great Western had laid a third rail from Niagara Falls to Windsor, permitting the railway to haul standard-gauge cars along its entire main line, leaving the transfer steamers at Windsor as the only roadblock left to establishing a through rail route between Chicago and the eastern seaboard.

The company's directors accepted that it was time to introduce a car ferry onto the Detroit River service. While construction on the main line was being carried out, a Scottish shipyard on the Clyde was commissioned to prefabricate an iron hull capable of withstanding the heavy ice conditions of the Detroit, and in 1866 the components arrived at the Jenkins yard in Windsor, where the hull was assembled. To that were added engines built in a Dundas, Ontario, machine shop, powering the ferry's side paddle wheels, with steam provided by boilers built in the Great Western's Hamilton shops. The most unique aspect of the ship, though, was on deck, or rather, what was over the deck. While more modern ferries of her type featured open decks on which the rails were laid, the Great Western's new ferry featured an enclosure completely covering her two sets of track and protecting the railway cars from the elements during the river crossing. Only two other ferries, both belonging to the Great Western, would be subsequently equipped with enclosed car decks.

When all was complete, she was launched as the *Great Western*, a 1,252-ton steamship capable of carrying up to 16 loaded freight cars or eight passenger cars on her two dual-gauge tracks. The *Great Western* could carry the narrow-gauge American cars as well as the broad-gauge Canadian equipment. On 1 January 1867 the *Great Western* made her debut on the Detroit River, and there spent the next 56 years providing faithful service not only to the Great Western, but later to the Grand Trunk and finally Canadian National. The only major alteration to the ferry occurred around 1882, when the structure covering her track deck was removed, giving her a more conventional appearance.

With the introduction of the *Great Western*, the railway placed the primary responsibility for transferring freight and passengers onto the *Great Western* and the *Union*. This probably enabled the company to dispose of the *Niagara* (although this is speculation on the author's part) and free up the *Transit* for local freight service around Windsor and Detroit. In 1869 the *Transit* was rebuilt at Toronto, and following her return to Windsor, she served the Great Western Railway well into the late-1870s.

Traffic on the railway continued to grow, and in 1872 the company felt that the construction of another car ferry was in order. Once again the work was carried out by Jenkins' Shipyard, who turned out the new 1,057-ton wooden car ferry later that year, sporting an enclosed car deck upon which two standard-gauge tracks had been laid (the Great Western having nearly completed its conversion to standard gauge), each track holding five freight cars. Since the new ferry was christened *Transit*, it is entirely possible that the old *Transit* was scrapped at this time with at least some of her machinery removed and placed in her namesake. *Transit* (II) started on her regular run early that September.

Just a couple of months before, another ferry had been ordered, this time from the Port Huron Drydock Company at Port Huron, Michigan. In their yard the small, 365-ton wooden ferry *Saginaw* was launched and delivered to the Great Western in May 1873. It is believed that *Saginaw* was equipped to carry passengers as well as four freight cars, although sources differ on this point. When *Saginaw* burned in 1892, for example, she was listed as a tug.[14] According to George Hilton's *The Great Lakes Car Ferries*, both *Transit* (II) and *Saginaw* were initially intended for a new service between Sarnia, at the end of the railway's branch from Komoka (west of London), and Port Huron, just across the St. Clair River. *Transit* was switched to the Windsor route before it was even launched, necessitating the construction of the *Saginaw*. Yet even the *Saginaw* saw very little service at Sarnia, spending at least the first six months of her career at Windsor instead.

To what extent the Great Western's plans for Sarnia had been developed at this time is difficult to say, but it should be noted that the Sarnia branch was never really considered by the company as more than a branch line, built to spite the Grand Trunk for invading the Great Western's territory in the 1850s as much as any other reason. Although warehouses and a grain elevator were later built at Sarnia for the benefit of attracting the lake trade, there is little evidence to suggest that any direct ferry crossing was ever made by the Great Western. At any rate, by the end of 1874 no ferry service was being provided at Sarnia by the railway, all ships being concentrated at Windsor.

The Great Western was still on the move when it ordered its last car ferry in 1873 from Jenkins' Shipyard after heavy winter ice stopped all but the *Great Western* from crossing the

Detroit River. At 1,465 tons, the *Michigan* was the largest ship ever to serve in the railway's fleet, and like the *Great Western*, she was equipped with side paddle wheels and a covered car deck. With the ability to carry up to 18 freight cars, *Michigan* greatly increased the company's transfer ability across the river and, more importantly, made it possible for whole passenger trains to cross between Detroit and Windsor for the first time. Now passenger trains from Toronto and Niagara Falls could run through to Chicago without change by way of the Michigan Central, providing the Great Western with a significant competitive advantage over the Grand Trunk until that company, too, introduced its own through trains not long after.

Michigan entered service in February 1874, but despite expectations she was never able to match the performance of her veteran sister, *Great Western*.

The early 1870s also brought a newcomer onto the scene, one which would threaten to take away the Great Western's primary source of American freight traffic, the Michigan Central Railroad. The Canada Southern Railway was being constructed across the southwestern Ontario peninsula to the south of the Great Western and promised to be an even better shortcut for the New York Central and the Michigan Central lines than the Great Western. By the 1880s the Canada Southern would be under the complete control of the Michigan Central, and the Great Western would lose an important source of traffic.

By 1882 the Great Western Railway was absorbed by the Grand Trunk Railway.

The Grand Trunk Railway of Canada
Canadian National Railways

Like the Great Western, the Grand Trunk also competed for the American transit trade, but by the time the Grand Trunk had reached Sarnia, its western terminus, in November 1856, the Great Western had already grabbed much of the business for itself. This was in part due to the Great Western's earlier completion, but it was also because the railway provided the shortcut the American railways needed. The Grand Trunk's route was well north of the Great Western and not only lacked a credible American railway from which to receive traffic at the Sarnia end, but its route was only practical if the goods were destined for the Atlantic seaboard at Portland, Maine, the railway's eastern terminal, or some point in between, such as Montreal or Toronto. That is why for many years the only ferry service provided by the Grand Trunk across the St. Clair River between Sarnia and Port Huron was the steamer *Canadian*. The *Canadian* was built for the railway in 1854 by Jenkins' Shipyard at Chatham and initially served as a supply ship during the Grand Trunk's construction.

By the end of the 1850s, the Grand Trunk had obtained its own access to Detroit through the lease of the Chicago, Detroit & Canada Grand Junction Railroad, running 59 miles between Port Huron and Detroit. Despite the fact that the newly acquired line was broad gauge, as was the Grand Trunk, no attempt to connect the two by means of a car ferry was made. The volume of traffic moving across the river must have been small, but at least it gave the railway a foothold into the Detroit market.

As cross-river tonnage slowly grew during the early 1860s, the need arose for a second transfer ferry to supplement the *Canadian*, and so in 1864 the Stead Shipyard at Sarnia constructed the 446-ton paddle-steamer *W.J. Spicer* for the Grand Trunk.

It is believed that a "swing ferry" for handling freight cars was also added around this time. Essentially a barge, the ferry was anchored near the American shore and was propelled from shore to shore by the strong river current.[15] The docks for the ferry were located upstream from Sarnia at Point Edward, Ontario, and at Fort Gratiot, Michigan.

Between 1872 and 1873 the Grand Trunk underwent the conversion to standard gauge in order to encourage through American traffic, just as the Great Western had done, opening up the possibility of interchanging equipment with the Michigan Central at Detroit, and thereby creating a new through line from Chicago to Portland, or by way of the newly acquired Buffalo & Lake Huron, from Chicago to Buffalo. The scheme would only be successful, however, if the Grand Trunk could put a self-propelled car ferry onto the St. Clair River.

Following a fire in 1892, the *Saginaw* was sold by the Grand Trunk, successor to the Great Western, and subsequently rebuilt as a wrecking tug. If this picture of the *Saginaw* is indeed thesame vessel, it shows that she must have been rebuilt again as a freighter before 1906, the year in which this photo was taken at Sault Ste. Marie. A careful examination of the vessel reveals that the hull is of an earlier vintage than the upper structures, possible proof that this is the same ship. — *PAC PA-145811*

The *International*, built at Fort Erie in 1872, was the Grand Trunk's first large car ferry. Photographed at Point Edward in 1890, she is seen loaded to capacity with 18 forty-foot stock cars of the Central Vermont. — *OA S13051*

Larger than the *International*, the *Huron* was built by the Grand Trunk in 1875 and together they ferried trains between Point Edward and Fort Gratiot until the opening of the St. Clair Tunnel in 1891. Both vessels were laid up as surplus with *International* being sold in 1898. *Huron*, on the other hand, was reactivated for service at Windsor in 1900 and sent south. Since the Windsor slips could only handle two-tracked ferries, *Huron* had her deck re-laid with only two tracks. In this view, the *Huron* is seen leaving Detroit in the late 1940s. — *CN X31259*

Here is a close-up view of *Huron*, again in the late 1940s leaving Detroit. In both views of the *Huron*, she is carrying three passenger cars and one baggage car (she is also carrying a Union Tank Line car in this view), indicating that both are part of train 16, The Ontario Limited, which left Detroit at 4:00 p.m. for Toronto and Montreal daily. According to the 25 November 1945 timetable, Canadian National assigned three cars from Detroit on this train — one coach (Detroit to Toronto), one parlour car (Detroit to Toronto) and one sleeper (Detroit to Montreal), all with air conditioning — with other cars, including a diner, being added at Windsor. Train 16 operated east of Toronto as The Maple Leaf although west of the city, The Maple Leaf (eastbound) was actually number 20 from Chicago by way of Sarnia. Both trains were joined at Toronto and operated as part of the Canadian National/Canadian Pacific pool train service between there and Montreal. — *CN X37567*

With the provision of a car ferry at Sarnia made imperative for the well-being of the railway, the Grand Trunk began planning for the new vessel as early as 1871, when the company ordered a prefabricated iron hull from the English firm of Palmer & Company of Yarrow-on-Tyne. The hull was delivered to the construction site at Fort Erie, Ontario, late in the year. This fact is interesting, for it suggests that the railway took advantage of crews employed in the erection of the International Bridge between Fort Erie and Black Rock (Buffalo) to carry out the assembly work, including the installation of engines and boilers manufactured in Montreal, and other necessary work.

Appropriately named *International*, the steamship could carry up to 21 freight cars on three tracks, laid to accommodate both broad-gauge and standard-gauge cars. Surprisingly enough, her gross tonnage was only 851 tons, yet she could carry more cars than any other ferry in the region, and she was also the first car ferry on the Great Lakes with three tracks.

International arrived to take up her duties at Sarnia by the end of August, but the actual crossing point was relocated upstream at Point Edward, where the company had rebuilt or replaced the swing ferry docks to accommodate the new ferry; the Fort Gratiot dock was treated likewise. As opposed to the crossing between Sarnia and Port Huron, this transfer point held the advantage of reduced crossing distance, while the swifter current at this point on the river aided in preventing winter freeze-up and ice accumulation, though ice could still pose operating problems.

No longer needed, the swing ferry was withdrawn and scrapped, as was the *Canadian*, leaving the *International* and the *W.J. Spicer* to handle all of the traffic.

With a new car ferry and standard-gauge track, the Grand Trunk was in a real position to compete for American traffic from Chicago, and soon the tonnages of freight handled began to climb, pleasing the railway's officials no end. One car ferry alone was no match for the newfound trade, and so in 1875 the Grand Trunk undertook the construction of a second car ferry, this time establishing a makeshift shipyard at Point Edward for the project. The new *Huron*, a 1,052-ton steel-hulled ship with a capacity of 24 freight cars on three tracks, was ready for service by the end of the year. With *Huron*'s entry, the *W.J. Spicer* was made redundant and soon after was sold, stripped of machinery and superstructure, and reduced to a barge.

Encouraged by the increasing volumes of Chicago freight the Grand Trunk was carrying, the railway made the push to extend its rails into Chicago, much to the resentment of the Michigan Central Railroad and Cornelius Vanderbilt, owner of both the Michigan Central and the New York Central lines. When the Grand Trunk finally reached Chicago in 1879, it was all-out war between the two systems, but the Grand Trunk wasn't worried. By 1883 it was carrying one third of all freight between Chicago and New England, much of it the same dressed-meat traffic the Michigan Central had turned its nose up at only a few years before. In one year alone, almost 200,000 freight cars were transferred across the St. Clair River by *Huron* and *International*, keeping the ferries busy 24 hours a day.[16]

The price of success took its toll as the cost of operating the ferries rose to $50,000 per year and soon it became clear that the car ferry service could not provide the capacity needed for future growth. The construction of a bridge was out of the question due to the heavy river traffic; ship owners objected to any structure that would restrict shipping on the St. Clair River, one of the busiest shipping lanes in the Great Lakes system. Tunnelling technology, however, had progressed far enough to offer a real alternative, and so in 1884 the Grand Trunk formed the St. Clair Tunnel Company with a mandate to engineer a single-track tunnel under the river between Sarnia and Port Huron. By 1888 actual construction began, and in 1891 the tunnel, all 6,032 feet of it, was opened to traffic. During the construction period, the St. Clair Tunnel Company employed the *W.J. Taylor*, a small nine-ton steamboat built in 1883 by Jenkins' Shipyard at Chatham. The *W.J. Taylor* remained with the company for several decades.

With the tunnel opened, the services of the *International* and the *Huron* were no longer needed and the ships were laid up. The *International* was sold in 1898 to the Lake Erie & Detroit River Railway, later consolidated into the Pere Marquette Railway. The *Huron* remained with the Grand Trunk and in 1900 was sent south to Windsor to augment the Grand Trunk's fleet there. The Grand Trunk's Windsor car ferry services date back to 1882, when the Grand Trunk consolidated the Great Western Railway into its system (made effective by 1884), thereby gaining a firm hold on rail services in southwestern Ontario. At the time the Grand Trunk assumed control, the Windsor fleet consisted of the car ferries *Great Western, Transit, Michigan* and *Saginaw*, and the transfer ferry *Union*, but except for the *Great Western*, all of the ferries were of wood construction, a material not only subject to rot but fire as well.

In an attempt to rectify the situation, the Grand Trunk commissioned the Detroit Dry Dock Company to construct an iron car ferry capable of carrying 16 freight cars. This new ferry was the 1,571-ton *Lansdowne*, launched in 1884. With steam supplied by boilers fabricated by the Grand Trunk in Montreal, the *Lansdowne* was powered with engines removed from the *Michigan*, which also lost part of its superstructure to the new vessel, Jenkins Shipyard making the installation as well as the final outfitting.

Once the *Lansdowne* was in service, the railway wasted no time in selling off the hull of the *Michigan* and the *Union*, both off the railway's property in 1885. The *Transit* was spared but only to be mothballed just in case future traffic increases required her reintroduction; this never happened, for on 4 March 1889 fire consumed the wooden ferry, leaving nothing but a charred hulk.

From 1884 the Grand Trunk's operating fleet consisted of the *Great Western*, the *Lansdowne*, and the *Saginaw*. It was indeed an eventful year for the service following the introduction of the *Lansdowne*, which resulted in the elimination of half the fleet. In fact, it largely overshadowed an incident earlier in April, when the *Great Western* collided with the new Michigan Central car ferry *Michigan Central* out on the Detroit River. Had it not been for the slow speed at which the ferries operated, both ships might have been lost.

For the most part, the acquisition of the Great Western allowed the Grand Trunk to split its traffic flow between the Windsor to Detroit and the Point Edward to Fort Gratiot crossings, and make use of the Great Western's superior main line. It was a boon to the old Great Western as well. The Michigan Central was now in firm control of the Canada Southern, and with its own railway line to Buffalo as well as a fleet of car ferries to rival the Grand Trunk's, it no longer had need to send its rail traffic over the old Great Western.

When the St. Clair Tunnel was opened in 1891, traffic flows once again shifted, this time north to Sarnia. The tunnel held the advantage over the car ferries in that trains could pass underneath the river without the need of breaking up the consists for loading onto a ferry, only to be reassembled on the other side of the river. While the Detroit River ferries still played an important role, they would no longer be responsible for the share of tonnage they previously enjoyed.

In May 1892 the wooden *Saginaw* caught fire and burned at Windsor. The company sold her soon after, but enough of the *Saginaw* was left to allow her new owners to rebuild her into a wrecking tug.

In 1897 the Grand Trunk secured an important source of income when the railway agreed to give the Wabash Railroad, which terminated at Detroit, trackage rights over the Grand Trunk between Windsor and Buffalo and Niagara Falls by way of the southerly "Loop Line" built originally by the Great Western as the Canada Air Line Railway. The Grand Trunk must have been happy, for in securing the Wabash as an ally, it also secured a railway with an animosity towards the Michigan Central equal to its own.

Not in possession of its own car ferries, the Wabash relied on the Grand Trunk to move its cars across the Detroit River. This extra traffic was sufficient enough that in 1900 the Grand Trunk reactivated the *Huron* and brought it down to Windsor. Because the Windsor car ferries and slips were built to accommodate two tracks only, the *Huron's* three tracks were lifted and replaced with two tracks, consequently reducing capacity to 14 freight cars.

The Wabash continued to send its cars across the river on board the Grand Trunk ferries until 1912 when, with the assistance of the Grand Trunk, the railway purchased its own ferries from the Michigan Central. The Michigan Central had completed its tunnel under the river two years earlier, freeing up its fleet for disposal.

The Grand Trunk car ferries were left once again with surplus capacity, and it might have resulted in the laying up of one or two of the ships had it not been for the outbreak of the First World War in August 1914. The demands of war stimulated rail traffic in general and with the industrial

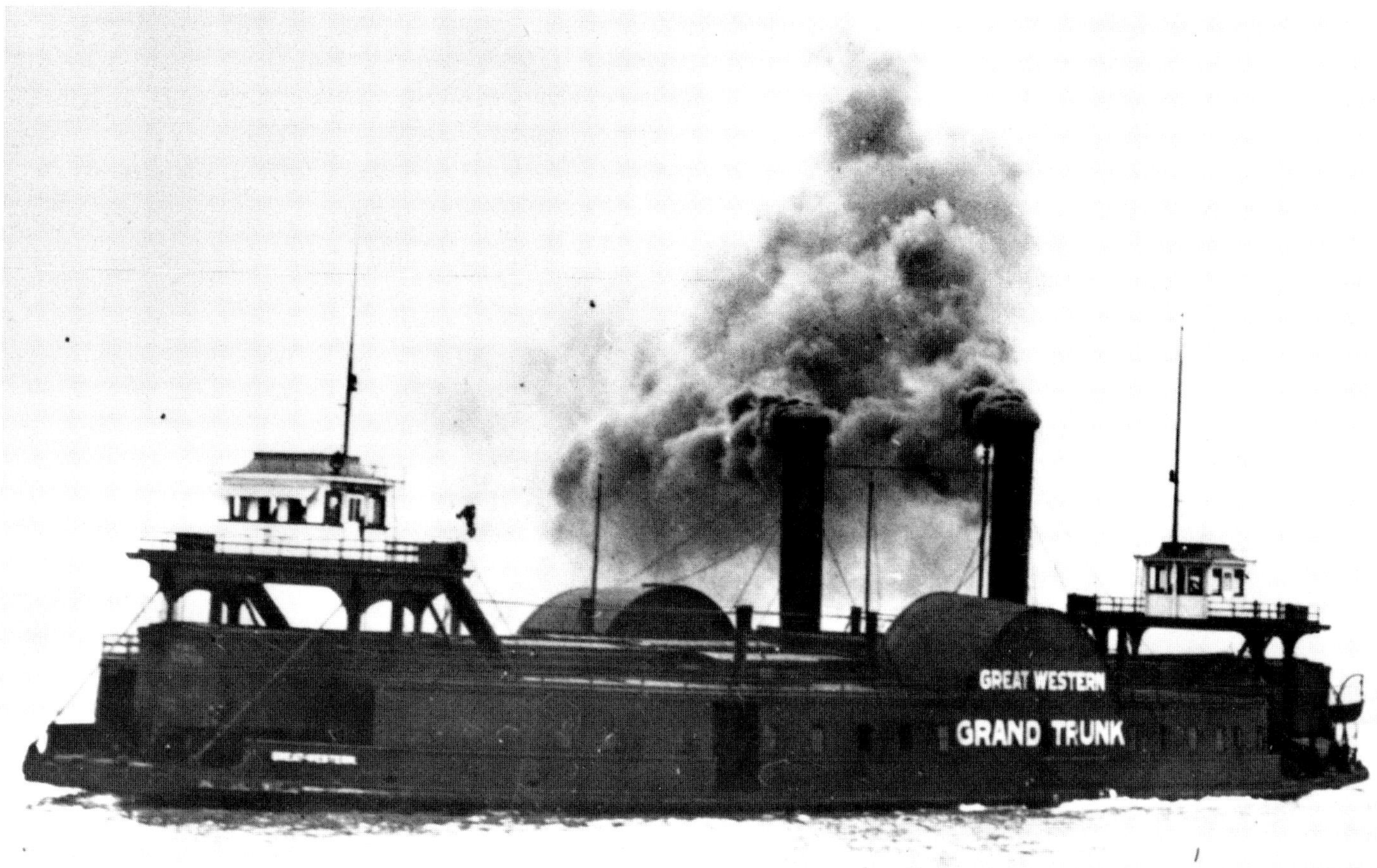

Around 1882, at about the time of the Grand Trunk takeover of the Great Western Railway, the *Great Western* was significantly altered by the removal of her superstructure above the train deck. As a result, the *Great Western* took on a more conventional appearance as this circa 1915 picture shows. — *UBL No. 8811*

W J TAYLOR — 1883

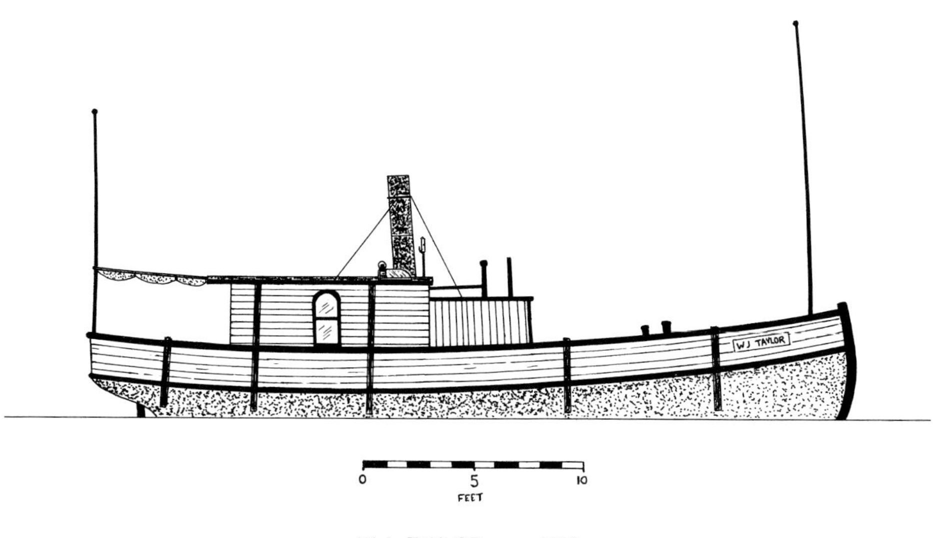

The St. Clair Tunnel Company's small steamer *W.J. Taylor.* — *Author*

Named in honour of the Governor-General and added to the Windsor fleet in 1884 by the Grand Trunk, the *Lansdowne* worked with the *Great Western* in providing the primary ferry service. A double-ender, *Lansdowne* followed closely the lines of the rebuilt *Great Western*, differing mainly in having two sets of double smoke stacks. This postcard view of *Lansdowne* leaving Windsor dates from about 1910. — *MTL*

Under the ownership of Canadian National, the *Lansdowne* was reduced to a single-ended ferry by the removal of her aft wheelhouse and bridge. Other minor modifications included the replacement of her wooden gunnel-railings fore and aft with steel railings fabricated from pipe sections. *Lansdowne* is seen here arriving at Windsor with several passenger cars in the late 1940s or possibly the 1950s. — *CN X39238*

might of Detroit just across the river, the ferries must have been very busy indeed. After the Armistice, however, volumes returned to normal levels.

The war and expansion in western Canada took their toll on the Grand Trunk though, and in January 1923 the Grand Trunk was officially consolidated into the newly formed Canadian National Railways. When Canadian National's management examined the Detroit River ferry service, they realized that they could get by with one ferry less. The aging *Great Western* was the obvious choice, and on 3 December 1923 the ferry was sold to the Essex Transit Company, who converted her to a sand barge, leaving the *Huron* and the *Lansdowne* to maintain the route.

By the end of the 1920s, the Windsor car ferries carried only ten percent of all traffic handled by Canadian National between Ontario and Michigan, the Sarnia Tunnel being responsible for the other 90 percent. In 1929, for example, the *Huron* and the *Lansdowne* handled 685,200 tons of freight, of which 333,900 tons were bound for American destinations while 351,300 tons were imported into Canada, roughly a 50-50 split.[17] The Sarnia Tunnel by contrast handled 5,761,805 tons of freight. But it is worth noting that twice as much freight, 3,808,278 tons, passed east through the tunnel, with westbound movements amounting to only 1,953,527 tons.[18]

Generally speaking, this pattern reflects the traffic flows experienced by both the Grand Trunk and Canadian National as far as the Windsor ferries and the Sarnia Tunnel are concerned, though tonnages varied considerably, especially during the Depression of the 1930s, when total Windsor tonnage fell below 200,000 tons and imports from the United States were at times double or even triple exports. Principal commodities carried to the United States during this period at Windsor were paper, canned goods and general merchandise. Coal, automobiles and parts, and general merchandise made up most of the import traffic into Canada.[19]

World War II provided a stimulus to traffic and the ferries were once again busy, but with the termination of the war volumes dropped. By the 1950s only the *Lansdowne* saw regular service, leaving the *Huron* sitting idle much of the time. Later in 1971 the *Huron* returned to its old stomping grounds at Sarnia, handling some of the modern rail cars too large to pass through the Sarnia Tunnel. Both ferries were converted to car floats in 1970, but by the end of the decade the *Lansdowne* and the *Huron*, representing the last operating vestiges of the Grand Trunk, were sold.

Sometime during the 1960s, the 1,858-ton car ferry *Scotia II*, built in 1915 at Newcastle, England, for service between Nova Scotia and Cape Breton Island, was transferred to Windsor. She was similar to the other car ferries in design and was eventually withdrawn in the 1970s.

The Canada Southern Railway

The Michigan Central Railroad

The Canada Southern Railway was, in concept, almost as old as the Great Western Railway, sharing many of the same goals, yet it was not until the 1870s that construction actually began on the line.

Strongly backed by capitalists south of the border, the Canada Southern consisted of a 229-mile main line running between Fort Erie, St. Thomas and Amherstburg, with a branch from St. Thomas to Courtright on the St. Clair River (named for Milton Courtright of Erie, Pennsylvania, President of the Canada Southern Railway), along with rail lines in Michigan between Toledo and Detroit, and between St. Clair (opposite Courtright) and Ridgeway. Canada Southern was essentially vying with the Great Western for control of the transit trade by providing a bridge line between the Michigan Southern and the Michigan Air Line companies in the west with the New York Central and the Erie Railroads at Buffalo, thereby forming the shortest route between Chicago and Buffalo, in fact 28 miles shorter than the Great Western's Canada Air Line.

When the Canada Southern opened in 1873, it was in direct connection with Buffalo by way of the International Bridge, but at Amherstburg it was unable to bridge the Detroit River, and so the railway introduced its first car ferry, the *Transfer*, by 1874.

The *Transfer*, a 1,222-ton wooden side-wheeler, was launched by Jenkins' Shipyard at Windsor in 1873, and while she was similar to her Great Western counterparts at Windsor, the

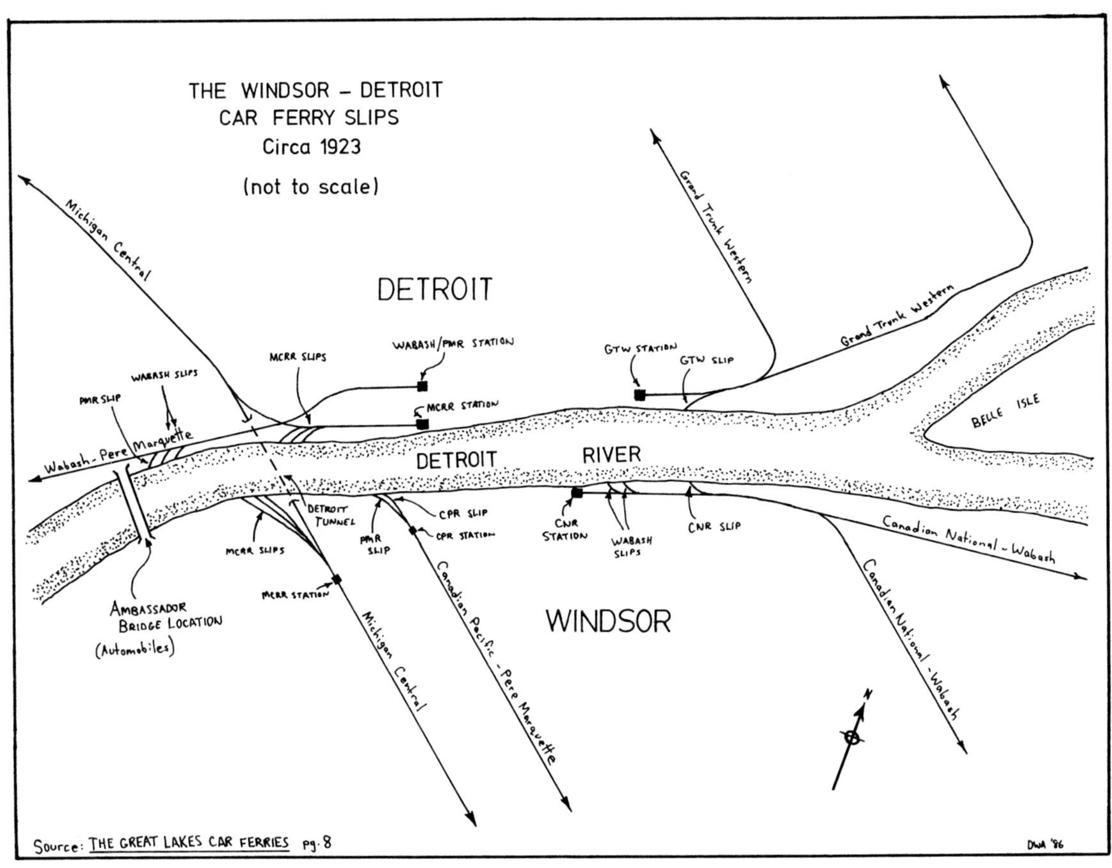

In response to increased traffic demands, the Canada Southern added the *Transport*, the railway's second car ferry, in 1880. The *Transport* passed to the Michigan Central Railroad in 1883 with that company's takeover of the Canada Southern, serving until 1912 when she, together with the *Transfer (II)* and the *Detroit* were sold to the Wabash Railroad. This view shows *Transport* sometime around 1920 when she was under the Wabash flag. — *UBL No. 8796-A*

Transfer differed by having three tracks rather than two, giving it a capacity of 21 freight cars. This track arrangement was introduced on the Grand Trunk's ferry *International* and, with the exception of the Great Western ferries, became standard along the Detroit and St. Clair rivers.

The Amherstburg crossing was a complicated one and was actually located about a mile north of the town centre, at Gordon. At this point on the Detroit River, an island, Grosse Isle, Michigan, separated the river into two channels. One, a navigable channel, was located on the Canadian side, and as it could not be bridged it had to be crossed with a car ferry. The channel on the other side of Grosse Isle was not used for shipping, and through its subsidiary, the Canada Southern Bridge Company, the railway erected a bridge across the river to Trenton, Michigan, where the railway connected with its lines to Detroit, Toledo and southwest Michigan. Although it has been a long time since the last train passed over the bridge in 1929, Canada Southern's assets on Grosse Isle (the railway at one time owned most of the island) have greatly increased in value, for the island has since become a prosperous suburb of Detroit and the old right-of-way comprises some of the last undeveloped land.

It did not take long for the Canada Southern to attract freight traffic, and by 1875 the *Transfer* was moving over 170,000 cars across the river each year.[20] By the end of the decade, levels reached a point where one ferry was no longer adequate, and so in 1880 the company ordered a new car ferry from the Detroit Dry Dock Company at Wyandotte, Michigan. The new ferry, named *Transport,* was a 1,595-ton iron paddle-steamer, and like *Transfer* she could carry 21 freight cars on her three tracks. *Transport's* introduction doubled the railway's transfer capacity across the river.

Throughout the 1870s the Michigan Central Railroad purchased stock in Canada Southern with an aim to gaining control of the company. Since 1854 the Michigan Central had been obliged to send freight across southern Ontario by way of the Great Western Railway, the only line able to provide a through connection with the New York Central Railroad for New York, but it meant losing freight revenue to the Great Western. The Canada Southern was an alternative that the Michigan Central was quick to take advantage of, and when it assumed control of the company on 1 January 1883, it finally had its own through line from Chicago to Buffalo.

Because the Michigan Central's principal eastern terminal was located at Detroit, several miles upstream from Amherstburg, the company made the construction of a new line between Windsor and the Canada Southern main line at Essex a top priority, along with the addition of another ferry to handle the extra Michigan Central traffic. The new line was completed in 1884, and with its opening all regular ferry operations were moved to Windsor and Detroit. There the *Transfer* and the *Transport* were joined by the newly completed *Michigan Central,* a 1,522-ton iron car ferry built by Detroit Dry Dock. From that time on the ferries would use the Amherstburg crossing only when ice conditions at Windsor and Detroit made passage across the Detroit River impossible.

In 1888 the wooden *Transfer* had reached such a state of decay that its hull was declared unseaworthy and the railway was forced to build a new *Transfer. Transfer (II)* was similar to the previous car ferries in having a capacity of 21 freight cars on three tracks and in being a side-paddlewheeler, but this 1,511-ton steel ship, a product of the Cleveland Ship Building Company, differed in that it was equipped with a screw propeller as well. The reason for the addition of the screw may have been the possibility of improved performance when plowing through ice. Side paddle wheels did not perform well in heavy ice, whereas screw propellers, located below ice level, were free to provide maximum power. Side-wheelers, however, were better suited when it came to manoeuvering into the ferry slips. The old *Transfer* had her machinery removed and was sold on 4 December 1888 and converted into a floating dry dock.

By the late 1890s Michigan Central traffic across the river had reached 500,000 cars a year and was still rising.[21] The company had to make a decision: either continue to build more car ferries and thereby continue paying money out on the ferry service, or build a tunnel under the river, keeping in mind that a bridge was out of the question due to heavy river traffic.

In 1904 the railway made the choice and found in favour of the tunnel. In 1905 the Detroit River Tunnel Company was formed by Michigan Central to design and build the tunnel, its

This turn of the century view shows the *Michigan Central* arriving at Windsor. — *UBL No. 8794*

When the wooden hull of the original car ferry *Transfer* became badly deteriorated, a new ferry was ordered. Delivered as the *Transfer (II)*, the new vessel incorporated a steel hull along with the unique combination of a paddle wheel and screw propeller propulsion system. It is highly probable that much of the first *Transfer*'s equipment found its way onto its new namesake. This photo of *Transfer (II)* probably dates from the early 1900s, before her sale to the Wabash. — *UBL No. 8795*

Built in 1904, the *Detroit* was the last car ferry purchased by the Michigan Central, arriving in the same year in which the decision to build the Detroit Tunnel was made. After serving for less than eight years, *Detroit* was sold to the Wabash, in whose service she is seen here in this circa 1950 view. — *UBL No. 8793A*

Perhaps dating from around 1910, this photograph shows two ferries on the Detroit River during winter. The ferry on the right is typical of many passenger ferries that once plyed between Windsor and Detroit; it is heading for Windsor. The car ferry on the left, however, is a mystery since it does not match the description of any of the car ferries on the river at that or any other time, particularly with its four separate funnels. The author suspects that it may in fact be the *Detroit* as built. Again, this is a matter of speculation. — *OA S16276*

approaches, and all the necessary trackwork and electrical installations needed for the electric locomotives which would pull trains through the tube. It would be a few years yet before the tunnel would be ready for regular use and in the meantime the railway still had to get its cars across the river by ferry, something that was becoming increasingly difficult.

It was therefore deemed that the railway would order one last car ferry for the Detroit River in order to bolster the service until the tunnel was finished. Appropriately named *Detroit*, the propeller-driven ferry was built in 1904 by Great Lakes Engineering at Ecorse, Michigan, and at 2,232 tons, she was the largest ferry employed by the railway on the Detroit. When built, the *Detroit* could carry 26 freight cars on three tracks.

The fleet now consisted of the *Transport*, the *Michigan Central*, the *Transfer(II)* and the *Detroit*, giving Michigan Central the largest car ferry fleet on the Detroit River at that time, and for good reason. By 1909 the railway was moving over 730,000 cars across the river each year, and when the tunnel was opened the following year, it was none too soon for the Michigan Central. In September 1910 regular freight trains started running through the tunnel, followed in October by all regular passenger trains.

With the tunnel officially opened, all car ferries were laid up, although there was no rush on the part of the Michigan Central to sell any of the ships. Perhaps they were holding back just in case problems arose with the tunnel, flooding always being a possibility with submarine tunnels. By 1912, however, the railway was ready to sell and it found an eager buyer in the Wabash Railroad, who purchased the *Transport*, the *Transfer* and the *Detroit*. The *Michigan Central* was not sold until the following June, finally ending her life in October 1926 when, after being converted to a barge, she sunk. Today, of the entire Michigan Central fleet, only the *Detroit* remains, still serving the Wabash's successor, the Norfolk & Western, though now only as a car float.

It should be mentioned that the Canada Southern at one time considered starting a car ferry service between Courtright and St. Clair, across the St. Clair River. Some dock construction was carried out during the 1870s, but no further developments ever took place. Canada Southern only had a short, isolated segment of line running out of St. Clair that wouldn't have generated enough traffic to warrant a car ferry. It served more as a branch line for the Grand Trunk in Michigan than it ever did Canada Southern.

The Canadian Pacific Railway

Of the car ferry services operated across the Detroit and St. Clair rivers, Canada Pacific's has remained the shortest-lived service.

Initially built to link Canada coast to coast and insure British Columbia's entry into Confederation, the Canadian Pacific was quick to grasp the importance of an Ontario network in order to broaden the company's revenue base and to provide a source of traffic to the line. In the push to acquire lines, the railway took control of the Credit Valley Railway in 1884 by way of the Ontario & Quebec Railway, and with it obtained a route into St. Thomas and the heart of southwestern Ontario, much to the resentment of the Grand Trunk. Canadian Pacific knew it needed to reach the traffic-rich American Midwest, but that demanded a direct connection with Detroit. The Credit Valley was pointed in the right direction, but it was far short of the mark.

The West Ontario Pacific Railway had been incorporated earlier by private concerns to construct a line from Woodstock, on the Credit Valley, to the St. Clair River and had already completed the railway as far as London when the Canadian Pacific purchased the company in 1888. It was the perfect vehicle to extend the railway to Detroit, and by 1890 Canadian Pacific had reached Windsor, just across the Detroit River from Detroit. The next step was the implementation of car ferry service.

In anticipation of the service, Canadian Pacific ordered the construction of two steel car ferries in 1889, the 1,730-ton *Michigan* and the 1,615-ton *Ontario*. While built to the same overall design, each side-wheeler being capable of carrying 16 freight cars on two tracks, the difference in tonnage can be attributed in part to the fact that each was built by a different company. The *Michigan* was a product of F.W. Wheeler & Company of Bay City, Michigan, and was an all-American effort, whereas the *Ontario* contract was let to the Polson Iron Works of Owen Sound, Ontario.

This rare and unusual photograph shows the *Ontario* at the Polson Iron Works yard at Owen Sound nearing completion in 1890. At this point, crews are completing the painting of the ship, evident by the two men on the scaffold beneath the aft bridge, as well as laying the track on the deck. Note too that the boilers are being fired-up, with smoke being visible above the port funnel (the right-hand funnel in this view). This photo was taken from the forward bridge looking aft.

— PAC PA-135426

The Canadian Pacific ferry slips at Windsor were adjoined by those of the Père Marquette (on the left), with the Canadian Pacific holding responsibility for moving the Père Marquette cars from the ferry slip to the Père Marquette yard at Walkerville. In this postcard view from around 1910, the *Père Marquette 14* appears on the left with Canadian Pacific's *Michigan* on the right.

— MTL

Polson Iron Works had just launched the Canadian Pacific lake steamer *Manitoba*, the first steel ship built in this country, and the quality of her construction so impressed Canadian Pacific's management that they had no qualms about awarding Polson's the *Ontario* contract. The works not only built the hull of the *Ontario* but the engines and boilers as well, the largest of their kind built in Canada up to that time, being fabricated at Polson's Toronto plant and sent by rail to Owen Sound. Each boiler alone weighed 37 tons and with diameters of 13 feet 3 inches were the largest ever carried by a North American railway to that date.[22]

Car ferry service between Windsor and Detroit commenced in the spring of 1890, at first carrying freight cars only, but by June passenger cars were also carried. Although Canadian Pacific was hoping to compete with the Grand Trunk for the American freight traffic, Canadian Pacific's lack of its own rails into Chicago and its failure to obtain trackage to the American railways at Niagara Falls and Buffalo resulted in limited traffic gains. Canadian Pacific suffered on New England-bound freight traffic as well, once again because it did not possess its own railway line into that region, unlike the Grand Trunk. As a result, the ferries were seldom overworked and during slow periods they were often leased to other railways operating across the Detroit River.

Following the opening of the Detroit Tunnel by the Michigan Central Railroad in 1910, Canadian Pacific made arrangements for its own trains to use the tunnel, starting with freight trains in 1915 and passenger trains by 1916. Canadian Pacific, unlike the Grand Trunk, was no threat to the Michigan Central and, in fact, they often co-operated, the joint ownership of the Toronto, Hamilton & Buffalo Railway by the New York Central, Michigan Central, and Canadian Pacific being a prime example.

With no further work, the *Michigan* and the *Ontario* were laid up, though it was not until 1924 when, stripped of boilers, engines, and other equipment, they were sold. The Port Arthur-based Newaygo Timber Company was the purchaser, and under its ownership the *Michigan* served until November 1942, when it was wrecked on Georgian Bay, outlasting the *Ontario*, which was lost on Lake Superior in October 1927. Both vessels were employed as pulpwood barges.

The Lake Erie & Detroit River Railway
The Pere Marquette Railway
The Chesapeake & Ohio Railway

The Lake Erie & Detroit River Railway was built by Hiram Walker of Windsor, founder of the distillery that now bears his name, and was initially a local line running between Walkerville (Windsor) and Leamington. By 1893 the railway was extended to St. Thomas and the lease of the London & Port Stanley Railway was obtained, forming the basis of a miniature railway system. Yet, as small as the system may have been, it served an important and growing industrial and agricultural region of Ontario, holding great prospects for future traffic growth.

It may have been the hope for increased traffic that inspired the railway's management to purchase the Grand Trunk car ferry *International* in 1898. The *International* was built in 1872 for the Grand Trunk's St. Clair River car ferry service and served there actively until 1891, when the Sarnia Tunnel was opened. Made surplus, it was subsequently laid up. The Lake Erie & Detroit River Railway must have had intentions to operate the ferry but no immediate action was taken. The company had just absorbed the Erie & Huron Railway running from Sarnia south to Lake Erie, and there may have been plans to start a car ferry service at Sarnia, but no definite action was taken.

In 1902 the railway entered into an agreement with the Michigan-based Pere Marquette Railway, the terms of which required the Lake Erie & Detroit River line to institute a car ferry service at Sarnia, while the Pere Marquette would implement a cross-lake car ferry service on Lake Erie (discussed in a later chapter). Within a short period of time the boilers of the *International* were fired up again and she commenced her second career carrying railway cars across the St. Clair River between South Sarnia, Ontario, and Port Huron, Michigan, where connection was made with the Pere Marquette.

In 1903 the Pere Marquette gained control of the Lake Erie & Detroit River Railway, and in 1904 the Pere Marquette obtained running rights over the Michigan Central line from St. Thomas

Having freed the icebound tug *Sarnia,* the *International* prepares to escort the *Sarnia* back to open water. Unlike the Grand Trunk's crossing at Point Edward, the Pere Marquette's at Sarnia to the south tended to experience greater ice build-up as this photograph demonstrates. — *PAC PA-60683*

Built in 1904, the *Pere Marquette 14* was the railway's first new car ferry built for service at Windsor. Owing to the need to repair the *International,* then serving at Sarnia, the *Pere Marquette 14* actually spent her first year of service running between Sarnia and Port Huron until 1905 when the *International* was reinstated. The *Pere Marquette 14* is seen here arriving at Windsor around the late 1940s. — *UBL No.8799*

The 1920s saw a surge in traffic for the Pere Marquette with the result that a second car ferry was needed at Sarnia to work with the aging *International.* Delivered in 1927, the *Pere Marquette 12* entered service at Sarnia, but what the 1920s brought to the railway, the Depression took away, ultimately forcing the railway to give up its St. Clair River service and concentrate its ferries at Windsor to handle what traffic remained. When the *International* was sold in 1934, only the *Pere Marquette 14* and the *Pere Marquette 12* remained. This photo shows *Pere Marquette 12* arriving at Windsor in the late 1940s. — *UBL No. 8798-A*

Built in 1945, the *Pere Marquette 10* was the last ferry delivered to the Pere Marquette before being acquired by the Chesapeake & Ohio Railway in 1946. In this view the ferry is moving northbound on the Detroit River as it approaches the Ambassador Bridge linking Detroit and Windsor. Probably photographed around 1950, it would not be too many years before the ferries would be transferred to Sarnia following the Chesapeake & Ohio's acquisition of trackage rights through the Detroit Tunnel in 1954. — *UBL No. 8797*

to Niagara Falls and Fort Erie. With that, the Pere Marquette became a high roller in the railway competition for American bridge traffic across southwestern Ontario.

By this time the old *International*, which for the past 13 years had remained idle, was in desperate need of repair and would soon be unfit for service. A new ferry was needed and in 1904 the Detroit Ship Building Company delivered the *Pere Marquette 14*, a 2,531-ton steel car ferry with a capacity of 30 freight cars on three tracks. The odd name, *Pere Marquette 14*, can be explained by noting that the Pere Marquette numbered its car ferries rather than giving them individual names and the number "14" was the number available at the time the ferry was built. Note also that the Pere Marquette operated most of its car ferries on Lake Michigan, one of the first companies to do so, which is why all subsequent car ferries operated by the railway on the St. Clair and Detroit rivers bore relatively high numbers.

After the company took delivery of the *Pere Marquette 14*, she was immediately sent to Sarnia, allowing the *International* to be withdrawn and repaired. When the *International* returned to service at Sarnia in 1905, the *Pere Marquette 14* was sent south to Windsor to establish Pere Marquette's Windsor to Detroit car ferry service. Access from Pere Marquette's Walkerville yard to the Windsor ferry slip was gained through trackage rights over the Canadian Pacific line into Windsor. Except for a short time between June and October 1906, when the *International* and the *Pere Marquette 14* exchanged routes, possibly due to traffic fluctuations, the *International* having a lesser capacity, the *Pere Marquette 14* spent her entire life on the Detroit River.

Traffic on the Pere Marquette made slow gains and it was not until 1927 that the railway added another car ferry. The new ship was the 2,767-ton *Pere Marquette 12*, a steel vessel built by the Manitowoc Shipbuilding Company of Manitowoc, Wisconsin, and was capable of carrying 27 freight cars on three tracks. *Pere Marquette 12* found immediate employment alongside the *International* at Sarnia.

Then the Depression came and freight tonnages slumped. The railway examined its position and found that the remaining traffic could be more expeditiously handled if they concentrated the ferry service on the Windsor to Detroit route, Windsor being better situated with respect to the main line. With that reasoning, the Sarnia ferries were withdrawn and the *Pere Marquette 12* was sent to Windsor to join the *Pere Marquette 14*. The *International*, on the other hand, was getting old, and to the railway she represented surplus capacity, an expensive luxury the company could do without. In 1934 the *International* was sold to the Sincennes-McNaughton Line Limited and rebuilt as a derrick barge.

Traffic patterns on the Pere Marquette were firmly established by this time, with the car ferries largely carrying through freight to and from American points. This fact is borne out by a look at the 1933 tonnages. Eastbound, of the 1,368,361 tons of freight carried across the Detroit River by the ferries, 1,368,361 tons were carried to Niagara Falls, New York, for interchange with the American railways terminating there.[23] Fort Erie, as an eastern terminus, was seldom used by the Pere Marquette after about 1930. The 473,878 tons of westbound freight goods received by the railway at Niagara Falls were transferred across the Detroit River on the car ferries. Not one ton of freight either received from or destined to a Canadian point on the Pere Marquette was handled by that railway's Detroit River car ferries.

Of the eastbound freight, 23 percent was made up of agricultural products, 35 percent comprised of mine and animal products, much of it coal, with manufactured and other goods representing the other 42 percent. Westbound, no agricultural products were carried, while manufactured and other goods outweighed mine and animal products three to one.[24] It was the classic transit trade pattern, making the Pere Marquette second only to the Michigan Central in total traffic carried between Windsor and Detroit, and ranking the railway third behind Michigan Central and Canadian National in total traffic carried across (or under) both the Detroit and the St. Clair rivers.

World War II brought a recovery in tonnages handled by the Pere Marquette, requiring the construction of the railway's last Detroit River car ferry, the *Pere Marquette 10*. Built by

Manitowoc Shipbuilding in 1945, the *Pere Marquette 10* was dimensionally similar to the *Pere Marquette 12* built 18 years earlier.

The Pere Marquette lost its identity in 1946 when control of the railway passed into the hands of the Chesapeake & Ohio Railway, although the Pere Marquette's Canadian lines continued to be known as the Pere Marquette Division.

With three ferries in operation, the service now made an average of about 16 trips each day, 12 months of the year, as reported to the U.S. Army Corps of Engineers in 1949. That lasted until 1953, when the Sarnia ferry route was revived, followed a year later by the elimination of the Windsor service when the Chesapeake & Ohio obtained the right to run freight trains through Michigan Central's Detroit Tunnel.

In 1957 the *Pere Marquette 14* was sold, taken to Hamilton, and scrapped. The *Pere Marquette 10* was later converted to a car float and has since continued to serve with the *Pere Marquette 12* on the St. Clair River.

The Wabash Railroad

The Norfolk & Western Railway

The Wabash was the last railway to establish a car ferry service across the Detroit River, and as discussed earlier, it all started when the railway obtained trackage rights over the Grand Trunk Railway between Windsor and Buffalo and Niagara Falls, New York in 1897. For many years the Grand Trunk had the responsibility for transferring Wabash freight cars across the Detroit River, until the Wabash purchased its own ferries in 1912 with the assistance of the Grand Trunk.

Until the Michigan Central Railroad opened the Detroit Tunnel in 1910, Michigan Central operated a fleet of four car ferries: *Transport, Michigan Central, Transfer* and *Detroit*. All were made redundant when the tunnel was completed, and by 1912 they were put up for sale. For the Wabash, it was an opportunity too good to pass up, and in October 1912 the company agreed to purchase the *Transport*, the *Transfer* and the *Detroit*, with a freight car capacity of 21, 21 and 24 cars respectively. All were steaming across the Detroit River by the following spring.

The Wabash handled reasonably large volumes of freight between Michigan and New York state, and by the 1920s the abilities of the aging ferries *Transport* and *Transfer* were being taxed to the limit. As a result, the Wabash began a program of fleet renewal.

In 1926 the company took delivery of the *Manitowoc* from the Manitowoc Shipbuilding Company. A large, 3,093-ton steel car ferry, the *Manitowoc* could carry 30 freight cars on four tracks, arranged in such a fashion as to allow the ferry to unload at a three-track slip, as used by the other ferries. The four-track system, though, was accepted as the new fleet standard, and in the following year the *Detroit* was reequipped with four tracks, boosting its capacity to 32 cars.

Another car ferry was added in 1930. Built by the Toledo Shipbuilding Company at Toledo, Ohio, the new *Windsor* was the Wabash's largest car ferry, weighing in at 3,131 tons, with a total capacity of 31 freight cars. The *Windsor's* arrival permitted the railway to sell the *Transport* and the *Transfer*, leaving the company with three of the biggest car ferries on the river.

A large-capacity fleet was vital to the Wabash. In 1933 the railway transferred 1,623,487 tons of freight across the Detroit River, making the company the third-largest mover of freight between Windsor and Detroit, and second-largest ferry operation on the river, only about 200,000 tons behind the Pere Marquette. Of the total tonnage moved, 954,237 tons consisted of eastbound freight, with westbound traffic amounting to 669,250 tons.[25] Traffic was generally split equally in the East between Buffalo and Niagara Falls, and except for a small percentage of traffic generated in Canada, the Wabash was chiefly a through line, since it only had the right to run through trains along the Canadian National line.[26] Wabash traffic across the Detroit in 1933 was broken down approximately as follows: eastbound, 33 percent animal products, 31 percent agricultural products, 30 percent manufactured goods, 6 percent forest products, and 1 percent mineral products; westbound, 61 percent manufactured goods, 30 percent mineral products, and 9 percent agricultural products.[27]

Since that time there have been changes. In 1939 the *Detroit* was rebuilt, and at some point all the ferries were converted to oil instead of coal. Since about the 1950s, the automakers have had

The *Detroit* was purchased from the Michigan Central in 1912 when the Wabash Railroad decided to take over responsibility for ferrying its cars across the Detroit River from the Grand Trunk. This photo shows how the *Detroit* appeared in the 1920s when she carried three stacks. In 1927, *Detroit,* built with three tracks, was refitted with four tracks, during which time the extra stack (in this view the one on the right) was removed. — *UBL No. 8793*

Named for the city of its construction, the *Manitowoc* was built in 1926 to allow the Wabash to begin the phase-out of the aging car ferries *Transfer* and *Transport. Manitowoc* was the first car ferry on the Detroit River to have four tracks on her deck. Since she had to operate from ferry slips designed for only three tracks, her centre two tracks joined at the bow into one track by means of a switch. This view, taken from Windsor, probably dates from the late 1930s or the 1940s. — *UBL No. 1168*

a strong influence on the ferry operations, and the railway now carries large quantities of auto parts and automobiles between the factories in Windsor and Detroit.

In 1969 the ferries were converted to car floats and two tugs were purchased to provide motive power. Today the fleet consists of the car floats *Detroit*, *Windsor*, *Manitowoc* and *Roanoke* (a recent addition of 1930 vintage), with capacities of 22, 28, 27 and 26 freight cars respectively, and the tugs *R.G. Cassidy*, built in 1953, and *F.A. Johnson*, built in 1952.

Since 1964, the Wabash Railroad has been under the control of the Norfolk & Western Railway Company.

Built at Toledo, Ohio, in 1930, the *Windsor* was almost identical in appearance to the *Manitowoc*. Photographed in the 1930s, the *Windsor* is seen here arriving at Windsor with two locomotives amongst her cargo: number 1880 on the left and number 2029 on the right. As a rule, car ferries did not carry steam locomotives due to their weight. In this case, the two engines, placed on either side of the ferry to balance the load, are probably returning after major repair work at the Wabash's main shops in the United States. Note how the *Windsor*'s centre track at the bow splits into two separate tracks. Two Canadian National passenger cars and an unidentified ferry can be seen at the left. — *UBL No. 1170- A*

Passenger Service on the St. Clair and Detroit River Car Ferries

Little has been mentioned so far about passenger accommodation on board the car ferries across the St. Clair and Detroit rivers, and by no means should it be assumed that passengers and passenger trains were not carried. In fact just the opposite is true, the ferries having carried some of North America's biggest-name trains. Even local passengers were taken across.

A quick survey of trains carried across the rivers in the late 1800s tallies up to well over 20 trains each day travelling between Chicago, New York and Boston by way of southern Ontario, as well as trains to Toronto and Montreal.

The Grand Trunk ran eight named trains, six through Sarnia and two through Windsor, as follows:

Eastbound

LIMITED EXPRESS	Chicago to New York via Sarnia
ATLANTIC EXPRESS	Chicago to New York, Boston via Sarnia
ERIE LIMITED EXPRESS	Chicago to New York via Sarnia
ST. LOUIS EXPRESS	St. Louis, Chicago to New York via Windsor

Westbound

CHICAGO EXPRESS	New York to Chicago via Sarnia
ERIE LIMITED EXPRESS	New York to Chicago via Sarnia
PACIFIC EXPRESS	New York, Boston to Chicago via Sarnia
ST. LOUIS EXPRESS	New York to Chicago, St. Louis via Windsor

All trains passed through Buffalo and Niagara Falls — an important tourist attraction which allowed the Grand Trunk to advertise itself as "The Great Niagara Falls Route between New York, Boston and Chicago," not forgetting the Grand Trunk's other slogan, "The Great International Route between East & West." With the exception of the St. Louis connection, all these through trains were linked with New York and Boston by way of the West Shore Railroad at Buffalo. Niagara Falls was a great sales feature and the railway offered passengers stopover privileges at the Falls as an added incentive to travel the Grand Trunk. But the Grand Trunk was not the only railway to make Niagara Falls its selling point.

The Michigan Central ran 12 through trains, four more than the Grand Trunk, calling itself "The Niagara Falls Route." All Michigan Central trains ran by way of Windsor and Detroit to Buffalo, where the New York Central took over for points east. All named passenger trains travelled by way of Niagara as follows:

Eastbound

NEW YORK & CHICAGO LIMITED	Chicago to New York, Boston
THE NORTH SHORE SPECIAL	Chicago to New York, Boston
NEW YORK & EASTERN EXPRESS	Chicago, Toledo to New York
ATLANTIC EXPRESS	Chicago to New York, Boston, Portland
NIAGARA FALLS & BUFFALO SPECIAL	Chicago to Buffalo
NEW YORK & BOSTON EXPRESS	Detroit to New York, Boston

Westbound

NEW YORK & CHICAGO LIMITED	New York, Boston to Chicago
THE NORTH SHORE LIMITED	New York, Boston to Chicago
CHICAGO & WESTERN EXPRESS	New York, Boston to Chicago
PACIFIC EXPRESS	Portland, Boston, New York to Chicago
CHICAGO SPECIAL	Buffalo to Chicago
CHICAGO DAY EXPRESS	Buffalo to Chicago

The Canadian Pacific Railway was far more limited during the late 1800s, offering two daily trains each way, one train each way Sundays, between Montreal, Toronto and Chicago by way of Windsor and Detroit, in connection with the Wabash Railroad from Detroit to Chicago.

When the Grand Trunk and the Michigan Central each built their tunnels, only a few trains continued to make the trip on a car ferry, Grand Trunk trains at Windsor specifically. The Grand Trunk, and later Canadian National, continued to send an average of one or two trains each way between Windsor and Detroit up until the 1950s, but all of the elite Canadian National trains used the Sarnia Tunnel.

The Wabash and Pere Marquette ferries seldom if ever carried passenger equipment. By the time those lines established their services, freight was the big revenue generator, and without their own railway lines east, there was no reason to operate through passenger trains. Trackage rights usually allowed through freight trains, but other freight and passenger services were not permitted.

This brief survey of passenger service across the Detroit and St. Clair rivers is by no means complete, but it does serve to illustrate the important roles the car ferries once played to passenger traffic.

CHAPTER FOUR - NOTES

1) 4 volumes of *Great Lakes Insurance Registers* for the period 1854 to 1874 (namely for years 1854, 1869, 1873 and 1874) are on deposit with the Archives of Ontario on microfilm, code Ms 401.
2) Anna G. Young, *The Great Lakes Saga* (Toronto, 1965), p. 44.
3) J.M. & Edw. Trout, *The Railways of Canada* (Toronto, 1970/1871), p. 145: Edward Fordes Bush, *Manuscript Report Number 424: Overland Transportation in the Rideau Region, 1800-1930* (Ottawa, 1979), pp. 995-6.
4) Nick and Helma Mika, *Railways of Canada* (Toronto, 1972), p. 87.
5) George W. Hilton, *The Great Lakes Car Ferries* (Berkeley, 1962), p. 246.
6) (J.B. Mansfield), *The Saga of the Great Lakes* (Toronto, 1980/Chicago, 1899), p. 262.
7) William John Wilgus, *The Railway Interrelations of the United States and Canada* (Toronto, 1937), p. 115.
8) Ibid., p. 115.
9) G.R. Stevens, *Canadian National Railways, Vol. 2* (Toronto, 1962), p. 365.
10) Frank N. Walker, "Buffalo, Brantford & Goderich Railway," *Upper Canada Railway Society 'Newsletter'* (Toronto), July-August 1975, p. 14.
11) J.M. & Edw. Trout, op. cit., pg. 80.
12) Ibid.
13) John N. Jackson and John Burtniak, *Railways in the Niagara Peninsula* (Belleville, 1978), p. 53.
14) (J.B. Mansfield), *Adventures on the Great Lakes* (Toronto, 1980/Chicago, 1899), p. 169.
15) George W. Hilton, op. cit., p. 13.
16) William H. Middleton, *When the Steam Railroads Electrified* (Milwaukee, 1974), p. 134.
17) William John Wilgus, op. cit., p. 112.
18) Ibid., p. 112.
19) Ibid., p. 112.
20) William H. Middleton, op. cit., p. 147.
21) Ibid., p. 142.
22) G. Mercer Adam, *Toronto Old and New* (Toronto, 1974/1891), p. 181.
23) William John Wilgus, op. cit., p. 118.
24) Ibid., p. 102.
25) Ibid., p. 101.
26) The exception was an auto assembly plant at Walkerville for which the Wabash (and now Norfolk & Western) had exclusive switching rights.
27) William John Wilgus, op. cit., p. 101 (based on).

V

THE IRON ORE CARRIERS

The search for and production of iron ore has had a profound effect on several of Ontario's railways, including the Central Ontario and the Kingston & Pembroke lines in the East and the Canadian Northern, the Algoma Central, and Canadian National railways in the North, to name but a few. Yet it was the shipping lines of the Great Lakes that were the greatest beneficiaries of the Industrial Age's hunger for iron ore, as they could provide the cheapest means of transportation to the blast furnaces of the industrial South. Railways became only the means of transferring the ore from the mine to the water's edge.

While many companies both here and in the United States were satisfied with this arrangement, others were not, chosing to develop what might be termed "integrated" mining companies who would mine, transport (by rail and water), and market their ore to the steel mills. In the United States, most of these companies operated out of mines located in northern Minnesota and Michigan, such firms as the Minnesota Iron Company, the largest American company of its kind operating at the turn of the century, which owned and operated the Minnesota Steamship Company and the Duluth & Iron Range Railroad Company; and the Cleveland-Cliffs Iron Company and its associated Cleveland-Cliffs Steamship Company and Lake Superior & Ishpeming Railroad Company.

Ontario, too, has had its "integrated" mining companies, the earliest dating back to 1866, when the Cobourg, Peterborough & Marmora Railway & Mining Company was formed out of the ruins of the Cobourg & Peterborough Railway.

The Cobourg & Peterborough Railway
The Cobourg, Peterborough & Marmora Railway & Mining Company

When railway fever swept the country during the 1850s, many bitter rivalries were sparked off between neighbouring communities as each fought the other for railway supremacy. Some fought over who would get a railway station and who would be left without, while others battled for control of territory through the construction of railway lines into underdeveloped hinterlands. Nowhere was this more true than the competition between the Lake Ontario ports of Port Hope and Cobourg in the push to build their respective railways north into Peterborough.

The citizens of Port Hope stood firmly behind the Port Hope, Lindsay & Beaverton Railway, first incorporated in 1846 as the Peterborough & Port Hope Railway, which reached Peterborough in 1858. The Port Hope railway was not just a favourite with Port Hope citizens, it received equally strong support from Peterborough as well. The people of Peterborough had no such love for the Cobourg project, which received absolutely nothing from the city.

Plans to build a railway north from Cobourg were made as early as 1834 and in their various incarnations ranged from plank roads to railroads. It was not until 1852 that plans were put into action with the incorporation of the Cobourg & Peterborough Railway, and by December 1854 the

Built in 1871 and purchased soon after by Henry Calcutt, the *Whistle-Wing* was the last privately operated steamer known to have provided regular passenger connections with the Cobourg, Peterborough & Marmora Railway on Rice Lake. Note the Masonic device on the vessel's paddle box, just above her name. This photo was probably taken in the late 1870s while the *Whistle-Wing* was on a passenger excursion. — *Peterborough Museum & Archives*

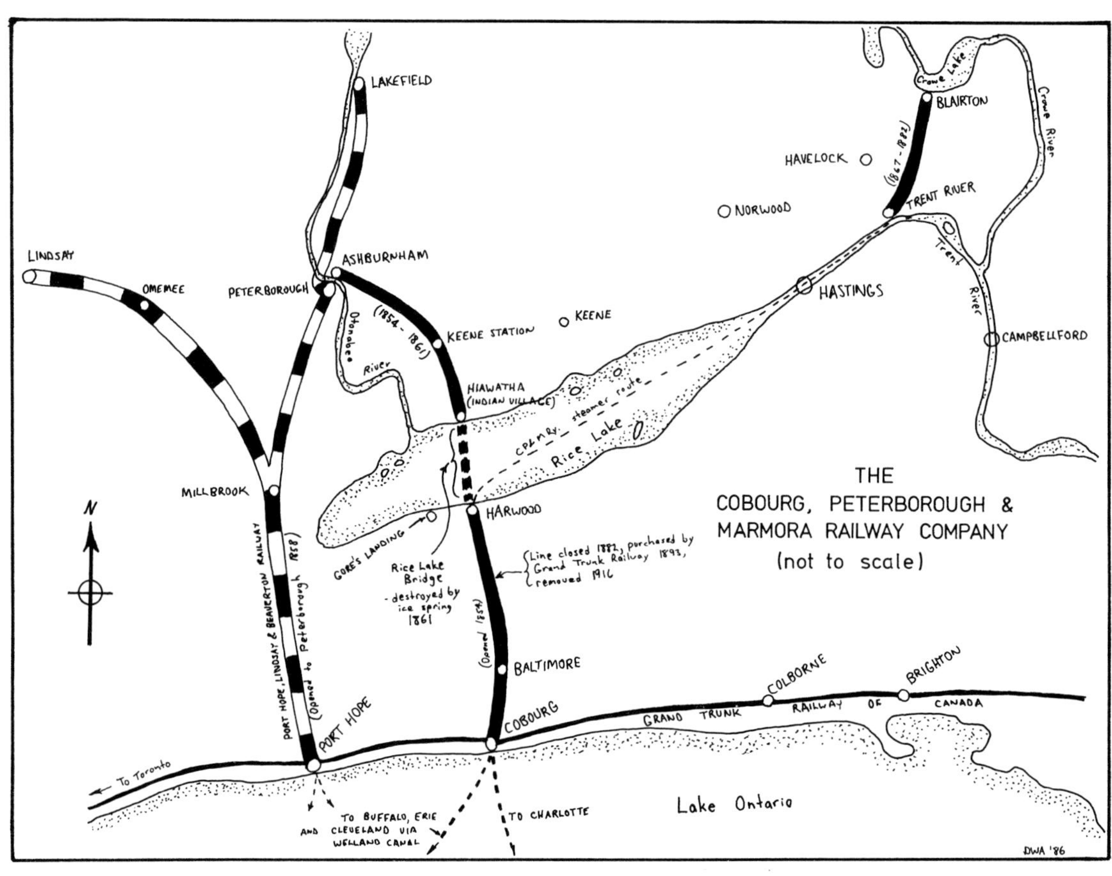

railway was opened to traffic between Peterborough and Cobourg, even if it was only temporary. The Cobourg & Peterborough had problems.

First of all, the railway was built on a very low budget, resulting in poor construction standards which were costly to remedy — much of the blame here rested on the shoulders of Samuel Zimmerman, primary contractor for the railway, who was notorious for his construction "shortcuts." But the biggest problem of all was the bridge over Rice Lake.

Unlike the Port Hope, Lindsay & Beaverton Railway, which possessed a dry-land route to Peterborough, the Cobourg & Peterborough was faced with Rice Lake, a large body of water running east and west in such a fashion as to either force the railway into a long and expensive detour around it, or into the construction of some sort of bridge or causeway across it. The railway chose to bridge the waterway, and so constructed a three-mile-long wooden trestle between Harwood on the south shore and Hiawatha on the north. The problem was not so much the bridge, but rather its terrible construction, which crumpled with the first ice of 1855, closing down the line. After a series of expensive repairs the bridge was reopened later that year, but it demanded continuous maintenance which ate into the railway's meagre revenues. In 1860 an attempt was made at filling in the trestle, but work was halted before the fill was completed, leaving much of the bridge exposed. During the following winter and spring, the ice and the lake finally had their revenge and the bridge unceremoniously "took its departure and sailed down the Lake." The railway had lost its connection with Peterborough and Peterborough could have cared less, for it was served by the superior Port Hope, Lindsay & Beaverton.

The Cobourg & Peterborough was in bad straits without its Peterborough connection, and so in 1863 it purchased the ten-year-old *Otonabee*, an 84-ton wooden side-wheeler, to provide a regular service between Harwood and Hiawatha initially, but by the end of the year the ship was making the passage all the way to Peterborough, up the Otonabee River. It was not enough, however, and the railway was sold in 1865 for $100,000.

The buyers of the railway turned out to be a group of steel men from Pittsburgh, Pennsylvania, led by George K. Schoenberger, one of the richest men in the state, to whom the railway was the means to an end. They had just acquired the Marmora Iron Company at Blairton, some miles east of Rice Lake, and needed a way of shipping the ore out. The mines, established in 1820, were far from the railway, but the owners had a plan which would link the mines by railway to the Trent River, where connection with Harwood would be made by steamer, and thence to Cobourg for shipment to the United States. It was certainly a round-about route, but there were no other railways or suitable canals in the region, and there would not be for some time to come.

The next step came in the following year when the two companies were merged on August 15 to form the Cobourg, Peterborough & Marmora Railway & Mining Company. This permitted the owners to move into action. They soon commenced the construction of an 8½-mile line of railway from the village of Trent River Bridge on the River Trent, commonly referred to at the time as the "Narrows," to the Blairton mine site. The task was completed by the summer of 1867 and allowed the company to move its construction crews in to the Blairton mine on Crowe Lake. It had been many years since any ore had been mined and it was therefore necessary to relocate a suitable body of iron ore plus erect all of the necessary buildings, including the mine pit head, railway facilities such as the station and enginehouse, and 60 tenement accommodations for the workers. The company also owned part of the village of Marmora, where it built saw and grist mills as well as storage sheds. In all, although costly, the facilities were necessary when one considers the relative remoteness of the mining community, something almost all mining towns have in common. The mills also provided additional outgoing traffic, diversifying the company's revenue base.

For the handling of the iron ore, specialized structures and equipment were introduced. Bottom-unloading ore cars were built for the railway by the Cobourg Car Works in Cobourg, totalling 150 in all between 1867 and 1875. Similar to today's ore hopper cars, these wooden four-wheeled vehicles could be loaded from the top and were equipped to discharge their loads from a bottom hatch into waiting scows or ships. This was accomplished by means of trestles built over the water. At the Narrows, the trestle was erected to allow the scows used to move the ore to Harwood, to be positioned directly underneath the cars, which would discharge their ore through openings in the deck of the trestle. A larger trestle resembling modern ore docks was erected at Cobourg, permitting the railway cars to use chutes to unload directly into waiting ships positioned alongside. In both cases, gravity did the work, but at Harwood it was necessary to transfer the ore from the scows up into the hopper cars for the trip south to Cobourg. Here a steam-powered elevator had to be used. All of these facilities were finished by 1869 or 1870.

Ready or not, the company began to ship ore out of Blairton in the fall of 1867, and shipping arrangements had to be made. On Rice Lake the steamer *Otonabee* was taken off the Peterborough run and teamed up with eight scows to provide the needed link between Trent River Bridge and Harwood. At the Cobourg end the railway possessed no such vessel and had to advertise for ships. The following appeared in the Toronto *Globe* of 1 July 1867, Dominion Day:

> Office of the Cobourg, Peterborough
> and Marmora Railway and Mining Company.
>
> Cobourg, June 25, 1867
>
> Proposals will be received until 5th prox, for the transportation of Iron Ore, during the season of 1867, from Cobourg C.W., to Charlotte, Buffalo, Erie and Cleveland, U.S.
>
> Bids may be made for either port, or for any quantity up to 400 tons per day.
>
> Address J.H. Dumble,
> Cobourg.

By 1870 transportation on Lake Ontario was in the charge of the company's own steamship *Otonabee (II)*, running regularly between Cobourg and Charlotte, New York, the Port of Rochester. Most of the ore made its way to Pittsburgh by rail from Charlotte.

Rice Lake services also underwent a change. In August 1869 the old *Otonabee* was sold and replaced by the newer 63-ton steamer *Enterprise*, but it only lasted until 1871, when it too was sold. It was later rebuilt as the *Clyde*. For two years chartered vessels filled in, until the paddle-steamer *Isaac Butts* was constructed for the company at Peterborough in 1873. A 132-ton wooden ship, the *Isaac Butts* was named after the Cobourg, Peterborough & Marmora's president and entered service either late in 1873 or in the following spring. By this time ore shipments from Blairton were in excess of 300 tons per day, making the mines the most productive in Canada at that time, greatly enhancing the company's profits.[1] The big steamer did much to further the company's gains, but its size did cause one problem. The locks at Hastings, located between Trent River Bridge and Rice Lake, were too narrow to allow the *Isaac Butts* passage and, as a result, the locks had to be rebuilt at considerable expense.

In 1876, while docked at Harwood, the *Isaac Butts* was severely damaged when the *Clyde* caught fire while lying alongside. The *Clyde* was destroyed, but enough of the *Isaac Butts* was saved that the company was able to rebuild her the following year, altering the ship's layout and increasing its gross tonnage to 199 tons.

By the end of the decade, the company was running out of ore to mine, and because of the availability of cheaper American iron ore, the Cobourg, Peterborough & Marmora's management saw no point in making any further explorations for ore. The last major shipments of ore were made in 1878, and in 1879 the mine was shut down entirely. Between 1879 and 1881 no iron ore shipments were made from Blairton. In an attempt to recoup something from the venture, the management decided to move out what remained of the firm's stockpile of ore at Blairton in 1881, a task completed by the following year. A tragic incident took place at Trent River Bridge during this period and was described in a newspaper dated 9 August 1881: "The third and last victim [at the Blairton Mine] was Samuel Bray, an old pensioner of the British Army, who took pride in showing many scars received in fierce engagements in six years, his last being the taking of Alma Heights in the Crimea War. Bray was drowned at the dumping ground at Trent Bridge. The track over the piers and dump openings was raised to allow the scows to go under and so receive the ore dumped from the cars. The train in question was nearly unloaded, and the boy, who was firing, made several useless attempts to push the loaded cars to the dumping. The engineer, who was amusing himself a few rods away, became angered at the necessity of being disturbed, took charge of the engine and, with language too unsavory for your columns prefacing the expression 'I'll put them up,' put on fearful speed knocking away the guard construction and plunging five empty cars over the outer pier."[2]

With the cars went old Samuel Bray, but if there is anything to be gained from the accident, it is worth noting that it was the article above that prompted Arthur Dunn, a professional engineer, to search for the five cars in 1979. In 1980 he and his associates were rewarded when, through their efforts, Parks Canada lifted four of the five cars out of the river, the fifth and most complete being left pending future preservation. It was truly a remarkable find.

During the mine's last years, the *Isaac Butts* continued to operate carrying freight and passengers only when there was no ore to move, finally taking the last of the ore out in 1881 and 1882. With the last shipment from Trent River Bridge, the ship's days were numbered, and on 22 July 1882 the *Isaac Butts* was laid up at Harwood, ultimately being scrapped in the fall of 1886. There is no record as to the disposition of the *Otonabee (II)* and it can only be assumed that the steamer was sold or scrapped sometime around the beginning of the decade.

Ore traffic provided the bulk of the Cobourg, Peterborough & Marmora's revenues, and without it the company was unable to keep the trains running. By the late 1880s the railway had fallen into disuse, and despite attempts to reactivate the company, no further trains were operated. In 1893 the property was acquired by the Grand Trunk Railway. In 1916 the rails between Cobourg and Harwood were removed and sent over to Europe for use by the Canadian Army's railways during the First World War.

During the 1870s passenger service was still maintained by the Cobourg, Peterborough & Marmora, even though the company was concentrating its efforts on the iron ore traffic. In 1875 the railway provided four trains each day, two northbound and two southbound, for the convenience of its passengers along the 14½-mile Cobourg to Harwood line as follows:

Northbound					Southbound	
A.M.	A.M.				P.M.	P.M.
9:00	6:30	lv.	Cobourg	ar.	3:00	6:00
9:20	6:50		Baltimore		2:40	5:40
9:45	7:15		Summit		2:15	5:15
10:00	7:30	ar.	Harwood	lv.	2:00	5:00

At Harwood passengers could transfer to either the company's own *Isaac Butts* for the Blairton Mines or onto Henry Calcutt's steamer *Whistle-Wing* for Hastings, Keene and Gores Landing. Calcutt purchased the railway's steamer *Enterprise* in 1871 but replaced her soon after with the *Whistle-Wing*. Steamboat connections could also be made for Peterborough, but in general all of these routes catered chiefly to local traffic, especially from points on Rice Lake, with little being derived from Peterborough. It is these steamer connections which partially explain why all northbound trains left in the morning for Harwood, returning in the afternoon, in co-ordination with steamer runs into and out of Harwood. As the Cobourg, Peterborough & Marmora only had two "second-class" coaches, each train must have had only one passenger car, perhaps suggesting that trains were mixed with freight cars.

The importance of the ore traffic can best be shown by a survey of the railway's revenues and expenditures of 1869 as outlined in Trout's *Railways of Canada*:

Receipts	
Received from sales of Iron Ore	$72,960.00
Received for carriage of lumber	17,757.89
Received for carriage of grain and flour	983.10
Received from miscellaneous freight	2,283.89
Received from rents	700.00
Total:	$94,684.88

Expenditures	
Permanent Improvements	
Fifty iron ore dumping cars	$12,500.00
Elevated Dock at Cobourg	3,000.00
Wharf Extension at Harwood	600.00
Steam Elevator at Harwood	500.00
Tanks and Telegraph Line	500.00
McDougall's and Campbell's Sidings	2,000.00
Total:	$19,100.00

Operating Expenses	
Mining Ore	$21,000.00
Operating Road	10,000.00
Staff Salaries	4,000.00
Lake Freights on Ore	12,000.00
Duty on Ore	4,800.00
Handling Ore	2,400.00
Harbour Tolls on Ore	1,200.00
Rice Lake Transportation	3,100.00
Total:	$58,500.00

Interest	
One year's Interest on Bonds	$10,984.00
Bank Interest	2,780.00
Total:	$13,764.00
Total Expenditures	$91,364.00

On the positive side of the operation, we can see that revenues from iron ore sales made up a clear 77 percent of total receipts, with lumber traffic contributing only 19 percent of the company's revenues, making the transportation of lumber more of a sideline than a mainstay.

The expenses also say a lot about the importance of the iron ore traffic. With the exception of the sidings installed to McDougall's and Campbell's lumber mills, and the water tanks and the telegraph lines, all of the permanent improvements made were made expressly for the iron ore business. And if we accept that the water tanks and telegraph lines were installed for the overall improvement of railway operations, including ore trains, 90 percent of improvement expenses were made to facilitate the iron ore traffic. Operating expenses are even more conclusive, showing that most of the costs to operate the company went toward the production, transportation and sale of the iron ore, 36 percent of the cost being devoted just to the mining of the ore.

Perhaps the biggest surprise about the Cobourg, Peterborough & Marmora in 1869 was its profit of just over $3,300 following years of losses. There is no record on the railway's performance through the 1870s, but based on its 1869 showing, the company must have done well until it was finally put under by cheaper American ore.

As a final note on the importance of ore traffic, it should be stated that the railway never made the change to standard gauge. Since all of the ore was shipped south by boat from Cobourg, the company had no reason to worry about interchanging traffic with other railways, especially the Grand Trunk, which passed through Cobourg. With ships, trains and mines all devoted to the iron ore trade, it can truly be said that the Cobourg, Peterborough & Marmora Railway & Mining Company was an integrated company.

The Algoma Central & Hudson Bay Railway

Almost a century ago, an American of modest beginnings came to Sault Ste. Marie, Ontario, and changed the face of that community forever. His name was Francis Hector Clergue, and despite his own lack of capital, he used his persuasive powers to attract money from financiers south of the border. By 1896, only two years after his arrival in Sault Ste. Marie, he was in control of the hydro-electric utility, the Lake Superior Power Company, and had opened up the Sault Ste. Marie Pulp & Paper Company, one of the largest mills of its type when built. The entire key to Clergue's growing empire was the exploitation of the natural resources that surrounded the city. Electricity was produced from the St. Mary's Rapids, forming the nucleus of his developments, which in turn supplied power for the pulp mill, which also used the water plus timber cut from the shores of Lake Superior to the north. Further acquisitions included the Gertrude and the Elsie nickel mines in Sudbury, along with the Manitoulin & North Shore Railway Company, later to become the Algoma Eastern Railway.

Possibly the most important purchase made by Clergue, however, was that of the Helen Mine, the site of which was discovered by a gold prospector in 1897. It was essentially a large hill of hematite, a high-grade iron ore, located on Wawa Lake north of Sault Ste. Marie. Clergue was quick to grasp the significance of the find, for in it he foresaw the development of the steel industry at the Sault. And so it was that in 1898 he acquired the rights to the mine.

It would seem that the future of steel-making at Sault Ste. Marie was assured with the Helen Mine, at least in the mind of Francis Clergue, but the remoteness of the mine required more than just vision, it needed a way to transport the ore. The logical solution was the construction of a railway north from Sault Ste. Marie which would connect the mine with a proposed steel mill in the city and also serve to bring timber down to the pulp mill. The result was the Algoma Central Railway Company, incorporated by act of Parliament on 11 August 1899 to build a line north from Sault Ste. Marie to a point on the Canadian Pacific main line which would later be named Franz. Time would be an important factor, for the railway was to be built through some of the roughest terrain in the province, making heavy rock cuts and expensive bridges the rule rather than the exception.

Clergue was in no position to wait, and while the railway was under construction, he had to find an alternative method of shipping ore out of the Helen. Fortunately the mine was located only ten miles away from Michipicoten Harbour, a sheltered bay open to navigation eight months of the year. It was one of the best natural harbours on Lake Superior, and it was therefore decided to construct a line from Michipicoten east to the Helen Mine (an open-pit mining operation), and from there, carry on to the route of the main line a further 17 miles east. Thus when Michipicoten Harbour was made ready, it would not only serve the ore traffic, but it would also provide a supply route to the railway construction inland, much as had been done from that same location during the building of the Canadian Pacific 25 years before. Construction of the Michipicoten branch commenced in 1899 at around the same time as the main line from Sault Ste. Marie was started. By July 1900 the branch was opened to the mine site, 12 years before the mine would obtain direct rail access to the Sault.

Along with the branch line, Michipicoten Harbour also needed work if it was to be of any use, particularly dredging in order to accept the free passage of freighters. By the time the railway was opened to the mine in 1900, dredging was completed, along with 4,000 feet of dockage, under the personal supervision of Francis Clergue. Facilities included an elevated iron ore dock built of wood and containing 12 ore pockets for the transfer of ore from railway hopper cars into ships

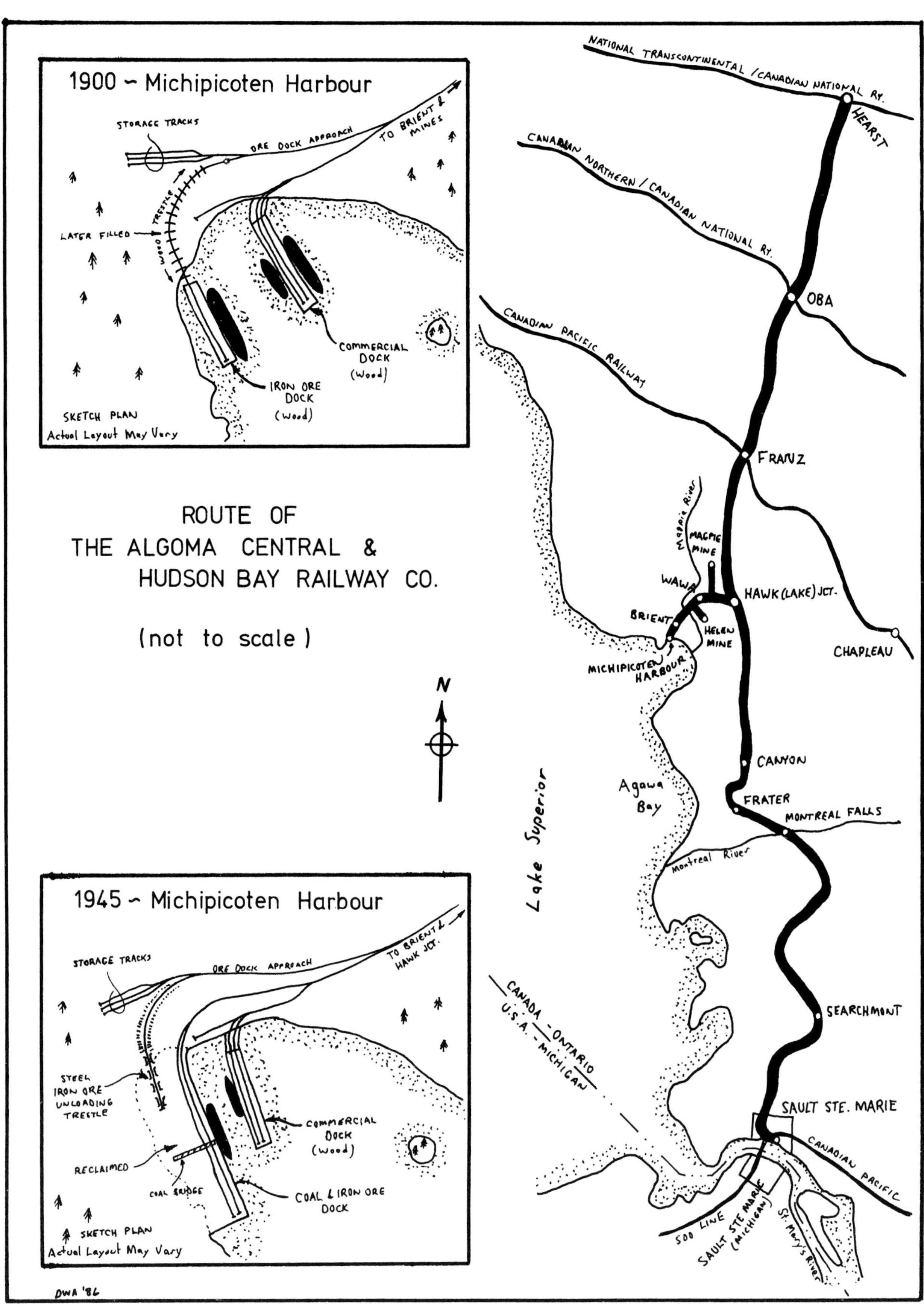

ROUTE OF
THE ALGOMA CENTRAL &
HUDSON BAY RAILWAY CO.
(not to scale)
1900 - Michipicoten Harbour
STORAGE TRACKS
ORE DOCK APPROACH
TO BRIENT & MINES
LATER FILLED
WOOD TRESTLE
COMMERCIAL DOCK (Wood)
IRON ORE DOCK (Wood)
SKETCH PLAN
Actual Layout May Vary
1945 - Michipicoten Harbour
STORAGE TRACKS
ORE DOCK APPROACH
TO BRIENT & HAWK JCT.
STEEL IRON ORE UNLOADING TRESTLE
COMMERCIAL DOCK (Wood)
RECLAIMED
COAL BRIDGE
COAL & IRON ORE DOCK
SKETCH PLAN
Actual Layout May Vary
DWA '86
N
NATIONAL TRANSCONTINENTAL / CANADIAN NATIONAL RY.
HEARST
CANADIAN NORTHERN / CANADIAN NATIONAL RY.
OBA
CANADIAN PACIFIC RAILWAY
FRANZ
Magpie River
MAGPIE MINE
WAWA
HAWK (LAKE) JCT.
BRIENT
HELEN MINE
CHAPLEAU
MICHIPICOTEN HARBOUR
CANYON
Agawa Bay
Lake Superior
FRATER
MONTREAL FALLS
Montreal River
CANADA - ONTARIO
U.S.A. - MICHIGAN
SEARCHMONT
SAULT STE. MARIE
CANADIAN PACIFIC
SOO LINE
SAULT STE MARIE (MICHIGAN)
St. Mary's River

docked alongside. Clergue even built his summer cottage on an island at the harbour! Transportation from the mine to Michipicoten Harbour would be provided by three steam locomotives and an array of cars.

During the initial period of construction on the branch, the company had to charter two steamers, the *Caribou* and the *Manitou*, along with a fleet of scows to move all the needed supplies to Michipicoten Harbour. That included rails and workers as well as locomotives and railway cars. When the time came to actually ship the ore, Clergue settled for nothing less than his own fleet of ships. Since the Algoma Central was already in the transportation business, it was only appropriate that the new steamship line be formed as an operating component of the railway, and thus, in 1900, the Steamship Department of the Algoma Central Railway was born.

To start the fleet off, four ocean-going freighters were purchased from British owners early in the year. The vessels were the English-built *Leafield, Monkshaven,* and *Paliki* of 1,454, 2,097 and 1,578 tons respectively, and the 952-ton *Theano,* constructed in the Netherlands. Together they gave the new shipping line a combined capacity of 9,000 tons of freight. Passengers also had to be catered to, since there was no other way into the mine except by water to Michipicoten Harbour and then by rail to the Helen Mine. For this purpose two American passenger steamers were purchased, the 447-ton *Minnie M.* and the 632-ton *Ossifrage,* and like the freighters, they were also previously owned.

No sooner had the ships arrived and the branch opened to traffic than the mine was ready to ship, and so it was that in July 1900 the first boatload of iron ore from the Helen Mine was sent forth from Michipicoten on board the *Theano* — but not to Sault Ste. Marie. Clergue had no steel- or iron-making facilities of his own at this time and instead had to send the ore, almost 60,000 tons by year end, to the blast furnaces of the Canadian Furnace Company at Midland, Ontario, erected during the previous year. Even so, this made that first shipment more than just a business transaction, for it became the first load of Canadian iron ore to be shipped to a Canadian port. While the Cobourg, Peterborough & Marmora Railway may have been responsible for the first shipment of Canadian ore, all of its product went to the United States, since no furnaces existed in Canada at that time.

In recognition of Francis Clergue's new aim of building the Algoma Central northward beyond the Canadian Pacific line, thereby connecting with the projected Canadian Northern Railway and the projected National Transcontinental Railway, and ultimately reaching Hudson Bay, the railway received a new name on 23 May 1901: the Algoma Central & Hudson Bay Railway Company. The Algoma Central never got past Hearst on the National Transcontinental (now Canadian National) and the reference to Hudson Bay was finally dropped in 1965.

The year 1901 also brought an addition to Clergue's empire at Sault Ste. Marie. Early that year construction was started on the Algoma Steel Works, which consisted of two small blast furnaces, a Bessemer steel plant, a blooming mill, and a rail mill (the Bessemer plant and the rail mill were purchased used in Pennsylvania, dismantled, and re-erected at the steel works). A year later, on February 18, Algoma Steel's Bessemer converter produced the first steel ever in Canada, followed in May by the rolling of the first rails ever manufactured in this country. Problems did arise, however. The first rails were inferior products, plant engineers had to acquire sufficient experience, and then there were the blast furnaces, first designed to burn charcoal but altered during construction to burn coke instead, forcing the steel works to use pig iron from Midland until 1905. It was a shaky start, but it was a start all the same, laying the foundations of the Algoma Steel Corporation, today Canada's third-largest steel producer.

Between the mine and the steel works, the steamships were kept busy and were further bolstered in 1902 by the addition of a new steel barge, the *Agawa,* built by Collingwood Shipbuilding. At 3,759 tons, with a freight capacity of 3,308 tons, the *Agawa* was Algoma Central's largest vessel to date, despite being unpowered. Another passenger steamer was also acquired. Christened the *King Edward,* the 355-ton paddle-wheeler came fresh from the builders in Hull, England.

By 1903 Clergue's empire, or the Consolidated Lake Superior Company, as the umbrella organization was known, was in serious financial trouble. In ten years Francis Clergue had accumulated 14 companies ranging from utilities and heavy industry to railways and streetcar lines, backed largely by American capital, but in so doing Clergue had overextended his company. By the end of 1903 labour riots became the order of the day when the company failed to meet its payroll,

One of the first freighters owned by the Algoma Central, the *Leafield* was lost on Lake Superior in 1913. *Leafield* is seen here at Sault Ste. Marie in 1910. — *PAC PA-144165*

On 5 December 1905, the *Monkshaven* ground on Angus Island in Lake Superior, leaving her crew stranded for 68 days. Pulled off the rocks in the spring of 1906, she returned to service following repairs. *Monkshaven* served the railway for eight more years before sinking for the last time. *Monkshaven* is seen here on Angus Island shortly before being freed. — *OA S13165*

Paliki is viewed here unloading iron ore at the Algoma Steel Works at Sault Ste. Marie in 1903. The *Paliki* was sold by the railway in 1924.
— OA S13083

In this photograph from 1901, the *Theano* is seen unloading what appears to be iron ore at Midland. If the location is at the Canada Iron Furnace dock, the manual unloading taking place is unusual since the iron company was using "whirly" cranes for most unloading at the time. Possibly the only explanation for the archaic hand unloading process viewed here, short of saying that this is not the Canada Iron Furnace dock, could be that the *Theano*'s masts, located in between the hatch openings, would have interfered with the whirly cranes which normally unloaded Great Lakes type freighters with relatively clear decks.
— OA Acc. 2375 S5280

The Canada Iron Furnace Company at Midland in the early 1900s. Towering in the background is the smelter and furnace complex while the freighters *Iroquois* and *Neebing* wait at the dock for unloading by the "whirly" cranes. The small steamboat is unidentified. — *OA Acc. 2375 S5416*

Photographed at Sault Ste. Marie, the *Minnie M.* is seen while on an excursion charter. In the years before through rail service was inaugurated between Michipicoten and Sault Ste. Marie, the Algoma Central's passenger and freight steamers *Minnie M.*, *Ossifrage*, and *King Edward* provided the only passenger service between the two. — *OA S17926*

requiring the militia to be called out to restore order. Clergue fought to retain control of his company, but despite his efforts the Consolidated Lake Superior Company was placed into receivership, and the following May a new company, the Lake Superior Corporation, was formed to take over the assets. By 1908 control of the corporation had passed from the United States into British hands. At this point Francis Clergue left Sault Ste. Marie for good.

Two vessels appeared around 1905 in Algoma Central's fleet, the barge *Barlum* and the passenger steamer *Slesta*. These ships were probably not owned by the railway and there is no further record of their employment by the company. It is possible that the barge *Barlum* may have been the *Thomas Barlum*, a ship later purchased by Algoma Central.

In November 1906 the *Theano* sank in Thunder Bay with a cargo of rails, the first loss of many the line would experience. Almost a year earlier, on 5 December 1905, the *Monkshaven* grounded on Angus Island, Lake Superior. The crew were stranded for 68 days before being rescued. The *Monkshaven* remained intact and was eventually pulled off and returned to service.

Under the new management of the Lake Superior Corporation, Algoma Steel began to grow again in an effort to meet the demand for rails and rail fittings brought about by the construction of the Canadian Northern, Grand Trunk Pacific, and National Transcontinental railways. In 1909 the need to secure a stable supply of raw materials led to the acquisition of a West Virginian coal company and the purchase of limestone properties in Michigan. On the Michipicoten branch, the Magpie iron mine was opened.

All of this served to keep Algoma Central's steamship line active. Freighters carried limestone from Michigan to the Sault, while ore from Michipicoten not only found its way to the furnaces of Algoma Steel but was also shipped southward to American Lake Erie ports such as Toledo, where the ships took on coal for the coke ovens back in Sault Ste. Marie. When there was no inbound or outbound cargo for the steel mills, the freighters carried western grain from Port Arthur to terminals on the lower lakes. Passenger traffic, on the other hand, did not experience any real growth and consequently Algoma Central sold off the *Minnie M.* in 1910, putting the proceeds toward the construction of a new freighter, the *Thomas J. Drummond*. A product of McMillan & Sons of Dumbarton, Scotland, the 2,201-ton *Thomas J. Drummond* had a capacity of 2,500 tons of freight. During the First World War, the company would use the ship's ocean-going capabilities when, in 1915, the *Thomas J. Drummond* made the longest voyage of any Algoma Central vessel, carrying steel billets from Algoma Steel across the Atlantic to France.

At the end of 1910 Algoma Central's fleet consisted of the freighters *Leafield, Monkshaven, Paliki* and *Thomas J. Drummond*, the barge *Agawa*, and the passenger steamers *King Edward* and *Ossifrage*.

In 1912 all five steel-production facilities at Sault Ste. Marie were merged by the Lake Superior Corporation into the Algoma Steel Corporation, at the same time giving control of the limestone and coal interests in the United States to the new company. This was but one of many changes made by the parent Lake Superior Corporation in the city. In 1911 the pulp and paper mill was sold off, eventually becoming Abitibi Pulp & Paper, and the Lake Superior Power Company was disposed of in 1916 in order to raise capital for wartime production at Algoma Steel. The result was the Great Lakes Power Company.

Algoma Central was also having difficulties, but none that the Lake Superior Corporation could fix. In 1913 the *Leafield* and her entire crew were lost on Lake Superior with a cargo of rails destined for Port Arthur. In 1914 the *Monkshaven* sank. Then in December 1915, only a month after the railway had reached Hearst, the Algoma Central & Hudson Bay Railway went bankrupt when the company failed to pay its bondholders. Although the railway remained in the hands of the Lake Superior Corporation, control passed to the bondholders until the railway's financial affairs were settled — no less than 44 years later. This all came at a time when the steamship line needed every vessel it could get, and it was to the company's credit that it was still able to replace the ships lost. In 1913 the barge *Agawa* was given its own engines and rejoined the fleet as a steamer in its own right. In addition, the freighters *Uranus* and *Saturn* were purchased from the Cleveland, Ohio, based Gilchrist Transportation Company. Both ships were built in 1901 by American Shipbuilding and were virtually identical, their 3,429 gross tons giving each a capacity of 6,200 tons of freight.

The *Ossifrage*, probably photographed at Sault Ste. Marie around 1905. — *UBL PB No. 1280*

The steel barge *Agawa*, seen here on the left at Midland, was the Algoma Central's largest vessel in terms of size and capacity when delivered from Collingwood Shipbuilding in 1902. Relying on other freighters to tow her, Agawa was equipped with a small steam engine to provide power for steering and winches, explaining the presence of the funnel behind her small wheelhouse on the rear deck. Barges such as the Agawa always carried a small crew. The other two ships in the photo are the *Turret Chief* (centre) and the *Strathcona* (right). The elevator is probably the Playfair Elevator built by James Playfair, a Midland shipowner. The photo dates from around 1905 or 1910. — *J.W. Bald Collection, Huronia Museum, Midland*

The paddle steamer *King Edward* was purchased new from England in 1902. In 1917 she was sold to the Royal Canadian Navy and served until 1942 as a fleet auxiliary. The *King Edward* is pictured here at the Algoma Central's first station beside the power canal near the hydro-electric station and the pulp mill founded by Francis Clergue at Sault Ste. Marie.
— *OA S13057*

Upon acquisition the *Uranus* was renamed the *W.C. Franz* and the *Saturn* became the *J. Frater Taylor.*

In 1917 the need for increased capacity led the Algoma Central into a deal with the Great Lakes Transportation Company of Midland, whereby the railway's *Thomas J. Drummond* was exchanged for Great Lakes Transportation's *William S. Mack*, operated by Algoma Central as the *Home Smith*. It was also a move in the direction of standardization, since the *Home Smith*, like the *W.C. Franz* and the *J. Frater Taylor*, was built in 1901 by American Shipbuilding at Lorain, Ohio, and differed mainly in tonnage and capacity, the 3,495-ton *Home Smith* having the lesser capacity of 5,850 tons of freight. The company also began its complete withdrawal from the water-borne passenger trade in 1917 with the sale of the *King Edward* to the Royal Canadian Navy for use as a fleet auxiliary. The paddle-steamer would survive to see World War II before being scrapped in 1942. The *Ossifrage* remained with the railway but unfortunately was wrecked in 1919, otherwise it too would probably have been sold eventually.

With the close of the First World War, Algoma Central was left with a fleet of five freighters — *Paliki, Agawa, W.C. Franz, Home Smith* and *J. Frater Taylor* — translating into a combined fleet capacity of 23,000 tons of freight, an increase of just over 150 percent from the original 1900 fleet. During this same period, Algoma Steel's production rose from 36,500 tons of rails in 1902 to over 500,000 tons of steel by 1917, mainly in the form of shell steel for the war effort, a whopping increase of more than 1,300 percent, although this was largely due to war production. Similarly, production of ore at the Helen and Magpie mines rose to meet the demands of Algoma Steel, but by war's end the supply of high-grade iron ore had been exhausted. In 1918 the Helen Mine became the first casualty. After producing more than 3,100,000 tons of ore since 1900 it was shut down. Three years later the Magpie was closed, thus putting an end to iron ore production in Canada for the next 18 years.

The closure of the iron mines was by no means the end of Algoma Steel nor the Algoma Central. It was simply a matter of obtaining ore elsewhere, and that wasn't difficult since there was plenty of iron ore available in neighbouring Michigan and Minnesota, and without having to build any facilities. All Algoma Central's ships had to do was to tie up at the appropriate ore dock and take on the cargo of iron ore.

Finding a supply of iron ore was simple enough for Algoma Steel, but finding buyers for its rails and rail products after the war was another matter entirely. The war bankrupted the Grand Trunk/Grand Trunk Pacific and the Canadian Northern railway systems, and the Crown-owned Canadian National Railways was formed from the ruins. The market for rails had dried up, leaving the company greatly overstocked and despite attempts to branch out into other steel products, the company finally succumbed to bankruptcy itself and in 1935 was reorganized. The parent Lake Superior Corporation disappeared about this time, leaving the Algoma Steel Corporation and the Algoma Central & Hudson Bay Railway as separate and independent entities.

As difficult as the twenties were for Algoma Steel, Algoma Central's fortunes were somewhat better. The closure of the mines almost finished Michipicoten Harbour for good, along with the Michipicoten branch. In time, however, the railway realized that the harbour was in a prime location to serve the locomotive coal needs of Canadian National's lines across northern Ontario and Quebec, as well as the new pulp-and-paper-oriented industries built along those lines. Isolated from cheap water transportation, the closest Canadian National harbour was located at Thunder Bay, where Canadian Northern formerly operated a coal dock. But while this may have been convenient for the Canadian Northern, which passed through that locality, the old National Transcontinental line was further north, lacking any direct contact with Great Lakes shipping. For that line only the Algoma Central offered a convenient inroad for coal by way of Michipicoten Harbour and Hearst. Even the old Canadian Northern line which crossed the Algoma Central at Oba would benefit due to the significantly shorter haulage distance.

Anticipating great rewards from the traffic the coal would bring, Algoma Central commenced construction of a new coal dock at Michipicoten Harbour in 1929. In providing a suitable platform on which to stockpile the incoming coal, the dock was built out into the water on a site in front of the old ore dock (by this time demolished) using dirt and rock fill; the railway even tapped the remaining iron ore stockpiles at the Helan and Magpie mines for fill! Completed by September 1929,

Built in 1901 as the *Uranus*, the *W.C. Franz* was acquired in 1913 and served the Algoma Central until 1934 when she was lost in a collision on Lake Huron. In this view, the *W.C. Franz* is seen taking on iron ore at Michipicoten Harbour around the time of World War I. Working on the ore dock is Algoma Central locomotive number 37, a class C-1, 2-8-0 built by Montreal Locomotive Works in 1911 and scrapped in the early 1950s. — *PAC PA-29349*

A starboard side view of the *J. Frater Taylor* from 1930. Acquired as the *Saturn* in 1913, she was first named *J. Frater Taylor* by the Algoma Central. When the railway changed its naming policy in the 1930s, the vessel was renamed *Algosoo* in 1936, operating as such until her sale and scrapping in 1965. — *PAC PA-145719*

Acquired new by the Algoma Central in 1910, the 2,201-ton *Thomas J. Drummond* proved to be too small for the railway's purpose and so in 1917, she was traded to the Great Lakes Transportation Company of Midland in return for their 3,495-ton *William S. Mack* (renamed *Home Smith*). The *Thomas J. Drummond* was sold not long after the trade to the grain firm of N.M. Paterson Company, Limited, of Fort William, in whose employ she is seen in this photograph from 1925.

— *PAC PA-145718*

the coal dock held a water frontage of 550 feet initially, just enough to dock one of the company's freighters, and was finished off with an overhead coal bridge for handling the coal. Later additions would triple the dock's frontage and storage capacity, with the original coal bridge serving its purpose until its removal in the late 1970s.

In addition to the new coal dock, two big 2-10-2 Santa Fe-type locomotives were delivered to the railway from the Kingston Locomotive Works to improve the railway's coal-haulage capacity. Similar to engines previously placed into service by Canadian National, these 550,000-pound units cost the railway over $83,500 each, a substantial investment and the company's only locomotive acquisitions between the two world wars.

Despite all that effort and offers of cheap freight rates, Algoma Central was unable to convince Canadian National that it was in that railway's best interests to ship its coal through Michipicoten, Canadian National countering that it had to run the trains no matter what. The pulp and paper companies had no such vested interests and were quick to switch to the Algoma Central route. Canadian National later had a change in heart, for by the end of World War II, it too was bringing in coal by way of the Algoma Central.

The year 1929 was one the Algoma Central would remember for more than just the opening of the coal dock that September, for it was quickly followed by the big financial crash on New York City's Wall Street. The Great Depression was on.

By this time the steamship line was down to only three ships: *W.C. Franz*, *Home Smith* and *J. Frater Taylor*. Reductions in freight tonnage carried after the First World War resulted in the railway disposing of the *Paliki* in 1924, in an attempt to further rationalize the line into a fleet of Great Lakes-type bulk freighters. Three years later the *Agawa* ran aground off Manitoulin Island and was abandoned, only to be salvaged the following spring and sold off, serving a number of owners until scrapped in 1965 at Bilbao, Spain.

While the additional coal traffic may have prompted Algoma Central to replace the *Agawa* or even expand the fleet, the Depression put a damper on such plans, and it was further complicated in 1930 when the Canadian government placed transportation subsidies on Nova Scotian coal, shifting a good portion of the coal supply in the North away from the Algoma Central and its American coal and back into Canadian National's hands.

The 1930s were years of struggle for Algoma Central. Reduced traffic translated into meagre returns, and after paying out for wages and other expenses, there was no money left for upkeep and maintenance. Only the steamship line seemed to have a future, even if it was bleak. For most of Algoma Central's history, the steamers were responsible for the majority of tonnage handled by the company, and when the line lost the *W.C. Franz* in a collision on Lake Huron in November 1934, it was imperative that a replacement be found. Fortunately certain railway bondholders held the ownership on two American vessels ideally suited to the railway's needs. The ships were at that time laid up at Buffalo, New York. The railway's management quickly went to work on a purchase agreement and, despite some difficulties in raising the money, took possession of the steamships *John J. Barlum* and *Thomas Barlum* in 1935.

Oldest of the two was the *Thomas Barlum*, built in 1907 by Detroit Shipbuilding. At 6,117 gross tons, the *Algosteel*, as she was renamed, gave the company 9,500 tons of additional freight capacity. The *John J. Barlum*, built by American Shipbuilding, operated as the *Algocen* under Algoma Central ownership, its 6,893 tons providing a further 9,800 tons of freight capacity. If not for the timely acquisition of these two ships, the steamship line, if not the entire railway, would surely have ceased to exist.

Now with four ships — *Home Smith*, *J. Frater Taylor*, *Algocen* and *Algosteel* — the line's combined capacity reached 31,150 tons of freight, 8,000 tons more than at the close of World War I. The new ships also set a trend in naming vessels, each name somehow related to the company and prefixed by "Algo." Subsequently, in 1936, the *Home Smith* became the *Algorail* and the *J. Frater Taylor* the *Algosoo*.

During the Depression, relations between Algoma Central and Algoma Steel reached a low ebb as each followed its own path, often pitting company against company. Such was the case when Algoma Steel decided to reopen the Helen Mine in 1937. Algoma Steel did not wish to have anything to do with the railway, instead proposing to construct a road from the mine to Michipicoten

Harbour over which dump trucks would haul the ore to the steel company's own ore dock. It would have been an expensive scheme, the success of which was wholly dependent on a federal government commitment to dredge a new harbour, but some backroom persuasion by the local Member of Parliament on behalf of the Algoma Central Railway quickly squashed that scheme. Without any alternative, Algoma Steel turned to the Algoma Central for transportation.

Recalling that supplies of hematite ore composed of 53 percent iron had been previously mined out, only siderite ore with about a 35 percent iron content remained. Under normal circumstances, low-grade ore such as siderite was uneconomical to mine and transport due to the low levels of real iron contained versus waste. A newly developed sintering process solved this problem by processing the ore into pellets containing 51 percent iron called "sinter" that are easily transported.

Once an agreement was achieved between the two organizations, Algoma Central started immediately on rebuilding the old branch into the mine from Wawa, enabling new equipment to be brought into the Helen. At Michipicoten, new facilities for loading ore onto the ships had to be installed, but instead of the usual elevated ore dock for dumping ore directly into the ships, a conveyor-belt system was built. This decision was based on the fact that the coal bridge interfered with the construction of a normal ore dock and building a new ore dock out into the water would have been too expensive. The make-up of the ore pellets also influenced the railway's decision, for their small uniform size made them aptly suited to a conveyor loading system. Even so, it was still necessary to build a trestle for the ore hopper cars, and for this purpose the original approach to the old ore dock was used with the addition of a steel trestle on the end, complete with bins underneath to receive the sinter. In all, it cost the railway a quarter of a million dollars, an investment soon to prove its worth. The first shipment of sinter left the harbour in the spring of 1939.

The original 1937 contract called upon the Algoma Central Railway to move four million tons of sinter ore for Algoma Steel, a figure long since passed, translating into an annual tonnage of about 450,000 tons. For Algoma Central it meant a return to better times and provided the extra capital to rebuild the railway line and its equipment. Traffic demand was further accelerated following the outbreak of World War II, leading the railway into the purchase of another ship, the *Algoway*, in 1940.

Built in 1903 by American Shipbuilding at Cleveland, the *Algoway* was rebuilt in 1912, again by American Shipbuilding, resulting in a gross tonnage of 3,785 tons with a corresponding capacity of 6,200 tons of freight. The fleet now consisted of five vessels — *Algocen*, *Algorail*, *Algosoo*, *Algosteel* and *Algoway* — and with the exception of the *Algosteel*, all were constructed by American Shipbuilding. Fleet capacity had now reached 37,350 tons.

The war brought a strong recovery for Algoma Central as well as Algoma Steel, whose management was only slowly warming to the railway. For the steamships, these would be busy days that even the end of the war couldn't halt. In 1948, for example, business at Michipicoten Harbour tallied 194 shiploads into and out of the port. Outbound, 73 loads of sinter and 53 loads of pulpwood were handled, while inbound 62 loads of coal and five of sulphur were received.[3] While Algoma Central steamships were not responsible for every shipment at Michipicoten, it is safe to assume that they carried the bulk of the freight handled.

From the prosperity of the forties, the early fifties brought the downfall of Michipicoten Harbour. Algoma Steel, for example, found that shipping its ore south by rail held advantages over water transport, particularly during winter, thus reducing the company's need to stockpile ore for winter use. From handling almost 910,000 tons of ore in 1950, tonnage declined to only 410,000 tons by the mid-1960s and has continued to drop. Conversely, ore shipments by rail increased five-fold. Only ore destined for American ports continued to be shipped by way of Michipicoten. Coal traffic also took a down turn as the railways switched to diesel power and as fuel oil became more popular as a heating fuel. Today Michipicoten Harbour is almost abandoned, except for the occasional ship calling for ore.

The decline of Michipicoten Harbour did not result in a corresponding decline of the steamship line. There was a loss in business at first, but other cargoes were found and the line made a steady comeback. By the mid-1960s the company had entered a new phase of fleet renewal and the

Acquired as the *William S. Mack* through a trade in 1917, the *Home Smith* served the Algoma Central until 1963, first as the *Home Smith,* then as the *Algorail* after 1936. Here, the *Home Smith* is discharging her cargo of coal at the Michipicoten Harbour coal dock in the early 1930s. The coal bridge was powered by steam. — *OA Acc. 10456 S16391*

The *Algosteel* was acquired by the railway in 1935 as the *Thomas Barlum.* She is seen here at the locks at Sault Ste. Marie, Michigan. — *UBL PB No. 2611*

five older ships were sold: *Algorail* in 1963; *Algoway* in 1964; *Algosoo* in 1965; *Algosteel* in 1966; and *Algocen* in 1968. They have been replaced by a fleet of large, modern freighters.

Today Algoma Central's steamship department is known as Algoma Central Marine and is the oldest continuously operated Canadian shipping line on the Great Lakes. Since 1950 the line has purchased 20 new and used ships, and it would be an oversight if these ships were not mentioned. They are: *A.S. Glossbrenner**, *Agawa (II)*, *Agawa Canyon**, *Algobay**, *Algocen (II)**, *Algolake**, *Algoport**, *Algorail (II)**, *Algosea*, *Algosoo (II)**, *Algoway (II)**, *Algowest**, *Algowood**, *E.B. Barber**, *Goudreau*, *John B. Aird**, *Michipicoten*, *Sir Denys Lowson*, *Roy A. Jodrey*, *V.W. Scully**. Ships marked with an asterisk (*) are currently serving with the fleet. Additional details may be found in the appended shipping list.

The Railway Iron Ore Docks

So far we have seen how two of Ontario's railways developed their own shipping lines to handle iron ore traffic, while only briefly touching upon the provision of iron ore docks by other railway companies. The following list attempts to rectify this by identifying the province's railway-owned ore docks according to railway company (subsequent railway affiliations are shown in parentheses) and location. Brief descriptions outline the history of, and facilities provided at, each dock where known.

While the descriptions are generally self-explanatory, docks listed as *pocket trestle type* are those resembling a railway trestle bridge into which storage bins were built. The photographs provided in this chapter of the Algoma Central's first Michipicoten Harbour ore dock and of Canadian National's Port Arthur ore dock are typical of the pocket-trestle-type dock. These docks were "gravity" operated as opposed to mechanical docks which used conveyor belt systems to handle the ore and which often showed no major physical structures.

a) **Algoma Central Railway**

Michipicoten Harbour: first dock built 1900, wood, dock 275 feet long by 40 feet high, pocket trestle type, twelve 50-ton pockets on one side, one track, approach embankment 350 feet long, demolished 1920s; second dock built 1939, steel unloading trestle, electrically-operated mechanical ore dock using conveyor-belt system, ore dock incorporated into coal dock.

b) **Canadian National Railways**

Port Arthur (Thunder Bay): built 1944-45, concrete, dock as built 600 feet long by 65 feet wide by 82 feet high, pocket trestle type, 100 ore pockets at 50 per side, 33,000 tons total capacity, four tracks, single track approach 2 ½ miles long including 4,000 feet of trestle, dock doubled in size with 600-foot extension in 1954, slated for demolition in 1986, having been superseded by newer mechanical dock.

c) **Canadian Northern Railway (CNR)**

Key Harbour: built 1908, wood (assumed), possibly pocket trestle type, details unknown, closed 1920s.

Port Arthur (Thunder Bay): some ore shipped through coal dock of subsidiary Canadian Northern Coal & Ore Dock Company, little specialized ore-handling equipment.

d) **Central Ontario Railway**

Weller's Bay: built 1882-84, wood, dock 1,812 feet long by 30 feet high, pocket trestle type, 45 pockets on one side, two tracks, capacity unknown, not used after 1885.

The freighter *Alex. Nisick* of Vermillion takes on a load of ore at the iron ore dock at Michipicoten Harbour. On the trestle, Algoma Central locomotive 22 (Algoma Central class C-1, 2-8-0, built by Baldwin Locomotive Works 1900 and scrapped 1924) works diligently as it shoves loaded ore hoppers onto the dock. Photographed only a few years after completion, the approach trestle shows signs of subsidence as indicated by the shims under the right hand rail to the right of the picture. — *OA S16388*

Canadian National's iron ore dock at Port Arthur (Thunder Bay) as it appeared around 1960. — *OA 22-G-1058*

e) **Cobourg, Peterborough & Marmora Railway & Mining Company**

Cobourg: built 1869, wood, pocket trestle type.

Harwood: built 1869, wood, steam-powered "elevator" for transferring ore from scows to rail cars.

Trent River Bridge: built 1869, wood, trestle type, ore dumped directly from rail cars into scows beneath trestle.

f) **Grand Junction Railway**

Belleville: small quantity of ore shipped by Grand Junction Railway through its general freight dock at Belleville.

g) **Grand Trunk Railway (CNR)**

Point Edward: Canada Steamship Lines dock, "whirly" cranes used to unload ore from ships into rail cars for shipment to the Hamilton steel mills, operation lasted from 1915 until 1932, when the present Welland Canal opened.

CHAPTER FIVE - NOTES

1) Donald M. Wilson, *Lost Horizons* (Belleville, 1983), p. 162.
2) Arthur D. Dunn, "In search of history (1) — The Trent River ore cars," *CIM Bulletin* (Montreal), May 1981, p. 142.
3) Mick Lowe, "Wawa's 'dream' may thrive again," *Globe & Mail* (Toronto), 3 October 1983.

VI

THE COAL BOATS

During the late decades of the last century, coal was gradually supplanting wood as the primary energy source for Ontario's homes and industries. In the forefront were the railways, who soon recognized the efficiency of coal in firing their larger engines, especially in light of the dwindling supplies of cordwood, as centuries-old tracts of timber fell to the axe.

Unfortunately Ontario was without its own coal supply and the nearest to be found was located in the Pennsylvania coal fields miles to the south. Coal could be delivered by rail, but it was an expensive proposition. An alternative lay with the many freighters and schooners plying the lakes. They were able to cut costs by picking up cargoes of coal at American ports such as Charlotte (Rochester), New York, and Ashtabula, Ohio, and delivering them with considerable savings to Canadian ports, much to the delight of coal merchants and consumers but providing little benefit to the railway companies.

For the railways, there had to be a better way of bringing the coal, a way that combined the efficiency of rail transportation with the economy of water transport. It was obvious that some sort of car ferry was the answer, but not the type developed for use on the rivers, for in open water those ferries would be vulnerable to the wind, weather and high waves commonly encountered out on the lakes. By the early 1890s such a ferry had been developed for use on Lake Michigan by combining a shallow-draught rugged hull capable of smashing through winter ice, with powerful engines and weatherproof accommodations for railway cars and passengers alike. Over a dozen were on the lake by mid-decade.

The first such service to Ontario was introduced by the American-owned United States & Ontario Steam Navigation Company on Lake Erie.

The United States & Ontario Steam Navigation Company
The Marquette & Bessemer Dock & Navigation Company

The Pittsburgh, Shenango & Lake Erie Railroad Company was a moderate-sized railway built at the end of the last century from Butler, Pennsylvania, in the coal fields near Pittsburgh, north to the Lake Erie ports of Erie, Pennsylvania, and Conneaut, Ohio. From the beginning the line was closely associated with the steel mills of Pittsburgh, for the railway's chief source of income was derived from southbound movements of Lake Superior iron ore from Erie to Pittsburgh. But such traffic patterns were by no means profitable, since northbound trains were largely comprised of empty cars returning for another load of ore.

The company knew that coal was a valuable commodity and with its strategic position within the coal fields, it had a perfect opportunity to develop northbound coal traffic for transferal to freighters on Lake Erie. The railway already had the empty ore cars available to carry the coal, but it soon found that facilities at Erie were inadequate for the railway's purpose. Conneaut, on the other hand, was well suited to the railway and possessed an excellent harbour just waiting to be fully developed. With no choice but to move, the railway commenced construction at the harbour in the spring of 1892; by November the company had received its first cargo of ore through the new port.

While excellent progress was made in developing the railway's ore traffic, great difficulty was encountered in finding customers willing to ship coal north to Conneaut, most shippers favouring such ports as Ashtabula, a few miles to the west. In search of a solution to their dilemma, the Pittsburgh, Shenango & Lake Erie instigated a feasibility study in 1894 to determine the potential of a car ferry service across Lake Erie from Conneaut to Port Dover, Ontario. Such a service would not only allow the railway to interchange freight cars with the Grand Trunk Railway at Port Dover, but more importantly it would also provide access to the steel mills then under construction at Hamilton and soon to be volume users of coal. Since a ferry would cut over 80 miles off an all-rail route to Hamilton, the company would be in a position to undercut existing all-rail freight rates.

The results of the study were positive and the railway promptly went to work on obtaining the necessary ships and building new ferry slips. Unlike Conneaut, Port Dover harbour was unable to accommodate any vessel larger than a schooner, requiring the company not only to build the ferry slips but also to dredge the harbour and its approaches. Fortunately for the Pittsburgh, Shenango & Lake Erie, successful negotiations with Canada's Department of Public Works were concluded on 5 November 1894, by which the railway would receive a subsidy of $15,000 upon completion of the work.[1] Still, by 1896 $45,200 had been paid out by the company, not including the subsidy, with little or no assistance from the Grand Trunk, which had effective ownership of the harbour. This was probably an early indication that the Grand Trunk held little hope for a successful Lake Erie car ferry service, therefore leaving all the risk to the Pittsburgh, Shenango & Lake Erie Railroad.

Up until now the railway had made no provisions for the future management of the ferry service. Often such operations were set up as subsidiaries of the parent organization for the sake of keeping such activities separate so far as profit and loss were concerned, as well as ensuring effective management. It was not until July 1895 that such a subsidiary was set up by the Pittsburgh, Shenango & Lake Erie, when the railway formed the United States & Ontario Steam Navigation Company to acquire and operate the railway's car ferries and ferry slips.

Delivery of the company's two new car ferries took place in August. Ordered by the railway during the previous year, the ferries were constructed by the Craig Shipbuilding Company of Toledo, Ohio. Sharing the same basic design, each vessel was built of wood and had a capacity of 26 freight cars on four tracks. Christened *Shenango No. 1* and *Shenango No. 2*, their gross tonnages were 1,941 tons and 1,938 tons respectively. By no means huge vessels, they were largely comparable in size to car ferries already operating on the Detroit and St. Clair rivers, differing mainly by having enclosed decks rather than the open decks favoured for river ferries. The choice of wood in their construction was unusual since by this time most large ships were being built out of steel, especially for vessels capable of breaking through ice, such as *Shenango No. 1* and *Shenango No. 2*. Manoeuvrability was enhanced by equipping the ferries with screw propellers fore and aft.

Operations were kicked off at Conneaut Harbour on 22 August 1895 with a "grand excursion" to Port Dover, the first regular car ferry operation on Lake Erie. It would be interesting to know how they made out on the trip, for the ships were only fitted out to carry a limited number of overnight passengers. Even so, they were licensed to carry up to 1,000 people for excursions, leaving one to imagine the upper decks laid out with assorted deck chairs for the convenience of dignitaries and guests.

Despite the celebrations, business for the ferries failed to materialize, resulting in the *Shenango No. 2* being leased for the 1897 season. Operated by the Detroit, Grand Rapids & Western Railway, *Shenango No. 2* initiated that company's new ferry service across Lake Michigan between Muskegon, Michigan, and Milwaukee, Wisconsin. A year later the *Shenango No. 2* was formally purchased by the Detroit, Grand Rapids & Western and renamed *Muskegon*. The ship passed into the hands of the Pere Marquette Railway in 1900 and on 9 October 1901 became the *Pere Marquette 16*. Withdrawn from service in 1907, the ferry was sold in 1917 and, as a barge, sunk on Lake Superior in 1922.

Shenango No. 1 is docked at the Port Dover ferry slip in this photograph taken from the deck of *Shenango No. 2*. Visible beyond *Shenango No. 1* are strings of gondola cars loaded with Pennsylvania coal bound for Hamilton and other Ontario communities. This scene probably dates from the winter of 1895-96. — *OA S18150*

Shenango No. 1 (right) pushes backwards in the ice with her bow propeller outside of Conneaut Harbour in the winter of 1896-97 in an effort to create a channel for *Shenango No. 2* (left). Taken only a year after the Port Dover photograph, both ships are painted in a revised colour scheme in contrast to their original colours. The Maltese Cross painted on the ships' bows was the logo of the Pittsburgh, Shenango & Lake Erie Railroad. As a point of detail, note that the *Shenango No. 2* had three portholes on either side of her bow while the *Shenango No. 1* has one rectangular window per side along with what appears to be two portholes on her port (left) side. — *UBL No. 8776*

The lease and subsequent sale of the *Shenango No. 2* provided some relief to the United States & Ontario line, but the problem still remained. At Conneaut during 1897, 589,368 tons of freight were handled, principally by the Pittsburgh, Bessemer & Lake Erie Railroad. Of that, incoming tonnage amounted to 560,198 tons, of which 551,417 tons was iron ore. Outbound shipments represented only 29,700 tons, 29,170 tons of which was coal.[2]

On the whole, the tonnage handled by the railway at Conneaut proved that the railway made the right choice in locating there, with further yearly increases reinforcing it. For the ferries and coal traffic in general, the statistics tell a different story. Assuming that the entire outbound tonnage was handled by the *Shenango No. 1* and delivered to Port Dover, there was only sufficient freight for 57 trips north at full capacity (assuming that one freight car held 20 tons of coal or freight). Expressing that in another way, since the ferry made one round trip per day (leaving Conneaut at 9:30 a.m., returning leaving Port Dover at 7:00 p.m.), five days a week for a nine-month season, each northbound journey averaged no more than a load of 171 tons, compared to a maximum capacity of approximately 520 tons (once again assuming that each car held 20 tons). Southbound, tonnage was almost negligible. Under these circumstances it would be impossible to make a profit.

For that reason the United States & Ontario signed a traffic agreement with the Lake Erie & Detroit River Railway in 1898 permitting *Shenango No. 1* to dock at Port Stanley, at a slip to be constructed by the railway. The first trip to Port Stanley was made on August 18, and thereafter *Shenango No. 1* alternated between Port Dover and Port Stanley.

Meanwhile the Pittsburgh, Bessemer & Lake Erie Railroad was having financial difficulties at home, and the losses experienced with the United States & Ontario were not helping the situation. Faced with the possible termination of the ferry service and the resulting loss in traffic, the Lake Erie & Detroit River Railway took out a five-year lease on the United States & Ontario commencing January 1899. By the end of the year the new management had spent $20,000 to establish a third terminal at Erieau, Ontario, following its acquisition of the Erie & Huron Railway, and the *Shenango No. 1* now alternated between all three terminals.

Year by year Port Dover became more of a liability than an asset. Traffic volumes were less than adequate and silting at the port became an operational headache, as the *Shenango No. 1* often hit bottom when fully loaded, though fortunately without serious damage. In 1901 Port Dover was dropped, leaving Port Stanley and Erieau, neither of which had facilities owned by the United States & Ontario. Of the two, Port Stanley held the greatest advantage in that it held direct access to the Grand Trunk and the Canadian Pacific railways as well as the cities of London and St. Thomas.

The year 1901 also saw the Pittsburgh, Bessemer & Lake Erie become the Bessemer & Lake Erie Railroad Company, under which name it continues to operate.

In the meantime a traffic agreement taking place between the Canadian-based Lake Erie & Detroit River Railway and the American-owned Pere Marquette Railway was about to change the future of the United States & Ontario Steam Navigation Company forever. Under the agreement, the Lake Erie & Detroit River Railway would institute a car ferry service between Windsor and Detroit for the purpose of exchanging freight with the Pere Marquette if the Pere Marquette established a car ferry operation across Lake Erie. In reality it was a prelude to the Pere Marquette's acquisition of the Lake Erie & Detroit River Railway in 1903, but nevertheless it was still a binding contract.

The Pere Marquette had gained considerable experience with cross-lake car ferries on Lake Michigan but had never operated on Lake Erie, the United States & Ontario being the only such service on the lake. Recognizing that both companies shared a mutual interest in a successful Lake Erie service, the Pere Marquette approached the United States & Ontario's parent company in 1903, proposing that the Bessemer & Lake Erie and the Pere Marquette join forces and form a new car ferry company.

The Pere Marquette not only offered an infusion of new capital but a network of railway lines in Ontario over which the Bessemer & Lake Erie could deliver. It was an offer too good to pass up. As a result the Marquette & Bessemer Dock & Navigation Company was incorporated on 2 April 1903, with each parent company holding 50 percent of the stock. For its part the Bessemer & Lake Erie transferred its assets in the United States & Ontario Steam Navigation Company over to the new line, including the *Shenango No. 1*, which became the Marquette & Bessemer's first car ferry.

The first new acquisition by the Marquette & Bessemer Dock & Navigation Company came in 1904 with the delivery of the *Marquette & Bessemer No. 1*, a steel ship built in the yards of the Buffalo Dry Dock Company. This unusual vessel was something of a hybrid, for it was not a car ferry, but it was equipped with two railway tracks. This 1,525-ton ship was in fact a bulk coal carrier much like other Great Lakes freighters with the addition of railway tracks. At Conneaut hopper cars of coal were pushed on board the ship, allowing the coal to be unloaded directly into the hold without the use of any special apparatus other than the existing ferry slip. Upon reaching Port Stanley or Erieau, the rails and hatches were removed, allowing the coal to be transferred to awaiting coal cars by a clam-shell bucket. In all, 2,500 tons of coal could be shipped by this method at any one time, considerably more than could be carried on a conventional car ferry.

The *Shenango No. 1* was destroyed on 11 March 1904 when it caught fire at Conneaut after being locked in the ice just outside the harbour since January. One crewman was killed.

As a replacement for the *Shenango No. 1*, a new steel car ferry was ordered from the American Shipbuilding Company of Cleveland. Arriving in September 1905, the *Marquette & Bessemer No. 2* followed an established design, adopted during the 1890s by Pere Marquette for its Lake Michigan car ferries, which provided space for 30 freight cars on four tracks. At 3,514 tons she would be the largest ferry operated by the Marquette & Bessemer and also the most tragic.

On 7 December 1909, while on its regular route between Conneaut and Port Stanley, the *Marquette & Bessemer No. 2* ran into a heavy storm on the lake and within a short period of time sunk with a full load of 30 cars carrying coal and steel. Nine members of the crew managed to get to a lifeboat, but when they were found a week later, all were frozen to death. Altogether, 32 crewmen lost their lives.

A new *Marquette & Bessemer No. 2* was ordered from American Shipbuilding in 1910 at a cost of over $340,000 (according to the 1938 book value) and except for a lower gross tonnage of 2,583 tons and an increased beam, both No. 2's were identical. Entering service in September, she represented the last purchase made by the company.

This would have left the Marquette & Bessemer without a car ferry for most of the 1910 season had it not been for the Pere Marquette Railway, which loaned one of its Lake Michigan car ferries, the *Pere Marquette*, to the company. The *Pere Marquette*, constructed in 1896 by W.F. Wheeler & Company at West Bay City, Michigan, for the Flint & Pere Marquette Transportation Company (a subsidiary of the Flint & Pere Marquette, later the Pere Marquette Railway), was the prototype for the Pere Marquette's fleet, as well as the Marquette & Bessemer's, and first operated between Ludington, Michigan, and Manitowoc, Wisconsin. As the Pere Marquette purchased more car ferries for Lake Michigan, the *Pere Marquette* was freed up, permitting it not only to be loaned to the Marquette & Bessemer for part of the 1910 season but also at certain other times when traffic demanded another car ferry.

One railway which benefitted greatly from the operations of the Marquette & Bessemer ferries was the London & Port Stanley, leased by the Pere Marquette until 1914, after which it operated as an independent electric line. In 1910 the railway delivered 486,302 tons of freight, including 16,134 tons of anthracite coal and 99,528 tons of bituminous coal. Because of the delay in replacing the original *Marquette & Bessemer No. 2*, only 24 percent of the volume of freight carried that year was made up of coal. By 1913 the railway was moving 642,920 tons of freight, of which anthracite represented 67,446 tons and bituminous coal 506,460 tons.[3] Coal had rebounded to 89 percent of all freight handled. It was not to last, however, for in the following years freight traffic tended to be rather erratic, up one year and down another, seldom reaching the levels experienced during the years immediately before the First World War. The separation between the London & Port Stanley and the Pere Marquette Railway in 1914 had no major effect on the ferry operations, for the *Marquette & Bessemer No. 2* continued to serve Port Stanley regularly.

Throughout the twenties, due to diminishing coal traffic and rising operating costs, it became increasingly difficult for the Marquette & Bessemer Dock & Navigation Company to make a profit. It was true that when the Marquette & Bessemer was formed, significant savings could be gained by sending cars across Lake Erie by ferry rather than around it, but as costs rose and volumes fell, those savings soon disappeared. The *Marquette & Bessemer No. 1*, for example, often made

The first ship built expressly for the Marquette & Bessemer Dock & Navigation Company was the *Marquette & Bessemer No. 1* delivered in 1903. Essentially a bulk Great Lakes freighter, she could be loaded directly from railway hopper cars at a ferry slip through having a split afterstructure and removable rails along her deck. Unloading, however, could only be carried out by conventional means such as the use of clamshell buckets as seen here at either Conneaut Harbour, Toledo or, possibly Erieau (though unlikely), owing to the presence of the Père Marquette gondolas. The four derricks along the vessel's port side were used in removing and replacing the hatches and rails. — *UBL No. 8778-A*

The *Marquette & Bessemer No. 1* with what appears to be a load of sawn lumber and a missing derrick. The location could be either the Detroit or the St. Lawrence River, possibly in the 1920s. — *UBL No. 8778*

The *Père Marquette,* built for the Flint & Père Marquette Transportation Company's Lake Michigan service in 1896, was the prototype for all steel cross-lake car ferries to follow. Along with railway cars, the *Père Marquette* accommodated 25 passengers in the cabin behind her wheelhouse, the crew having the cabin behind the funnels. The Père Marquette frequently sent the *Père Marquette* to Lake Erie to assist the Marquette & Bessemer. — *UBL No. 8779*

The first *Marquette & Bessemer No. 2,* built in 1905. She sank in a violent storm on 7 December 1909 with the loss of her entire crew. — *University of Western Ontario*

trips carrying coal and other bulk commodities to various ports on the Great Lakes and the St. Lawrence River when there was insufficient traffic on its regular route to Erieau. At other times it was not uncommon for the ship to pick up coal at other Lake Erie harbours such as Toledo, instead of Conneaut, for delivery to Erieau. When a storm damaged the company's installations at Erieau in November 1927, the Marquette & Bessemer decided to drop the route.

Even with the company concentrating all of its efforts onto the shorter Conneaut to Port Stanley run, traffic continued on its downward slide. In 1929, 258,752 tons of freight were carried between Port Stanley and Conneaut, but by 1931 cross-lake traffic had dropped to only 100,222 tons. During the same period losses rose from just over $3,500 to almost $76,000 per year.[4] On 25 July 1932 the company received permission from the Interstate Commerce Commission to abandon its car ferry service, and on August 25 the *Marquette & Bessemer No. 2* made its last run.

The *Marquette & Bessemer No. 1* was sold in 1937, but the *Marquette & Bessemer No. 2* was not sold until 1942, when she was purchased by the Filer Paper Company, who converted the ship into a barge. During the years preceding the sale, the *Marquette & Bessemer No. 2* was even used as a showboat. The barge was sold once again in 1946 and became the *Lillian* in 1948.

The Pennsylvania-Ontario Transportation Company

Like the Pere Marquette, the Canadian Pacific Railway also developed a market for coal in southwestern Ontario, not to mention locomotive coal for its own needs. Taking the lead from the Marquette & Bessemer line, Canadian Pacific approached the Pennsylvania Railroad with a proposal for the establishment of a cross-lake car ferry service on Lake Erie. As a major coal-hauling road willing to expand its territory, the Pennsylvania had no apprehensions about going into partnership with the Canadian line, and so on 16 February 1906 the Pennsylvania-Ontario Transportation Company Limited was formed under American law, with both parent companies taking a 50-percent stake.

Soon afterwards an order was placed with the Great Lakes Engineering Works of St. Clair, Michigan, for the construction of a new steel car ferry of 2,670 gross tons. Christened *Ashtabula*, she was capable of carrying 26 freight cars on four tracks, six cars on each outer track and seven cars on the inner tracks. She was delivered in time to finish out the 1906 navigation season.

The company's choice of *Ashtabula* for the ferry's name was by no means arbitrary. Ashtabula, Ohio, was the Pennsylvania Railroad's foremost coal- and ore-handling port on Lake Erie and the obvious southern terminus for the new service. Canadian Pacific's chosen port was Port Burwell, a small fishing port at the end of a newly finished branch line from Ingersoll, and had the ferry service been more successful, it too might have had a car ferry named for it.

Despite attempts at attracting commodities other than coal, especially for southbound journeys, the *Ashtabula* spent most of her time carrying locomotive coal for the Canadian Pacific. So long as high volumes of coal were carried, such an operation could remain profitable, as it did until the 1930s. This was particularly true if southbound movements of miscellaneous forest products and manufactured goods helped offset return trips with empty hoppers.

The Depression put an end to that. A drop in goods being shipped not only resulted in the end of southbound freight, but it also meant that fewer trains were required, hence a reduced demand for locomotive coal. In 1929, for example, 361,216 tons of freight consisting chiefly of coal was carried north by the ferry, with 36,659 tons of freight being returned to the United States, totalling 397,875 tons. A steady decline following the crash brought a low in 1934 of 158,515 tons carried north and only 1,178 tons shipped south.[5] That's a total of only 159,693 tons, representing a 60-percent drop in volume compared to 1929. Faced with those conditions, the company was forced to lay the *Ashtabula* up whenever traffic shortages occurred, operating the ferry only when required.

The outbreak of World War II gave the ferry service a boost, and by 1943 approximately 245,000 tons of freight were being transferred across Lake Erie, with northbound coal making up 237,000 tons.[6] Despite that, the increase in traffic was only temporary, and once the war was over, service returned to an "as required" operation during its nine-month navigation season. Dieselization during the 1950s caused a further decline in traffic as the Canadian Pacific withdrew its coal-fired steam engines.

By the end of the 1950s it was clear that the *Ashtabula* had outlived her usefulness, but before the company was able to gain permission to abandon the car ferry operation, the *Ashtabula* collided with the freighter *Ben Moreel* in Ashtabula harbour. The date was 18 September 1958. Had this happened 30 years earlier, there can be no doubt that the ferry would have been repaired. Unfortunately it was the 1950s and the steamship was no longer looked upon as an asset; as the last surviving Lake Erie car ferry, she was simply an expensive burden.

Refloated later on, the *Ashtabula* made one final journey back from whence she came, to the Great Lakes Engineering Works, there to be scrapped. On 29 September 1961 the Pennsylvania-Ontario Transportation Company officially ceased to be.

The Toronto, Hamilton & Buffalo Navigation Company

The last company to start a car ferry service on Lake Erie, as well as being the first to cease operations, was the Toronto, Hamilton & Buffalo Navigation Company, a wholly owned subsidiary of the Toronto, Hamilton & Buffalo Railway.

Like many railway companies, the original legislation of 1884 incorporating the Toronto, Hamilton & Buffalo Railway gave the railway the right "to build, purchase or charter, and to manage, work and navigate, in connection with (its rail operations), steam vessels, sailing vessels and barges . . ."[7] At that time the Toronto, Hamilton & Buffalo was a small local venture to link Hamilton with Waterford on the Canada Southern-Michigan Central main line in an attempt to break the railway monopoly the Grand Trunk held on the city. Eleven years later control of the Toronto, Hamilton & Buffalo passed to the Canadian Pacific, New York Central, Michigan Central, and Canada Southern railways in an effort to expand the company's operations into the Niagara Peninsula, thereby forming an effective bridge between the New York Central lines (including the Michigan Central and Canada Southern), the Canadian Pacific, and the City of Hamilton, which by then was a developing steel and industrial centre. By the end of 1897 this support was justified when the line was completed from Welland to Waterford by way of Hamilton.

Developments during this period were strictly confined to railway construction and operations, and for many years the steamship provisions in the charter went unnoticed. That is until 1910.

In 1910 the Town of Dunnville, previously by-passed by other railways, proposed to the Toronto, Hamilton & Buffalo a plan by which the railway would construct a branch line from Smithville, on the railway's main line, to Dunnville and on to Port Maitland on Lake Erie. Because the railway was experiencing problems in getting freight through Buffalo as a result of traffic congestion, the town additionally proposed that a car ferry service be established at Port Maitland linking that port with some other port on the American side of the lake.

Although the initial proposal made by the town met with a cool reception from the railway's management, the scheme to build to Port Maitland and develop a car ferry link with the United States piqued the company's interest. Following a lengthy delay, construction of the new branch began in the spring of 1914 and was opened to Dunnville that November. By 1916 Port Maitland was reached. All that remained was the installation of docking facilities and, of course, the construction of the car ferry.

For the sake of operating convenience, the Toronto, Hamilton & Buffalo Navigation Company was formed in 1916 to assume control of all ferry operations. As Canada was at war in 1916, the company was incorporated in Ohio, a move which protected the company from having any ship under its ownership taken for war service by the Canadian government. It also solved the problem of paying customs duty on any ferry which was built in the United States.

The ferry purchased to start the car ferry service was ordered from the Great Lakes Engineering Works of Ecorse, Michigan, the same company that had built the Pennsylvania-Ontario Transportation Company's *Ashtabula* a decade earlier. The resulting family resemblance was obvious, for the new 2,751-ton *Maitland No. 1* delivered to the navigation company incorporated

The *Ashtabula* at Port Burwell around 1950. Some of the hopper cars at the lower right bear the insignias of the Pennsylvania Railroad and the Nickle Plate Road. The Pennsylvania-Ontario logo on *Ashtabula*'s bow is a "P" for Pennsylvania surrounded by an "O" for Ontario on a white background. — *UBL No. 8800*

Here is an early view of *Maitland No. 1* in the ice at Ashtabula Harbour. — *PAC PA-145140*

the same general design as the *Ashtabula*, with the only significant exception being its capacity, *Maitland No. 1* taking 32 cars, six more than the *Ashtabula*.

In addition to owing its name, *Maitland No. 1*, to Port Maitland, the adoption of the numerical system of naming its ferries provides some insight into the navigation company's original plans. When the contract was let to Great Lakes Engineering, three car ferries were actually ordered: *Maitland No. 1*; *Maitland No. 2*, similar to *No. 1* but with passenger accommodations; and *Maitland No. 3*. Logically *Maitland No. 1* was the first to be completed, but due to delays in finishing the ferry slips and rail yard at Port Maitland, the ship was leased to the Ann Arbor Railroad immediately upon delivery, resulting in a four-month stint on Lake Michigan.

The Ann Arbor at this time was operating at least two established routes on Lake Michigan, one between Frankfort, Michigan, and Gladstone and Menominee, Michigan, and the other from Frankfort to Kewaunee and Manitowoc, Wisconsin. It not only needed the extra ferry, but it was so impressed with *Maitland No. 1*'s performance that it purchased sister-ship *Maitland No. 2* while still under construction, renaming it *Ann Arbor No. 6*. Apparently the Toronto, Hamilton & Buffalo had a change of heart and decided against operating three ferries, for it not only sold *Maitland No. 2*, it cancelled *Maitland No. 3* as well.

With only one car ferry, regular service commenced on 1 November 1916, when *Maitland No. 1* left the New York Central dock at Ashtabula with a load of coal hoppers for the Toronto, Hamilton & Buffalo Railway at Port Maitland. Because of the railway's close relationship with Hamilton's steel producers, much of the coal carried across Lake Erie would find its way to the steel mills for conversion to coke. Typically the southbound run would net a significantly lower tonnage, with newsprint making up the largest proportion of freight destined for the American markets.

Most ferry companies have had their share of close encounters as well as disasters and the Toronto, Hamilton & Buffalo was no exception. On 23 December 1919 the three-year-old *Maitland No. 1* ran aground on Lowes Point and was forced to spend the next five days marooned until the *Marquette & Bessemer No. 2* could come to pull the stranded ferry off. Another incident occurred in 1927 that almost resulted in the loss of the ferry entirely. Pushing through heavy ice on March 25, *Maitland No. 1* grounded on Tecumseh Shoal, inflicting serious hull damage. She pulled through, however, avoiding the fate of other ships who were either sunk or crushed by the pack ice. Such were the risks of winter operation and serve to explain why many companies ceased operations between January and April.

The years before the Depression were good and profitable years for the navigation company, resulting in dividend payments to the railway of over $600,000, compared to the original investment of almost $400,000 for the ferry and the slip at Port Maitland.[8] Such a performance was impressive but was in many ways encouraged by the inadequate capacity of the Welland Canal, whose small size discouraged the passage of large bulk freighters. When it came to coal, that meant that the *Maitland No. 1* could remain competitive so long as ships passing through the Welland were restricted to small steamers or "canalers."

For the shipping interests on the Great Lakes, the Welland Canal has always been a bottleneck and over the years has resulted in several rebuildings. Such was the case during the twenties, when the government was working on enlarging the canal to accommodate larger ships up to a maximum length of 730 feet, enough for a freighter of over 25,000 tons in capacity. The project had actually started in 1913 but was delayed during the First World War. As the new canal neared completion towards the end of the 1920s, it was becoming increasingly clear that its opening would take a large amount of freight away from the Toronto, Hamilton & Buffalo.

When the steel mills began to obtain coal by way of Sodus Point, New York, on Lake Ontario, in 1928, a sizable volume of the Toronto, Hamilton & Buffalo's coal business was lost. If that wasn't enough, the Wall Street crash of 1929 ended the economic boom of the 1920s forcing many manufacturers to drastically reduce production and still more to close entirely.

With insufficient volumes of freight being shipped, the railway and the ferry service soon succumbed, slowly at first, but by 1932 tonnage was dropping rapidly with no prospects for a turnaround. For the Toronto, Hamilton & Buffalo Navigation Company, the writing was on the wall. Once the new and enlarged Welland Canal was opened, most of their remaining coal traffic would

Viewed at Ashtabula Harbour in the late 1920s, the *Maitland No. 1* sports an enclosed upper-wheelhouse added in the 1920s to improve visibility in all weather. — *UBL No. 8801*

Laid down as the *Maitland No. 2,* the ship was sold to the Ann Arbour Railroad during construction and she was launched as the *Ann Arbor No. 6. Ann Arbor No. 6* was rebuilt in 1959 as the *Arthur K. Atkinson* and is still in service on Lake Michigan. — *UBL No. 889*

disappear. Without any alternative, the navigation company was forced to discontinue service. On 28 June 1932 the *Maitland No. 1* was laid up at Ashtabula. On August 6 the new canal was officially opened.

Idle until 1935, *Maitland No. 1* was finally leased, once again for service on Lake Michigan. Operated by the Nicholson Universal Steamship Company, the ferry served to carry automobiles across the lake between Muskegan, Michigan, and Milwaukee, Wisconsin, until 1937, when she had to be withdrawn due to a legal technicality. Under American law, any service between two or more American ports had to be provided by American-owned vessels. Despite *Maitland No. 1's* United States registry, the navigation company's stock was held entirely by the Toronto, Hamilton & Buffalo Railway, which was incorporated in Canada, therefore making the ship ineligible for Lake Michigan service. In order to get around the law, the railway decided to redistribute the stock among its parent railways according to their ownership in the railway, resulting in a third going to the Canadian Pacific Railway and the rest going to the New York Central System. Thus the navigation company achieved American majority control, making it re-eligible for service on Lake Michigan. It was too late, however, and she remained laid up at Ashtabula.

In 1942 the ship was requisitioned by the American government, who removed the engines and sold the hull. Reduced to a pulpwood barge soon after, *Maitland No. 1* has continued to serve on the lakes, more recently carrying a variety of bulk freight.

The Ontario Car Ferry Company

When it came to shipping coal out by water, Lake Erie ports tended to be favoured above all others due to their close proximity to the coal fields of Pennsylvania and Ohio, an arrangement which permitted coal to be shipped cheaply and efficiently to any harbour on the upper Great Lakes by iron ore carriers who would have normally returned empty. Lake Ontario ports, on the other hand, were not as well placed and generally were far from any major coal consumer. Of these ports, by the turn of the century only Charlotte, the port of Rochester, New York, developed a significant coal trade.

The credit for Charlotte's success as a coal port must ultimately go to one company, the Buffalo, Rochester & Pittsburgh Railway Company, a line whose history dates back to the 1880s. With a main line running from Rochester down to the heart of the Pennsylvania coal fields, it was ideally located for the delivery of coal north to Lake Ontario, and through its mining subsidiary, the Rochester & Pittsburgh Coal & Iron Company (sold in 1906), coal traffic was assured.

It therefore comes as no surprise that by the end of the nineteenth century, Charlotte had become the principal coal port on Lake Ontario as well as the biggest American port on the lake. Of the 385,981 tons of freight handled at Charlotte in 1897, for example, 97 percent or 372,713 tons consisted of Pennsylvania coal delivered to the harbour by the Buffalo, Rochester & Pittsburgh.[9] Interestingly enough, 302,270 tons of coal were shipped down the St. Lawrence River, while only 5,963 tons passed through the Welland Canal to Lake Erie.[10] The remaining 64,479 tons found its way to the various Canadian harbours dotted along the north shore of Lake Ontario on board the many schooners that once plied the lakes. It was very clear that the future for coal traffic along the railway was bright indeed, especially if the company could break into the Ontario market just across the lake.

The Grand Trunk Railway during those years was still in a period of expansion, consolidating its railway lines in southern Ontario, building bigger and better locomotives, and planning its western expansion through the Grand Trunk Pacific Railway. Coal to fuel its expansion was a sorely needed commodity, and the Grand Trunk was forced to import coal from the south by whatever method it could. This usually came down to bringing coal into the province by way of Fort Erie and Niagara Falls, resulting in time-consuming and expensive all-rail movements of coal, particularly when that coal had to be sent to northern or eastern Ontario.

In light of these facts the Grand Trunk and the Buffalo, Rochester & Pittsburgh conducted several meetings with a view to establishing a cross-lake ferry link for the purpose of carrying locomotive coal north for the Grand Trunk, and any other freight as may be required. These meetings concluded in 1905 with the formation of the Ontario Car Ferry Company, Limited, as a joint venture, with each company assuming 50 percent of the stock. The company's head office was located at Toronto.

One of the new company's first tasks was the selection of a new car ferry for the route. The design most favoured was that of the Pennsylvania-Ontario Transportation Company's steamer *Ashtabula*, built by Great Lakes Engineering, with the addition of passenger accommodations on the upper deck. Unfortunately for Great Lakes Engineering, a ship of that size could not have passed through the Welland Canal, and so far as the construction of the hull, that company could not be considered. As a second choice, the contract for the new ship was given to the Canadian Shipbuilding Company at Toronto, with Great Lakes Engineering obtaining the engine contract and probably the design work as well. Three hundred and seventy thousand dollars later, the *Ontario No. 1* was commissioned for service, a 5,146-ton steel car ferry capable of carrying 28 freight cars and up to 1,000 passengers.

Along with the construction of the *Ontario No. 1*, ferry terminals also had to be established. The Buffalo, Rochester & Pittsburgh was already well entrenched at Charlotte and, with no reason to change, installed its ferry slip at Genesee Dock, a location originally served by the New York Central years earlier, at a cost of $51,797.01.[11] The Grand Trunk had no such port but finally decided on Cobourg, which, although requiring the installation of two concrete piers as protection from storms, was almost opposite Charlotte and was easily linked to the main line.

On 19 November 1907 *Ontario No. 1* made her first revenue run out of Charlotte with a full load of coal hoppers for the Grand Trunk. When she arrived at Cobourg, the ferry was greeted by a crowd of local citizens, fascinated by the huge ship as it manoeuvred into the dock. This process, by the way, took almost an hour due to the inexperience of the crew. Later, this time was drastically reduced and docking could be completed in a matter of minutes. In the afternoon *Ontario No. 1* returned to Charlotte with a load of empties.

Unlike its Lake Erie counterparts, the Ontario Car Ferry Company actively solicited passengers, a practice started in 1909 after *Ontario No. 1* had proved herself during the 1908 season. Encouraged by such accoutrements as berths for 90 overnight passengers, a music room and a restaurant, passengers were offered four trips per week based on the following timetable:

Lv. Cobourg, Ont.	3:30 p.m.
Ar. Genesee Docks, N.Y.	8:00 p.m.
Ar. Rochester, N.Y. (B.R. & P. Ry.)	8:30 p.m.
Lv. Rochester, N.Y. (B.R.& P. Ry.)	8:30 a.m.
Lv. Genesee Docks, N.Y.	9:00 a.m.
Ar. Cobourg, Ont.	2:00 p.m.

The provision of a special boat train between Genesee Docks and Rochester by the Buffalo, Rochester & Pittsburgh Railway was unique, for no other Great Lakes car ferry operation offered such a service to its passengers. Passenger arrangements between Cobourg and Toronto, the service's main source of passenger traffic, were by way of regularly scheduled trains stopping at Cobourg station with no special connections. Because of operating problems such as storms and ice during the winter months, passengers were carried only from May until September each year.

By 1912 traffic levels had reached such a level that a dividend of $12,000 was paid to each parent organization. Within two years *Ontario No. 1* was operating to capacity, resulting in the company placing an order for a second car ferry in 1914 with the Polson Iron Works at Toronto. The *Ontario No. 2* would cost $457,718.58.[12] At 5,568 gross tons, she was the largest vessel to operate on Lake Ontario in her day, becoming the flagship of the Ontario Car Ferry Company. *Ontario No. 2's* extra size permitted the ferry to carry an additional 200 passengers and two freight cars over *Ontario No. 1*, and with bigger engines, she also proved to be a steadier ship than her older sister.

The *Ontario No. 1* at her slip at Charlotte (Rochester), New York, around 1920. Both *Ontario No. 1* and *Ontario No. 2* had ample capacity for passengers as indicated by the number of lifeboats carried and the large cabin area. — *UBL No. 854*

This stern view of *Ontario No. 2* leaving Cobourg dates from 1927 and gives a good look at her stern pilot house, used in guiding the ship into its slip, as well as her open ended train deck. On all other car ferries of this type on the Great Lakes, sea-gates which could be raised or lowered into position, were used to prevent waves from breaking over the stern and flooding the train deck and lower decks. These gates were never used on the Ontario Car Ferry Company's two ships.
— *PAC PA-87722*

Delays during construction prevented *Ontario No. 2* from entering service until late 1915, when she made her first trip across Lake Ontario on September 15. As part of her sea trials she would return to the builder for the final finishing touches.

The year 1916 was the first full season in which service was provided by two car ferries. Not only did this double the line's freight capacity, it enabled passenger service to be increased as well, allowing a daily summer service, Sundays excepted, as the following schedule from the Grand Trunk timetable of 20 May 1916 illustrates:

ONTARIO CAR FERRY SERVICE

May 20th to June 29th	— Mondays, Thursdays and Saturdays
July 1st to Sept. 4th	— Daily except Sunday
Sept. 7th to Sept. 30th	— Mondays, Thursdays and Saturdays

Lv. Cobourg, Ont.	3:15 p.m.
Ar. Genesee Docks, N.Y.	8:00 p.m.
Ar. Rochester, N.Y. (B.R. & P. Ry.)	8:30 p.m.
Lv. Rochester, N.Y. (B.R. & P. Ry.)	8:30 a.m.
Lv. Genesee Docks, N.Y.	9:00 a.m.
Ar. Cobourg, Ont.	2:00 p.m.

On the whole, the ferries were fortunate when it came to storms and mishaps, but there is probably one storm that will always be remembered. On Sunday, 6 January 1924, a powerful winter storm swept Lake Ontario, whipping up the water into 20-foot waves and reducing visibility to zero in the blizzard conditions. When *Ontario No. 1* came out of the safety of Charlotte harbour on her regular run to Cobourg, the ship's captain soon realized that it would be impossible to reach Cobourg under such conditions and decided to try for Toronto instead. Throughout the afternoon and evening, the ship progressed slowly through the storm as giant waves broke over her bow and the spray froze in thick layers on the decks. Down below, water flooded into the hull through the train deck, threatening the vessel with foundering.

When Toronto was finally reached, it was 2 a.m. Monday morning and there was no let-up in the storm. With high winds preventing the ferry from entering the safety of Toronto Harbour, the captain pressed on to Port Credit, where he anchored to wait out the storm. After the storm had passed, *Ontario No. 1* limped back to Toronto to make repairs and pump out the hull. On Tuesday she left for Cobourg, where she arrived during the afternoon, two days late, much to the relief and joy of the townspeople who gathered to greet her.

Throughout its adventure, *Ontario No. 1's* progress was monitored by Captain C.H. Nicholson, the line's manager at Toronto, by way of wireless telegraph. As the first ship to be so equipped on the Great Lakes, she was further proof of the viability of radio for shipping.

During the storm, *Ontario No. 2* had been on her southbound run to Charlotte and was able to make port by Sunday evening.

The Ontario Car Ferry Company reached its peak during the 1920s, benefitting from the great financial upturn following the First World War. Seasonal totals reaching 70,000 passengers became commonplace and, in 1925 alone, 12,863 freight cars were ferried across the lake.[13] As a reflection of the rise of the automobile, motor cars carried on flatcars made their appearance by mid-decade, an extra service provided for those who preferred to drive. The motor cars were carried on railway flatcars because Genesee Dock lacked adequate roadway access. The true test of the line's success, however, was the profit it made, and there the company passed with flying colours. In 1929 the Ontario Car Ferry Company paid Canadian National (successor to the Grand Trunk) and the Buffalo, Rochester & Pittsburgh $75,000 each in dividend payments, three times that paid two years earlier, in 1925.[14]

Passenger traffic was very important during this period of the company's history, resulting in a four-day-a-week service during the off-season and a daily service during the summer months. Even Sunday service was offered, as shown in the following schedule from the 23 June 1929 Canadian National timetable:

ONTARIO CAR FERRY SERVICE
between
Cobourg, Ont. and Rochester, N.Y.

From May 30th to June 30th and Sept. 5th to Sept. 30th	Sundays Mondays Thursdays Saturdays
From July 1st to Sept. 2nd	Daily

Table No. 204

Lv. Cobourg, Ont. (Steamer)	3:15 p.m.
Ar. Genesee Dock, N.Y. (Steamer)	8:00 p.m.
Ar. Rochester, N.Y. (B.R. & P. Ry.)	8:30 p.m.
Lv. Rochester, N.Y. (B.R. & P. Ry.)	8:00 a.m.
Lv. Genesee Dock, N.Y. (Steamer)	8:35 a.m.
Ar. Cobourg, Ont. (Steamer)	1:35 p.m.

C.H. NICHOLSON, Manager, TORONTO, ONT.

The Buffalo, Rochester & Pittsburgh Railway took advantage of the good economic times to complete its purchase of the Charlotte Docks Company in January 1930, resulting in the railway gaining control of the Port of Rochester. With similar reasoning, the Baltimore & Ohio Railroad obtained permission from the Interstate Commerce Commission a month later to acquire a controlling interest in the Buffalo, Rochester & Pittsburgh, culminating on 1 January 1932 with the Baltimore & Ohio taking over all operations of the railway. It was an advantageous arrangement for all concerned, since the Buffalo, Rochester & Pittsburgh finally gained access to Pittsburgh itself, along with an assured source of traffic, while the Baltimore & Ohio gained access to the markets of Buffalo and Rochester as well as Canada through connecting railways and the Ontario Car Ferry Company.

Unfortunately the deal came right at the beginning of the Depression and traffic levels soon began to slide. In 1929 the ferries carried 786,195 tons of freight across Lake Ontario, of which 635,532 tons consisting chiefly of coal were brought to Canada and 150,663 tons made up of flour, feldspar, forest products and paper being returned to the United States. By 1933 that same traffic had plummetted to only 218,529 tons, with 197,208 tons carried north and only 21,321 tons moved south.[15]

Although there was a very slight recovery made during 1934, the ferry company had to wait until the outbreak of World War II before traffic levels returned to the volumes experienced during the twenties. Passenger traffic recovered modestly, reaching almost 50,000 annually during the war years, but it was in freight that the biggest gains were made. In 1945 the ferries transported 854,916 tons of freight, of which coal made up 601,073 tons. It was only temporary, for after the close of the war volumes fell to only 425,651 tons by 1949, with coal comprising only 192,773 tons.[16] From a small profit in 1945, the company reached an operating deficit of almost $200,000 by the end of the decade.

The drop in passenger traffic to only 22,000 in 1949 was a result of two contributing factors, the first and most important being the popularity of the automobile. The second factor was the cessation of boat trains between Genesee Dock and Rochester by the Baltimore & Ohio in 1942. With no direct connections, passenger traffic was discouraged.

The following table from the 25 November 1945 Canadian National timetable not only reflects the lack of a train connection at Genesee Dock (as shown by the elimination of Rochester as a destination), but also winter arrangements for freight:

ONTARIO CAR FERRY SERVICE
BETWEEN
COBOURG, ONT., and GENESEE DOCK (PORT OF ROCHESTER)
Subject to change without notice.

Ferries operate in freight service during winter months without definite schedule. Approximate times may be secured from Canadian National Railways Agent at Cobourg and Baltimore & Ohio Railroad Agents at Rochester or Genesee Dock, N.Y.

ONTARIO CAR FERRY CO. STEAMSHIP "ONTARIO"

Lv.	GENESEE DOCK, N.Y.	Ar.
Ar.	COBOURG, ONT.	Lv.

The above would be one of the last timetables released for the Ontario Car Ferry Company. With a high operating deficit in 1949 and declining traffic volumes, the company mothballed *Ontario No. 1* in August. In December the company filed to abandon service with the Interstate Commerce Commission, who granted permission soon afterward. On 30 April 1950 *Ontario No. 2* made her last voyage to Cobourg.

Both ships had reached the extent of their certification when they were withdrawn and with no possible traffic increases in the future, the Ontario Car Ferry Company could see little reason in making the necessary repairs (which were estimated at almost $1 million) to meet the certification requirements, especially after the *Noronic* disaster at Toronto in September 1949 caused the Canadian government to tighten standards even more.

As a result, *Ontario No. 1* was scrapped at Port Colborne in 1951, and in 1952 *Ontario No. 2* was broken up at Hamilton. The reign of the Ontario Car Ferry Company was over.

Incan Marine

Brief mention should be made of the recent car ferry operation of Incan Marine on Lake Superior. Incan Marine was formed as a joint venture between Canadian Pacific and the London (U.K.)-based Inchcape Group in 1972. In 1974 the company took delivery of two identical car ferries from Burrard Dry Dock of North Vancouver, British Columbia: *Incan Superior* and *Incan St. Laurant*. Each ship was diesel-powered and could carry up to 26 modern freight cars on five tracks.

The 3,838-ton *Incan Superior* was put into service on Lake Superior between Thunder Bay, Ontario, and Superior, Wisconsin, thus forming another link between Canadian Pacific and its Soo Line subsidiary south of the border. The *Incan St. Laurant* was built for service on the St. Lawrence, but as that service was cancelled before the ship was delivered, she spent her first two years on the Pacific coast. In 1977 the *Incan St. Laurant* was purchased by Canadian National Railways for service between the St. Lawrence River ports of Baie Comeau and Matane, Quebec, and subsequently renamed *Georges Alexandre Lebel*.

The Railway Coal Docks

When the railways were unable to import American coal by direct rail or by car ferry due to cost or location, they often resorted to the construction of specialized coal docks to handle coal received by freighter. With a few exceptions, the majority of Ontario's railway coal docks were located on Georgian Bay and Lake Superior.

What follows is a brief listing of the known railway coal-handling docks built in the province according to company (subsequent railway affiliations appear in parentheses) and location. A short description of each dock is included.

a) **ALGOMA CENTRAL RAILWAY**

Michipicoten Harbour: first dock built 1899, wooden general freight dock, two tracks, coal unloaded by small self-propelled railway cranes, coal-receiving function superseded by new coal dock in 1929; second dock built 1929-30, steel steam-powered coal bridge, dock face 550 feet long, storage capacity 100,000 tons, storage area and dock face doubled in mid-1930s, coal bridge removed 1960s.

Sault Ste. Marie: built 1914, steel electrically-powered coal bridge with 248-foot span, storage capacity 125,000 tons, dock area redeveloped 1970s.

b) **ALGOMA EASTERN RAILWAY (CPR)**

Little Current (Turner Yard): built 1913, steel steam-powered coal bridge, stockpile area approximately 700 feet long (increased to 1,100 feet in 1928) by 250 feet wide, bridge removed 1960s.

c) **CANADA ATLANTIC RAILWAY (GTR/CNR)**

Depot Harbour: built 1896, wood structure, archaic steam-powered mechanical dock, dock adjacent to grain elevator, coal dock removed by 1920s.

d) **CANADIAN NORTHERN RAILWAY (CNR)**

Key Harbour: some facilities may have been installed in 1905, harbour closed 1920s.

Port Arthur (Thunder Bay): built 1905, steel coal bridge and three steel unloaders, steam-powered mechanical transfer system, wooden trestles and storage structures, storage capacity 500,000 tons in the open and 160,000 tons under cover, owned by subsidiary Canadian Northern Coal & Ore Dock Company, sold 1920s.

e) **CANADIAN PACIFIC RAILWAY**

Fort William (Thunder Bay): first dock built circa 1885, five wooden coal bridges, possibly steam-powered, replaced in 1902 by new dock; second dock built 1902, steel Hulett-type unloaders and steel coal bridges, electrically-powered (assumed).

Prescott: built circa 1895, wooden structure, archaic mechanical dock, possibly removed by 1920s.

f) **LAKE ERIE & DETROIT RIVER RAILWAY (PMR)**

Erieau: built 1904, unloading accomplished with small self-propelled railway cranes.

Port Stanley: some bulk coal shipments may have been handled using small self-propelled railway cranes.

g) **TORONTO, HAMILTON & BUFFALO RAILWAY**

Port Maitland: built circa 1920, dock face 800 feet long (later extended to 1,000 feet), no specialized facilities known to have been employed (at time of writing).

Unloading coal the old-fashioned, manual way, at Depot Harbour about 1895 or 1896. The buckets and wheel barrows would be replaced within a few months by a mechanical unloader. The grain elevator is barely visible at the top of the photograph. — *OA Acc. 13098-50*

A view of the Depot Harbour elevator (right) and coal dock (left), dating from around 1908. The steamship *Ottawa* of the Canada Atlantic Transit Company is unloading grain, while behind it, an unidentified wooden freighter is unloading coal. — *OA S2543*

The Canadian Pacific Railway coal dock at Fort William on the Kaministiquia River around 1890. Five movable wooden coal bridges were utilized at the dock. The sizable stockpile of coal suggests that this photograph was taken in the late summer or autumn since such a large amount would be required for winter, when the navigation season was closed.
— *TBHMS 972.16.56*

Here is a close-up view of the Canadian Pacific coal dock at Fort William dated 10 May 1893, showing the results of an ice jam on the Kaministiquia River. The small hoppers and chutes for directing the coal into the railway gondola cars can be seen suspended from the coal bridges above the string of box cars. Note the complete absence of a stockpile.
— *TBHMS 972.2.77*

The Canadian Pacific built this modern coal dock at Fort William in 1902 to replace its earlier facilities. While the coal bridge, visible in the background, handled coal for the stockpile, the battery of twin Hulett unloaders were responsible for actually unloading the ships. In this view, the Huletts can be seen straddling the line of hoppers used in delivering coal to railway cars (at the time this photo was taken, the railway tracks had yet to be laid). The tug *Siskiwit* is probably the same tug that was once owned by the Canadian Pacific. The name of the freighter arriving at the dock appears to be *Peter P. Ramsey* or *Peter P. Hussey* (it is too blurred to be certain). — *TBHMS 975.85.67*

The Ontario Coal Dock was established at Sault Ste. Marie by the Algoma Central Railway and opened in 1914. With the exception of being electrically operated, the coal bridge itself was identical to the one built at Little Current by the Algoma Eastern, the Algoma Central's smaller sister railway. The Algoma Central Railway's stone, three-storey station can be seen below the bridge at the extreme left of the photograph. The freighter in this circa 1920 view is the *A. (?) Watson French* of Duluth; only its after holds remain unloaded. — *PAC PA-13064*

A close-up look at the business end of the steam-powered coal bridge at Michipicoten Harbour from the early 1930s. The freighter *W.J. Crosby* of Port Arthur had only recently docked at the commercial wharf and is preparing to take on a load of pulp-wood; meanwhile, a string of pulp-wood cars wait on the old ore dock approach for a locomotive to switch them to the commercial dock for transfer to the ship.

— *OA Acc. 10456 S16392*

In the mid-1930s the Algoma Central doubled the size of its coal dock by reclaiming land from the harbour. In this aerial photograph, the dock face has been extended while dredgers busy themselves scooping mud from the harbour bottom. The wooden pile dock jutting out from shore, sometimes referred to as the commercial dock, handled general cargo at the harbour including significant quantities of pulp-wood. Before the installation of the coal dock, the commercial dock handled all coal shipments to the harbour. For unloading from ships, the railway utilized small, self-propelled railway cranes equipped with clamshell buckets, discharging the coal directly into railway cars standing by on an adjacent track.

— *OA RG 1/E 13-3, 1*

These three unloaders marked the south end of the Canadian Northern coal dock. Steam-powered (the location of the steam plant is identified by the short brick smoke stack to the right of the unloaders), each was capable of independent movement on tracks mounted on top of the wooden trestle. The chute at the extreme left of the photograph (probably one of several) represents the only provision made for handling iron ore at the dock. In this view, the *James P. Walsh* waits its turn while the wooden freighter *Gringco* is unloaded. It should be noted that the horizontal booms of the unloaders were swung to the side when not in use, otherwise they would foul the masts of the ships.
— PAC PA-43412

The size of the Canadian Northern coal dock at Port Arthur is clearly demonstrated in this circa 1920 view looking northward. As can be seen, the steel coal bridge spanned the entire width of the dock. Note the small cable-hauled coal cars running atop the trestles on either side of the central railway tracks. *— PAC PA-21726*

CHAPTER SIX - NOTES

1) (J.B. Mansfield), *The Saga of the Great Lakes* (Toronto, 1980/Chicago, 1899), p. 294.
2) Ibid., p. 282.
3) W. Glen Curnoe, *The London & Port Stanley Railway, 1915-1965* (London, 1976), p. 2.
4) George W. Hilton, *The Great Lakes Car Ferries* (Berkeley, 1962)
5) William John Wilgus, *The Railway Interrelations of the United States and Canada* (Toronto, 1937), pp. 98 and 115.
6) George W. Hilton, op. cit.
7) Norman Helm, *In the Shadow of Giants* (Cheltenham, 1978), p. 32.
8) Ibid. pp. 102 and 97.
9) (J.B. Mansfield), op. cit., p. 270.
10) Ibid., p. 270.
11) George W. Hilton, op. cit., p. 238.
12) Ibid., p. 240.
13) Ibid., p. 243.
14) ibid., p. 243.
15) William John Wilgus, op. cit., p. 112.
16) George W. Hilton, op. cit., p. 244.

The Canadian Pacific coal bridge and dock at Little Current was originally opened in 1914 by the Algoma Eastern Railway to serve the Sudbury district. Although this postcard view dates from the mid-1930s, the construction activity in the foreground suggests that the original photograph may have actually been taken in 1928 when the Algoma Eastern expanded the dock. Canadian Pacific acquired the Algoma Eastern in 1930 and there is no information available to indicate that the Canadian Pacific ever carried out such construction. *— OA Acc. 6673 No. 149*

One of the earliest vessels built for the Royal Mail Line was the *Passport*, launched at Kingston in 1846. Renamed *Caspian* in 1898, she survived until 1921. — *OA Acc. 12026-3*

VII

NAVIGATION COMPANIES LARGE & SMALL

The railways have been served by a number of navigation companies over the years, often through informal arrangements. Presented here are several steamship lines of various descriptions which in their own way played a role in the railway history of Ontario.

The Independents

The railways represented a true threat to the shipping and navigation companies on Ontario's lakes and rivers, but in time both sides learned to live with each other and eventually to co-operate. This was particularly so with the passenger trade on Lake Ontario when early on it became evident that the steamers could not compete with the speed of the trains and, conversely, the trains could not compete with the relative luxury of the ships. Luckily for both sides, the tourist trade was beginning to take hold.

Thus the venerable Royal Mail Line, whose roots on Lake Ontario dated back to the early 1830s, transformed itself through mergers first into the Canadian Navigation Company in 1857 and finally the Richelieu & Ontario Navigation Company in 1875. At each step, its business became increasingly linked to the tourist trade, luring travellers by such scenic highlights as the Thousand Islands and the exciting passage down the St. Lawrence rapids to Montreal.

By the 1880s the Richelieu & Ontario was being given special mention in certain Grand Trunk Railway timetables as an added attraction for its passengers, beginning a friendly relationship that was to last into the Canadian National Railways era, when special boat trains were provided between Montreal and either Prescott or Brockville for westbound steamer passengers. Sadly, the steamer operations went into decline in the 1930s and ended entirely in 1950 when the paddle-steamer *Kingston (II)*, the last of the regular overnight Lake Ontario steamships, made her final run.

Another Lake Ontario concern was the Lake Ontario & Bay of Quinte Steamboat Company. Amongst the company's regular routes was its cross-lake service between Charlotte (Port of Rochester), New York, and Port Hope with the steamship *North King*. Extremely popular with Americans from the 1880s until the outbreak of World War I, it was a valuable summer feeder route for Grand Trunk trains heading north from Port Hope to Lindsay, Peterborough and Lakefield in the Kawartha Lakes district.

The Kawarthas themselves were well served by a multitude of small steamboats which reached the summer resorts and cottages. By about 1910 the Kawartha Lakes trade was dominated by four companies: Kawartha Lakes Navigation Company and Trent Valley Navigation Company, both of Lindsay; Stoney Lake Navigation Company of Lakefield; and Peterborough & Lake Simcoe Navigation Company of Peterborough. Stoney Lake Navigation was particularly attuned to the needs of its passengers and co-ordinated all of its arrivals and departures at Lakefield with those of the trains.

A similar situation could be found on the Muskoka Lakes. When the Northern Railway arrived at Muskoka Wharf near Gravenhurst in 1875, several steamers, largely controlled by A.P. Cockburn, were already in operation, and a small yet burgeoning tourist business was beginning to take hold. The railway promoted development and with the resulting prosperity A.P. Cockburn expanded to the Lake of Bays east of Huntsville and then to Lake Nipissing. In 1881 his fleet was incorporated as the Muskoka & Nipissing Navigation Company. The extension of the Northern Railway to North Bay, completed in 1886, allowed Cockburn to introduce steamers onto the Magnetawan River at Burk's Falls (these ships were sold in 1906).

Reincorporated as the Muskoka & Georgian Bay Navigation Company in 1886, Cockburn experimented with steamer operations on Georgian Bay. Failing success, he withdrew in 1893 to concentrate on his inland routes.

Following the opening of the company's Royal Muskoka Hotel on Lake Rosseau in 1902, the enterprise was again reincorporated in 1903 as the Muskoka Lakes Navigation & Hotel Company. By 1906 all of the navigation company's steamer routes were concentrated on the profitable Muskoka Lakes.

None of this would have been possible without the Northern's successor, the Grand Trunk Railway. Since the 1890s the Grand Trunk had provided special train service to Muskoka Wharf from Toronto, such that by the Canadian National era of the 1920s Muskoka Lakes Navigation could count on the arrival and departure of six daily trains at the wharf each summer. This was a remarkable situation considering that Muskoka Wharf was located at the end of a spur running off the main line south of Gravenhurst — certainly the railways would not have committed themselves to such an operational headache had it not been for the high traffic demand and profitability. Other railway-steamship transfer points of lesser importance on the Muskokas included Bala Park, Footes Bay and Lake Joseph/Dock Siding stations on Canadian National's Bala Subdivision (formerly the Canadian Northern main line), Bala station on the Canadian Pacific, and Bracebridge north of Gravenhurst.

The Depression and the motor car took their toll on the navigation company throughout the 1930s and 1940s, such that in 1956 the steamship line not only lost its mail contract but Canadian National ended all service to Muskoka Wharf. Lack of patronage and poor service ultimately led to the end of the steamship service in 1958. Of Muskoka Navigation's fleet, only the steamship *Segwun* survives and now provides summer excursions from Gravenhurst as the oldest operating steamship in North America — *Segwun's* iron hull originally belonged to the steamer *Nipissing II*, built in 1887.

North of Gravenhurst, the Huntsville & Lake of Bays Navigation Company, established in 1895, operated steamers throughout the Huntsville Lakes district until the 1950s. It too relied on its railway connections and during the 1920s could count on the arrival and departure of four Canadian National trains daily at Huntsville Dock during the summer season, in association with its ships. Once again tourism played a key role in the company's development.

Besides the steamships, the firm also ran the Huntsville & Lake of Bays Railway, a 1¼-mile narrow-gauge portage railway built in 1903 to link the company's steamers on the Lake of Bays with those on Peninsula Lake. As the shortest chartered railway in the world, the railway was a tourist attraction in its own right and outsurvived the steamships. The railway — engines, cars and track — was sold in 1961 and removed to Pinafore Park in St. Thomas, Ontario.

Unfortunately this short review of the independent steamship connections cannot do full justice to the important role they played in the province's railway and transportation history, nor does it cover all of the interconnecting railway-steamship operations. Their story must be left to another time and to other authors.

With a view to providing improved passenger accommodations and generally increase its fleet capacity, the Richelieu & Ontario took delivery of the *Toronto* in 1899 from the Bertram Shipyards of Toronto. The *Toronto* ran between Toronto and Prescott until 1938, calling at Rochester, New York, Kingston, and Brockville along the way. — *OA S8445*

In 1901 the *Kingston (II)*, another product of Bertrams' Shipyard, joined the *Toronto* on the Lake Ontario-St. Lawrence run. — *OA Acc. 12026-150*

Rebuilt in 1891 from the *Norseman* (built 1868), the *North King* was the mainstay of the Lake Ontario & Bay of Quinte Steamboat Company, known as the "Bay of Quinte Line". This photo shows the *North King* on Lake Ontario about the time of the First World War. The *North King* was sold to the Ontario Navigation Company in 1917 and was broken up five years later. — *OA S8436*

The paddle-steamer *Sunbeam*, built in 1891, was typical of many small, individually owned and operated steamers on the Kawartha Lakes. Photographed here in the 1890s, she was later sold and renamed *Alexandra*. By 1912, she was running as the *Arthur C.* under the ownership of the Kawartha Lake Navigation Company of Lindsay. — *OA Acc. 14390-7*

Stoney Lake Navigation Company's steamers *Empress* (left) and *Stoney Lake* (right) at the government wharf at Lakefield in 1909. — *OA Acc. 3685 S18028*

The *Manita* of the Trent Valley Navigation Company was built in 1900 at Kingston. Seen here at Lindsay (or possibly Bobcaygeon) in the early 1900s, she was sold to the Stoney Lake Navigation Company in 1911 and operated by them until 1944 when she was scrapped. — *OA Acc. 2839-23*

PETERBORO AND LAKE SIMCOE NAVIGATION COMPANY, LIMITED

KAWARTHA LAKES AND LAKE SIMCOE ROUTE

S. S. OTONABEE

Largest and Best Equipped Steamer on Minor Inland Waters, open for Excursions on waters from Barrie, Orillia and Jackson's Point, Lake Simcoe; all Kawartha Lake Ports, and Peterborough to Hastings, and Rice Lake Waters.

LAKE SIMCOE STURGEON LAKE STONEY LAKE RICE LAKE	OPERATING STEAMERS OTONABEE MANITA LINTONIA	 GENEVA WATER LILLY MONARCH	TRENT CANAL AND FAMOUS LIFT LOCK ROUTE

Connecting at Peterborough, Bobcaygeon and Lindsay with Canadian Pacific Railway Trains from Toronto, Buffalo, Detroit and all points East and West; and with Grand Trunk Railway Trains at Peterborough, Lakefield and Lindsay.

Apply at Office of the Company, Peterboro, for information as to routes and camping locations.

E. F. MASON,
President.

R. PINCHIN,
Sec'y and General Manager

Ad advertisement of World War I vintage for another Kawartha Lakes steamer company, the Peterborough & Lake Simcoe Navigation Company, based at Peterborough. Worth noting are the company's railway connections as well as its operating area — from Rice Lake all the way to Lake Simcoe. — *OA S2596*

It is thought that A.P. Cockburn was inspired by the *Emily May* on Lake Simcoe when he built the *Nipissing* in 1871. Initially able to carry 148 passengers, she was enlarged in 1877 to a capacity of 243 passengers. — *OA S3628*

Muskoka Navigation's (left to right) *Medora, Muskoka* and *Nipissing*. Since the *Muskoka* appears as rebuilt in 1895 and since the *Nipissing* burned in 1896, this photograph can be dated to either 1895 or 1896. — *OA S1875*

The Muskoka & Georgian Bay Navigation Company's paddle steamer *Wenonah II* on the Magnetawan River around 1900. The ship is about to pick up a group of deer hunters. — *OA S18100*

A postcard view of Muskoka Lakes Navigation Company's *Sagamo* at Woodington on Lake Rosseau dating from around 1910. *Sagamo* was the largest steamer afloat on fresh water in Canada, not including the Great Lakes.
— *OA Acc. 13889-21*

The first *Algonquin* at Huntsville Dock on Dominion Day 1918. The close proximity of the railway tracks to the steamer dock greatly facilitated the transfer of passengers, baggage and freight between the ships and trains.
— *PAC PA-71078*

A postcard seen from about 1910 depicting a train on the Huntsville & Lake of Bays Railway. Both steam engines owned by the company are shown but only one of the baggage cars and one of the passenger cars are included. As a matter of note, the passenger car has been fabricated by splicing together two horse cars purchased from Toronto.
— *OA Acc. 13889-14a*

The Brockville & Ottawa Railway

The search for lumber has spawned many a railway in Ontario and the Brockville & Ottawa Railway was no exception. Chartered in 1853, the company was authorized to build from Brockville, on the St. Lawrence River, northward to Pembroke and the timber regions along the Ottawa River by way of Smith's Falls, where a branch was projected to Perth. By the spring of 1854 construction had begun, but like many small ventures, money was hard to come by and it was not until 1859 that the railway was finally opened. Even then it had only reached as far as Smith's Falls and Perth, a mere 40 miles from Brockville and far from the Ottawa.

Some relief for the line did come as an amendment to the charter in 1855 allowing the company to sell more shares, but many investors, already worried about the shaky state of the Grand Trunk Railway at the time, would not touch the new issue, forcing the Brockville & Ottawa to place itself into ever-increasing debt. Though other parts of the amendment allowed the construction of additional branch lines, demonstrating a naive sense of optimism on the part of the directors, the only significant part of the new legislation was the government's permission for the railway to operate its own steamers on the Ottawa and St. Lawrence rivers.

The Brockville & Ottawa finally reached the Ottawa River by 1867, when the line was opened to Sand Point on Chats Lake. Since the ultimate goal was still far into the future — Pembroke would not be reached until 1876 — the railway saw fit to use its powers to operate steamships gained in 1855 to fill in the gap. The new 240-ton wooden steamer *Alliance* was launched by Powers Shipyard at Sand Point in 1866 and held the dubious distinction of being the railway's only steamship. One fact that the company failed to comprehend was that there were already two companies running competing steamers on Chats Lake and the entry of a new rival did nothing but heat up an already touchy situation. In no time the rivalry got red-hot and it soon grew out of control, until in 1868 the parties concerned came together to find a settlement to the intolerable situation, resolving to merge the three separate operations under one new company.

Exactly how the Brockville & Ottawa came out of the whole mess is unknown, for in 1869 the *Alliance* was still registered with the railway, suggesting that its ownership was not assumed by the new steamship operation. On the financial side, the government's total reorganization of the railway in 1868 largely overshadowed other events, including the steamship fiasco. It is possible that the *Alliance* was initially chartered to the new steamship line, but the fact that she was dropped from the insurance register by 1873 may mean that she was laid up permanently by this time. When the company's timetable appeared in the 1875 edition of the *Rand McNally Railway Guide*, no mention was made of the *Alliance*, only a simple entry indicating that connections could be made at Sand Point with steamers for Portage, DuFort, Pembroke and other points. Nevertheless, the *Alliance* would not finally be scrapped until 1882.

The Deseronto Navigation Company
The Thousand Islands Railway Company

The Ontario lumbering industry of the last century spawned many a successful enterprise, but few firms could match the record of the Rathbun Company of Deseronto. Led by Edward Rathbun, this family enterprise grew into a small empire, diversifying from their sawmill operations to found charcoal and chemical works, cement and terra cotta plants, a pig iron smelter and a flour mill.

To meet the transportation needs of the expanding company, the family began to build and acquire its own railways starting in 1881. In that year they chartered the Bay of Quinte Railway & Navigation to construct a line from Deseronto, on Lake Ontario's Bay of Quinte, five miles north to the Grand Trunk Railway at Deseronto Junction, just west of Napanee. This needed outlet for their products encouraged the family to further expand their railway interests in 1883, when the Napanee, Tamworth & Quebec Railway (later to become the Kingston, Napanee & Western Railway) was purchased, opening up the region north of Deseronto. The Thousand Islands Railway and the Oshawa Railway (an electric street railway) were also added, along with the establishment of the Rathbun's own car shops, which not only supplied equipment to their own lines but built

The Bay of Quinte Railway station at Deseronto was a beehive of activity, servicing the freight and passenger needs of both the railway and the Deseronto Navigation Company. In this view from the early 1900s, the steamer *Alexandria* of the Richelieu & Ontario Navigation Company is making a brief stopover at the station wharf. Meanwhile, Bay of Quinte locomotive Number 9 takes charge of a box car, pausing briefly while passengers leave the station. Engine 9, a 4-4-0, built by the Grant Locomotive Works of Paterson, New Jersey, in the 1870s, was acquired by the railway second-hand in the 1880s and as Canadian Northern Number 60, was retired in 1912. The large "Deseronto Station" sign (to the right of the box car) reads: "Bay of Quinte Railway trains make close connection at Deseronto Junction with Grand Trunk Railway for all points east and west." — *Deseronto Public Library*

Deseronto station and wharf as seen from the Bay of Quinte. The lighthouse atop the Deseronto Cold Storage Warehouse originally sat on top of the original station structure and was relocated when the warehouse was added in the 1890s. The two-storey warehouse itself incorporates part of the station building for about one-third to one-half of its length. The three-storey brick office building at the left was the Rathbun Company's headquarters and was erected in the mid-1880s; from it, the Rathbuns could survey the Deseronto waterfront which was dominated entirely by the various Rathbun-owned industries and enterprises. The steam barge tied alongside the wharf may have belonged to the Deseronto Navigation Company but its name cannot be deciphered, making positive identification difficult. It is not, however, the *Reliance*, the *Resolute*, or the *Norman*, all of which comprised the only steam barges known to have been owned by Deseronto Navigation. This station was superceded shortly before the First World War by a new Canadian Northern station erected on that railway's Toronto to Ottawa line which incorporated the Bay of Quinte Railway in its route. — *Lennox & Addington County Museum, Napanee*

Armenia (right), *Ella Ross* (centre), and an unidentified steam launch (left), pose for the camera in the late 1890s somewhere on the Bay of Quinte. Oldest of the two Deseronto Navigation steamers was the *Ella Ross*, having been launched at Montreal in 1873. Rebuilt in 1879 as the *Gypsy*, she was renamed *Ella Ross* in 1887, possibly when she was purchased by the company. *Armenia* was built at Picton in 1876 by A.W. Hepburn, assumingly for the Rathbun Company. While *Armenia* initially saw service running tri-weekly between Deseronto and Ogdensburg, New York, both ships probably were running strictly on the Bay of Quinte by the 1890s. *Armenia* was broken up in 1905 while the *Ella Ross* was sold about 1907 and burned five years later at Parry Sound. — *LACM No. 1574*

work, passenger, freight and streetcars for many other railway and traction companies.

As important as the railway operations were to the Rathbun organization, water transport proved to be the mainstay in moving their lumber products for many years. Since the 1860s a great deal of Rathbun lumber was shipped to the United States, all lumber being sent by boat across Lake Ontario, but it may not have been until 1868 that the company began to assemble its own fleet. It was during that year that a yard was established at Oswego, New York, for the receipt of lumber from Deseronto for transshipment to New York City by way of the Oswego Canal or by railway, the New York & Oswego Midland Railroad (later the New York, Ontario & Western) becoming the main railway route. It is worth noting that by the 1890s, 60 percent of all vessels calling at Oswego were Canadian, many taking on coal, while others, such as the Rathbun ships, delivered lumber.

It was to the company's advantage to own their own ships for service on Lake Ontario, just as smaller tugs and "alligators" (steam-powered, shallow-draught lumbering boats capable of hauling themselves over dry land, a process known as "warping") had been used to bring logs down to the mill by river. Soon the steamers started to arrive at Deseronto, including some built by the Rathbuns at their own shipyard. Passenger and freight steamers, tugs and barges were all needed and by the time the Deseronto Navigation Company was formed to oversee the operation of the ships in 1880, the roster included seven major steamers, a number of tugs and barges as well as the alligators.

Under the Deseronto Navigation Company, the Rathbun fleet on Lake Ontario was in effect divided into two distinct segments, the passenger division and the freight division. The freight division, by the 1890s, was firmly entrenched with "freight lines between the Bay of Quinte and Charlotte, Oswego, Sodus Point, Fairhaven, Cape Vincent, Clayton and Ogdensburg, N.Y., with reliable steam transport, competent tugs, barges and powerful steam barges."[1] Connections with the Bay of Quinte Railway were available at Deseronto, although most of the freight probably originated from or was destined for Deseronto or other Bay of Quinte ports.

The passenger division was not as far-reaching as the freight line, the vast majority of passenger steamers being concentrated on the Bay of Quinte trade with two routes being offered. By far the most popular service was that operated between Napanee, Deseronto and Picton (see table 7-1), with three trips each way daily (two trips each way to Napanee) made by the company's Royal Mail steamers. One trip each day was provided from Picton to Trenton by way of Belleville, Deseronto and other smaller Bay of Quinte ports (see table 7-2).

Table 7-1
DESERONTO NAVIGATION COMPANY
NAPANEE, DESERONTO AND PICTON STEAMER SERVICE
1893

Napanee	Lv.	6:00 a.m.	...	3:30 p.m.
Deseronto	Lv.	7:00 a.m.	1:00 p.m.	5:00 p.m.
Picton	Ar.	8:30 a.m.	2:30 p.m.	6:30 p.m.
Picton	Lv.	8:30 a.m.	9:00 a.m.	3:00 p.m.
Deseronto	Lv.	10:30 a.m.	11:00 a.m.	5:00 p.m.
Napanee	Ar.	11:30 a.m.	...	6:00 p.m.

Source: *Travelers' Official Guide*, June 1893, p. 64.

Table 7-2
DESERONTO NAVIGATION COMPANY
TRENTON, BELLEVILLE, DESERONTO AND PICTON
STEAMER SERVICE
1893

Read Down					Read Up	
P.M.	A.M.				P.M.	P.M.
3:00	6:00	Lv.	Picton	Ar.	2:30	6:30
3:30	6:30		Thompson's		...	...
...	...		Cole's		...	...
...	...		Barnhart's		...	...
5:00	7:15		Deseronto		1:00	5:00
P.M.					P.M.	
	...		Cronk's			...
	...		Brant's			...
	8:15		Northport			4:00
	8:30		Big Island			3:45
	10:00		Belleville			3:00
	10:45		Rednersville			1:45
	11:30	Ar.	Trenton	Lv.		1:00
	A.M.					P.M.

Source: *Travelers' Official Guide*, June 1893, p. 64.

As home port, Deseronto's main steamer dock received a lot of attention from company officials and served not only as the navigation company's terminal but also as the railway station, resulting in a large and impressive structure. Constructed around 1881, the wood-and-fill dock was built out into the water, on top of which a combination railway station and freight warehouse was erected. With the building completely covering the tracks, passengers and freight could be transferred between the trains and the steamers no matter the weather. Later on the dock was extended by the addition of a cold storage warehouse to its outer end.

When the Rathbun fortunes took a down turn at the turn of the century, it was only a matter of time before the various components were sold off or closed. In 1910 control of the Bay of Quinte Railway passed into the hands of William Mackenzie and Donald Mann, in effect the Canadian Northern Railway. The Grand Trunk had its turn in 1911 when it purchased the Oshawa Railway and the Thousand Islands Railway from the Rathbuns, taking the last vestiges of the Rathbun railway empire.

Likewise, the Deseronto Navigation Company went into decline, but in this case there were no buyers. Small steamboat companies were no longer viable in the face of the larger navigation companies and railway competition, and it was left to the Rathbun Company to dissolve the Deseronto line ship by ship, year by year, until, by the close of the First World War, little remained.

Table 7-3
PRINCIPAL STEAMSHIPS OF THE
DESERONTO NAVIGATION COMPANY
1872-1920

Vessel	Built (Rebuilt)	Period Owned/Operated
AMERICA	1871 (1894)	-1920
ARMENIA	1876	1876-1905
COMET	1887	1887-
DESERONTO		
EMMA MUNSON		
GYPSY	1873 (1879)	1879-1887
- ELLA ROSS		1887-1907
NORMAN	1872	1872-1883

Two of the last vessels owned by the Deseronto Navigation Company were the *Varuna* (left) and the *America* (right), photographed here at Napanee around 1910. *Varuna*, built in 1880 at Picton, Ontario, served the company until 1920 when she was scuttled on Lake Ontario — the longest serving steamer in the fleet. *Varuna*'s relatively small size reflected her role as a Bay of Quinte passenger steamer, contrasting markedly with the *America*, one of the company's largest steamers, having been acquired around 1905. At the time this photo was taken, the *America* was probably operating to American ports on Lake Ontario and the St. Lawrence, explaining the presence of the American flag at her bow.

— *PAC C-45408*

Deseronto Navigation's *America* had a long and interesting history. She was first built in 1871 as the *Maude* by ship-owner Charles H. Gildersleeve at Kingston as a paddle-wheeler. Sold by her owner around 1894, she was rebuilt in that year as the *America*, pictured here. At this point, her actual ownership is unclear, but it is probable that it was a New York state company operating as the New York & St. Lawrence Steamboat Line. This company owned another steamer, the *St. Lawrence*, built in 1884, which operated out of Cape Vincent, New York, serving the vacation resorts of the Thousand Islands of the St. Lawrence. As rebuilt, the *America* appeared quite similar to the *St. Lawrence*. By the early 1900s, the *America* had been sold to the Deseronto Navigation Company with the only subsequent alterations being the relocation of the lifeboats to the next deck below. *America* was sold one last time in 1920. Renamed *Midland City*, she was taken to Georgian Bay and was later rebuilt with a diesel engine and screw propeller. She was scrapped in 1955. In this photograph, we see *America* departing one of the many St. Lawrence River resorts about 1900.

— *OA S8453*

PILGRIM		
QUINTE	1871	1882-1889
REINDEER		
RELIANCE	1881	1881-c.1912
RESCUE		
RESOLUTE	1883	1883-
ROCKET		
VARUNA	1880	1880-1920

Before leaving the Rathbun's entirely, it should be mentioned that the Thousand Island Railway also operated a steamer service, in this instance a steam ferry running between Gananoque and Clayton, New York, by way of the Thousand Islands. Whether or not the steamer or steamers used belonged to the railway directly or to the Deseronto Navigation Company is unclear, as is their identity. Odds are that only one steamer was in service at any one time, for the crossing of the St. Lawrence River was relatively short and the volume of passengers carried modest. After the Grand Trunk took control of the Thousand Islands Railway in 1911, any ferry service offered was provided by a privately owned steamer.

The decline of the lumber-oriented Rathbun Company was almost inevitable, for despite all attempts at diversification, all subsidiaries were primarily developed to serve or to supplement the lumber business. When the supply of timber from the regions around Deseronto ran out, the company had to go farther afield and bring logs in by train, but the supply was never enough. In 1916 the Deseronto mill was closed, with the Rathbun Company Limited officially being dissolved seven years later.

The Whitby & Port Perry Extension Railway
The Whitby, Port Perry & Lindsay Railway

The only railway-owned steamships to operate in the Kawartha Lakes region (excluding Rice Lake and the lower Otonabee River) were those of the Whitby & Port Perry Extension Railway Company, incorporated in March 1874 to link the newly completed Whitby & Port Perry Railway at Port Perry on Lake Scugog with Lindsay. Since it would take a few years to build the railway, the company purchased the steamers *Ogemah*, built in 1852, and the 191-ton *Victoria*, built in 1867, to provide a temporary lake service between Port Perry and Lindsay and Bobcaygeon.

For the 1874 season the railway offered the following steamer arrangements:[2]

Whitby and Port Perry Extension Railway
and Steamers
"OGEMAH" and "VICTORIA"

---

commencing Monday, May 18th, 1874,
Steamer "Ogemah"
(Captain C. Dawes)
will make a Daily Connection between
LINDSAY & PORT PERRY

Leaving Lindsay every morning (Sundays excepted) at 7 o'clock, calling at Port Hoover at 9:30 a.m., and arriving at Port Perry at 11 o'clock a.m., connecting with trains for Whitby, where connections will be made with G.T. trains East and West.

Returning will leave Port Perry every day at 1 o'clock p.m., connecting at Lindsay with Midland Railway trains North and South.

The steam barge *Resolute* was launched by the Rathbun Company at Deseronto in 1883 with a gross tonnage of 336 tons. Four years later, she was enlarged to 372 gross tons and rebuilt into the configuration as seen in this view of her. The *Resolute*'s construction followed by two years that of the *Reliance*, a 221-gross-ton steam barge, also built by the Rathbuns. Similar in appearance, they differed chiefly in the location of the wheelhouse — *Reliance*'s being located on top of the aft cabins, *Resolute*'s being located on the forecastle. Since both had similar octagonal wheelhouses, it is possible that the *Resolute*'s wheelhouse was relocated to the bow at the time of the ship's 1887 rebuilding. Both the *Reliance* and the *Resolute* provided freight service between Deseronto and Lake Ontario ports, following in the wake of the steam barge *Norman* which burned in 1883. This turn of the century photo was probably taken at Midland (an unusual port of call for a Rathbun boat, if indeed she was still under Rathbun ownership). It would be interesting to know why the lifeboat has been hung from the short mast at the centre of the ship. Wrecked in November 1906, *Resolute* was rebuilt in the following year as the *John Rolph*. She was broken up in the 1920s.

— *OA Acc. 2375 S5263*

The Whitby & Port Perry steamer *Victoria*, built in 1867. Aside from passenger service, she was often employed towing scows loaded with sawn lumber destined for the United States by way of the railway and Lake Ontario. — *OA S17887*

The Whitby & Port Perry's steamers *Ogemah* (left) and *Victoria* (right) together with two scows, photographed on one of the Kawartha Lakes in the early to mid-1870s. *Ogemah* was destroyed by fire in 1876 while *Victoria* may have survived until the second decade of this century. — *OA S12814*

A postcard view of Port Perry station from the turn of the century. The grain elevator is on the left, just behind the station, while Lake Scugog is to the right. The locomotive was typical of the Grand Trunk's branch line stock. — *OA S12820*

Tickets

Lindsay to Toronto	$2.00
Lindsay to Port Perry	1.00
Lindsay to Port Perry and Return	1.50
Lindsay to Port Hoover	.50
Port Perry to Port Hoover	.50
Return Tickets from Port Perry to Port Hoover	.75

Tickets can be obtained in Toronto at the GTR Station.

Pleasure Parties and Season Tickets at Reduced Rates.
Parties going by this route will please get Tickets from Agents.

STEAMER "VICTORIA"
(Captain G.W. Rose) will ply between Lindsay, Fenelon Falls and Bobcaygeon.
Through Freights from Montreal and Toronto at Low Rates.

The Port Whitby & Port Perry Railway, which at this time was separate from the extension railway, ran two trains each way per day similar to the following outline from the 1875 *Rand McNally Railway Guide*: "Trains leave Whitby Junction on the Grand Trunk Railway, 30 miles east of Toronto, for Whitby (pop. 2,732) on the north shore of Lake Ontario, 1 mile; Brooklin, (pop. 1,000) 6 miles; Manchester, (pop. 350) 15 miles; Prince Albert, (pop. 1,500) 17 miles; and Port Perry, (pop. 2,000) 19 miles, northern terminus at 9:00 a.m. and 7:23 p.m., arriving at Port Perry 10:30 a.m., and 8:53 p.m. Returning, leave Port Perry 6:30 a.m., and 1:00 p.m., arriving at Whitby Junction at 7:30 a.m. and 2:30 p.m."

Assuming that the 1874 and the 1875 railway schedules were identical (which is probably the case), the connections between the trains and the steamers at Port Perry were by no means close, but they were at least convenient.

In 1876 the Port Whitby & Port Perry Railway and the Whitby & Port Perry Extension Railway were merged to form the Whitby, Port Perry & Lindsay Railway Company, and within a year the railway was completed to Lindsay. The amalgamation of the two companies included the steamers *Ogemah* and *Victoria*, which continued to operate throughout the 1876 season. Late in the year, however, the *Ogemah* caught fire and burned on November 6, leaving the *Victoria* as the railway's sole remaining ship. After the railway was opened to Lindsay, there was no longer any need for a Port Perry to Lindsay steamer service, and it is therefore probable that after a short period on the route in 1877 the *Victoria* was returned to her regular run between Lindsay, Fenelon Falls and Bobcaygeon. This assumption is borne out by the fact that the *Victoria* was reported as having burned at Bobcaygeon in March 1884. After that time there is some question as to her fate. One source states that the *Victoria* was subsequently rebuilt as the *Esturion* and another states that she had been retired since 1882, when she was burned.

Nevertheless, as late as 1912 the *Victoria* was registered to the Whitby & Port Perry Railway Company, by which time the railway had passed into Grand Trunk control; it is not likely that an extinct ship would have remained on the official registers for that length of time.

Canadian Northern Steamships, Limited

Although it seems strange to include two North Atlantic liners in a history of Ontario railway shipping, an exception must be made for the Canadian Northern.

The Canadian Northern Railway was originally projected as a complete transportation system along the lines of the Canadian Pacific, with a transcontinental railway linked to the four corners of the world by large, sleek passenger liners. Unfortunately too much optimism and too little funding prevented the company's plans from being fulfilled on all oceans but the Atlantic, for which Canadian Northern Steamships, Limited, was chartered on 21 October 1909, with headquarters at the railway's head office in Toronto.

By good fortune, two ships built for the British-owned Egyptian Mail Steamship Company for service between Marseille, France, and Alexandria, Egypt, became available when that company went bankrupt in 1909. The ships were the 11,117-ton *Cairo* and the 11,146-ton *Heliopolis*, both constructed by the Fairfield Shipbuilding & Engineering Company at Govan, Scotland, in 1907, and while small by North Atlantic standards, they were barely two years old, almost new, and were capable of speeds over 20 knots. Removing them from service on the Mediterranean for the North Atlantic trade required the ships to be modified for the colder climate, and it was not until 1910 that they took up their new route, patriotically named *Royal Edward* (formerly *Cairo*) and *Royal George* (formerly *Heliopolis*) with home port at Toronto! In reality the liners never even saw Toronto, but since the steamship line was based in Toronto, Toronto was the most convenient port of registry.

Known as the "Royal Line," the Canadian Northern steamers were placed in service between Montreal and Avonmouth, England, during the summer months, switching the Canadian port to Halifax during the winter, when the St. Lawrence was frozen over. Business was brisk, especially with the flow of immigrants to Canada, and soon a third ship was contemplated. But it was never to be, for the outbreak of the First World War halted almost all immigrant traffic.

Shortly after hostilities commenced in August 1914, *Royal Edward* and *Royal George* were requisitioned by the Admiralty and were quickly converted to troopships. Just over a year later, on 13 November 1915, the *Royal Edward* was sunk by a German torpedo in the Aegean Sea. Almost 1,500 troops were on board at the time, and 200 were lost.

The *Royal George* was luckier, for she was sold to the Cunard Line on 10 May 1916, with the Canadian Northern Railway and Cunard agreeing to co-operate in all future service on the Atlantic and Pacific oceans. *Royal George* then took up a new route between New York and Liverpool or Southampton but was laid up in 1920 and scrapped in 1922 when Cunard deemed that she was not up to their standards — *Royal Edward* and *Royal George* were well known for their excessive rolling.

So ended the careers of two ships, not only among the few ocean liners ever to be registered under the Canadian flag, but also, so far as is known, the only two ocean liners ever to be registered at Toronto, a port they never even saw.

The London & Port Stanley Railway

One of Ontario's pioneer railways, the London & Port Stanley, was opened in 1856 between Port Stanley on Lake Erie and London by way of St. Thomas in order to provide that region with access to the Great Lakes and encourage development. Unlike the other railways then under construction, however, the London & Port Stanley received most of its capital from the local municipalities along the line and especially the City of London, which provided the lion's share and later went on to acquire complete control. The fact that the company never grew into a major money-maker was of no concern to them, for opening up the region and providing the Grand Trunk and Great Western railways with some competition was their main goal.

As it turned out, freight volumes on the line were surprisingly low, for the two major trunk lines tended to take most of the freight originating out of St. Thomas and London, leaving small amounts of agricultural produce and related freight for the London & Port Stanley.

It was no wonder, therefore, that Port Stanley failed to grow into a major harbour despite the railway. Even so, the harbour held some importance — construction began there in 1854 and most of the equipment and construction materials had to come in by ship. On 1 October 1859 control of

The "Royal Line" steamship *Royal Edward* as she appeared around 1910. — *PAC PA-49819*

The *Royal George* arriving at Bristol, England, shortly before the First World War. The *Royal George* and the *Royal Edward* were the only ocean liners ever to be registered at Toronto. — *PAC C-49597*

the port passed from the government to the railway on the condition that any tolls collected would be put towards the repair and improvement of the harbour.[3] Strangely enough, this was the turning point for passenger traffic on the railway. Ideally located on Lake Erie, with excellent beaches, Port Stanley held the potential of becoming a popular tourist attraction. Once this fact was recognized by the railway's management, the excursion business sent passenger volumes soaring, and by the mid-1860s passenger revenue almost equalled that of freight.

Much of the excursion business's success can be attributed to the railway's establishment of a "pleasure park" which remained popular until the 1950s, but an unknown factor was the railway's entry into the steamer business. In 1865 or 1866 the London & Port Stanley Railway purchased its first steamship, the 342-ton *Georgian*, built by the Potter Shipyard at Machedash on Georgian Bay for J.C. Graham of Toronto in 1864. In all probability, as either a passenger or a passenger-and-freight steamer, *Georgian* provided excursion trips out onto Lake Erie as well as regular services to American ports on the opposite shore.

Not long after the *Georgian* arrived, the Shickluna yards at St. Catharines launched the 361-ton *City of London* for the London & Port Stanley. As with the *Georgian*, it can only be assumed that the *City of London* ran excursion trips on Lake Erie along with regular journeys to the United States, for there is no hard evidence to the contrary. In 1875 the railway noted that steamer connections for Buffalo and Cleveland could be had at Port Stanley, but the ships would not have belonged to the company, for both the *Georgian* and the *City of London* had been sold by this time.

The most logical explanation for the disposal of the two ships may lay with the financial difficulties experienced by the company in the early 1870s, which ultimately resulted in the lease of the London & Port Stanley to the Great Western Railway in September 1872. It was probably around this time that the *Georgian* and the *City of London* were sold by the railway in an attempt to come up with some extra cash.

Of the two ships, the *City of London* had the shorter career. Sold to a Mr. Johnson of Port Stanley, she met her fate in August 1874 when fire broke out on board while at Colins Inlet, Georgian Bay, destroying the entire vessel.

Georgian was a little more fortunate, but just barely. In 1873 *Georgian* was serving the firm of Burgess & Company, and while docked at Ogdensburg, New York, in July she experienced considerable fire damage. She resumed her duties following some heavy repair work. A decade later *Georgian* was working for the Canadian Pacific as a supply ship during the construction of that railway around Lake Superior.

Following the sale of the *City of London* and the *Georgian*, the London & Port Stanley Railway made no further adventures onto the lakes. Port Stanley harbour, however, continued to be operated and maintained by the company more for the benefit of local fishermen and boat owners than the railway, for it would not be until 1898, when the Lake Erie & Detroit River Railway, London & Port Stanley leasee since 1893, was able to bring the railway ferry *Shenango No. 1* and the passenger steamer *Urania* to Port Stanley, that the harbour once again became a true railway port.

Nevertheless, excursion steamers continued to make frequent trips to Port Stanley, especially during the summer. For American vacationers from Cleveland and Erie across the lake, Port Stanley was an attractive destination on weekends and, joined by excursionists from London and St. Thomas, they guaranteed crowded beaches. The heyday of Port Stanley's fame, though, probably came after electrification, when the railway erected a large number of buildings (many to replace older structures) to serve the multitudes. During the heady days following the First World War, visits by steamships such as the steel sidewheeler *State of Ohio* were commonplace.

State of Ohio was owned by the Cleveland & Buffalo Transit Company (the C & B Line) and in partnership with sistership *State of New York* (superseded by the *City of Buffalo* in 1896), she provided regular overnight accommodations between Buffalo and Cleveland during the 1890s. By the twenties railway competition had forced the ships off their former route and the C & B Line made great inroads into the excursion trade as the Cleveland, Port Stanley, Cedar Point & Put In Bay Steamship Line. While Cleveland and Port Stanley are probably well known to readers by this time, it should be noted that Cedar Point and Put In Bay were vacation spots lying along the south shore of Lake Erie. In 1813 Put In Bay figured prominently in the Battle of Lake Erie during the war of 1812, giving it historic appeal as well.

The *City of London*, built at St. Catharines in 1866, was the second steamship acquired by the London & Port Stanley Railway. This photograph reveals a freshly painted, if not new, *City of London* possibly at St. Catharines or at Port Stanley. The initials "N.S.T.Co.", however, pose a question of ownership. Presumed to stand for "North Shore Transportation (or Transit) Company", was this the name of a London & Port Stanley Railway subsidiary (the registers indicate only the railway proper as owner in the late 1860s), was it a subsequent owner (a Mr. Johnson of Port Stanley is believed to be the only owner following the vessel's sale by the London & Port Stanley), or was it a previous owner (taking into account its very new appearance)? Two points worth noting on the vessel are the beaver figure mounted on top of the octagonal wheelhouse and the white ensign of the Royal Navy at the stern. Note also the schooner behind the *City of London* in the process of being rigged. — *UWO*

In later years, steamers of various companies made calls at Port Stanley, particularly after the railway turned the beaches of Port Stanley into a popular summer attraction. A regular visitor by the end of the First World War was the steamer *State of Ohio* of the Cleveland & Buffalo Transit Company's Cleveland, Port Stanley, Cedar Point & Put In Bay Steamship Line. The *State of Ohio*, along with her identical sister *State of New York* pictured here in the early 1900s, was built in 1882 for the Detroit & Cleveland Navigation Company as the *City of Mackinac* (the *State of New York* being originally called the *City of Alpena*). Both of these ships were made redundant and subsequently were sold in 1892 by the Detroit & Cleveland to its Cleveland & Buffalo affiliate. Later replaced by newer vessels, the *State of New York* eventually was sold back to the Detroit & Cleveland. The *State of Ohio*, however, remained with the Cleveland & Buffalo Transit Company, taking on a new role as an excursion steamer based out of Cleveland, becoming in essence the Cleveland, Port Stanley, Cedar Point & Put In Bay Steamship Line, making regular summer trips to Port Stanley. — *OA Acc.2713- 9*

The paddle steamer *Urania* was acquired by the Lake Erie Navigation Company as the *Flora* in 1898 and was placed into service between Erieau and Port Stanley, Ontario, and Cleveland, Ohio, in connection with the company's parent, the Lake Erie & Detroit River Railway. When sufficient passenger traffic failed to materialize, the *Urania* was sold back into American hands, becoming the *Flora* once again. This view of the *Flora* probably dates from around 1910. — *UBL No. 890*

The Lake Erie Navigation Company

The Lake Erie & Detroit River Railway, acquired by the Michigan-based Pere Marquette Railway in 1903, entered the Lake Erie steamship trade in 1898 (the year in which the Erie & Huron Railway, controlling the harbour at Erieau, was purchased) when the Lake Erie Navigation Company was chartered as an operating subsidiary. The first vessel acquired was the 899-ton passenger steamer *Flora*, a Lake Michigan veteran built in 1875. Upon arriving in Canada in 1898, she was immediately registered as the *Urania* and soon after took up her regular route between Erieau and Port Stanley, Ontario, and Cleveland, Ohio.

Passenger traffic could not have met with expectations, however, for in 1908 the *Urania* was sold back to American interests. The odds are that better connections could be had elsewhere.

Lake Erie Navigation remained dormant until 1927, when the Pere Marquette, anticipating the withdrawal of the Marquette & Bessemer's car ferry and collier, through which the railway imported its coal into Ontario, reactivated the company with the purchase of the 5,700-ton bulk carrier *H.A. Rock*. Renamed the *Alexander Leslie*, after a railway official, the freighter's acquisition assured the railway of a direct supply of coal for several years to come.

The *Alexander Leslie* was sold in the 1940s or 1950s and survived until 1969, when she was scrapped while under the ownership of the Norlake Steamship Company of Toronto.

The Lake Erie Navigation Company, Limited, was officially dissolved on 2 January 1970 after years of inactivity.

The *Alexander Leslie* was built in 1901 by the American Shipbuilding Company at Cleveland, Ohio, as the *J.T. Hutchinson*. While under American ownership, she was renamed *H.A. Rock* in 1923 and as such was acquired by Lake Erie Navigation in 1927 and rechristened *Alexander Leslie* under Canadian registry. Here she is shown downbound at Sault Ste. Marie with a cargo of pulpwood in 1929. Because the car ferry *Marquette & Bessemer No. 2 (II)* was not taken out of service until 1932, the *Alexander Leslie* was employed as a general freight carrier for several years, an advantage not held by the typical railway car ferry. — *PAC PA-145812*

Lake Simcoe and the Northern Railway

In chapter two the story of the Northern Railway's ventures on the Great Lakes was related, but Frederick Cumberland and the Northern did not just concern themselves with shipping on those waters alone. Lake Simcoe, with its various ports, also showed to be a potential source of traffic for the company. In 1853 the only steamer on Lake Simcoe was the 150-ton *Morning*, owned by Charles Thompson, a well-known Yonge Street stagecoach operator. Cumberland therefore recommended that the Northern purchase the *Morning* along with the docking facilities at Bradford and Orillia in order to secure the lake traffic for the railway. As Bradford was located on the Holland River some distance south of Lake Simcoe, Frederick Cumberland felt that the navigation season could be extended by establishing a new southern terminal for the Lake Simcoe service at what became Belle Ewart, completed in May 1854. Located on a branch line 1½ miles from the main-line station of Lefroy, Cumberland wrote of Belle Ewart in July 1854: "The right-of-way and a terminus of five acres was secured free, and the line, together with a steamboat pier, station and freight building have been constructed and are now in full operation."[4]

The Northern's Lake Simcoe steamship service commenced out of Bradford in 1853 with the newly acquired *Morning* serving such communities as Barrie, Orillia, Beaverton, Sutton and Keswick, all of which were without railway service at the time. The combined rail-and-water route provided the local residents with an inexpensive and comfortable way of travelling to Toronto. In May 1854 Belle Ewart became the main transfer point for the railway, replacing Bradford as the Northern's principal Lake Simcoe port.

Despite operating losses incurred on the Lake Simcoe service, the railway built a second 150-ton steamer in 1854, named the *J.C. Morrison* in honour of the president of the railway. In describing the ship, one newspaper wrote of her: "She has a very fine figurehead of the worthy gentleman himself, beautiful carving, gilded china and a piano on board. She cost $17,000 and is a failure. She is not safe in a gale and last summer she hardly earned enough to pay a cook."[5]

In 1857, the railway advertised that the *J.C. Morrison* "will leave Belle Ewart daily at 10 a.m. on arrival of trains and on Monday, Wednesday, and Friday run up the West side of the Lake, and return on the East side. On Tuesday, Thursday, and Saturday, up the East and down the West side."[6]

Excursion tickets were available for $3, which entitled the ticket-holder to a round trip from Toronto, around Lake Simcoe, and return, good for two days.

Built in 1849 by stagecoach operator Charles Thompson, the *Morning* was the first steamboat on Lake Simcoe. Acquired by the Northern Railway in 1853, she served until 1862.
— *MTL T-16233*

Lady of the Lakes and Barrie station as they appeared in the late 1870s. — *OA Acc. 12026-53*

The Huntsville, Lake of Bays & Lake Simcoe Navigation Company's steamship *Enterprise* at the Barrie station wharf at the turn of the century. The railway tracks in the foreground belong to the former Northern Railway main line (now Canadian National) from Toronto to North Bay and are still in active use. This photograph shows how the tracks hugged the western end of Kempenfeldt Bay from Allandale northward past Barrie. Note how the steamer wharf has been expanded since the time the previous picture showing the *Lady of the Lakes* was taken. — *OA Acc. 12026-51*

Like her Great Lakes counterparts in Northern Railway service, the *J.C. Morrison* was not a money-maker, and just at a time when the railway company was ready to abandon its Lake Simcoe steamship services, "the Lake Simcoe problem solved itself," as Col. G.R. Stevens put it. On 5 August 1857 the ship burned to the waterline. Five years later the *Morning* was lost, temporarily ending the Northern's monopoly of the Lake Simcoe trade.

A successor to the *Morning* and the *J.C. Morrison* was the privately owned *Emily May.* Built in 1861 by Captain H. Chisholm at Belle Ewart, the 181-ton *Emily May* was the largest steamer ever to sail Lake Simcoe, and through most of her life enjoyed an almost total monopoly of the trade. Providing the same service as that formerly offered by the Northern Railway's steamers, she was also a popular excursion boat, being frequently chartered. The *Emily May's* apparent success seemed to be too good to be true in light of the railway's failure, sparking the interest of the Northern's management. The result was the purchase of the ship by the company in 1874, rechristening her the *Lady of the Lakes*. By the late 1870s, however, freight and passenger traffic on the lake was on the decline and profits once again became scarce. By 1879 she was running mainly between Orillia and the nearby Atherly Narrows, finally being abandoned at Belle Ewart in 1883. She was the last of the Northern Railway's steamers.

By this time the Northern no longer held a monopoly on Lake Simcoe, and several steamships (as well as sailing vessels) were being operated to various points on the lake. The small 20-ton steamer *Carriella*, for example, offered cruises to patrons of the Northern's Couchiching Hotel, opened in 1873 at Couchiching Point near Orillia. The service lasted until the fall of 1876, when the hotel was destroyed by fire.

The 85-ton side-wheeler *Ida Burton* was built in 1866 at Orillia and for many years operated out of Barrie, connecting the Northern Railway there with Orillia and the Severn River where stages for Muskoka terminated. When the Northern was opened to Gravenhurst in 1875, the *Ida Burton's* usefulness was at an end, and in 1876 she was permanently laid up.

One of the last steamships to ply the waters of Lake Simcoe was the 148-ton *Enterprise*, the only twin-screw vessel ever to operate on the lake. *Enterprise* was originally built in 1869 as a schooner, but in 1883 she was rebuilt as a steamship. In 1899 *Enterprise* was purchased by the Huntsville, Lake of Bays & Lake Simcoe Navigation Company and operated under that flag until 3 August 1903, when she caught fire and burned at Barrie. By that time, Barrie, Orillia and Sutton (Jackson's Point) were the principal transfer points between the Lake Simcoe steamers and the Grand Trunk Railway.

The Temiskaming & Northern Ontario Railway
The Ontario Northland Transportation Commission

The provincially-owned Temiskaming & Northern Ontario Railway, running between North Bay and Moosonee, was strictly a railway-oriented operation until after the Second World War when, in 1945, the railway purchased the Temagami Navigation Company, operating on Lake Temagami, and the Nipissing Navigation Company, operating on Lake Nipissing. To supplement and reduce the equipment required, the railway added some newer vessels. For Lake Temagami, several wartime landing barges were obtained to serve the cottages and lumber camps, and a passenger boat, built in 1910, was purchased and refitted as the *Aubrey Cosens, V.C.* in honour of a local hero killed in the war. On Lake Nipissing, the new motorship *Chief Commanda* was introduced for service between North Bay and the French River.

These ships represented the railway's first real move towards diversification. In 1946 the Temiskaming & Northern Ontario was reorganized as the Ontario Northland Railway under the newly established Ontario Northland Transportation Commission, created by the Ontario government to ensure that adequate and reliable transportation services were provided in Ontario's north. Under the commission's auspices, more ships would be acquired through the purchase of the Owen Sound Transportation Company. As well, trucking operations, a highway bus service and an airline, the regional carrier Norontair, would be added.

In the mid-1950s the *Aubrey Cosens, V.C.* was retired, leaving the *Chief Commanda* as the commission's only operating inland vessel. In 1975 the *Chief Commanda* was withdrawn and sold

A postcard view of the steamer *Meteor* owned by the Temiskaming Navigation Company of Mattawa, Ontario (she was at one point owned by the Lumsden Boat Lines of Ottawa). Built in 1897 at Opemican, Quebec, the 299-ton steamer (131 feet long, beam 27 feet), replaced an earlier, 132-ton *Meteor* built in 1889, and in 1898 was joined by the 295-ton steamer *Temiscamique* (133 feet long, beam 23 feet) launched at Temiscamingue, Quebec. Before the Temiskaming & Northern Ontario Railway was built, communities along Lake Timiskaming could only be reached by water, and the *Meteor* and the *Temiskamique* provided that service, connecting with the Canadian Pacific at Mattawa on the Ottawa River.
— *OA S12696*

The Temagami Navigation Company's steamer *Belle of Temagami* in the 1940s.
— *OA S12876*

The Ontario Northland Transportation Commission's *Chief Commanda*, photographed 22 June 1949. — *OA 1-F-229*

to the Nipissing Indian Band following the 1974 launching of the new 305-passenger, catamaran-hulled *Chief Commanda II*, which currently maintains the Lake Nipissing service. The last inland vessel added was the 1956-vintage *Manitou Island II*, purchased in 1977 to ferry passengers, automobiles and trucks across the Moose River between Moosonee and Moose Factory.

The Owen Sound Transportation Company
The Ontario Northland Transportation Commission

The Owen Sound Transportation Company was founded by Captain Norman MacKay, an experienced Great Lakes captain who left Canada Steamship Lines to start the new venture. In 1931 the company received a franchise from the Ontario government to operate a summer ferry service between Tobermory on the Bruce Peninsula and the Manitoulin Island community of South Baymouth. To inaugurate the service Captain MacKay acquired the American fire tug *James R. Elliott*, built in 1902 at Port Huron, Michigan, by Jenks Shipbuilding. Following a complete refit at Midland's Georgian Bay Shipbuilding Company, the ship entered regular service as the passenger and freight steamer *Normac*. A few years later the company acquired the steamship *Manitoulin* from Canada Steamship Lines to bolster its Georgian Bay service. The Scottish-built vessel was launched in 1889 as the *Modjeska* for the Hamilton Steamboat Company and was transferred to Georgian Bay in 1927 by Canada Steamship Lines after she was refitted as the *Manitoulin*.

In 1936 the Owen Sound Transportation Company entered into a pooling arrangement with the Dominion Transportation Company, assuming complete management of Dominion a year later. Dominion Transportation owned the 470-ton *Manitou* and the 597-ton *Caribou*, similar steamers built by William Marlton at Goderich in 1903 and 1904 respectively. These two ships served as far north as Lake Superior in their earlier years, but Owen Sound to Sault Ste. Marie, Ontario, by way of Manitoulin Island and the north shore of Lake Huron was the *Caribou's* principal route from 1936 until 1944. She subsequently ran in the summer months only between Tobermory and South Baymouth until 1946, when she was sold. The *Manitou* was probably sold sometime in the late 1930s. Nevertheless, Dominion Transportation remained a separate entity until its last vessel, the *Caribou*, was sold.

After World War II the Owen Sound Transportation Company began to renew its fleet with the addition of new ships. In 1946 the 1,668-ton *Norisle* was constructed for the company by Collingwood Shipbuilding, entering service in September. In 1950 the 1,477-ton *Norgoma* was built, again by Collingwood Shipbuilding. Both ships carried 250 passengers and were later modified to carry automobiles — up to 50 on the *Norisle* and up to 37 on the *Norgoma*.

After *Norgoma's* introduction, the *Manitoulin* was retired and scrapped. It was not until 1964, however, that the *Norgoma* became a regular on the Tobermory to South Baymouth route, which was maintained until that time almost exclusively by the *Norisle*.

By 1973 the Owen Sound Transportation Company, now under the control of the Ontario Northland Transportation Commission, was operating the *Norisle* and the *Norgoma*, but by this time traffic levels were beginning to exceed the capacity of the two ships. In 1973 the Ontario government implemented the recommendations of a 1970 study for the upgrading of its newly acquired service, included in which was the construction of the $8.2 million ferry *Chi-Cheemaun* by Canadian Shipbuilding & Engineering at Collingwood. Launched in 1974, the new ferry was proclaimed to be the largest and most modern ferry ever built for service on the Great Lakes, having room on board for 600 passengers and 140 automobiles.

Chi-Cheemaun has since superseded the *Norisle* and the *Norgoma*, both of which have been sold.

The Canadian Pacific Railway — Devil's Gap Lodge

In 1923 the Canadian Pacific opened the Devil's Gap Lodge near Kenora on the Lake of the Woods. Since the lodge was located some distance from the railway's station at Kenora, two motor launches, *CPR No. 1* and *CPR No. 2*, were acquired to transfer passengers to and from the station

The *Manitou* of the Dominion Transportation Company, photographed at the Canadian Pacific steamship dock, presumably at Fort William (Thunder Bay), in the 1920s or 1930s. She was broken up in 1945 while under the ownership of the Sincennes-McNaughton Line of Montreal. The wooden *Caribou* and *Manitou* were similar in design to the other Owen Sound Transportation ships, all of which featured steel hulls. — *OA S13066*

Dominion Transportation's *Caribou*, photographed in the late 1930s or early 1940s somewhere on Manitoulin Island or the north shore of Lake Huron. *Caribou* and her sister *Manitou* were built for the Dominion Fish Company to carry fish from Lake Huron's north shore south, as well as supplies and passengers. The vessels were taken over by the Dominion Transportation Company in 1909, which in turn was taken over by Owen Sound Transportation in 1937.
— *OA Acc. 10456 S16407*

as well as to other parts of the lake. In 1929 the ten-ton launch *Nipigonian* was added and the fleet remained relatively unchanged until late 1947 or early 1948, when the *Nipigonian* was transferred to Lower Arrow Lake in British Columbia to replace the railway's tug *Columbian*. Since *Nipigonian* was far too small to act as an effective tug, her services were utilized only as long as it took to find a more suitable replacement. It can only be assumed that the *Nipigonian* was returned to the Devil's Gap Lodge later in 1948.

In the early 1950s the older boats were replaced by new cabin cruisers. *CPR No. 1* and *CPR No. 2* were scrapped with the introduction of the *Misty Mist* in 1953, while in 1954 the vessels *Misty Maid* and *Canadiana* were added. Both *Misty Mist* and *Misty Maid* were destroyed early in their careers by explosion.

The Devil's Gap Lodge was sold in 1961 in a deal which included the *Canadiana* and another small boat.

In addition to the power boats, the Devil's Gap Lodge also possessed a number of unpowered boats called "otter boats," which were towed by the motor boats during excursions around the lake.

CHAPTER SEVEN - NOTES

1) National Railway Publications Company, *Travelers' Official Guide - June 1893* (New York, 1972/1893), p. 64.
2) Richard Tatley, *Steamboating on the Trent-Severn* (Belleville, 1978), p. 68.
3) (J.B. Mansfield), *The Sage of the Great Lakes* (Toronto, 1980/Chicago, 1899), p. 194.
4) Frank N. Walker, *Four Whistles to Wood Up* (Toronto, 1953), p. 45.
5) G.R. Stevens, *Canadian National Railways, Vol. 1* (Toronto, 1960), p. 402.
6) Melba Morris Croft, *Fourth Entrance to Huronia — The History of Owen Sound* (Owen Sound, 1980), p. 68.

The *Modjeska*, built in 1889 for the Hamilton Steamboat Company, became the *Manitoulin* in 1927 after she was rebuilt with cabins by Canada Steamship Lines for service on Georgian Bay. Purchased by Owen Sound Transportation in the mid-1930s, she served until 1951. *Modjeska* is seen here while still in the service of the Hamilton Steamboat Company.
— *OA S15093*

The first steamship acquired by the Lake Superior Royal Mail Line was the *Algoma*, purchased in 1864 as the *Racine*. By no means a new ship, she was built in 1839 at Niagara as the *City of Toronto* for service on Lake Ontario. Sold to a group of Americans in 1863, she was rebuilt at Detroit as the *Racine* but, for various reasons, they decided to sell her and in 1864 she passed to the Lake Superior Line, becoming the *Algoma*. She was scrapped in 1888. — *PAC C-28537*

Launched at Port Robinson in 1871, the *Cumberland* bore the family name of Barlow Cumberland of the Lake Superior Royal Mail Line and of Frederick Cumberland of the Northern Railway. The ship ran aground on a reef off Isle Royale, Lake Superior, in 1877 and was later abandoned after salvage attempts failed. — *OA Acc. 14996-6*

VIII

THE LAKE SUPERIOR ROUTES

Ever since the American locks were completed at Sault Ste. Marie in 1855, Canadian ship owners, along with their American counterparts, have been eager to push their ships north to Lake Superior in search of new frontiers. For the Canadian lines in particular, these developments were spurred on by the completion of the Northern Railway to Collingwood, also in 1855, thereby providing a new and shorter route to the northwest.

At first the trade out of Collingwood was dominated by the ships involved in the American transit trade (especially those in connection with the Northern Railway) and by others serving ports on Georgian Bay. One such service was offered by Captain W.H. Smith of Owen Sound with the "fast-sailing, low-pressure steamer" *Canadian*. In a newspaper advertisement dated 27 May 1857 service "Through from Toronto to Owen Sound in Nine Hours, by way of the Ontario, Simcoe and Huron Railroad (Northern Railway) to Collingwood, and steamer CANADIAN to the Sound" was offered. The service also included such ports as Meaford and Cape Rich.[1]

The Lake Superior Royal Mail Line

By the mid-1860s service by Canadian ships to Lake Superior ports of call had become firmly established with the formation of the Lake Superior Royal Mail Line. With the steamers *Algoma* (417 tons), *Chicora* (931 tons), *Cumberland* and *Francis Smith*, the line maintained a twice-weekly service between Collingwood, Owen Sound, and Duluth, Minnesota, relying on its close connections with the Northern Railway for its supply of passengers; the fact that one of the company's founders was Barlow Cumberland, son of the Northern's general manager, Frederick Cumberland, did much to encourage relations between the two organizations.

The Great Northern Transit Company

As trade with Lake Superior and northern Georgian Bay ports continued to grow, so too did the number of companies making Collingwood their home base. The Great Northern Transit Company was one of the first steamship lines to follow the Lake Superior Royal Mail Line when, as early as 1875, Great Northern Transit placed the 513-ton steamer *Northern Belle* on the Sault Ste. Marie run in connection with the Northern Railway. By the end of the century the company had four steamers on the route offering a twice-weekly service.

Along with the *Northern Belle*, Great Northern Transit owned the 683-ton *Atlantic*, the 918-ton *Pacific*, and the pride of the line, the elegant 1,578-ton *Majestic*. Until it burned at Collingwood in 1896, the line also operated the steamer *Baltic*, acquired in 1888 as the *Francis Smith*, formerly of the Lake Superior Royal Mail Line.

The *Northern Belle* was built as the *Gladys* in 1875 but never delivered to her intended owners. As a result she was purchased by the Great Northern Transit Company and renamed, becoming the company's first steamship.

— *OA Acc. 14996-25*

The *Pacific,* built at Owen Sound in 1883, was the pride of the Great Northern Transit Company until she burned at Collingwood in 1898.

— *OA S13045*

The North Shore Navigation Company

In competition with Great Northern Transit came the North Shore Navigation Company in 1890, and by 1898 it boasted a total fleet of five steamers, including the 1,387-ton *City of Collingwood*, the 385-ton *City of London*, the 748-ton *City of Midland*, the 491-ton *City of Parry Sound*, and the 782-ton *City of Toronto*.

Using Collingwood as base, the steamers plied regularly from Collingwood and Owen Sound to Sault Ste. Marie by way of Mackinac Island, where passengers bound for Chicago and other ports on Lake Michigan and the American side of Lake Superior could transfer to one of the many American steamship lines, such as the Lake Michigan & Lake Superior Transportation Company or the Seymour Transportation Company.

Typically, the rivalry between the Great Northern Transit Company and the North Shore Navigation Company grew as each competed for the other's business until neither could operate profitably. There was only one solution, merge. As a result, the two lines were amalgamated in 1899 to form the Northern Navigation Company of Ontario, Limited. The new line, however, still had one drawback in that it lacked its own route to the Lake Superior harbours of Port Arthur and Fort William, or more importantly, the necessary class of steamer to start that profitable route. Even so, there was another company, the North West Transportation Company of Sarnia, with just the right ships for the purpose.

The North West Transportation Company

The North West Transportation Company was started in 1871 by James H. and Henry Beatty with the objective of forming a new line of steamers connecting the railways at Windsor and Sarnia with the head of Lake Superior. Beginning with the 465-ton *Waubuno*, the company quickly added the steamers *Asia* (350 tons), *Manitoba* (980 tons), *Ontario* (1,138 tons), *Quebec* (1,338 tons), and *Sovereign* (684 tons), until it was able to offer the following sailing times advertised in May 1879: "Running in connection with the Grand Trunk, Great Western, and Canada Southern Railway. On the opening of Navigation one of these steamers will leave Windsor every Friday, and Sarnia every Tuesday and Friday, calling the following day at Goderich, Kincardine, and Southampton for all points on Lake Huron and Superior, making close connections at Duluth with the Northern Pacific Railway for Winnipeg and all points west."

It was also claimed by the steamship line that "passenger rates from all points in Canada (were) $5.00 lower than by rail." This was no doubt true, considering the circuitous route through Chicago that one would have had to have followed travelling by rail. No fewer than three changes of train were required on the week-long journey, and considering the hard, uncomfortable seats and rough roadbeds common to railways in those days, it was no wonder that the shipping lines were so popular.

One ship acquired by the line in 1880 to replace the *Waubuno*, which sank in Georgian Bay in 1879, had the shortest career of any ship owned by the company. The 706-ton *Manitoulin* was brand new and served barely two years before it burned at Shoal Point on Georgian Bay in May 1882. It was rebuilt as the *Atlantic* the following year for the Great Northern Transit Company.

Also in 1882, Henry Beatty left the North West Transportation Company to take over the management of Canadian Pacific's steamship service. Only a few short years later, Canadian Pacific's ships under Henry Beatty would become brother James H. Beatty's major competitors.

The next 15 years brought about several other changes in the company. It was becoming increasingly evident that the Lake Superior trade required larger and better-appointed ships in order to meet the competition, and a program of fleet renewal was initiated. The first new ship was the 1,961-ton steamer *United Empire*, one of the last big wooden vessels built for the Great Lakes. Aside from having an increased freight capacity over the earlier ships, *United Empire* was given one of the finest passenger accommodations of any lake ship of her day.

In 1890 the 2,017-ton *Monarch* became the last ship built for the line. Strangely enough, she was constructed entirely of wood at a time when most large ships were being built with at least iron or steel hulls — old habits die hard, especially when the rest of the fleet was of wooden construction. There is one exception, however, for between 1890 and 1895 the 1,700-ton steel ship *Campana* was

The *City of Collingwood* was launched on 24 May 1893 for North Shore Navigation at Owen Sound by Polson Iron Works. A steel-hulled ship, she passed to the Northern Navigation Company in 1899 but her career was cut short when she caught fire and burned at Collingwood on 19 June 1905. *— OA Acc. 14996-35*

The *Waubuno*, built in 1865 and acquired in 1870, was the first ship operated by the North West Transportation Company. She sank in November 1879 on Georgian Bay. *— OA Acc. 12026-100*

The *Manitoba*, delivered in 1871, was the first new ship acquired by North West Transportation. Seen here at Fort William, the Hudson Bay Company's post at the Lakehead, in the 1870s, the *Manitoba* served the company until 1888 when she was sold to the Canada Transit Company and renamed *Carmona*. She was later resold and in 1900 was rebuilt as the *Pittsburgh*. She burned in 1903. — *OA S15996*

Asia, built in 1873, at the Lake Superior & Mississippi (later St. Paul & Duluth) Railroad dock at Duluth in the late 1870s. *Asia* sank on Georgian Bay off Byng Inlet on 2 September 1882. — *OA S13061*

The *Ontario* of 1874 as she appeared in an early stylized painting. Sold in 1888, she was wrecked eleven years later near Rossport on Lake Superior. — *Canadian Pacific Corporate Archives No. 16335*

Built in 1874, the *Quebec* featured a prominent arch truss supported hull, which, upon the arch, was proudly written "North West Transportation Company". Seen here around 1883 in the shadow of Thunder Bay's "Sleeping Giant" island, the *Quebec* later sank at the mouth of the Sault River (near Sault Ste. Marie) in July 1885 and afterward was salvaged by Americans. The ice visible in the photograph suggests that it may have been taken in the spring. — *OA S15985*

The *Manitoulin* of 1880 was a ship plagued by fire. *Manitoulin* was first struck by fire in May 1882 at Shoal Point, Georgian Bay. Rebuilt in the following year as the *Atlantic*, she was later sold to the Great Northern Transit Company. Passing ultimately to the Northern Navigation Company, she was completely destroyed by fire in 1902. She appears at Collingwood when still new, apparently bedecked for a Masonic excursion.
— *OA S17456*

The British-built *Campana* was launched in 1873 as a sea-going heavy cargo steamer but was taken to the upper lakes early in her career. Along with operating under charter to the Canadian Pacific in the late 1880s, she was chartered by North West Transportation from 1890 until 1895. She was later purchased by the Quebec Steamship Company and taken down to the Gulf of St. Lawrence, there plying between Quebec City and Pictou, Nova Scotia. This view probably dates from the early 1890s.
— *OA Acc. 14996-4*

operated under charter to the company. *Campana* was built in 1881 in Britain as an ocean-going cargo steamer, but not long after launching she was taken to the upper Great Lakes, becoming the first twin-screw steamer to ply those waters. From 1888 to around 1889 *Campana* was chartered to the Canadian Pacific Railway following the loss of the Canadian Pacific steamer *Algoma.*

By 1898 North West Transportation had reduced its fleet down to just the *United Empire* and the *Monarch,* yet together they could carry a total of 200,000 bushels of grain each month, a reasonably good record considering the fact that they were designed to carry freight and passengers. At this time they were running on a weekly schedule, connecting the Grand Trunk Railway at Windsor and Sarnia with Fort William and Duluth.

The Northern Navigation Company

In late 1899 North West Transportation merged with the fledgling Northern Navigation Company of Ontario, forming the Northern Navigation Company, Limited, which by 1901 boasted a fleet of nine ships: *Atlantic, Britannic, City of Collingwood, City of Parry Sound, City of Toronto, Germanic, Majestic, Monarch* and *United Empire. Britannic* and *Germanic* were the first ships acquired by Northern Navigation. The 1,014-ton *Germanic* arrived new in 1899 and was the last wooden ship built by the Collingwood Drydock Company at Collingwood. The 428-ton *Britannic,* on the other hand, was originally built in 1866 as the tug *Rocket* and was rebuilt in 1892 as a passenger steamer. She was added to the fleet in 1901.

From the start, the Lake Superior Division was given priority over the Georgian Bay services, especially when it came to upgrading the fleet. The *United Empire* and the *Monarch* were no longer able to cope with the passenger traffic and were in no condition to continue on without major rebuilding. In answer to this dilemma, the company placed an order with Collingwood Shipbuilding for the construction of a large new steel ship, delivered in 1902 as the 3,300-ton *Huronic.* She was the largest and best-equipped ship of her type on the lakes and quickly set a new fleet standard. *United Empire,* now a veteran of 20 seasons, was no match for *Huronic* and in 1903 put into Sarnia for a complete refitting. When she returned to service in 1904, she not only had a new lease on life but a new name as well — *Saronic.* There is little doubt that *Monarch* would have eventually been rebuilt as well, had it not been for her untimely loss in December 1906, when she was wrecked off Isle Royale on Lake Superior.

Accommodating package freight was another concern for company officials, since only a portion of the space on board the steamships was allocated to freight. Faced with ever-increasing volumes of freight being handled, especially during the spring and fall, Northern Navigation purchased its first ship totally devoted to package freight in 1906, the 1,708-ton steel freighter *Cuba.* Renamed *Ionic,* she was built at Buffalo, New York, in 1872 for the Delaware, Lackawanna & Western Railroad's shipping subsidiary, the Lackawanna Transportation Company, from whom she was acquired, and was therefore well suited to her role. A year later the freighter *Tadousac* was purchased and renamed *Doric.* Only four years old, the 2,359-ton *Doric* was built by the Bertram Shipyards at Toronto and was only second in size to the *Huronic* at this point.

Unlike the passenger ships *Huronic* and *Saronic* which operated between Windsor, Sarnia, Fort William and Duluth, *Doric* and *Ionic* ran out of Collingwood for Fort William.

The Georgian Bay fleet at the end of 1908 included the ships *City of Midland, City of Windsor, Germanic,* and *Majestic.* Of these vessels, all were Northern Navigation veterans with the exception of the *City of Windsor,* which operated under lease from 1906 to 1909. The *Britannic* and the *City of Toronto* were both sold in September 1908 as traffic on Georgian Bay declined.

Throughout the first decade of the company's history, its headquarters was located in Collingwood, but while much of Northern Navigation's trade was still handled through Collingwood, even more was being handled on the Lake Superior route out of Sarnia. That situation was emphasized in 1908 when, after years of informal relations, the Northern Navigation Company entered into an official traffic agreement with the Grand Trunk and Grand Trunk Pacific railways whereby the two railways undertook to deliver their entire lakebound freight and passenger traffic between Sarnia, the Lakehead and Duluth to the Northern Navigation Company, effective 1 January 1909.

Next only to the *Monarch*, the *United Empire*, built in 1882, was the grandest ship operated by the North West Transportation Company. Refitted by Northern Navigation in 1904 as the *Saronic*, she remained a popular ship until scrapped in 1915. This view was taken off Sarnia around 1900. — *OA Acc. 9912-2-16a*

The *Britannic* is seen here at the Grand Trunk wharf at Midland in the early 1900s. The ship on the right is the *Winona*, then owned by a Captain White of Midland. The *Britannic* was sold in September 1908. — *OA Acc. 2375 S5261*

Photographed leaving Midland in the early 1900s, the *City of Toronto* was built in 1895 for the North Shore Navigation Company and served Northern Navigation until her sale in September 1908. She burned at Cornwall in 1914.
— *OA Acc. 2375 S5292*

The first new ship purchased by Northern Navigation, the *Germanic* was also the last wooden vessel launched at Collingwood. *Germanic* was destroyed by fire at Collingwood in March 1917. — *OA Acc. 14996-42*

The *Monarch*, built in 1890, came to Northern Navigation by way of the North West Transportation Company. She was wrecked off Isle Royale, Lake Superior, in December 1906. This view dates from the early 1900s.
— *OA S17568*

Built in 1902, the *Huronic* outlived her larger sisterships *Hamonic* and *Noronic*. She was scrapped at Hamilton in 1950 after spending her last years in package freight service.
— *OA 14996-44*

The results of the contract were significant. In 1909 the navigation company took delivery of its grandest ship yet from the Collingwood Shipbuilding Company. The 5,265-ton *Hamonic* could carry 475 passengers, along with 3,500 tons of freight, and showed the line's commitment to run only the best ships on the new "Grand Trunk Line," the title all of the Lake Superior ships bore after 1909. Now with three ships, the following 1909 fall sailings were advertised out of Port Arthur for Sault Ste. Marie and Sarnia:

S.S. HURONIC leaves Port Arthur every Tuesday at 1:15 p.m.
S.S. SARONIC leaves Port Arthur every Thursday at 1:15 p.m.
S.S. HAMONIC leaves Port Arthur every Saturday at 1:15 p.m.

These times were effective from October 4 to December 19, while Duluth sailings would be discontinued after September 28.[2]

By the end of 1910 new facilities for handling freight and passengers had been completed at Sarnia and the corporate headquarters relocated there from Collingwood. The passenger dock and waiting rooms, general offices and a small freight terminal were built on the site of the former Great Western Railway station, while the main freight terminal, commissary and coaling dock were situated in Point Edward at the former Grand Trunk car ferry docks. This new arrangement allowed the recently introduced boat trains from Toronto to be run from the Sarnia Tunnel station directly to the dock, where passengers could make the transfer between ship and train without any delay or inconvenience.

Despite the fact that patronage on the Georgian Bay service was still on the decline, the company purchased its last ship for those waters in 1909 from Collingwood Shipbuilding. Christened *Waubic*, the 504-ton vessel would not only be the only steel ship placed in service on Georgian Bay by Northern Navigation, but she would be the last of the company's ships to operate there as well.

Named for the town of Waubaushene and built in 1909, the *Waubic* replaced the Georgian Bay steamers *Britannic* and *City of Toronto*. The only steel ship regularly operated by Northern Navigation in Georgian Bay service, the *Waubic* was sold years later. She was rebuilt as a motor ship in 1938 and burned in 1959.
— *OA S4519*

Table 8-1
LAKE SUPERIOR ROUTE
NORTHERN NAVIGATION COMPANY
VIA THE CANADIAN NORTHERN RAILWAY
Summer 1912

Westbound

			Time	SARONIC Day	HURONIC Day	HAMONIC Day
Sarnia	NNC	Lv.	3:30 p.m.	Mon.	Wed.	Sat.
Sault Ste. Marie	NNC	Lv.	3:30 p.m.	Tue.	Thurs.	Sun.
Port Arthur	NNC	Ar.	3:30 p.m.	Wed.	Fri.	Mon.
Port Arthur	CNoR	Lv.	4:30 p.m.*	Wed.	Fri.	Mon.
Fort William	CNoR	Lv.	4:42 p.m.*	Wed.	Fri.	Mon.
Winnipeg	CNoR	Ar.	9:00 a.m.*	Thurs.	Sat.	Tue.

Eastbound

			Time	SARONIC Day	HURONIC Day	HAMONIC Day
Winnipeg	CNoR	Lv.	5:50 p.m.*	Thurs.	Sat.	Tue.
Fort William	CNoR	Ar.	9:45 a.m.*	Fri.	Sun.	Wed.
Port Arthur	CNoR	Ar.	10:00 a.m.*	Fri.	Sun.	Wed.
Port Arthur	NNC	Lv.	1:30 p.m.	Fri.	Sun.	Wed.
Sault Ste. Marie	NNC	Ar.	12:00 noon	Sat.	Mon.	Thurs.
Sarnia	NNC	Ar.	11:00 a.m.	Sun.	Tue.	Fri.

* - Indicates Central Time. All other times Eastern Time.
NNC - Northern Navigation Company
CNoR - Canadian Northern Railway

Source: Canadian Northern Railway Timetable, 14 February 1912

The Northern Navigation Company's Lake Superior route was not only popular with Grand Trunk passengers, it also gained the favour of Canadian Northern Railway passengers as well. It therefore should come as no surprise to see the line's services listed in the Canadian Northern timetable as well as the Grand Trunk's, as table 8-1 shows from the Canadian Northern timetable of 14 February 1912.

By this time the old *Saronic* was approaching the end of a long and successful career. Plans were under way for the construction of a new ship at the Western Dry Dock Company at Port Arthur; she was the 6,905-ton *Noronic*, launched in 1913. The new flagship, *Noronic* (named for Northern Navigation) was built along the lines of the *Hamonic* and was equipped to carry 600 passengers. Her dining room alone measured 102 feet by 46 feet and could seat 300 diners at a time. *Noronic* would have been ready for service at the end of 1913 had it not been for a near disaster which occurred while she was berthed at Sarnia for her final fitting out. For some unknown reason *Noronic* listed to one side and had it not been for the support of the dock, she surely would have capsized. Fortunately this happened before she entered regular service, for such a situation would have resulted in a heavy casualty toll in open waters. The defect was remedied with the installation of sponson-type stabilizers on the lower hull. Certain superstitious crewmen, however, never really trusted the *Noronic* afterwards. *Noronic* finally commenced her regular duties in 1914, and in 1915 the *Saronic* was retired. *Saronic* was sold in 1917 and renamed *W.L. Kennedy.*

After months of negotiations, the Northern Navigation Company, along with several other shipping lines, including the Niagara Navigation Company, the Hamilton Steamboat Company, and the Richelieu & Ontario Navigation Company, merged on 4 December 1913 to form the Canada Steamship Lines. Under the new organization the Northern Navigation Company became the Northern Navigation Division of Canada Steamship Lines, although unlike many of the other companies that disappeared with the amalgamation, Northern Navigation retained much of its own identity right to the end, perhaps due in part to its remoteness from the other passenger operations.

By 1916 Northern Navigation's fleet consisted of the *Hamonic*, the *Huronic*, the *Noronic*, the *Doric* and the *Ionic* on the Lake Superior route, with *Germanic* and *Waubic* maintaining the Georgian Bay services following the loss of the *Majestic* by fire at Point Edward in 1915.

On the Lake Superior route, *Huronic* and *Hamonic* were the mainstays for the entire navigation season, while *Noronic* joined them only in summer. This arrangement freed *Noronic* up for cruises during the spring and fall, and in the entire history of the *Noronic* she never deviated from this. *Doric* and *Ionic* were never scheduled, at least as far as the public was concerned, for as package freighters, they carried no passengers.

Tables 8-2 and 8-3 from the Grand Trunk timetable issued 20 May 1916 show the regularly scheduled services for the spring and fall months, and the summer service when all three passenger steamers were running on the route. The steamship specials operated by the Grand Trunk between Toronto and Sarnia Wharf in connection with the Northern Navigation steamers were operated only

Ionic began her long career as the *Cuba*, launched at Buffalo in 1872 for the Lackawanna Transportation Company, a subsidiary of the Delaware, Lackawanna & Western Railroad, as a package freighter. Purchased by Northern Navigation in 1906 and renamed *Ionic*, she served until 1920 when she was sold, finally being scrapped in 1946. *Ionic* was photographed here at Sault Ste. Marie in 1917 with Canada Steamship Lines insignia. — *PAC PA-145814*

This postcard view of the Sarnia waterfront dates from about 1910 when it was still a hub of Northern Navigation activity in the south. At dockside are the *Huronic* (left) and the *Majestic* (right). This area was originally developed by the Great Western Railway in the late 1850s and it was the Great Western which was responsible for the construction of the grain elevator seen behind the freight-house, and most probably the brick station (the roof of which is visible in the lower left corner) and the brick freight-house. — *MTL*

Built in 1903 as the *Tadousac*, the *Doric* was purchased in 1907 and refitted as a package freighter. Pictured here at Sault Ste. Marie in 1917 wearing Canada Steamship Lines colours, *Doric* was requisitioned by the Canadian government for war service and sank that same year. — *PAC PA-145815*

This photograph of the *Majestic* was taken at the same time as the Sarnia waterfront postcard view shown nearby and in fact is an extension of that view. The *Majestic* was built for the Great Northern Transit Company in 1895 and subsequently served Northern Navigation well until her loss in 1915. At the left is the *Huronic*. Note the grain elevator across the river at Port Huron, Michigan. — *OA S17566*

during the summer, when *Hamonic*, *Huronic* and *Noronic* were all in service, and then only on the days when the ships either sailed or arrived, as shown in table 8-4.

On Georgian Bay, *Germanic* was assigned to the Sault Ste. Marie run out of Collingwood by way of Owen Sound (see table 8-5). As it turned out, 1916 was the last year this service was offered, for in March 1917 *Germanic* caught fire and burned at Collingwood; she was not replaced. *Waubic* operated on the popular 30,000 Islands route between Penetang and Parry Sound (see table 8-6). The service remained a favourite well into the 1930s, by which time the southern terminal at Penetang was moved to Midland. The Grand Trunk's successor, Canadian National, even placed special trains in service between Toronto and Midland Wharf during the summer months, apparently in connection with this route.

World War I appeared to have little impact on Northern Navigation's services with the exception of the package freight steamers. *Doric* was requisitioned around 1917 for war service, only to be sunk that same year. *Ionic*, possibly due to her age, escaped being requisitioned by the government and was sold to the Quebec-based Branch Line in 1920, at which time she was renamed *Maplebranch*, serving until 1946 when, after 74 years on the Great Lakes, she was scrapped. A temporary addition to the fleet was made in 1917 when the American steamer *Rochester* was chartered on Lake Erie to link Detroit with Cleveland.

The 1920s brought the Northern Navigation service its greatest popularity ever, especially with American tourists, and it was during this period that the line became the official "Canadian National Route" following the merger of the Grand Trunk system into Canadian National Railways in 1923. As a new ally, Canadian National offered several advantages over the Grand Trunk, not so much in the way of southern Ontario connections, which remained much as they had always been, but chiefly in the provision of new boat trains between Winnipeg and Port Arthur, and between Winnipeg and Duluth, Minnesota. In addition, a special excursion train was provided for passengers wishing to visit Kakabeka Falls west of the Lakehead; picnic lunches prepared on the ships were provided for all passengers taking part. This side trip was eliminated in later years in favour of Chippewa Park in Fort William. Similar excursions were also offered at Duluth. Even at Sarnia a bus trip was provided for the sake of Windsor and Detroit passengers who had to lay over at Sarnia until the Toronto boat train arrived.

At Sarnia the automobile-and-passenger ferry *Louis Phillippe* was acquired in 1923 and placed into service between Sarnia and Port Huron, Michigan. She was eventually replaced by the Bluewater Bridge.

Table 8-2
LAKE SUPERIOR ROUTE
NORTHERN NAVIGATION COMPANY
Spring & Fall 1916

Westbound - 22 Apr. - 10 June; 18 Sept. - close of navigation

			HURONIC	HAMONIC
		Time	Day	Day
Sarnia, Northern Navigation Dock	Lv.	3:30 p.m.	Wed.	Sat.
Sault Ste. Marie, New Ontario Dock	Lv.	11:00 a.m.	Thurs.	Sun.
Port Arthur, Canadian Northern Dock	Ar.	6:30 a.m.	Fri.	Mon.

Eastbound - 25 Apr. - 12 June; 21 Sept. - close of navigation

			HURONIC	HAMONIC
		Time	Day	Day
Port Arthur, Canadian Northern Dock	Lv.	3:30 p.m.	Sat.	Tue.
Sault Ste. Marie, New Ontario Dock	Lv.	11:00 a.m.	Sun.	Wed.
Sarnia, Northern Navigation Dock	Ar.	6:30 a.m.	Mon.	Thurs.

The above service will be supplemented by the addition of package freight steamers.

Source: Grand Trunk Railway Timetable, 20 May 1916.

Saronic (right) and *Hamonic* (left) at the Canadian Northern Railway dock at Port Arthur (now part of Thunder Bay) in the early 1910s. — *OA S13096*

The Canadian Northern Railway docks at Port Arthur (Thunder Bay) as they appeared about the time of the First World War. Among the ships at dock are the *Huronic* (upper right) and either the *Alberta* or the *Athabasca* of the Canadian Pacific Railway (upper left). These docks were inherited by Canadian National. The Canadian Northern station was located behind the photographer. — *OA S8086*

Table 8-3
LAKE SUPERIOR ROUTE
NORTHERN NAVIGATION COMPANY
Summer 1916

Westbound

Effective from Windsor, Ont. & Detroit Mich.
17 June - 16 Sept.
Effective from Sarnia, Ont. 12 June - 16 Sept.

			HURONIC	HAMONIC	NORONIC
		Time	Day	Day	Day
Windsor, Government Dock	Lv.	8:15 a.m.	Mon.	Wed.	Sat.
Detroit, Brush St. Dock	Lv.	9:00 a.m.	Mon.	Wed.	Sat.
Sarnia, Northern Navigation Dock	Lv.	5:00 p.m.	Mon.	Wed.	Sat.
Sault Ste. Marie, New Ont. Dock	Lv.	12:00 n'n	Tue.	Thurs.	Sun.
Port Arthur, CNoR Dock	Ar.	7:00 a.m.	Wed.	Fri.	Mon.
Fort William, CGR Dock	Ar.	8:00 a.m.	Wed.	Fri.	Mon.
Port Arthur, CNoR Dock	Lv.	11:00 p.m.	Wed.	Fri.	Mon.
Duluth, Minn., NPR Dock No. 4	Ar.	11:00 a.m.*	Thurs.	Sat.	Tue.

Eastbound

Effective from Duluth, Minn., 20 June - 19 Sept.
Effective from Fort William & Port Arthur
16 June - 20 Sept.

			HURONIC	HAMONIC	NORONIC
		Time	Day	Day	Day
Duluth, Minn., NPR Dock No. 4	Lv.	8:00 p.m.*	Thurs.	Sat.	Tue.
Fort William, CPR Dock	Ar.	10:00 a.m.	Fri.	Sun.	Wed.
Fort William, CGR Dock	Lv.	2:45 p.m.	Fri.	Sun.	Wed.
Port Arthur, CNoR Dock	Lv.	4:00 p.m.	Fri.	Sun.	Wed.
Sault Ste. Marie, New Ont. Dock	Lv.	12:00 n'n	Sat.	Mon.	Thurs.
Sarnia, Northern Navigation Dock	Ar.	7:00 a.m.	Sun.	Tue.	Fri.

* - Central Time. All other times Eastern Time.
CNoR - Canadian Northern Railway
CGR - Canadian Government Railways
NPR - Northern Pacific Railway

Source: Grand Trunk Railway Timetable, 20 May 1916.

Table 8-4
GRAND TRUNK RAILWAY
SCHEDULE OF STEAMSHIP SPECIAL TRAINS
BETWEEN TORONTO, LONDON AND SARNIA WHARF

Summer 1916

Number 23 Westbound Mondays, Wednesdays and Saturdays				Number 24 Eastbound Tuesdays, Fridays and Saturdays
11:15 a.m.	Lv.	TORONTO	Ar.	1:10 p.m.
11:24 a.m.	Lv.	Sunnyside	Ar.	12:55 p.m.
12:23 p.m.	Lv.	HAMILTON	Ar.	11:45 a.m.
1:15 p.m.	Lv.	Brantford	Ar.	11:05 a.m.

1:29 p.m.	Lv.	Paris	Ar.	10:49 a.m.
2:02 p.m.	Lv.	Woodstock	Ar.	10:21 a.m.
2:17 p.m.	Lv.	Ingersoll	Ar.	10:05 a.m.
2:47 p.m.	Lv.	LONDON	Ar.	9:30 a.m.
3:22 p.m.	Lv.	Strathroy	Ar.	8:55 a.m.
3:58 p.m.	Lv.	Wyoming	Ar.	. . .
4:20 p.m	.Ar.	Sarnia	Lv.	8:00 a.m.
4:30 p.m.	Ar.	SARNIA WHARF	Lv.	7:45 a.m.
Read Down				Read Up

Westbound trains commence Saturday, 17 June
Eastbound trains commence Sunday, 18 June

Source: Grand Trunk Railway Timetable, 20 May 1916.

Table 8-5
GEORGIAN BAY ROUTE
NORTHERN NAVIGATION COMPANY

Summer 1916

Steamship GERMANIC

Westbound		Eastbound
12:30 p.m. Sat.	Collingwood	11:45 a.m. Fri.
3:30 p.m. Sat.	Meaford	9:30 a.m. Fri.
11:00 p.m. Sat.	Owen Sound	6:00 a.m. Fri.
10:00 a.m. Sun.	Killarney	6:00 p.m. Thu.
1:00 p.m. Sun.	Manitowaning	3:30 p.m. Thu.
3:00 p.m. Sun.	Sheguiandah	1:30 p.m. Thu.
6:15 p.m. Sun.	Little Current	12:00 n'n Thu.
8:45 p.m. Sun.	Kagawong	9:30 a.m. Thu.
4:00 a.m. Mon.	Gore Bay	6:00 a.m. Thu.
6:30 a.m. Mon.	Spanish Mills	@
8:00 a.m. Mon.	Cutler	@
9:30 a.m. Mon.	John Island	@
11:30 a.m. Mon.	Spragge	@
3:00 p.m. Mon.	Blind River	10:45 p.m. Wed.
7:30 p.m. Mon.	Thessalon	7:15 p.m. Wed.
10:00 p.m. Mon.	Bruce Mines	4:45 p.m. Wed.
7:00 a.m. Tue.	Hilton	3:45 p.m. Wed.
8:30 a.m. Tue.	Richard's Landing	3:30 p.m. Wed.
11:30 a.m. Tue.	Sault Ste. Marie	12:00 n'n Wed.
Read Down		Read Up

@ - eastbound, will stop for carload freight only.

Source: Grand Trunk Railway Timetable, 20 May 1916.

Table 8-6
30,000 ISLANDS ROUTE
NORTHERN NAVIGATION COMPANY
16 June to 16 September 1916

Steamship WAUBIC

Northbound				Southbound
2:10 p.m.	Lv.	Penetang	Ar.	12:20 p.m.
3:00 p.m.		Honey Harbour		11:15 a.m.
3:30 p.m.		Minnecog		10:55 a.m.
3:45 p.m.		Whalens		10:40 a.m.

4:20 p.m.		Go-Home-Bay		10:05 a.m.
5:05 p.m.		Wahwahtaysee		9:20 a.m.
5:50 p.m.		Manitou		8:45 a.m.
6:05 p.m.		Copper Head		8:30 a.m.
6:20 p.m.		Sans Souci		8:20 a.m.
7:40 p.m.		Rose Point		7:10 a.m.
8:00 p.m.	Ar.	Parry Sound	Lv.	7:00 a.m.
Read Down				Read Up

Source: Grand Trunk Railway Timetable, 20 May 1916.

The schedules reproduced in tables 8-7 and 8-8 show Northern Navigation's Lake Superior service for the 1929 season in what was probably to be the line's last big year. It is interesting to compare the timetables for the steamship specials between Toronto and Sarnia for the summer of 1916 (table 8-4) and that of 1929 (table 8-9), in that despite an elapsed time of 13 years and a change in railway companies, little had really changed. The stations served were identical, the train numbers were similar, and even the running times were close.

Table 8-7
LAKE SUPERIOR ROUTE
NORTHERN NAVIGATION COMPANY
Spring & Fall 1929

Westbound - 11 May - 15 June; 10 Sept. - 1 Oct.

			HAMONIC	HURONIC
		Time	Day	Day
Sarnia, Pt. Edward Dock	Lv.	4:30 p.m.	Tue.	Sat.
Sault Ste. Marie	Lv.	12:00 n'n	Wed.	Sun.
Port Arthur	Ar.	6:45 a.m.	Thurs.	Mon.

Eastbound - 15 May - 15 June; 14 Sept. - 5 Oct.

			HAMONIC	HURONIC
		Time	Day	Day
Port Arthur	Lv.	1:00 p.m.	Sat.	Wed.
Sault Ste. Marie	Lv.	10:30 a.m.	Sun.	Thurs.
Sarnia, Pt. Edward Dock	Ar.	6:30 a.m.	Mon.	Fri.

Source: Canadian National Railways Timetable, 23 June 1929.

Table 8-8
LAKE SUPERIOR ROUTE
NORTHERN NAVIGATION COMPANY
Summer 1929

Westbound

Effective from Sarnia (Pt. Edward Dock) Ont.
18 June - 7 Sept.
Effective from Detroit, Mich., 17 June - 6 Sept.

			HAMONIC	HURONIC	NORONIC
		Time	Day	Day	Day
Detroit	Lv.	11:00 p.m.	Mon.	Wed.	Fri.
Sarnia, Pt. Edward Dock	Ar.	6:45 a.m.	Tue.	Thurs.	Sat.
Sarnia, Pt. Edward Dock	Lv.	4:30 p.m.	Tue.	Thurs.	Sat.
Sault Ste. Marie	Lv.	12:00 n'n	Wed.	Fri.	Sun.
Port Arthur	Ar.	5:45 a.m.*	Thurs.	Sat.	Mon.
Fort William		. . .	. . .	. . .	. . .

Port Arthur	Lv.	5:30 p.m.*	Thurs.	Sat.	Mon.
Duluth, Minn.	Ar.	8:00 a.m.*	Fri.	Sun.	Tue.

Eastbound

Effective from Duluth, Minn., 21 June - 10 Sept.
Effective from Port Arthur, Ont., 17 June - 11 Sept.

			HAMONIC	HURONIC	NORONIC
		Time	Day	Day	Day
Duluth, Minn.	Lv.	4:30 p.m.*	Fri.	Sun.	Tue.
Port Arthur	Ar.	6:30 a.m.	Sat.	Mon.	Wed.
Fort William		. . .	. . .	. . .	. . .
Port Arthur	Lv.	1:00 p.m.	Sat.	Mon.	Wed.
Sault Ste. Marie	Lv.	10:30 a.m.	Sun.	Tue.	Thurs.
Sarnia, Pt. Edward Dock	Ar.	6:30 a.m.	Mon.	Wed.	Fri.
Sarnia, Pt. Edward Dock	Lv.	Note(A)	Mon.	Wed.	Fri.
Detroit	Ar.	4:25 p.m.	Mon.	Wed.	Fri.

* - Central Time. All other times Eastern Time.
Note (A) - Will leave Sarnia between 10:00 a.m. and noon.

Source: Canadian National Railways Timetable, 23 June 1929.

Table 8-9
CANADIAN NATIONAL RAILWAYS
SCHEDULE OF STEAMSHIP SPECIAL TRAINS
BETWEEN TORONTO, LONDON AND POINT EDWARD
Summer 1929

Number 23 Westbound Tuesdays, Thursdays and Saturdays				Number 22 Eastbound Mondays, Wednesdays and Fridays
10:00 a.m.	Lv.	TORONTO	Ar.	1:15 p.m.
10:42 a.m.		Sunnyside		1:00 p.m.
10:38 a.m.		HAMILTON		12:03 p.m.
12:35 p.m.		Brantford		11:20 a.m.
12:49 p.m.		Paris		11:05 a.m.
1:20 p.m.		Woodstock		10:40 a.m.
1:35 p.m.		Ingersoll		10:24 a.m.
2:10 p.m.		LONDON		9:50 a.m.
2:40 p.m.		Strathroy		9:20 a.m.
. . .		Wyoming		8:48 a.m.*
3:40 p.m.	Ar.	Sarnia	Lv.	8:30 a.m.
4:10 p.m.	Ar.	SARNIA (PT. EDWARD DOCK)	Lv.	8:00 a.m.
Read Down				Read Up

* - Stops only to set off boat passengers.

Westbound trains operate from Tuesday 18 June - Thursday 12 Sept.
Eastbound trains operate from Wednesday 19 June - Friday 13 Sept.

Source: Canadian National Railways Timetable, 23 June 1929.

The mighty *Noronic* as she appeared within a few years of her 1913 launching. Built along similar lines to the smaller *Hamonic*, *Noronic* had a top-heavy appearance due to the addition of an extra deck. Indeed, it was probably that extra deck that caused her to nearly capsize at Sarnia in 1913 when she was still being fitted out, delaying her introduction until the following season. — *OA S13161*

In a tranquil scene, two competitors lie side by side at Fort William (now part of Thunder Bay) in the late 1930s. On the left is the Canadian Pacific steamer *Keewatin*; on the right is the larger *Hamonic* of the Northern Navigation Division of Canada Steamship Lines. — *OA Acc. 9254 S14298*

Table 8-10
CANADIAN NATIONAL RAILWAYS
SCHEDULE OF STEAMSHIP SPECIAL TRAINS
BETWEEN WINNIPEG AND PORT ARTHUR AND DULUTH
Summer 1929

Eastbound					Westbound	
Thu., Sat. and Mon.	Fri., Sun. and Tue.				Thu., Sat. and Mon.	Fri., Sun. and Tues.
5:20 p.m.	10:30 p.m.	Lv.	Winnipeg	Ar.	9:10 p.m.	8:50 p.m.
...	1:30 a.m.	Lv.	Minaki	Ar.	5:54 p.m.	...
...	5:40 a.m.	Lv.	Sioux Lookout	Ar.	1:40 p.m.	...
...	11:15 a.m.	Lv.	Fort William	Lv.	7:45 a.m.	...
...	11:25 a.m.	Ar.	Port Arthur	Lv.	7:30 a.m.	...
9:10 a.m.	...	Ar.	Duluth	Lv.	...	9:00 a.m.
Fri., Sun. and Tue.	Sat., Mon. and Wed.				Thu., Sat. and Mon.	Fri., Sun. and Tue.
Read Down					Read Up	

N.B. - All times in Central Time.

Source: Canadian National Railways Timetable, 23 June 1929.

The same cannot be said for the steamship service, particularly during the summer. Following the formation of Canadian National, the ships only docked at the former Canadian Northern dock at Port Arthur, where the boat trains to and from Winnipeg (see table 8-10) could be readily handled, instead of docking at the three separate wharfs of the Canadian Pacific and the former Canadian Government Railway at Fort William and the Canadian Northern at Port Arthur. This also resulted in a time saving in terms of excessive manoeuvring at the Lakehead, put to good use accommodating the transfer of passengers and baggage between the steamships and trains. Note too that the ships now docked at Point Edward Dock, not Sarnia Wharf as in the 1916 timetable. Mention should also be made of the Winnipeg boat trains to Duluth by way of the Duluth, Winnipeg & Pacific Railway (table 8-10), a Canadian National subsidiary acquired by way of the Canadian Northern Railway.

Traffic gradually fell throughout the Depression years, and by 1940 the smaller *Huronic* had been withdrawn from passenger service and placed in package freight service between Sarnia and Port Arthur. This left the *Hamonic* and the *Noronic* to maintain the route (except the spring and fall seasons when the *Noronic* was cruising, during which time only *Hamonic* was used) until 17 July 1945, when a fire broke out on the *Hamonic*. It was while *Hamonic* was on the St. Clair River just off Point Edward that the fire was discovered, and within a short time it began to spread throughout the ship. The captain, seeing that there was little that the crew could do, put the ship into a safe dock at Point Edward, where the passengers and crew could disembark and allow the fire department on shore to quell the blaze. Unfortunately the fire was out of control by that point, and once *Hamonic* had been evacuated, there was little for the firemen to do other than prevent the flames from spreading elsewhere. Although *Hamonic* was a complete loss, casualties were small.

Noronic was left as the sole remaining passenger ship operating from Windsor and Sarnia to the Lakehead, and in keeping with her traditional role, she only operated on that route during the summer months. In 1946 the *Noronic* service offered American vacationers a seven-day cruise from Detroit to Duluth and return, leaving every Thursday from June 14 to September 6. "Over 2,000 miles of cruising" was advertised by Canada Steamship Lines, "visiting Sarnia, the Soo, Port Arthur and Duluth. Fare includes Berths and All Meals." All of this could be had for the price of $70 for an inside berth and $80 for an outside berth.

For the rest of the season *Noronic* could be found cruising almost anywhere on the Great Lakes, even on Lake Ontario after the Welland Canal was enlarged. Some cruises might run from Cleveland and Detroit to Lake Huron and Georgian Bay, for instance, while others took the ship as far east as Prescott on the St. Lawrence River and the Thousand Islands. It was on one of these cruises to Lake Ontario that the *Noronic* met with a disastrous end. She was tied up at Toronto on 17 September 1949 when a fire broke out in a linen closet at about 1:30 in the morning. Most of the 571 passengers had already retired for the evening when the flames were discovered by a steward, but the smoke was spreading fast, aided in part by the ventilation system. It should be pointed out that of the crew of 171, only 15 were on duty.

By the time the fire department arrived, the fire was out of control and there was little that they could do. After an all-night ordeal, the fire was put out but the death toll was rising. Some passengers had been ashore when the fire started and therefore escaped, but for those left on board, the smoke and flames proved too much. Many escaped but many more died in the inferno, mainly from the smoke, although several drowned after jumping overboard. In all, 119 lives were lost, mainly residents of Ohio and Michigan. It was one of the worst disasters ever to hit the Great Lakes and one which would have severe consequences on safety standards for all other ships.

Just as the loss of the *Titanic* off Newfoundland in 1912 prompted governments to rule that all ships must carry sufficient lifeboats to take all passengers and crew, the *Noronic* disaster resulted in new fire protection standards for all vessels on the Great Lakes. It was true that the *Noronic* was primarily a steel ship, but much of her interior was made of wood, with little consideration for fire control such as fire blocks and sprinklers — and *Noronic* was still far better equipped than many other ships of her type. Despite that, however, a Royal Commission found Canada Steamship Lines and the *Noronic's* captain at fault, with the result that the company had to pay out a total of $2,150,000 in damages among 669 claimants.[3] New fire codes were passed by governments on both sides of the border, codes many vessels failed to meet. One by one, ships were withdrawn when owners deemed reconstruction uneconomical in the face of falling traffic levels. Such was the case with the Lake Ontario car ferries *Ontario No. 1* and *Ontario No. 2*, as well as Canadian Pacific's steamer *Manitoba*, to mention but a few.

Huronic was left as the last Northern Navigation steamer, but she too was without a future, and in 1950 made one last voyage, this time to Hamilton for scrapping.

The Canadian Pacific Railway

Though destined to become the parent of one of the world's greatest ocean shipping lines, Canadian Pacific's venture into water transportation really began on the Great Lakes.

The railway company was faced with two problems during its construction years in the early 1880s. First was the fact that the railway was built in two distinct sections, with the line west of the Lakehead to the Rocky Mountains being completed before the line around Lake Superior could be finished. Since it was the policy of the Canadian government to keep the railway entirely in Canada, steamships had to be used to fill in the gap between east and west. Second, in constructing the railway through the rugged country around Lake Superior, sections of track were often located in isolated regions accessible only by water, necessitating the purchase of supply ships to carry in raw materials, food and labourers.

Few if any company officials, however, were familiar with steamship operations, as their expertise lay mainly in railway construction or banking. In obtaining just the right person for the task of setting up the steamer service, general manager William Van Horne approached Henry Beatty of the North West Transportation Company. In September 1882 Beatty became the manager of Canadian Pacific's newly formed steamer service. Under Beatty's command, Canadian Pacific would grow to become one of the principal shipping lines on the Great Lakes.

Beatty's first job was to organize a line of supply boats to keep the numerous construction camps around Lake Superior in provisions and materials. This was no mean feat, for enormous volumes of supplies had to be delivered to makeshift harbours dotted along the Lake Superior shoreline during the season of navigation, which lasted no longer than six or seven months. If insufficient quantities of supplies were delivered, work parties would have to go without until the following spring — while game could be shot for food, there was no substitute for steel rails and dynamite.

For its part, Canadian Pacific assembled a small fleet of steamers as the backbone of the supply line. In 1883 the 323-ton side-wheel passenger tug *Champion No. 2* became the railway's first ship and was soon followed by the 61-ton *Siskiwit* and the former Toronto Island ferry *Juliette* which, as it happened, sank that same year at Pine Tree Harbour on the Bruce Peninsula. The year 1884 brought with it four more ships: The *Dolphin*, the *Emily:* the 377-ton *Georgian*, originally belonging to the London & Port Stanley Railway; and the 18-ton *Magdalena*. For the most part these ships served as tugs, towing barges between Port Arthur, Owen Sound and the depot harbours on Lake Superior, along with the occasional trip to a southern port. Due to their size, *Champion No. 2* and *Georgian* were fully capable of carrying passengers and freight by themselves.

Along with the ships belonging to Canadian Pacific, Beatty employed steamers of the North West Transportation Company and the Owen Sound Steamship Company, plus ships of several smaller firms under various contracts and agreements, both formal and informal. These vessels were responsible for transporting everything from workers to supplies. The ships *Butcher's Boy* and *Butcher's Maid*, for example, carried cattle between Port Arthur and the construction harbours along Lake Superior's shore.[4]

Following the completion of Canadian Pacific's main line around Lake Superior, the supply ships were no longer required and the privately owned steamers resumed their regular duties elsewhere. The company itself was left with a fleet no longer deemed useful and quickly set out to relieve itself of many of the ships. By the end of 1885 *Champion No. 2, Dolphin* (assumed), *Emily* and *Magdalena* had been sold, while *Georgian* and *Siskiwit* were retained. These latter two ships were to serve as railway steamers, with *Siskiwit* by and large working on the Kamistikquia River at Fort William, where she was placed in 1883 to assist ships (particularly sailing vessels) up the river to the railway's elevators and docks, and to carry out any other towing as required. *Siskiwit* was sold in 1894, reportedly to C. Drinkwater of Montreal, but the steamer remained at Fort William, where she burned in August 1895.

Georgian was still owned by Canadian Pacific as late as 1912, even though she was listed as having sunk at Owen Sound in May 1888. She was apparently salvaged, but the event suggests that much of her time was spent around Owen Sound during this period, Owen Sound having become the home port for Canadian Pacific's Great Lakes steamers in 1884. Furthermore, it was indicated in one report of the sinking that *Georgian* was a steambarge, a forerunner to the modern lake freighter, which was primarily designed to carry freight, although limited passenger accommodations were often included.[5] Whether or not *Georgian* took this form during her days with the London & Port Stanley Railway is uncertain, for rebuildings were commonplace and, in the case of the *Georgian*, repairs due to fire damage while in the employ of Burgess & Company of Toronto may very well have resulted in the alteration of her configuration.

If in fact *Georgian* was a steambarge, she may have remained under the Canadian Pacific flag to supplement the package freight business handled by the line's passenger ships between Owen Sound and Fort William, perhaps even travelling to Lake Michigan ports. Dropped from the registers in 1913, *Georgian* survived long enough to see the last two ships, *Assiniboia* and *Keewatin*, purchased by the railway for service on the lakes.

As working boats, the above ships were not alone in Ontario, for Canadian Pacific also owned the steamers *Lottie* and *Mattawan*, both registered at Ottawa, for service on the Ottawa River. Of these two ships, the 22-ton *Mattawan* was probably the first to be acquired, having been built at Portsmouth, Ontario, in 1876 and probably purchased as a supply vessel or a tugboat sometime during the early 1880s, when the old Canada Central main line was being pushed north from Pembroke to North Bay, a route which parallelled the Ottawa River. *Lottie*, at only ten tons, was the smaller of the two and was built for the railway in 1907 at Aylmer, Quebec. Judging by her size, she too must have been a tugboat, since Canadian Pacific did not operate any hotels or resorts along the river for which she could have carried passengers. *Lottie* and *Mattawan* were still owned by Canadian Pacific at the outbreak of World War I.

As important as the railway's working boats were, it was Canadian Pacific's Great Lakes passenger steamers who received the greatest accolades. At the time of Henry Beatty's appointment

The cattle and meat supply boat *Butcher's Boy* at an unidentified supply base on Lake Superior. *Butcher's Boy*, along with the steamer *Butcher's Maid*, was owned by Messrs. Smith & Mitchell of Port Arthur who had the meat supply contract for the Canadian Pacific construction crews working around Lake Superior.

— *OA S1326*

Smith & Mitchell's supply boat *Butcher's Maid* entering Port Caldwell, a scene in which the ruggedness of the Lake Superior shoreline is clearly in evidence.

— *OA S1328*

as manager of shipping services, the company was fully aware of the fact that it would be several years before any passenger train would be able to travel through from Montreal to Port Arthur and on to Winnipeg, and for the interim the railway would have to rely on steamers to fill in the gap. It was therefore among Beatty's first duties to see to the construction of three new steamships, and in 1882 he travelled to the Clyde, Scotland, to place the orders, valued at $300,000 per ship.

The contract went to the shipyard of Charles Connell & Company of Glasgow, for the 2,282-ton *Alberta* while the Kelvinbaugh firm of Aitken & Mansell received the orders for the 1,773-ton *Algoma* and the 2,269-ton *Athabasca.* Despite differences in tonnage, all ships followed the same basic design: 263 feet in length with a beam of 38 feet, a capacity of 2,000 tons of freight and 374 passengers, with stateroom accommodations for 240 in first and tourist class.

After the ships were launched in 1883, they steamed across the Atlantic to Montreal where, owing to the limited size of the St. Lawrence and Welland canals, they had to be cut in two and towed to Buffalo, New York. At Buffalo they were rejoined and taken back to Port Colborne, there to winter over and be outfitted for regular service. After spring break-up, they sailed for Owen Sound.

Originally the railway's engineers had planned to operate the steamers out of the harbour of Algoma Mills at the end of a branch line running west from Sudbury. It was their intention to equip Algoma Mills — which up to this time had acted only as a supply depot — as a fully fledged lake terminal complete with a hotel (construction of which had commenced in 1884). However, in 1884 Canadian Pacific gained control of the Ontario & Quebec Railway, which included a main line under construction from Perth through to Toronto and on to St. Thomas by way of the Credit Valley Railway, as well as branches from Toronto to Orangeville and Owen Sound by way of the Credit Valley and the Toronto, Grey & Bruce railways. In effect, the Ontario & Quebec acquisition gave Canadian Pacific a complete system in southern Ontario independent of its rival, the Grand Trunk.

Perhaps the most important property acquired in the Ontario & Quebec deal at the time was the Toronto, Grey & Bruce Railway, for it gave the company an established harbour at Owen Sound with easy access to Toronto and, once the Ontario & Quebec line was complete, Montreal. In the meantime the Grand Trunk would fill in the distance between Toronto and Montreal. All that Algoma Mills could offer was a lengthy connection to Montreal and an incomplete harbour. As a result, all development at Algoma Mills was cancelled and activity switched to Owen Sound, the new home port for Canadian Pacific steamships on the Great Lakes.

Regular service out of Owen Sound commenced on 11 May 1884, when the *Algoma* departed for Port Arthur carrying 1,000 passengers (mainly immigrants squeezed in on the decks) and a load of freight, thus replacing the makeshift arrangements offered in 1883, the year in which the railway was opened from Port Arthur to Winnipeg. During that season passengers could travel to Winnipeg by three different routes in connection with Canadian Pacific — the North West Transportation Company out of Sarnia; the Lake Superior Royal Mail Line out of Collingwood; and the Owen Sound Steamship Company out of Owen Sound — together advertised by the railway as the "Thunder Bay Route" (see table 8-11). Canadian Pacific claimed as "Undeniable Facts" that "in comparison with the ALL RAIL LINE to Winnipeg, passengers via this NEW ROUTE will save over $10.00 in fare. Will save over 300 miles of travel, and make almost same time through having the advantage of a sailing." This statement was very much directed at the Grand Trunk, whose line, as discussed earlier, represented the only all-rail route to the Northwest, albeit by way of connecting American railroads. Even so, what the Grand Trunk lost the Grand Trunk gained, for at least two of the routes required passengers to travel part of the way over the Grand Trunk, and even the route through Owen Sound by way of the Toronto, Grey & Bruce Railway indirectly involved the Grand Trunk, since the company owned a considerable interest in the Toronto, Grey & Bruce before selling its stocks to the Ontario & Quebec Railway.

Alberta as she appeared prior to departure from Owen Sound in 1884. — *OA S15998*

Algoma, photographed at Owen Sound in 1884. Of the three ships — *Alberta, Athabasca* and *Algoma* — the *Algoma* was the smallest in terms of tonnage. — *OA S15989*

Athabasca at Owen Sound in 1884. — *OA S15988*

Table 8-11
CANADIAN PACIFIC RAILWAY
THUNDER BAY ROUTE
STEAMER CONNECTIONS TO PORT ARTHUR AND WINNIPEG
1883

	Via the Owen Sound Steamship Company		
Lv.	Toronto (TG & B)	4:25 p.m. Tuesday	1:45 p.m. Saturday
Lv.	Owen Sound	10:00 p.m. Tuesday	7:00 p.m. Saturday
Lv.	Port Arthur (CPR)	7:25 p.m. Friday	7:25 p.m. Monday
Ar.	Winnipeg (CPR)	8:00 p.m. Saturday	8:00 p.m. Tuesday
	Via the Collingwood Lake Superior Line		
Lv.	Toronto (GTR/NNWR)	12:00 n'n Tuesday	12:00 n'n Friday
Lv.	Collingwood	4:30 p.m. Tuesday	4:30 p.m. Friday
Lv.	Port Arthur (CPR)	7:25 p.m. Friday	7:25 p.m. Monday
Ar.	Winnipeg (CPR)	8:00 p.m. Saturday	8:00 p.m. Tuesday
	Via the North West Transportation Company		
Lv.	Sarnia	9:00 p.m. Tuesday	9:00 p.m. Friday
Lv.	Port Arthur (CPR)	7:25 p.m. Friday	7:25 p.m. Monday
Ar.	Winnipeg (CPR)	8:00 p.m. Saturday	8:00 p.m. Tuesday

TG & B - Toronto, Grey & Bruce Railway
CPR - Canadian Pacific Railway
GTR - Grand Trunk Railway
NNWR - Northern & North Western Railway

Source: Canadian Pacific Railway poster, "Thunder Bay Route" 1883.

Dependence upon other companies was far from Canadian Pacific's original intentions, thus making the company's 1884 steamship schedule (table 8-12) such a change from 1883. Not only did the railway control the line between Winnipeg and Port Arthur, but with the three new steamers and control of the Ontario & Quebec Railway, the Canadian Pacific was in the position of controlling the entire route from Montreal and Toronto all the way to Manitoba, and that meant profits. Moreover, a steamship express train was added to work in conjunction with the steamers, running only on sailing days and always consisting of at least one parlour car along with the usual coaches and baggage cars.

Canadian Pacific also took pride in the fact that its steamers were the largest then operating on the Great Lakes, boasting in its timetable issued 9 September 1884: "The magnificent Steamships of this line are complete in every detail, their furnishing is luxurious, being equal to the finest ocean steamers, and their menu compares with that of the leading hotels of our large cities." Special emphasis was placed on the fact that the ships were "lighted throughout with Edison's Electric Lights," an important selling point at a time when most other ships were using coal-oil lamps.

Table 8-12
CANADIAN PACIFIC RAILWAY
LAKE AND RAIL CONDENSED TIMETABLE
Fall 1884

Westbound

			Time	ALBERTA Day	ATHABASCA Day	ALGOMA Day
Toronto	CPR	Lv.	10:45 a.m.	Tue.	Thurs.	Sat.
Owen Sound	CPR	Ar.	3:05 p.m.	Tue.	Thurs.	Sat.
Owen Sound	CPSS	Lv.	4:00 p.m.	Tue.	Thurs.	Sat.
Port Arthur	CPSS	Ar.	8:00 a.m.	Thurs.	Sat.	Mon.
Port Arthur	CPR	Lv.	9:15 a.m.*	Thurs.	Sat.	Mon.
Winnipeg	CPR	Ar.	7:00 a.m.*	Fri.	Sun.	Tue.

* - Indicates Central Time. All other times Eastern Time.
CPR - Canadian Pacific Railway
CPSS - Canadian Pacific Steamships

Source: Canadian Pacific Railway Timetable, 9 September 1884.

Steamship passengers were handled in five separate classes. First- and tourist-class ticket-holders were entitled to meals and a berth in one of 58 staterooms arranged around the upper saloon deck, each containing (on average) an upper and lower berth as well as a sofa which could be converted into an additional berth. Second-class, colonist and emigrant passengers were given passage on the main deck only, which included deck berths but neither bedding nor meals. These passengers had to provide their own bedding and meals, although meals could be purchased for 25 cents if so desired.

In common with most inland steamers of the day, the ships were equipped with a central clerestoried saloon for first- and tourist-class passengers; this doubled as a lounge and a 110-seat dining room where "first rate" meals were served. On this point William Van Horne, himself a lover of food, took particular notice. In June 1884 Van Horne carried out an inspection tour of the *Alberta* and shortly thereafter reported to Henry Beatty that, while the food was excellent, there were "altogether too many dishes offered." Instead, Van Horne suggested this combination which guided the menus of the steamship line for the next 80 years: "Fewer varieties, but plenty of each, I have always found to be better appreciated than a host of small, made-up dishes. Poultry of any sort when it can be had is very desirable. Two entrees will be plenty. Deep apple, peach and etc., pie should be the standard in the pastry line; and several of the minor sweets should be left out. Plenty of fresh fish . . . is what people expect to find on the lakes and it is, as a rule, the scarcest article in the steamers' larders."[6]

Not even the coffee escaped Van Horne's scrutiny. He found it bad, "being too weak until I spoke to the steward about it and poor in quality as well containing a considerable percentage of burnt peas."[7] No doubt improvements were made. After all, when William Cornelius Van Horne spoke, people listened!

The year 1884 was a good one for the steamship line, marred only by a collision between the *Alberta* and the steamer *J.M. Osborn* on Lake Superior in July. The *J.M. Osborn* was sunk and three of her crew lost, but fortunately the *Alberta* survived relatively unscathed. The year 1885 would have been even better, but again the line suffered what proved to the worst disaster ever to hit Canadian Pacific's Great Lakes fleet. Late in the season, on November 7, the *Algoma* was steaming across Lake Superior on her way to Port Arthur during a blinding snowstorm. Unbeknownst to the crew, Isle Royale was posed directly in the path of the *Algoma*, and by the time the island was sighted, there was no time to take evasive action. The ship was dashed on the rocks and completely wrecked. Thirty-eight of the passengers and crew were drowned. The few survivors, including two passengers, were later rescued in poor condition by the *Athabasca*. Only the *Algoma's* engines were fit for salvage.

On the same day *Algoma* was wrecked, company officials were driving home the last spike of the Canadian Pacific Railway at Craigelachie, British Columbia.

At first the railway took little interest in replacing the *Algoma*. The main line was almost complete and the company assumed that the shift in passengers travelling from Montreal to the all-rail route around Lake Superior would make the construction of a third ship unnecessary. How wrong they were. The minor loss in traffic experienced by the steamship line was only temporary, and by 1887 Canadian Pacific was taking steps to secure another ship.

As a temporary measure, the company chartered the 1,700-ton steamer *Campana* in 1888. *Campana* was built on the Clyde in 1873 as an ocean-going heavy cargo steamer, but in 1882 she was taken to the upper lakes, becoming the first twin-screw steamship to sail those waters. Running between Owen Sound and Port Arthur, *Campana* made history when she left Port Arthur on 14 May 1883 with the first express shipment to be carried from the West by an entirely Canadian route. Certainly no stranger to the Canadian Pacific, *Campana* fitted into the railway's lake service with ease, showing no difficulty in keeping up with the schedules of *Athabasca* and *Alberta*, as the 1888 steamship timetable (table 8-13) indicates.

Table 8-13
CANADIAN PACIFIC RAILWAY
LAKE AND RAIL CONDENSED TIMETABLE
1888

Westbound

				CAMPANA	ATHABASCA	ALBERTA
			Time	Day	Day	Day
Toronto	CPR	Lv.	11:00 a.m.	Mon.	Wed.	Sat.
Owen Sound	CPSS	Lv.	3:30 p.m.	Mon.	Wed.	Sat.
S.S. Marie, Mich.	CPSS	Ar.	11:00 a.m.	Tue.	Thurs.	Sun.
Port Arthur	CPSS	Ar.	8:30 a.m.	Wed.	Fri.	Mon.
Port Arthur	CPR	Lv.	2:25 p.m.*	Wed.	Fri.	Mon.
Winnipeg	CPR	Ar.	9:30 a.m.*	Thur.	Sat.	Tue.

Eastbound

				CAMPANA	ATHABASCA	ALBERTA
			Time	Day	Day	Day
Winnipeg	CPR	Lv.	6:00 p.m.*	Sun.	Wed.	Fri.
Port Arthur	CPR	Ar.	2:15 p.m.*	Tue.	Thurs.	Sat.
Port Arthur	CPSS	Lv.	3:00 p.m.	Tue.	Thurs.	Sat.
S.S. Marie, Mich.	CPSS	Ar.	11:00 a.m.	Wed.	Fri.	Sun.
Owen Sound	CPSS	Ar.	8:00 a.m.	Thurs.	Sat.	Mon.
Toronto	CPR	Ar.	12:00 n'n	Thurs.	Sat.	Mon.

* - Indicates Central Time. All other times Eastern Time.

Source: Canadian Pacific Railway Timetable, 9 July 1888.

Supplementing the company's regular Lakehead sailings, Canadian Pacific also added the steamers *Carmona* and *Cambria* on a twice-weekly local timetable between Owen Sound and Sault Ste. Marie, and to Mackinac Island during July and August. However, these ships were not owned by Canadian Pacific, rather they were owned by the Canada Transit Company, Limited, and operated in close connection with the line. *Carmona* was acquired by the company in 1888 from the North West Transportation Company, where she was known as the *Manitoba*. Similarly, *Cambria* was purchased as the *Champion No. 2* from Canadian Pacific in 1887 and shortly afterward enlarged at Owen Sound.

Cambria was built in 1877 as the passenger tug *Champion No. 2* and became the first steamship ever owned by the Canadian Pacific when the railway purchased her in 1883 as a supply ship. Sold by the railway in 1885, she passed to Canada Transit who had her rebuilt as the *Cambria* in 1887. The ship was broken up in 1902. — *OA Acc. 2375 S5387*

Built as the *Manitoba* in 1871 for the North West Transportation Company, the *Manitoba* was sold in 1888 to the Canada Transit Company, becoming their *Carmona.* Although owned by Canada Transit, the *Carmona* was operated in close connection with the Canadian Pacific and even carried the railway's smoke stack colours as can be seen in this photograph from the 1890s. *Carmona* was sold to the Georgian Bay Navigation Company and rebuilt as the *Pittsburgh* in 1900, burning two years later. — *OA S13162*

Until a replacement for the wrecked *Algoma* could be built, the Canadian Pacific chartered the steamship *Campana*. *Campana* is seen here at Collingwood in 1889 or 1890, the Canadian Pacific red and white stack colours having been recently painted out. The Northern Railway grain elevator appears at the left while the *Atlantic* of the Great Northern Transit Company is on the right.
— *OA Acc. 14996-37*

Here is a rare view of *Manitoba*'s launching at Owen Sound in 1889, taken just as *Manitoba*'s stern entered the water. The locomotive at the lower left, presumably at the head of a special director's train, is an unidentified 4-4-0 equipped with footboards at the front, suggesting she was used for switching at Owen Sound, and was probably inherited from the Toronto, Grey & Bruce Railway.
— *OA S15976*

Cambria and *Carmona* provided the railway with valuable connections to points along the north shore of Georgian Bay and Lake Huron, as well as to the holiday community on Mackinac Island, frequented by many of the United States' most powerful and influential citizens. Round-trip excursions to Sault Ste. Marie and Mackinac Island were especially promoted during the summer by the railway, which was becoming increasingly conscious of the tourist trade. The following is from the 9 July 1888 timetable: "This trip is an exceedingly charming and invigorating one. Leaving Toronto, at 4:40 p.m. by the CANADIAN PACIFIC RAILWAY, we arrive at the thriving town of OWEN SOUND, where we embark on the "CAMBRIA" or "CARMONA," first stop being Killarney, where all are delighted, enraptured at the unexpected richness and variety of the scenery. The steamer passes on past islands of all sorts and sizes, up Manitowaning Bay, calling at MANITOWANING, SHEGUINDAH, LITTLE CURRENT, KAGAWONG and GORE BAY, all ports on the Great Manitoulin Island. Leaving Gore Bay the steamer crosses over to the main land, calling at SPANISH and SERPENT RIVERS, and ALGOMA MILLS, from which the Canadian Pacific Railway Algoma Branch, extends to SUDBURY and Sault Ste. Marie, a distance of about 90 miles in either direction. Leaving ALGOMA MILLS the route is along the coast to BLIND RIVER, THESSALON (where excellent sport is offered to fishermen), and BRUCE MINES, ST. JOSEPH'S ISLAND is then called at, and several small lakes crossed until the mouth of the St. Mary River is reached, at the head of which is the coming great city, SAULT STE. MARIE, the terminus of the Sault Branch of the Canadian Pacific Railway, which is connected with the American shore by a superb steel bridge. The Great Ship Canal, the largest and finest structure of the kind in the world, forms the navigable link between Lakes Superior and Huron, and the Falls of St. Mary will in themselves warrant a visit. Leaving Sault Ste. Marie, the steamer will proceed via the American channel past Sailors' Encampment, to the southwest of St. Joseph's Island, through Detour passage, to Mackinac Island, which is looked upon as the Gem of the Great Lakes."

Whether passengers travelled by way of the regular Lake Superior steamers or by way of the *Cambria* or the *Carmona*, Sault Ste. Marie, Michigan, offered them a choice of connecting services. By rail, the Minneapolis, Sault Ste. Marie & Atlantic Railway would take passengers as far as St. Paul and Minneapolis, Minnesota, while the Duluth, South Shore & Atlantic catered to various northern Michigan communities. In both cases, the Canadian Pacific held considerable interests, hence their inclusion in the steamship lines' 1888 timetable. They are still owned by the Canadian Pacific today, operated as the "Soo Line."

By water the Lake Superior Transit Company offered service to Duluth, leaving Sault Ste. Marie at 8 a.m. Sundays, Mondays, Wednesdays and Saturdays, and along the way calling at Marquette, L'Anse, Portage Lake, and Ontonagon, Michigan; Ashland, Washburn and Bayfield, Wisconsin; and finally Duluth, Minnesota. Steamers of the Delta Transportation Company left Sault Ste. Marie daily at 6 a.m., Sundays excepted, for the Michigan ports of Detour, Mackinac Island, St. Ignace, Mackinac City and Cheboygen. Returning ships left Cheboygan at 6 a.m. daily except Sundays.

Like the railways, who always outlined connecting timetables, the steamship lines felt the benefits of providing schedules for other companies, giving passengers a variety of destinations — more than any one company could offer — and despite the fact that any one of which could be reached by an alternate route, they were encouraged to take that company's own ships. For example, the North West Transportation Company ran ships between Sarnia, Sault Ste. Marie, Port Arthur and Duluth without change of ship. But passengers would have had to reach Sarnia by way of the Grand Trunk, and unless they were to board a Canadian Pacific train at Port Arthur, for instance, the line could provide no source of revenue for the Canadian Pacific. Therefore, by offering connecting services at Sault Ste. Marie, Canadian Pacific guaranteed that it would make money from passengers at least to that point, since they would have to take a train to Owen Sound and then board a Canadian Pacific steamer. It was just that kind of arrangement that the company encouraged. As William Van Horne so often said, why should he let others skim off the cream and leave the skim milk for the railway.

Price-wise the company's return fares in 1888 were advertised as being "Cheaper than Ice," implying the economy of the Canadian Pacific line over all others. From Toronto, Port Arthur could be reached for $30, Sault Ste. Marie $16, Mackinac $16, and Duluth $32. All prices included meals and berths and were return.

In August 1888 work began on the company's replacement for the wrecked *Algoma* at the newly established Owen Sound yard of Polson Iron Works. The new ship, the first built of steel in Canada, was launched a mere nine months later, in May 1889, as the *Manitoba*, and at 2,616 tons, it held the distinction of being the largest vessel then afloat on fresh water. Her engines were salvaged from the *Algoma* and were supplied with steam from boilers fabricated at Polson's Toronto works; shipped by rail to Owen Sound, the boilers represented the largest shipment ever to be made by rail in North America to that time. *Manitoba's* extra size enabled her to hold an extra ten staterooms over her sister ships *Alberta* and *Athabasca*. Following her outfitting, *Manitoba* took over from the *Campana* later in 1889.

Campana eventually returned to salt water when she was purchased by the Quebec Steamship Company in the 1890s and placed in service between Montreal and Pictou, Nova Scotia.[8] Even *Carmona* and *Cambria* were gone from the Canadian Pacific timetables by 1891, the year they were sold by Canada Transit.

The year 1892 found *Alberta, Athabasca* and *Manitoba* providing the same basic service between Owen Sound and the Lakehead as always, but there were a few changes. By this time Canadian Pacific had adopted Fort William as its principal Lakehead port, relegating Port Arthur to second place and, when water levels on Lake Superior were low, omitting Port Arthur entirely. There were also the usual timetable changes, as table 8-14 shows, but these were generally limited to minor differences in arrival and departure times. Unfortunately the 19 July 1892 Canadian Pacific *Annotated Timetable* from which these times were obtained did not indicate which ships left or arrived on which days, resulting in the ship assignments being extrapolated from the 1888 schedule, replacing *Campana* with *Manitoba*.

An interesting item of note in the 1892 timetable is the appearance of the *Cambria*, now under the ownership of the Port Arthur & Duluth Steam Packet Company, providing connections to Duluth as follows:

Westbound

Port Arthur	Lv.	7:00 p.m.	Wed., Sat., Mon.
Duluth	Ar.	1:00 p.m.	Thurs., Sun., Tue.

Eastbound

Duluth	Lv.	7:30 p.m.	Thurs., Sun., Tue.
Port Arthur	Ar.	1:30 p.m.	Fri., Mon., Wed.

Cambria indeed had a very busy schedule, made necessary in order to provide reasonably close connections with Canadian Pacific's steamships.

During the late 1890s Canadian Pacific ran the *Alberta* out of Windsor between June 26 and August 28, running her directly to Fort William without detouring to Owen Sound. Departure from Windsor took place every Saturday at 3 o'clock in the afternoon, arriving at Fort William on Monday. Returning, *Alberta* left the Lakehead on Tuesday, arriving back at Windsor at noon Thursday.[9] It is not known whether these sailings were offered in connection with a Toronto boat train or not, but in all likelihood the answer is no. Regular trains from Toronto were fully adequate, since it would appear that this service was operated largely for the benefit of American tourists from nearby Detroit and the Midwest.

Alberta always returned to Owen Sound in September, just in time to help in transporting the western grain harvest. Together, *Alberta, Athabasca* and *Manitoba* could move about 400,000 bushels of grain a month between the Canadian Pacific elevators at Fort William and Owen Sound,

Manitoba departing Owen Sound in July 1904. Note the red and white checkered Canadian Pacific house-flag flying from *Manitoba*'s centre mast.
— *OA S13232*

An aerial view of the *Manitoba* from the 1930s. The raised forecastle and wheelhouse represent some of the later alterations made to the *Manitoba* in this century.
— *OA RG 1/E 13-Book 5, 16*

Table 8-14
CANADIAN PACIFIC RAILWAY
LAKE AND RAIL CONDENSED TIMETABLE
1892

Westbound

				MANITOBA	ATHABASCA	ALBERTA
			Time	Day	Day	Day
Toronto	CPR	Lv.	11:10 a.m.	Mon.	Wed.	Sat.
Owen Sound	CPR	Ar.	3:20 p.m.	Mon.	Wed.	Sat.
Owen Sound	CPSS	Lv.				
Sault Ste. Marie	CPSS	Ar.	11:00 a.m.	Tue.	Thurs.	Sun.
Sault Ste. Marie	CPSS	Lv.	11:30 a.m.	Tue.	Thurs.	Sun.
Port Arthur	CPSS	Ar.	. . .	. . .	. . .	. . .
Fort William	CPSS	Ar.	10:00 a.m.	Wed.	Fri.	Mon.
Fort William	CPR	Lv.	3:10 p.m.*	Wed.	Fri.	Mon.
Winnipeg	CPR	Ar.	2:20 p.m.*	Thurs.	Sat.	Tue.

Eastbound

				ALBERTA	MANITOBA	ATHABASCA
			Time	Day	Day	Day
Winnipeg	CPR	Lv.	5:45 p.m.*	Wed.	Fri.	Mon.
Fort William	CPR	Ar.	12:30 p.m.	Thurs.	Sat.	Tue.
Fort William	CPSS	Lv.	12:45 p.m.	Thurs.	Sat.	Tue.
Port Arthur	CPSS	Lv.	. . .	. . .	. . .	. . .
Sault Ste. Marie	CPSS	Ar.	11:00 a.m.	Fri.	Sun.	Wed.
Sault Ste. Marie	CPSS	Lv.	11:30 a.m.	Fri.	Sun.	Wed.
Owen Sound	CPSS	Ar.	10:00 a.m.	Sat.	Mon.	Thurs.
Owen Sound	CPR	Lv.				
Toronto	CPR	Ar.	2:00 p.m.	Sat.	Mon.	Thurs.

* - Indicates Central Time. All other times Eastern Time.
Note - Ships assigned departure and arrival days based on the 1888 timetable and therefore may have differed.

Source: Canadian Pacific Railway Timetable, 19 July 1892.

twice the capacity of the North West Transportation Company.[10] Of course bulk carriers were more efficient and offered greater carrying capacities, but it should be remembered that Canadian Pacific's steamers carried passengers as well as package freight and that any grain carried had to be bagged. This fact later resulted in the steamers concentrating mainly on southbound feed and flour shipments. Northbound cargoes consisted of anything packaged, from binder twine to household goods.

By 1900 or 1901 all three ships were sailing out of Owen Sound for the entire season. Perhaps competition from the Northern Navigation Company at Windsor and Sarnia gave the Canadian Pacific's management second thoughts about basing the *Alberta* at Windsor for the summer. Nevertheless, business was improving, especially with tourists, who looked upon the lake voyage as a delightful alternative to taking the train through northern Ontario. This trade demanded the very best in first-class accommodation, and in comparison with newer ships such as Northern Navigation's *Huronic*, the *Alberta*, *Athabasca* and *Manitoba* were becoming increasingly inadequate.

Around 1906 plans were finalized for two new ships that would cater exclusively to first-class passengers (plus package freight) in a style more like the transatlantic liners than the fresh-water

The Canadian Pacific Railway yard at Owen Sound as it appeared in 1898. The station is at the right while the steamer docks are beyond the freight sheds on the left. Rising in the background are the railway's two grain elevators: Elevator A on the left; Elevator B on the right. — *CPCA A12289*

The *Alberta* was rebuilt by Collingwood Shipbuilding in 1911. The most notable changes made were the raised forecastle and the passenger deck built over the clerestoried cabin roof. — *OA S15957*

vessels. Even though Canadian shipbuilders on the lakes were fully equipped to construct such vessels, Canadian Pacific awarded the contracts to the Fairfield Shipbuilding & Engineering Company of Govan, Scotland, who had just completed the Canadian Pacific liners *Empress of Ireland* and *Empress of Britain* for the Atlantic service. Launched in 1907, the sister ships were christened *Assiniboia* and *Keewatin*, grossing 3,880 tons and 3,856 tons respectively, thereby continuing the railway's tradition of naming its new lake boats after districts and provinces in the Northwest Territories and Ontario. The names *Alberta* and *Manitoba* are by now self-explanatory, both having become provinces. The others, however, are more obscure to modern ears. Athabasca District originally took in much of northern Alberta and Saskatchewan around Lake Athabasca, while Algoma District covered most of the land lying north of Lake Huron and east of Lake Superior, including the city of Sault Ste. Marie Ontario; the region is still known as *Algoma*. Assiniboia District once covered all of southern Saskatchewan and took its name from the Asiniboine Indians, while the Keewatin District comprised of most of northwest Ontario. It was around the time that the *Keewatin* and the *Assiniboia* were launched that most of these districts geographically became part of the provinces of Ontario, Manitoba, Saskatchewan and Alberta.

When *Keewatin* and *Assiniboia* arrived at Levis, Quebec, in 1907, they were cut in two by the Davie Shipyard and towed through the St. Lawrence and Welland Canal systems to Buffalo, where they were rejoined by Buffalo Dry Dock in an exercise reminiscent of the time in 1883 when *Algoma*, *Athabasca* and *Alberta* followed the same procedure to reach the upper Great Lakes. The final fitting-out for *Keewatin* and *Assiniboia* was done at Owen Sound.

The new ships were much larger than their older sisters, each having a capacity of 147,000 cubic feet of freight and 181 first-class cabins. The new ships were delivered in the same basic colour scheme as the older ships, namely black hull with white upper decks and trim. However, by this time the funnel colours, originally black decorated with two wide red rings separated by a narrow white ring, had been altered to a mustard-yellow colour capped with black. In later years the colour scheme was altered again, resulting in an overall white scheme (including the hull) with black trim. This scheme was in use by the early 1920s.

Another contrast to the earlier vessels, whose cabins were situated around a single saloon deck, was that the new ships accommodated their passengers in staterooms on two decks, boasting "a flower lounge two decks high with stained-glass skylight and many pot plants, a dining saloon seating 120, and a ballroom lounge depicting various countries of the Commonwealth."[11]

As for the cabin arrangements themselves, cabins 1 through 29 were located on the upper deck and were described in the 1953 Canadian Pacific brochure *Great Lakes Way* as follows: "Each room except 1, 4, 5 and 6 has two berths and one sofa berth. Room 1 has four berths and a long seat. Rooms 4 and 5 have two berths and a long seat. Room 6 is De Luxe Room with twin beds and private bathroom." Rooms 30 through 181 on the main deck were equipped as follows: "All Inside Rooms except 101 and 149 have two berths and a long seat, Rooms 101 and 149 have two berths and a short seat only. Each Outside Room except 166, 168, 171, 173, 174 and 177 has two berths and a sofa berth; Rooms 168 and 177 are De Luxe Rooms with double bed, sofa berth and private bathroom. Rooms 166, 171, 173 and 175 are De Luxe Rooms with twin beds and private bathroom."

Following the introduction of the new ships in 1908, the line was in a position to offer five departures a week instead of three, but even so, the fleet's days at Owen Sound were numbered. Work on a new main line running north from Toronto to Sudbury had just been completed, lessening to some extent the need for the steamers. Since 1905 the railway had been working on a new line from Bethany Junction on the former Toronto-Montreal main line through Peterborough to a point on Georgian Bay named, by the company, Port McNicoll. This new route was established to provide a shorter rail route to Montreal in order to facilitate the important grain trade and also compete in this lucrative market with the Grand Trunk, already entrenched at Midland, near Port McNicoll. The new harbour received the latest in modern facilities, including elevators and an up-to-date terminal for the Great Lakes fleet. When the grain elevators at Owen Sound burned in 1911, no attempt was made to rebuild, since they were now redundant.

By the spring of 1912 all of the ships had transferred to Port McNicoll, including the *Athabasca* and the *Alberta*, both newly rebuilt and enlarged by Collingwood Shipbuilding in 1910

Assiniboia leaving Owen Sound, quite possibly on her first revenue voyage in 1908. The Canadian Pacific Elevator A is on the left along with the marine tower of Elevator B. — *OA S15991*

A publicity photo of *Assiniboia* from around 1930. Much of the water has been retouched to accentuate the waves. — *CPCA No. 6700*

and 1911 respectively. Under the 1912 schedule reproduced in table 8-15, all ships except for *Manitoba* ran directly between Port McNicoll and the Lakehead without calling in at Owen Sound; only *Manitoba* made the stop on her way west, but eastbound she omitted Owen Sound entirely. The running times of all ships should be noted here, with the new ships proving to be the fastest.

All boat trains during the 1912 season ran to Port McNicoll, and for the first time since 1884 Owen Sound was without its own express train.

In 1916 *Alberta* and *Athabasca* were relegated to freight service only, resulting in a major readjustment in the steamer schedules by the time the 1918 timetable was published (see table 8-16). While *Keewatin* and *Assiniboia* continued to run out of Port McNicoll, *Manitoba* was returned to her Owen Sound home and a steamship special of sorts was once again running into the town. Actually the "special" was the regular train, number 707 northbound and number 706 southbound, which operated daily except Sunday and was equipped with a buffet-parlour car along with the regular consist of coaches. On sailing days *Manitoba's* arrival and departure times were co-ordinated with these trains. Before 1912 only the steamship express trains carried "luxury" coaches such as parlour cars.

Table 8-15
CANADIAN PACIFIC RAILWAY
LAKE AND RAIL CONDENSED TIMETABLE
1912

Westbound

		KEEWATIN ASSINIBOIA		MANITOBA		ATHABASCA ALBERTA	
		Time	Day	Time	Day	Time	Day
Toronto	Lv.	12:45 p.m.	Tue., Sat.	12:45 p.m.	Wed.	12:45 p.m.	Mon., Thu.
Port McNicoll	Ar.	3:55 p.m.	Tue., Sat.	3:55 p.m.	Wed.	4:00 p.m.	Mon., Thu.
Port McNicoll	Lv.	4:00 p.m.	Tue., Sat.	4:00 p.m.	Wed.	4:00 p.m.	Mon., Thu.
Owen Sound	...	...		10:30 p.m.	Wed.	...	
Sault Ste. Marie		11:30 a.m.	Wed., Sun.	6:30 p.m.	Thu.	2:30 p.m.	Tue., Fri.
Port Arthur	Ar.	6:30 a.m.	Thu., Mon.	4:30 p.m.	Fri.	1:00 p.m.	Wed., Sat.
Fort William	Ar.	7:30 a.m.	Thu., Mon.	5:30 p.m.	Fri.	2:00 p.m.	Wed., Sat.
Fort William	Lv.	8:30 a.m.*	Thu., Mon.	9:50 p.m.*	Fri.	9:50 p.m.*	Wed., Sat.
Winnipeg	Ar.	9:15 p.m.*	Thu., Mon.	11:30 a.m.*	Sat.	11:30 p.m.*	Thu., Sun.

Keewatin in the 1930s, probably at Port Arthur. — *CPCA No. 6699*

Eastbound

		KEEWATIN ASSINIBOIA		MANITOBA ATHABASCA ALBERTA	
		Time	Day	Time	Day
Winnipeg	Lv.	9:25 p.m.*	Thu., Mon.	9:25 p.m.*	Sat., Wed., Fri.
Fort William	Ar.	10:20 a.m.*	Fri., Tue.	10:20 a.m.*	Sun., Thu., Sat.
Fort William	Lv.	2:00 p.m.	Fri., Tue.	2:00 p.m.	Sun., Thu., Sat.
Port Arthur		3:00 p.m.	Fri., Tue.	3:00 p.m.	Sun., Thu., Sat.
Sault Ste. Marie		12:00 n'n	Sat., Wed.	1:00 p.m.	Mon., Fri., Sun.
Owen Sound		. . .		. . .	
Port McNicoll	Ar.	8:30 a.m.	Sun., Thu.	11:30 a.m.	Tue., Sat., Mon.
Port McNicoll	Lv.	8:45 a.m.	Sun., Thu.	11:45 a.m.	Tue., Sat., Mon.
Toronto	Ar.	12:00 n'n	Sun., Thu.	3:00 p.m.	Tue., Sat., Mon.

* - Indicates Central Time. All other times Eastern Time.

Source: Canadian Pacific Railway Timetable, 1 July 1912.

Table 8-16
CANADIAN PACIFIC RAILWAY
LAKE AND RAIL CONDENSED TIMETABLE
1918

Westbound

		KEEWATIN ASSINIBOIA		MANITOBA		ATHABASCA ALBERTA	
		Time	Day	Time	Day	Time	Day
Toronto	Lv.	5:25 p.m.	Mon.	2:00 p.m.	Wed.	2:00 p.m.	Sat.
Owen Sound	Ar.	10:30 p.m.	Mon.	. . .		. . .	
Owen Sound	Lv.	10:30 p.m.	Mon.	. . .		. . .	
Port McNicoll	Ar.	. . .		5:15 p.m.	Wed.	5:15 p.m.	Sat.
Port McNicoll	Lv.	. . .		5:30 p.m.	Wed.	5:30 p.m.	Sat.
Sault Ste. Marie	Ar.	6:00 p.m.	Tue.	12:00 n'n	Thu.	12:00 n'n	Sun.
Sault Ste. Marie	Lv.	6:00 p.m.	Tue.	12:30 p.m.	Thu.	12:30 p.m.	Sun.
Port Arthur	Ar.	3:00 p.m.	Wed.	7:00 a.m.	Fri.	7:00 a.m.	Mon.
Fort William	Ar.	4:00 p.m.	Wed.	8:30 a.m.	Fri.	8:30 a.m.	Mon.
Fort William	Lv.	11:05 p.m.*	Wed.	8:30 a.m.	Fri.	8:30 a.m.	Mon.
Winnipeg	Ar.	12:00 n'n*	Thu.	10:05 p.m.*	Fri.	10:05 p.m.*	Mon.

Eastbound

		MANITOBA		KEEWATIN		ASSINIBOIA	
		Time	Day	Time	Day	Time	Day
Winnipeg	Lv.	9:10 p.m.*	Wed.	9:10 p.m.*	Fri.	9:10 p.m.*	Tue.
Fort William	Ar.	10:00 a.m.*	Thu.	10:00 a.m.*	Sat.	10:00 a.m.*	Wed.
Fort William	Lv.	12:00 n'n	Thu.	12:00 n'n	Sat.	12:00 n'n	Wed.
Port Arthur	Lv.	1:00 p.m.	Thu.	1:00 p.m.	Sat.	1:00 p.m.	Wed.
Sault Ste. Marie	Ar.	9:00 a.m.	Fri.	12:30 p.m.	Sun.	12:30 p.m.	Thu.
Sault Ste. Marie	Lv.	9:00 a.m.	Fri.	1:00 p.m.	Sun.	1:00 p.m.	Thu.
Owen Sound	Ar.	6:00 a.m.	Sat.	. . .		. . .	
Owen Sound	Lv.	6:40 a.m.	Sat.	. . .		. . .	
Port McNicoll	Ar.	. . .		8:00 a.m.	Mon.	8:00 a.m.	Fri.

Port McNicoll	Lv.	. . .	8:30 a.m. Mon.	8:30 a.m. Fri.
Toronto	Ar.	11:35 a.m. Sat.	11:45 a.m. Mon.	11:45 a.m. Fri.

* - Indicates Central Time. All other times Eastern Time.

Source: Canadian Pacific Railway Timetable, 14 July 1918.

As we shall see in more detail later, the regular season of the steamers was gradually being cut back. In 1918 *Manitoba's* scheduled sailings started on May 2 with her first trip out of Owen Sound, ending with her return on September 29, following which time unscheduled freight service was provided, though passengers were accommodated. The regular season for *Keewatin* and *Assiniboia* was even shorter, lasting from June 1 through to September 28. Similar to *Manitoba*, these ships operated in freight service during May and during October and November.

Traffic for Canadian Pacific remained buoyant throughout the twenties, allowing the railway to make significant consolidations and improvements. On the Great Lakes, the company's steamers continued their popular service, particularly in regards to tourist traffic, which had by and large replaced the earlier immigrant movements westward. Package freight, too, was holding its own and kept *Alberta* and *Athabasca* busy during these years as well as supplementing the revenue derived from the passenger steamers. When the Depression came in late 1929, however, traffic suffered, and by 1932 the railway was experiencing losses in traffic by as much as 40 to 50 percent over the preceding decade. In the face of hard times, the company was forced to rationalize its Great Lakes service, and by the mid-1930s *Alberta* and *Athabasca* were laid up pending improved conditions in the future.

Fortunately for *Keewatin*, *Assiniboia* and *Manitoba*, conditions never resulted in their withdrawal, for despite the general loss of business for the railway, there were always passengers with wealth enough to patronize the steamers. In 1930, the last big revenue year before the effects of the financial crash were really felt by the company, steamship service was being provided on the basis of the schedule reproduced in table 8-17. As can be seen, there was little change over the 1918 timetable (table 8-16) and, for that matter, there would not be any significant alterations until after the Second World War.

Table 8-17
CANADIAN PACIFIC RAILWAY
LAKE AND RAIL CONDENSED TIMETABLE
1930

Westbound

		MANITOBA	KEEWATIN	ASSINIBOIA
		Time Day	Time Day	Time Day
Toronto	Lv.	5:10 p.m. Mon.	12:30 p.m. Wed.	12:30 p.m. Sat.
Owen Sound	Ar.	9:40 p.m. Mon.	. . .	. . .
Owen Sound	Lv.	9:40 p.m. Mon.	. . .	. . .
Port McNicoll	Ar.	. . .	3:40 p.m. Wed.	3:40 p.m. Sat.
Port McNicoll	Lv.	. . .	4:00 p.m. Wed.	4:00 p.m. Sat.
Sault Ste. Marie	Ar.	4:40 p.m. Tue.	10:30 a.m. Thu.	10:30 a.m. Sun.
Sault Ste. Marie	Lv.	4:40 p.m. Tue.	12:00 n'n Thu.	12:00 n'n Sun.
Port Arthur	Ar.	1:30 p.m. Wed.	6:30 a.m. Fri.	6:30 a.m. Mon.
Fort William	Ar.	2:30 p.m. Wed.	8:00 a.m. Fri.	8:00 a.m. Mon.
Fort William	Lv.	8:20 p.m.* Wed.	7:30 a.m.* Fri.	7:30 a.m.* Mon.
Winnipeg	Ar.	7:45 a.m.* Thu.	6:30 p.m.* Fri.	6:30 p.m.* Mon.

Eastbound

		MANITOBA	KEEWATIN	ASSINIBOIA
		Time Day	Time Day	Time Day
Winnipeg	Lv.	6:30 p.m.* Wed.	10:00 p.m.* Fri.	10:00 p.m.* Tue.
Fort William	Ar.	5:35 a.m.* Thu.	10:00 a.m.* Sat.	10:00 a.m.* Wed.

Fort William	Lv.	12:00 n'n Thu.	12:30 p.m. Sat.	12:30 p.m. Wed.
Port Arthur	Lv.	1:00 p.m. Thu.	1:30 p.m. Sat.	1:30 p.m. Wed.
Sault Ste. Marie	Ar.	10:30 a.m. Fri.	9:00 a.m. Sun.	9:00 a.m. Thu.
Sault Ste. Marie	Lv.	10:30 a.m. Fri.	1:00 p.m. Sun.	1:00 p.m. Thu.
Owen Sound	Ar.	6:00 a.m. Sat.	...	...
Owen Sound	Lv.	7:00 a.m. Sat.	...	...
Port McNicoll	Ar.	...	8:00 a.m. Mon.	8:00 a.m. Fri.
Port McNicoll	Lv.	...	8:20 a.m. Mon.	8:20 a.m. Fri.
Toronto	Ar.	11:20 a.m. Sat.	11:15 a.m. Mon.	11:15 a.m. Fri.

* - Indicates Central Time. All other times Eastern Time.

Source: Canadian Pacific Railway Timetable, 1 March 1930.

In 1937, just before the outbreak of World War II, an increase in traffic resulted in the reactivation of the *Alberta* and the *Athabasca* to package freight service. This time the ships were placed on a new route running between Port McNicoll and the Lake Michigan ports of Chicago and Milwaukee. When the war ended, the two veterans once again became redundant, and in August 1946 they were sold off as fruit carriers to a Florida company. They were scrapped in 1948.

Following the *Noronic* disaster in 1949, the whole question of safety on board Great Lakes steamers came to the forefront, and for the first time in the history of Canadian Pacific's steamship line on the Great Lakes, the possibility of scrapping the fleet seemed entirely feasible. The aging *Manitoba* was no longer deemed worthy of rebuilding, and after being withdrawn in 1950 she was sold and scrapped the following year. *Assiniboia* and *Keewatin* were more fortunate. They were solid, relatively modern ships, and since there was still a demand for their services, the cost of making the necessary repairs and alterations would more than pay for itself. As a result, they were outfitted with sprinklers and fire bulkheads at Midland during the winter of 1950-51, at the same time losing their three wooden masts in favour of two of steel.

Throughout most of the 1950s and 1960s, the steamers provided a twice-weekly service along the lines of the 1955 schedule shown in table 8-18. Unfortunately the earlier rebuildings and other modifications made to the vessels were only stopgap measures and could not hide the fact that the ships were reaching the end of their useful lives. By the mid-1960s Canadian Pacific had reached the conclusion that it was no longer economical to operate the ships, nor was it feasible to build even one new vessel to replace *Keewatin* and *Assiniboia*. In 1965 the railway steamers carried their last passengers and were placed into strictly freight service. *Keewatin* served until November 1966, when she was sold for scrap, but fortunately she was sold again the following June and towed to Douglas, Michigan, to become a marine museum. On 26 November 1967 *Assiniboia* made her last voyage for Canadian Pacific, ending almost 90 years of Canadian Pacific navigation on the lakes. In August 1968 Assiniboia was towed to West Deptford, New Jersey, to become a floating restaurant. She caught fire and burned in November 1969.

Table 8-18
CANADIAN PACIFIC RAILWAY
LAKE AND RAIL CONDENSED TIMETABLE
1955

Westbound

				KEEWATIN	ASSINIBOIA
			Time	Day	Day
Toronto	CPR	Lv.	12:01 p.m.	Wed.	Sat.
Port McNicoll	CPR	Ar.	3:00 p.m.	Wed.	Sat.
Port McNicoll	CPSS	Lv.	3:15 p.m.	Wed.	Sat.
Sault Ste. Marie	CPSS	Ar.	9:45 a.m.	Thurs.	Sun.
Sault Ste. Marie	CPSS	Lv.	11:45 a.m.	Thurs.	Sun.
Port Arthur	CPSS	Ar.	6:30 a.m.	Fri.	Mon.
Fort William	CPSS	Ar.	7:45 a.m.	Fri.	Mon.
Fort William	CPR	Lv.	7:50 a.m.*	Fri.	Mon.

Winnipeg	CPR	Ar.	7:30 p.m.*	Fri.	Mon.
			Eastbound		
				KEEWATIN	ASSINIBOIA
			Time	Day	Day
Winnipeg	CPR	Lv.	6:35 p.m.*	Fri.	Mon.
Fort William	CPR	Ar.	4:55 a.m.*	Sat.	Tue.
Fort William	CPSS	Lv.	12:30 p.m.	Sat.	Tue.
Port Arthur	CPSS	Lv.	2:00 p.m.	Sat.	Tue.
Sault Ste. Marie	CPSS	Ar.	9:00 a.m.	Sun.	Wed.
Sault Ste. Marie	CPSS	Lv.	12:30 p.m.	Sun.	Wed.
Port McNicoll	CPSS	Ar.	8:00 a.m.	Mon.	Thurs.
Port McNicoll	CPR	Lv.	8:15 a.m.	Mon.	Thurs.
Toronto	CPR	Ar.	11:15 a.m.	Mon.	Thurs.

* - Indicates Central Time. All other times Eastern Time.

Source: Canadian Pacific Railway Timetable, 24 April 1955.

The Canadian Pacific Railway Boat Trains

To the very end of passenger service on the Great Lakes, Canadian Pacific's steamers operated in close connection with steamship express trains. As a matter of fact the trains which ran out of Toronto in connection with *Keewatin* and *Assiniboia* until 1965 were the last boat trains to operate in North America. A review of some of these boat trains is therefore in order, for their evolution was inextricably mixed with that of the steamships.

Oldest of the boat train routes was that following the old Toronto, Grey & Bruce Railway between Toronto and Owen Sound. It was the Toronto, Grey & Bruce that started the tradition around 1882 or 1883 when the Owen Sound Steamship Company began running its steamers *Spartan*, *Africa* and *Magnet* to Port Arthur in connection with the Canadian Pacific for Winnipeg. However, it was following the Canadian Pacific takeover of the railway in 1884 (through the Ontario & Quebec Railway), along with the introduction of the Canadian Pacific lake steamers, that the steamship express trains became a prominent feature.

From 1884 until 1908, the steamship expresses operated only on the days that the steamers arrived and departed, making regular stops at West Toronto (formerly Toronto Junction), Melville Junction, and Orangeville on the way between Toronto and Owen Sound (see table 8-19). For passengers, Orangeville was the most important intermediate stop; up until the late 1890s they were allowed a brief 15 minutes for lunch at the station restaurant on their northbound journey. The express trains were shifted to an afternoon schedule at the turn of the century, making the lunch stop unnecessary, while southbound trains were always timed to arrive at Toronto around noon. At various times, timetables also included stops at Parkdale, Alton East and Fraxa Junction (formerly Orangeville Junction), but these quite often appear to have been included as a result of operational considerations as much as any.

Table 8-19
CANADIAN PACIFIC RAILWAY
STEAMSHIP EXPRESS SCHEDULES
TORONTO TO OWEN SOUND
1892, 1900 and 1910

	Northbound Read Down				Southbound Read Up	
#17 1910	S.S. Express 1900	S.S. Express 1892		S.S. Express 1892	S.S. Express 1900	#18 1910
1:00 p.m.	1:30 p.m.	11:10 a.m.	Lv. Toronto Ar.	2:00 p.m.	12:55 p.m.	12:45 p.m.
1:08 p.m.	. . .	11:20 a.m.	Parkdale	. . .	12:45 p.m.	12:36 p.m.
1:19 p.m.	1:48 p.m.	11:30 a.m.	West Toronto (Toronto Junc.)	. . .	12:38 p.m.	12:29 p.m.
. . .	3:03 p.m.	1:05 p.m.	Melville Junc.	. . .	11:16 a.m.	. . .
. . .	. . .	1:05 p.m.	Ar. Lv.	. . .	11:10 a.m.	11:12 a.m.
			Orangville			
2:45 p.m.	3:10 p.m.	1:20 p.m.	Lv. Ar.	. . .	. . .	. . .
. . .	3:18 p.m.	. . .	Fraxa Junction (Orange. Junc.)	. . .	11:00 a.m.	. . .
. . .	. . .	. . .	Shelburne	. . .	. . .	10:37 a.m.
. . .	. . .	. . .	Markdale	. . .	. . .	9:45 a.m.
4:50 p.m.	5:20 p.m.	3:20 p.m.	Ar. Owen Sound Lv.	10:00 a.m.	9:00 a.m.	8:50 a.m.
Daily ex. Sun.	Tue. Thurs. & Sat.	Mon. Wed. & Sat.		Mon. Thurs. & Sat.	Sun. Tue. & Thurs.	Daily ex. Sun.

With the arrival of the ships *Assiniboia* and *Keewatin* in 1908, the railway was able to offer five sailings a week out of Owen Sound, and it was realized that operating the boat trains only in connection with the steamers no longer made practical sense, since at least one train northbound or southbound was required each and every day of the week, Sundays excepted. Two new trains were therefore introduced, number 17 northbound and number 18 southbound (see table 8-19), to provide regular service between Toronto and Owen Sound. In addition to the usual consist of first- and second-class coaches, a buffet-parlour car was added to the trains around this time (if not before) to provide refreshment service and a touch of added luxury. Southbound runs included Shelburne and Markdale, while Parkdale, West Toronto and Orangeville comprised the only regular intermediate stops.

Following the removal of Canadian Pacific's steamship facilities to Port McNicoll in 1912, all trips by Canadian Pacific's steamers originated and terminated there, with only *Manitoba* calling at Owen Sound, and even then it was only on the northbound trip. Since Owen Sound no longer figured prominently in the railway's plans, express trains 17 and 18 were cancelled and replaced with local trains 707 and 706. When *Manitoba's* terminus was returned to Owen Sound on a permanent basis during World War I, trains 707 and 706 assumed the responsibility for carrying all *Manitoba* passengers. While a buffet-parlour car was added to the trains, they continued to stop at virtually every station between Toronto and Owen Sound, resulting in a total trip time of about 4½ hours. Trains 17 and 18 covered the same distance in an average time of around 3 hours and 50 minutes, stopping only at a handful of stations. Table 8-20 shows the schedules of trains 707 and 706 for 1930, which were little changed since the war. Because the trains were operated through the evening supper and morning breakfast hours, the 15-minute stop at Orangeville was reintroduced to the steamship passengers.

In the mid-thirties the section of track between Bolton and Melville Junction, including the scenic Horseshoe Curve, was lifted and all Owen Sound trains subsequently followed the old Credit Valley Railway line to Orangeville and Owen Sound by way of Streetsville Junction.

Table 8-20
CANADIAN PACIFIC RAILWAY
LOCAL SCHEDULE OF TRAINS 707 AND 706
BETWEEN TORONTO AND OWEN SOUND
1930

Northbound Train 707 Daily ex. Sun. P.M.				Southbound Train 706 Daily ex. Sun. A.M.
5:10	Lv.	Toronto	Ar.	11:25
5:20		Parkdale		11:10
5:30		West Toronto		11:06
5:37		Weston		f10:59
f5:44		Emery		. . .
5:52		Woodbridge		f10:47
f5:57		Elder		. . .
6:03		Kleinburg		f10:38
6:13		Bolton		10:25
6:24		Mono Road		10:15
6:45		Caledon		9:55
6:54		Melville		9:42
7:00	Ar.	Orangeville	Lv.	9:37
7:15	Lv.	Orangeville	Ar.	9:25
7:25		Fraxa		9:15
f7:31		Laurel		f9:07
f7:39		Crombies		f9:00
7:49		Shelburne		8:52
f7:56		Melancthon		f8:42
8:03		Corbetton		8:36
8:11		Dundalk		8:28
8:20		Proton		8:18
8:27		Saugeen		8:14
8:34		Flesherton		8:08
8:45		Markdale		7:56
8:54		Berkeley		7:45
9:02		Holland Centre		7:37
9:16		Chatsworth		7:24
f9:26		Rockford		f7:14
9:40		Owen Sound		7:00
P.M.				A.M.

f - Stops on signal only.

Source: Canadian Pacific Railway Timetable, 1 March 1930.

Table 8-21
CANADIAN PACIFIC RAILWAY
BOAT TRAIN SPECIALS
TORONTO TO PORT McNICOLL
Summer 1955

Northbound Train 703 Wed. & Sat. P.M.				Southbound Train 704 Mon. & Thurs. A.M.
12:01	Lv.	Toronto	Ar.	11:15
12:07		Parkdale		11:06
12:15		West Toronto		11:58
1:55		Midhurst		9:18
3:00	Ar.	Port McNicoll	Lv.	8:15
P.M.				A.M.

Northbound trains operate from 11 June to 10 September.
Southbound trains operate from 13 June to 12 September.

Source: Canadian Pacific Railway Timetable, 24 April 1955.

After *Manitoba* made her return to Owen Sound, Port McNicoll boat trains were provided for *Assiniboia* and *Keewatin* passengers only. Up until the Second World War these trains ran from late May until late September, but by the mid-fifties the regular steamship season was reduced to mid-June through mid-September and the boat specials were cut back accordingly. Schedules, however, remained relatively constant, and the timetable for the 1955 season (table 8-21) was typical for most of the period up to the last specials in 1965. All of these trains carried coaches and parlour cars in order to cater to the first-class passengers carried by *Keewatin* and *Assiniboia.*

Boat trains between the Lakehead and Winnipeg were not as common and passengers were generally accommodated on the regular transcontinental trains after the completion of the railway line around Lake Superior in 1885. In the preceding years, however, all trains running westward out of Port Arthur were co-ordinated with the steamship line, as the following westbound condensed timetable from 1884 shows:

		Time	Day of the Week
Lv.	Port Arthur	9:15 a.m.	Thurs., Sat., Mon.
Ar.	Savanne (Dining Hall)	12:45 p.m.	Thurs., Sat., Mon.
Ar.	Ignace (Dining Hall)	4:40 p.m.	Thurs., Sat., Mon.
Ar.	Rat Portage	1:05 a.m.	Fri., Sun., Tue.
Ar.	Whitemouth	4:25 a.m.	Fri., Sun., Tue.
Ar.	Winnipeg (Dining Hall)	7:00 a.m.	Fri., Sun., Tue.

There were no dining cars on the Canadian Pacific in 1884 and all meals had to be provided in "dining halls" located at key stations along the line. Because it took almost 24 hours to travel from Port Arthur to Winnipeg, it comes as no surprise that two intermediate dining halls were located along the 431 miles between the two cities.

By 1892 through transcontinental trains to and from Montreal were carrying steamship passengers between Fort William, Winnipeg and the West. While the trains were operated daily except Tuesday westbound from Fort William, and Thursday eastbound from Winnipeg, running times were little changed. Dining cars were being operated on every train for the benefit of first-class ticket-holders, but the other passengers found better prices in the dining halls. For the sake of comparison with the 1884 timetable, the 1892 westbound schedule is reproduced below in condensed form:

Lv.	Fort William	3:10 p.m.	Wed., Thurs., Fri., Sat., Sun., Mon.
Ar.	Savanne (Dining Hall)	6:45 p.m.	Wed., Thurs., Fri., Sat., Sun., Mon.
Ar.	Ignace (Dining Hall)	10:15 p.m.	Wed., Thurs., Fri., Sat., Sun., Mon.
Ar.	Rat Portage	5:00 a.m.	Thurs., Fri., Sat., Sun., Mon., Tue.
Ar.	White Mouth	7:57 a.m.	Thurs., Fri., Sat., Sun., Mon., Tue.
Ar.	Winnipeg (Dining Hall)	2:20 p.m.	Thurs., Fri., Sat., Sun., Mon., Tue.

When the *Assiniboia* and *Keewatin* were brought into service to handle most of the railway's first-class steamer passengers, the need for a Winnipeg boat train became evident. Since the railway's premier transcontinental trains, *The Imperial* and *The Dominion*, already gave excellent regular service between Winnipeg and the Lakehead, the boat trains were restricted to the peak summer months and were scheduled to co-ordinate with the regular transcontinentals at Winnipeg. For the 1930 season the following arrangements were made:

Westbound

"June 6 to Sept. 15 Boat Special with Coaches, Diner, Parlour Cars and Fort William to Banff Standard Sleepers leaving Fort William 7:30 a.m. Fridays and Mondays connects at Winnipeg with No. 1 'The Imperial.'

"Prior to June 6 and after Sept. 15 passengers make connection with train 3 'The Dominion' leaving Fort William 8:20 p.m. (C.T.) which in addition to carrying coaches and diner handles a Fort William to Winnipeg Standard Sleeper daily arriving Winnipeg 7:45 a.m."

Eastbound

"June 13 to Sept. 5 Boat Special with Coaches, Diner and Standard Sleepers leaves Winnipeg 10:00 p.m. on Fridays and Tuesdays.

"Prior to June 13 and after Sept. 5 passengers leave Winnipeg by train 4 'The Dominion' at 6:30 p.m. which in addition to carrying coaches and diner handles a Winnipeg to Fort William Standard Sleeper daily arriving Fort William 5:35 a.m. — occupancy by passengers until 8:00 a.m."[12]

Passengers travelling on board the *Manitoba* were not as fortunate as their first-class counterparts and were required to make connections with *The Dominion* at Fort William or Winnipeg throughout the navigational season. Table 8-22 briefly outlines the schedules of *The Imperial* (trains 1 and 2) and *The Dominion* (trains 3 and 4) for 1930. Both trains ran to Vancouver, but as a point of clarification, *The Imperial* was Canadian Pacific's original transcontinental train based out of Montreal, while *The Dominion* ran out of Toronto.

The Imperial was replaced by the stainless-steel streamliner *The Canadian* in 1955 and downgraded to become trains 17 and 18. Train 17 (westbound) and train 6 (eastbound) were the regular transcontinental trains assigned to carry steamship passengers during the 1950s and 1960s, since boat trains between Fort William and Winnipeg no longer operated. On sailing days these trains were brought shipside to allow passengers to make the transfer between ship and train.

Table 8-22
CANADIAN PACIFIC RAILWAY
TRANSCONTINENTAL SERVICE
BETWEEN FORT WILLIAM AND WINNIPEG
1930

Westbound					Eastbound	
No. 1	No. 3				No. 4	No. 2
A.M.	P.M.				A.M.	P.M.
6:20	9:20	Lv.	Fort William	Ar.	4:45	9:50
8:27	. . .		Savanne		. . .	7:45
10:20	1:10	Ar.	Ignace	Lv.	1:10	6:05
10:30	1:20	Lv.	Ignace	Ar.	1:00	5:55
2:35	4:55	Ar.	Kenora*	Lv.	9:25	1:40
2:45	5:05	Lv.	Kenora*	Ar.	9:15	1:30
4:48	6:58		Whitemouth		7:21	11:25
6:15	8:45	Ar.	Winnipeg	Lv.	5:40	10:00
P.M.	A.M.				P.M.	A.M.

* - Kenora formerly Rat Portage.

Source: Canadian Pacific Railway Timetable, 1 March 1930.

CHAPTER EIGHT - NOTES

1) Melba Morris Croft, *Fourth Entrance to Huronia — The History of Owen Sound* (Owen Sound, 1980), p. 68.
2) Joseph M. Mauro, *A History of Thunder Bay* (Thunder Bay, 1981), p. 196.
3) *Sunday Star (Toronto Star)*, 16 September 1984, p. D5.
4) Canadian Pacific, *Early History of Canadian Pacific* (Montreal, 1971), p. 10.
5) (J.B. Mansfield), *Adventures on the Great Lakes* (Toronto, 1980/Chicago, 1899), p. 158.
6) Pierre Berton, *The Impossible Railway* (New York, 1972), p. 440.
7) Ibid., p. 440.
8) James Croil, *Steam Navigation* (Toronto, 1973/1898), p. 235.
9) (J.B. Mansfield), *Trading and Shipping on the Great Lakes* (Toronto, 1980/Chicago, 1899), p. 286.
10) James Croil, op. cit., p. 286.
11) George Musk, *Canadian Pacific — The Story of the Famous Shipping Line* (Toronto, 1981), p. 107.
12) Canadian Pacific Railway timetable, *Eastern Lines Folder B*, 1 March 1930, p. 55.

A bow view of *Michigan Central* from the early 1900s. — *UBL No. 8794-A*

LIST OF RAILWAY SHIPPING

Contained in this list are all known railway-owned vessels that have operated within Ontario to the present date, along with certain other ships that operated in close connection with the railways, the latter including the steamships of the Niagara Navigation Company and the Northern Navigation Company. With the principal exception of certain American railway vessels, namely car ferries, all of the ships listed fell under Canadian ownership.

This list is not intended to be definitive, rather it is intended to provide a framework for future studies. Consequently, details such as hull numbers, engine and boiler builders, engine dimensions, etc., have been omitted for the sake of clarity.

Among the major sources consulted in the list's preparation were the *Great Lakes Insurance Registers* for the years 1854, 1869, 1873 and 1874; the Canadian shipping registers published by the government; John M. Mills' *Canadian Coastal and Inland Steam Vessels 1809-1930*; George Musk's *Canadian Pacific: The Story of the Famous Shipping Line*; and George Hilton's *Great Lakes Car Ferries.*

All ships have been listed alphabetically. Wherever a ship has had two or more names, only one primary entry (i.e. the numbered entries) has been made, to which the alternate names are referred. Each primary entry lists ownership, year acquired, year built or rebuilt (as indicated by the prefix "r" such as r1903), builder or rebuilder, gross tonnage in short tons, length x beam in feet, principal hull construction, propulsion system, disposition and notes.

The following abbreviations are used in the list:

a) Under OWNER

AC & HBR - Algoma Central & Hudson Bay Railway
AARR - Ann Arbor Railroad
B & OR - Brockville & Ottawa Railway
Brown - A.P. Brown & Company, Hamilton
BB & GR - Buffalo, Brantford & Goderich Railway/Buffalo & Lake Huron Railway
Burgess - Burgess & Company, Toronto
CAR - Canada Atlantic Railway
CATC - Canada Atlantic Transit Company
CSR - Canada Southern Railway/Michigan Central Railroad
CTC - Canada Transit Company
CNR - Canadian National Railways
CNoSS - Canadian Northern Steamships Limited
CPC & PTC - Canadian Pacific Car & Passenger Transfer Company
CPR - Canadian Pacific Railway
CPRDGL - Canadian Pacific Railway — Devil's Gap Lodge
Chisholm - Captain H. Chisholm
C & PR - Cobourg & Peterborough Railway/Cobourg, Peterborough & Marmora Railway
DL & WRR - Delaware, Lackawanna & Western Railroad

DNC - Deseronto Navigation Company
Doty - Doty Ferry Company, Toronto
F & PMTC - Flint & Pere Marquette Transportation Company/Pere Marquette Railway
GBNC - Georgian Bay Navigation Company
GTR - Grand Trunk Railway of Canada
GTR1 - Grand Trunk Railway of Canada/Canadian National Railways
GNTC - Great Northern Transit Company
GWR - Great Western Railway of Canada
GWR1 - Great Western Railway of Canada/Grand Trunk Railway of Canada
GWR2 - Great Western Railway of Canada/Grand Trunk Railway of Canada/Canadian National Railways
Heron - Captain Dick & Andrew Heron
Incan - Incan Marine
JC & C - John Counter & Company/Wolfe Island, Kingston & Toronto Railway
LE & DRR - Lake Erie & Detroit River Railway/Pere Marquette Railway/Chesapeake & Ohio Railway
LENC - Lake Erie Navigation Company
L & PSR - London & Port Stanley Railway
Macklem - Oliver T. Macklem, Queenston
NiaNav - Niagara Navigation Company
NStC & TN - Niagara, St. Catharines & Toronto Navigation Company
NSNC - North Shore Navigation Company
NWTC - North West Transportation Company
NorNav - Northern Navigation Company
NRRNY - Northern Railroad of New York/Ogdensburg Railroad/Ogdensburg & Lake Champlain Railroad
NRC - Ontario, Simcoe & Huron Railway/Northern Railway of Canada
OCFC - Ontario Car Ferry Company
OSTC - Owen Sound Transportation Company/Ontario Northland Transportation Commission
P-OTC - Pennsylvania-Ontario Transportation Company
StCTC - St. Clair Tunnel Company
T & NOR - Temiskaming & Northern Ontario Railway/Ontario Northland Transportation Commission
TH & BN - Toronto, Hamilton & Buffalo Navigation Company
US & OSNC - United States & Ontario Steam Navigation Company/Marquette & Bessemer Dock & Navigation Company
Wabash - Wabash Railroad/Norfolk & Western Railway
WR - Welland Railway
W & PPR - Whitby & Port Perry Railway

b) Under BUILDER

A & M - Aitken & Mansell, Kelvinbaugh, Scotland
AmerC - American Shipbuilding Company, Cleveland, Ohio
AmerL - American Shipbuilding Company, Lorain, Ohio
Ault - George N. Ault, Portsmouth, Ontario
AW & C - A.G. Armstrong, Whitworth & Company, Newcastle, England
Aylmer - built at Aylmer, Quebec
B & B - Bidwell & Banta, Buffalo, New York
B & G - Bartley & Gilbert, Montreal, Quebec
Banta - J.W. Banta, Buffalo, New York
BDDC - Buffalo Dry Dock Company, Buffalo, New York
Beauch - Beauchemin et Fils, Sorel, Quebec
Bertram - Bertram Shipyards, Toronto, Ontario

Blumer	- J. Blumer, Sunderland, England
Burl	- built at Burlington, Ontario
Burrard	- Burrard Dry Dock Company, North Vancouver, British Columbia
Bushn'l	- J. Bushnell, Detroit, Michigan
CanS	- Canadian Shipbuilding Company, Toronto, Ontario
CanSC	- Canadian Shipbuilding & Engineering Company, Collingwood, Ontario
Cantin	- Augustin Cantin, Montreal, Quebec
CBC	- Central Bridge Company, Trenton, Ontario
Chatham	- built at Chatham, Ontario
Chicago	- Chicago Shipbuilding Company, Chicago, Illinois
ChisB	- Captain H. Chisholm, Belle Ewart, Ontario
ChisM	- Captain H. Chisholm, Meaford, Ontario
Clayton	- Martin Clayton, Kingston, Ontario
Cleve	- Cleveland Shipbuilding Company, Cleveland, Ohio
CollDD	- Collingwood Dry Dock Company, Collingwood, Ontario
CollS	- Collingwood Shipbuilding Company, Collingwood, Ontario
Connl	- Charles Connell & Company, Glasgow, Scotland
CraigT	- Craig Shipbuilding Company, Toledo, Ohio
D & P	- Messrs. Dyble & Parry, Sarnia, Ontario
D & W	- Robert Davis & Z.W. Wright, Clayton, New York
Davie	- Davie Shipbuilding Company, Lauzon, Quebec
DavieL	- G.T. Davie Shipyards, Levis, Quebec
Davis	- Davis Shipyard, Kingston, Ontario
DDDW	- Detroit Dry Dock Company, Wyandotte, Michigan
Doty	- F.W. Doty, Toronto, Ontario
DSBW	- Detroit Shipbuilding Company, Wyandotte, Michigan
Dunbar	- John Dunbar, Coteau Landing, Quebec
F'field	- Fairfield Shipbuilding & Engineering Company, Govan, Scotland
Gild	- Charles H. Gildersleeve, Kingston, Ontario
Glasgow	- built at Glasgow, Scotland
GLEng	- Great Lakes Engineering Works, Ecorse, Michigan
GLEngSC	- Great Lakes Engineering Works, St. Clair, Michigan
GTRFE	- Grand Trunk Railway, Fort Erie, Ontario
GTRPE	- Grand Trunk Railway, Point Edward, Ontario
Ham	- built at Hamilton, Ontario
Harson	- Harrison & Company, Hamilton, Ontario
Hawley	- Hawley & Sons, Boston, Massachusetts
Hebburn	- built at Hebburn-on-Tyne, England
Hepburn	- A.W. Hepburn, Picton, Ontario
Hmlton	- Hamilton Bridge Company, Hamilton, Ontario
Hull	- built at Hull, Quebec
HullUK	- built at Hull, England
Hunter	- Hunter Boats Limited, Orillia, Ontario
JC & C	- John Counter & Company
JenkC	- Jenkins' Shipyard, Chatham, Ontario
JenkW	- Jenkins' Shipyard, Windsor (Walkerville), Ontario
JSC	- Jenks Shipbuilding Company, Port Huron, Michigan
King	- King Iron Works, Buffalo, New York
Kingstn	- built at Kingston, Ontario
Manit	- Manitowoc Shipbuilding Company, Manitowoc, Wisconsin
Marlin	- Marlin Yacht Company
Marlton	- William Marlton, Goderich, Ontario
McM & S	- McMillan & Sons, Dumbarton, Scotland
MifordB	- built at Miford Bay, Ontario

Miller - J.W. Miller & Sons, Liverpool, England
Milw - Milwaukee Shipyard Company, Milwaukee, Wisconsin
Mont - built at Montreal, Quebec
MPoint - built at Mill Point, Ontario
Newport - built at Newport (Marine City), Michigan
NiaDk - Niagara Dock & Harbour Company, Niagara (-on-the-Lake), Ontario
NS & B - Napier, Shanks & Bell, Yoker, Scotland
Oades - Oades Shipbuilding Company, Detroit, Michigan
OLake - built at Opinicom Lake, Ontario
Orillia - built at Orillia, Ontario
OSound - built at Owen Sound, Ontario
P & B - J. Potter & A. Bauckharn, Huntsville, Ontario
PArt - Port Arthur Shipbuilding Company, Port Arthur (Thunder Bay), Ontario
P'boro - built at Peterborough, Ontario
PColbne - built at Port Colborne, Ontario
Pearson - Harrison C. Pearson, Ogdensburg, New York
PHDDC - Port Huron Dry Dock Company, Port Huron, Michigan
P'mouth - built at Portsmouth, Ontario
PolOS - Polson Iron Works, Owen Sound, Ontario
PolT - Polson Iron Works, Toronto, Ontario
Potter - Potter's Shipyard, Machedash, Ontario
Power's - Power's Shipyard, Sand Point, Ontario
P'tang - built at Penetang, Ontario
Quebec - built at Quebec City, Quebec
Rama - built at Rama, Ontario
Rathbun - Rathbun Company, Deseronto, Ontario
Readh'd - J. Readhead & Company, South Shields, England
Renfrew - built at Renfrew, Scotland
Rich - Richardson Boat Works, Orillia, Ontario
Roberts - E.K. Roberts, Detroit, Michigan
Russel - Russel Hipwell Engines, Owen Sound, Ontario
Sarnia - built at Sarnia, Ontario
SH & WR - Swan, Hunter & Wigham Richardson, Wallsend-on-Tyne, England
Shick - L. Shickluna Shipyard, St. Catharines, Ontario
SimpOS - Melancthon Simpson, Owen Sound, Ontario
SimpPR - Melancthon Simpson, Port Robinson, Ontario
Smit - P. Smit, Slikkerveer, Netherlands
Smith - W. Smith, Sorel, Quebec
Stead - Stead's Shipyard, Sarnia, Ontario
Strand - Strand Slipway Company, Sunderland, England
T & J - Taylor & Jewett, Buffalo, New York
Thomp - Charles Thompson, Johnston's Landing, Ontario
Toledo - Toledo Shipbuilding Company, Toledo, Ohio
Toronto - built at Toronto, Ontario
TorS - Toronto Shipbuilding Company, Toronto, Ontario
Turner - Turner Boat Works, Vancouver, British Columbia
Union - Union Dry Dock Company, Buffalo, New York
WDDC - Western Dry Dock Company, Port Arthur (Thunder Bay), Ontario
Wheeler - F.W. Wheeler & Company, West Bay City, Michigan
Windsor - built at Windsor, Ontario
Wood - A. & J.W. Wood, Ogdensburg, New York
W'peg - built at Winnipeg, Manitoba

c) Under CONSTRUCTION

a - aluminum
f - fibreglass
i - iron
s - steel
w - wood

d) Under PROPULSION

bg - barge
ds - diesel engine, screw propeller
gs - gasoline engine, screw propeller
ogs - outboard gasoline engine, screw propeller
sp - steam engine, side paddle wheels
ss - steam engine, screw propeller
sts - steam turbine, screw propeller

e) Under DISPOSITION

A - abandoned
B - burned
L - lost at sea or sunk
S - sold
W - wrecked
X - scrapped

(Any of the above followed by a small "c" — e.g. Sc 1949 — indicates date is approximate.)

NOTES TO SHIPPING LIST

1) Acquired from Diamond Shamrock Company; vessel formerly belonged to Labrador Steamship Company of Montreal.
2) Built as unpowered barge; engined 1913.
3) Built as *Howard M. Hanna Jr. (I)*; renamed *Glenshee* in 1915, renamed *Marquette (II)* in 1926; renamed *Goderich (I)* in 1927; sold 1968 to Goderich Elevators for grain storage and renamed *Lionel Parsons.*
4) Built as *J.T. Hutchinson*, renamed *H.A. Rock* 1923; renamed *Alexander Leslie* on acquisition; last owner Norlake Shipping of Toronto.
5) Acquired as *John J. Barlum.*
6) *Algosea* statistics not available; ship no longer owned by Algoma Central.
7) Rebuilt by American Shipbuilding at Cleveland 1912.
8) Ship built as bulk freighter; converted to self-unloader at Collingwood 1964, thereby becoming the first Algoma Central self-unloader.
9) Operated as *Coatzacoalcos* 1859-1862.
10) Built as *Maude*; rebuilt about 1894 as *America*; renamed *Midland City* 1920 and later rebuilt as a motor ship.
11) Built for C.W. Elphicke & Company; lengthened 52 feet by Chicago Shipbuilding around 1898 or 1899; last owner Overlakes Freight Corporation; believed scrapped 1947.
12) Chartered to Canadian Pacific Railway 1888-1889; chartered to North West Transportation Company 1890-1895; later acquired by Quebec Steamship Company; built as *North* and renamed *Campana* 1881 when brought to upper lakes.
13) Renamed *Mississippi* 1859.
14) Before launching named *Kitche Cheemaun* with capacity of 500 passengers and 113 automobiles.

15) Built as Civil War blockade runner *Letter B.*; renamed *Chicora* when brought to upper lakes by Lake Superior Royal Mail Line; rebuilt as barge *Warrenko* 1921.
16) Sold to Nipissing Indian Band.
17) Catamaran hull.
18) Hull prefabricated in Glasgow, Scotland, by Dalzell Company.
19) Sold to Prescott & Ogdensburg Ferry Company.
20) Built as *Kathleen*; scrapped 1920.
21) Built as *Favourite* and renamed 1895.
22) Named *City of Windsor* 1890; chartered by Northern Navigation Company 1906-1909; renamed *Michipicoten* 1911.
23) Sold to Owen Sound Mail Line and operated briefly; reduced to barge at Owen Sound 1866.
24) Sold to Branch Line and renamed *Maplebranch.*
25) Sold to Inland Lines Limited of Montreal and renamed *Island King II.*
26) Original name unknown; rebuilt 1879 as *Gypsy*; probably acquired as *Gypsy* and renamed *Ella Ross.*
27) Operated as *Grimsby* 1913 only.
28) Renamed *Norseman* 1895.
29) Chartered to Great Western Railway 1855-1856.
30) Acquired through purchase of Lakeside Navigation Company.
31) Built for C.W. Elphicke & Company; requisitioned by American government 1917.
32) Rebuilt 1873 following fire.
33) Acquired from Great Lakes Transportation Company as *William S. Mack*; renamed *Algorail* 1936.
34) Chartered to Northern Railway.
35) One source claims built by John Smith at Point Edward.
36) *Incan St. Laurant* (renamed *George Alexandres Lebel* 1977) identical to *Incan Superior* and sold to Canadian National Railways in 1977.
37) Rebuilt 1877 after fire in 1876.
38) Acquired as *Saturn* from Gilchrist Transportation Company; renamed *Algosoo* 1936.
39) Sold to Royal Canadian Navy as fleet auxiliary 1917, serving until 1942.
40) Builder and dimensions are for *Kingston* owned by the Royal Mail Line and is assumed to be same ship since both built in same year; *Kingston* of Royal Mail Line burned in 1872 and rebuilt as *Bavarian*; rebuilt as *Algerian* 1874 after another fire; renamed *Cornwall* 1904; sold for scrap by Richelieu & Ontario Navigation Company 1930.
41) Sold late 1930s to Sincennes-McNaughton Line Ltd.
42) Built as *Modjeska* for Hamilton Steamboat Company; rebuilt with overnight cabins in 1927 by Canada Steamship Lines and renamed *Manitoulin.*
43) Renamed *Carrollton* 1937.
44) Reduced to barge; renamed *Lillian* 1948.
45) Converted to barge 1924.
46) Converted to barge 1913.
47) Sent to Lower Arrow Lake, B.C., in 1947 or 1948 to replace Canadian Pacific tug *Columbia* (built 1896) which had been retired; operated there from 1 February 1948 until late April 1948 when new replacement arrived.
48) Built as fire tug *James R. Elliott*; converted to passenger and freight steamer 1931 by Georgian Bay Shipbuilding of Midland and renamed *Normac.*
49) Hull prefabricated at Dumbarton, Scotland.
50) Acquired as *Beauharnois.*
51) Sold to Ontario & Quebec Navigation Company of Picton, Ontario.
52) First Algoma Central ship built as a self-unloader; sunk up-bound on St. Lawrence River near Alexandria Bay, New York, with load of iron ore pellets 20 November 1974; no lives lost.
53) Acquired as *Cairo*; torpedoed 1915 as troopship.
54) Acquired as *Heliopolis*; sold to Cunard Line.
55) Registered with Canadian Minister of Transport; carried 239 passengers and 18 freight cars on

three tracks.

56) Requisitioned by Canadian government 1917.
57) Traded 1917 for *William S. Mack* of Great Lakes Transportation Company.
58) Overall width 75 feet.
59) Renamed *W.L. Kennedy* 1915.
60) Purchased from American interests as *Flora*; resold to American interests and name *Flora* restored.
61) Some sources claim *Victoria* burned March 1884 at Bobcaygeon and later rebuilt as *Esturian*; however, *Victoria* still registered to Whitby & Port Perry Railway as late as 1912.
62) Acquired as *Uranus* from Gilchrist Transportation Company.
63) Built as passenger steamer; rebuilt 1882 as car ferry; resold by Prescott & Ogdensburg Ferry Company 1912 and converted to barge *Mons Meg*.
64) Sold to Windsor Detroit Barge Line.
65) Sold to Windsor Detroit Barge Line; converted to barge.

The *Pontiac*, built in 1889 by the Cleveland Ship Building Company at Cleveland, Ohio, was typical of the freighters operated by the American iron mining companies. Owned by the Cleveland Iron Mining Company, *Pontiac* was a 2,298-gross-ton (1,788 net tons) steel steamship measuring 320 feet in length with a beam of 40 feet, and was notable not only for her relatively modern design but also for being the first steel freighter built for an iron ore company for service on the Great Lakes. Seen here at Sault Ste. Marie, Michigan, around 1889, the *Pontiac*'s parent became the Cleveland-Cliffs Iron Company in 1890 following the Cleveland Iron Mining Company's successful takeover of the Iron Cliffs Company. — *OA S15983*

NUMBER	VESSEL	OWNER	ACQUIRED	BUILT	BUILDER	GROSS TONNAGE	LENGTH X BEAM	CONSTRUCTION	PROPULSION	DISPOSITION	NOTES
001	A.S. GLOSSBRENNER	AC & HBR	1971	1966	Davie	17,995	730 x 75	s	ds	-	1
002	AGAWA (I)	AC & HBR	new	1902	CollS	3,759	379 x 46	s	ss	S1927	2
003	AGAWA (II)	AC & HBR	1963	1908	AmerC	-	500 x 54	s	ss	S1968	3
004	AGAWA CANYON	AC & HBR	new	1970	CanSC	16,290	647 x 72	s	ds	-	
005	ALBERTA	CPR	new	1883	Connl	2,282	263 x 38	s	ss		
		CPR		r1911	CollS	2,829	310 x 38	s	ss	S1946, X1948	
006	ALEXANDER LESLIE	LENC	1927	1901	AmerC	3,509	354 x 48	s	ss	S?, X1969	4
	ALGERIAN See #104, KINGSTON										
007	ALGOBAY	AC & HBR	new	1978	CanSC	22,466	730 x 75	s	ds	-	
008	ALGOCEN (I)	AC & HBR	1935	1909	AmerL	6,893	513 x 54	s	ss	S1968	5
009	ALGOCEN (II)	AC & HBR	new	1968	CanSC	18,089	730 x 75	s	ds	-	
010	ALGOLAKE	AC & HBR	new	1977	CanSC	22,851	730 x 75	s	ds	-	
011	ALGOMA	CPR	new	1883	A & M	1,773	263 x 38	s	ss	W1885	
012	ALGOPORT	AC & HBR	new	1979	CanSC	20,222	650 x 72	s	ds	-	
	ALGORAIL (I) See #086, HOME SMITH										
013	ALGORAIL (II)	AC & HBR	new	1968	CanSC	16,157	640 x 72	s	ds	-	
014	ALGOSEA	AC & HBR	-	-	-	-	-	s	ds	-	6
	ALGOSOO (I) See #096, J. FRATER TAYLOR										
015	ALGOSOO (II)	AC & HBR	new	1974	CanSC	21,715	730 x 75	s	ds	-	
016	ALGOSTEEL	AC & HBR	1935	1907	DSBW	6,117	488 x 52	s	ss	S1966	
017	ALGOWAY (I)	AC & HBR	1940	1903	AmerC	3,785	366 x 50	s	ss	S1964	7
018	ALGOWAY (II)	AC & HBR	new	1972	CanSC	16,186	649 x 72	s	ds	-	
019	ALGOWEST	AC & HBR	new	1982	CanSC	20,309	730 x 75	s	ds	-	
020	ALGOWOOD	AC & HBR	new	1981	CanSC	22,558	730 x 75	s	ds	-	
021	ALLIANCE	B & OR	new	1866	Power's	240	139 x 20	w	sp	X1882	
022	AMERICA	GWR	new	1854	NiaDk	1,100	288 x 38	w	sp	S1857, B1869	9
023	AMERICA	DNC	-	1871	Gild	-	153 x 33	w	sp	S1920, X1955	10
	ANN ARBOR #6 See #113, MAITLAND #2										
	ARGYLE See #074, EMPRESS OF INDIA										
024	ARMENIA	DNC	-	1876	Hepburn	110	100 x 18	w	ss	X1905	
	ARTHUR K. ATKINSON See #113, MAITLAND #2										
025	ARTHUR ORR	CATC	1898	1893	Chicago	2,745	334 x 41	s	ss	S1947	11
026	ASHTABULA	P-OTC	new	1906	GLEngSC	2,670	338 x 56	s	ss	X1958	
027	ASSINIBOIA	CPR	new	1907	F'field	3,880	337 x 44	s	ss	S1968, B1969	
028	ATHABASCA	CPR	new	1883	A & M	2,269	263 x 38	s	ss		
		CPR		r1910	CollS	2,784	299 x 38	s	ss	S1946	
	ATLANTIC See #120, MANITOULIN										
029	AUBREY COSENS V.C.	T & NOR	1945	1910	Hawley	58	77 x 15	s	ss	X1950s	
	BAVARIAN See #104, KINGSTON										
	BEAUHARNOIS See #169, QUINTE										
030	BOSTON	NRRNY	new	1852	Quebec	334	170 x 23	w	sp	S1863	

NUMBER	VESSEL	OWNER	ACQUIRED	BUILT	BUILDER	GROSS TONNAGE	LENGTH X BEAM	CONSTRUCTION	PROPULSION	DISPOSITION	NOTES
	BRITANNIC See #176, ROCKET										
	CAIRO See #180, ROYAL EDWARD										
	CAMBRIA See #041, CHAMPION #2										
031	CAMPANA	-	-	1873	Glasgow	1,620	225 x 45	s	ss	W1909	12
032	CANADA	GWR	new	1854	NiaDk	1,100	288 x 38	w	sp	S1857, L1862	13
033	CANADA ATLANTIC TRANSFER	CAR	new	1884	Dunbar	619	171 x 70	w	sp	S1894	
034	CANADIAN	GTR	new	1854	JenkC	339	162 x 47	w	sp	Xc1873	
035	CANADIAN GUNNER	-	new	1919	CollS	2,415	251 x 44	s	ss	S1926	
	CANATCO ('26)	CATC	1926	r1927	CollS	2,415	251 x 44	s	ss	S1947	
036	CANADIAN HARVESTER		new	1921	WDDC	2,394	251 x 44	s	ss	S1926	
	DALWARNIC ('26)	CATC	1926	r1927	CollS	2,394	251 x 44	s	ss	S1947	
037	CANADIANA	CPR-DGL	new	1954	Rich	-	26 x ?	w	gs	S1961	
	CANATCO See #035 CANADIAN GUNNER										
038	CARIBOU	CPC & PTC	new?	1868	Cantin	114	89 x 18	w	ss		
		CPC & PTC		r1888	-	144	89 x 18	w	ss	X1901	
039	CARIBOU	DTC	new	1904	Marlton	597	149 x 27	w	ss	S1946, A1955	
	CARMONA See #116, MANITOBA										
	CARROLLTON See #123, MARQUETTE & BESSEMER #1										
040	CAYUGA	NiaNav	new	1907	CanS	2,196	312 x 36	s	ss	S1953, X1958	
041	CHAMPION #2	CPR	1883	1877	DavieL	323	131 x 23	w	sp	S1885	
	CAMBRIA ('87)	CTC	1885	r1887	OSound	-	175 x 23	w	sp	X1902	
042	CHARLES LYON	CPC & PTC	new	1908	PolT	1,658	280 x 40	s	ss	S1937, X1941	
043	CHI-CHEEMAUN	OSTC	new	1974	CanSC		365 x 62	s	ds	-	14
044	CHICORA	NiaNav	1877	1864	Miller	931	235 x 26	i	sp		
		NiaNav		r1877	PColbne	931	235 x 26	i	sp	S1921, L1939	15
045	CHIEF COMMANDA	T & NOR	new	1945	CBC	243	99 x 22	s	ds	S1975	16
046	CHIEF COMMANDA II	T & NOR	new	1974	Marlin	347	94 x 36	s	ds	-	17
047	CHIPPEWA	NiaNav	new	1893	Hmlton	1,514	309 x 36	s	sp	X1939	
048	CIBOLA	NiaNav	new	1886	Rathbun	-	-	s	sp	B1895	18
049	CITY OF BELLEVILLE	CPC & TPC	new	1878	Shick	101	90 x 15	w	ss	S1909, B1914	19
050	CITY OF COLLINGWOOD	NorNav	1899	1893	PolOS	1,387	213 x 34	s	ss	B1905	
051	CITY OF LONDON	L & PSR	new	1866	Shick	361	145 x 27	w	ss	S?, B1874	
052	CITY OF LONDON	NorNav	1899	1888	Clayton	385	120 x 27	w	ss	S1901	20
053	CITY OF MIDLAND	NSNC	new	1890	PolOS	748	176 x 28	s	ss	S1899	
		NorNav	1899	r1893	CollDD	974	176 x 28	s	ss	B1916	
054	CITY OF PARRY SOUND	NorNav	1899	1888	ChisM	491	130 x 25	w	ss	B1915	21
055	CITY OF TORONTO			1864	NiaDk	512	207 x 24	w	sp	B1883	
056	CITY OF TORONTO	NorNav	1899	1895	PolOS	782	150 x 24	s	sp	S1908, B1914	
057	CITY OF WINDSOR	-	-	1883	Roberts	511	117 x 25	w	ss	B1927	22
058	CLIFTON	-	-	1854	NiaDkC	236	187 x 26	w	sp	S1865	23
	COATZACOALCOS See #022, AMERICA										

NUMBER	VESSEL	OWNER	ACQUIRED	BUILT	BUILDER	GROSS TONNAGE	LENGTH X BEAM	CONSTRUCTION	PROPULSION	DISPOSITION	NOTES
059	COMET	DNC	new	1887	MifordB	20	60 x 12	w	ss	-	
	CORNWALL See #104, KINGSTON										
060	CORONA	NiaNav	new	1896	PolT	1,247	270 x 32	s	sp	X1937	
061	CPR #1	CPR DGL	new	1923	-	-	26 x ?	w	gs	X1952	
062	CPR #2	CPR DGL	new	1923	-	-	30 x ?	w	gs	X1952	
063	CUBA	DL & WRR	new	1872	King	1,708	238 x 36	s	ss	S1906	
	IONIC ('06)	NorNav	1906	1872	King	1,708	238 x 36	s	ss	S1920	24
064	DALHOUSIE	WR	new	1869	Shick	353	144 x 26	w	ss	B1872	
065	DALHOUSIE CITY	NStC & TN	new	1911	CollS	1,256	200 x 37	s	ss	S1950, B1960	25
	DALWARNIC See #036, CANADIAN HARVESTER										
066	DESERONTO	DNC	new?	-	-	-	-	w	ss	-	
067	DETROIT	CSR	new	1904	GLEng	2,232	308 x 77	s	ss	S1912	
		Wabash	1912	r1927	-	2,232	308 x 77	s	ss		
		Wabash		r1969	-	2,232	308 x 77	s	bg	-	
068	DOLPHIN	CPR	1884	-	-	-	-	w	s	-	
	DORIC See #119, TADOUSAC										
069	E.B. BARBER	AC & HBR	new	1953	PAS	10,419	574 x 59	s	sts	-	8
070	ELLA ROSS	DNC	-	1873	Mont	325	99 x 28	w	sp	-	
		DNC	-	r1907	-	228	99 x 28	w	sp	S?, B1912	26
071	EMILY	CPR	1884	-	-	-	33 x ?	w	s-	S1885	
072	EMILY MAY	Chisholm	new	1861	ChisB	181	144 x 21	w	sp	S1874	
	LADY OF THE LAKES ('74)	NRC	1874	1861	ChisB	181	144 x 21	w	sp	B1883	
073	EMMA MUNSON	DNC	-	-	-	-	-	w	sp	-	
074	EMPRESS OF INDIA	-	new?	1876	MPoint	579	170 x 26	w	sp	S1899	
	ARGYLE ('99)	-	1899	r1899	-	700	185 x 26	w	sp	S1912	
	FRONTIER ('12)	-	1912	r1899	-	700	185 x 26	w	sp	L1918	27
075	ENTERPRISE	WR	new	1864	Shick	600	177 x 31	w	ss	S1881, L1912	28
076	EUROPA	Brown	new	1854	Harsn	341n	224 x 28	w	sp	S1857, X1873	29
077	F.A. JOHNSON	Wabash	1969	1952	-	286	-	s	ds	-	
	FAVOURITE See #054 CITY OF PARRY SOUND										
	FLORA See #202, URANIA										
	FRONTIER See #074 EMPRESS OF INDIA										
078	GARDEN CITY	NStC & TN	1902	1892	Bertram	673	178 x 26	s	sp	S1916, X1935	30
079	GEORGE ORR	CATC	1898	1896	Chicago	2,872	326 x 42	s	ss	S1917, L1918	31
	GEORGE ALEXANDRE LEBEL See #090, INCAN SUPERIOR										
080	GEORGIAN	L & PSR	c1865	1864	Potter	342	130 x 22	w	ss	S?	
		Burgess	c1872	r1873	-	377	130 x 22	w	ss	S1884?	32
		CPR	1884	-	-	377	130 x 22	w	ss	Xc1913	

NUMBER	VESSEL	OWNER	ACQUIRED	BUILT	BUILDER	GROSS TONNAGE	LENGTH X BEAM	CONSTRUCTION	PROPULSION	DISPOSITION	NOTES
081	GERMANIC	NorNav	new	1899	CollDD	1,014	184 x 32	w	ss	B1917	
	GLENSHEE See #003, AGAWA (II)										
	GODERICH (I) See #003, AGAWA (II)										
082	GOUDREAU	AC & HBR	-	-	-	12,500	552 x 56	s	sp	-	
083	GREAT WESTERN	GWR2	new	1866	JenkW	1,252	220 x 40	i	sp	-	
		GWR2	new	r1882	JenkW?	1,080	220 x 40	i	sp	S1923	
	GRIMSBY See #074, EMPRESS OF INDIA										
	GYPSY See #070, ELLA ROSS										
	H.A. ROCK See #006, ALEXANDER LESLIE										
084	HAMONIC	NorNav	new	1909	CollS	5,265	350 x 50	s	ss	B1945	
	HARRIET B. See #187, SHENANGO #2										
	HELIOPOLIS See #181, ROYAL GEORGE										
085	HENRY PLUMB	CPC & PTC	-	-	-	-	-	-	ss	S1909	19
086	HOME SMITH	AC & HBR	1917	1901	AmerL	3,495	346 x 48	s	ss	S1963	33
	HOWARD M. HANNA JR. (I) See #003, AGAWA (II)										
087	HUNTER	-	-	1857	Banta	667	193 x 31	w	ss	L1869	34
088	HURON	GTR1	new	1875	GTRPE	1,052	239 x 54	s	ss	S1970	35, 65
089	IDA BURTON	-	-	1866	Orillia	85	84 x 14	w	sp	X1876	
	INCAN ST. LAURANT See #090, INCAN SUPERIOR										
090	INCAN SUPERIOR	Incan	new	1974	Burrard	3,838	382 x 66	s	ds	-	36
091	INTERNATIONAL (I)	BB & GR	new	1854	NiaDkC	500	160 x 32	w	ss	B1854	
092	INTERNATIONAL (II)	BB & GR	new	1857	B & B	1,120	226 x 41	w	sp	B1874	
093	INTERNATIONAL	GTR	new	1872	GTRFE	851	210 x 40	i	ss	S1898	
		LE & DRR	1898	1872	GTRFE	851	210 x 40	i	ss	S1934	
	INTERNATIONAL See #190, SOUTH EASTERN										
	IONIC See #063, CUBA										
094	ISAAC BUTTS	C & PR	new	1874	P'boro	67	110 x 30	w	sp		
		C & PR	new	r1877	-	174	108 x 17	w	sp	X1886	37
	ISLAND KING II See #065, DALHOUSIE CITY										
	JAMES R. ELLIOTT See #144, NORMAC										
095	J.C. MORRISON	NRC	new	1854	ChisB	150	150 x ?	w	sp	B1857	
096	J. FRATER TAYLOR	AC & HBR	1913	1901	AmerL	3,429	346 x 48	s	ss	S1965	38
	J.T. HUTCHINSON See #006, ALEXANDER LESLIE										
097	JOHN COUNTER	JC & C	new	1853	JC & C	296	206 x 34	w	sp	S1854, X1857	
098	JOHN B. AIRD	AC & HBR	new	1883	CanSC	22,881	730 x 75	s	ds	-	
	JOHN J. BARLUM See #008, ALGOCEN (I)										
	JOHN ROLPH See #174, RESOLUTE										

NUMBER	VESSEL	OWNER	ACQUIRED	BUILT	BUILDER	GROSS TONNAGE	LENGTH X BEAM	CONSTRUCTION	PROPULSION	DISPOSITION	NOTES
099	JULIETTE	CPR	1883	1878	Burl	-	-	w	s-	L1883	
100	JUMBO	CPC & PTC	new	1880	Sorel	150	136 x 20	w	bg	S1920s	
	KATHLEEN See #052, CITY OF LONDON										
101	KEARSARGE	CATC	1899	1894	Chicago	3,092	340 x 44	s	ss	S1943	
102	KEEWATIN	CPR	new	1907	F'field	3,856	337 x 44	s	ss	S1966	
103	KING EDWARD	AC & HBR	new	1902	HullUK	355	156 x 24	s	sp	S1917, X1942	39
104	KINGSTON	GTR	new	1854	B & G	344	174 x 26	i	sp	Sc1855, X1930	40
105	LADY ELGIN	-	-	1851	B & B	1,038	252 x 33	w	sp	L1860	34
	LADY OF THE LAKES See #072, EMILY MAY										
106	LAKESIDE	NStC & TN	1902	1888	Windsor	348	121 x 26		sp	S1911, L1929	30
107	LANSDOWNE	GTR1	new	1884	DDDW	1,571	294 x 41	i	sp	S1970	65
108	LEAFIELD	AC & HBR	1900	1892	Strand	1,454	249 x 35	s	ss	L1913	
	LETTER B. See #044, CHICORA										
	LILLIAN See #125, MARQUETTE & BESSEMER #2 (II)										
	LIONEL PARSONS See #003, AGAWA (II)										
109	LOTTIE	CPR	new	1907	Aylmer	10	40 x 8	w	ss	-	
110	LOUIS PHILLIPPE	NorNav	1923	-	-	-	-	s	-	-	
111	MAGDALENA	CPR	1884	1875	Union	18	48 x 12	w	ss	-	
112	MAITLAND #1	TH & BN	new	1916	GLEng	2,751	338 x 56	s	ss	S1942	
113	MAITLAND #2	TH & BN	nd	1916	GLEng	-	350 x 56	s	ss	S1916	
	ANN ARBOR #6 ('16)	AARR	1916	1916	GLEng	-	350 x 56	s	ss		
	ARTHUR K. ATKINSON ('59)	AARR	1916	r1959	Manit	3,241	384 x 56	s	ds	-	
114	MAITLAND #3	TH & BN	nd	1916	GLEng			s		Construction	cancelled
115	MAJESTIC	NorNav	1899	1895	CollDD	1,578	230 x 36	w	ss	B1915	
116	MANITOBA	NWTC	new	1871	SimpPR	980	173 x 25	w	sp	S1888	
	CARMONA ('88)	CTC	1888	r1888	-	937	173 x 25	w	sp	S1900	
	PITTSBURGH ('00)	GBNC	1900	r1900	-	-	173 x 25	w	sp	B1902	
117	MANITOBA	CPR	new	1889	PolOS	2,616	305 x 38	s	ss	X1951	
118	MANITOU	DTC	new	1903	Marlton	470	137 x 24	s	ss	S1930s, X1944	41
119	MANITOU ISLAND II	T & NOR	1977	1956	Russel	45	49 x 18	s	ds	-	
120	MANITOULIN	NWTC	new	1880	OSound	706	147 x 30	w	ss	B1882, S1883	
	ATLANTIC ('83)	GNTC	1883	r1883	-	683	147 x 30	w	ss	S1899	
		NorNav	1899	-	-	683	147 x 30	w	ss	B1902	
121	MANITOULIN	OSTC	1930s	1889	NS & B	678	178 x 31	s	ss	X1951	42
122	MANITOWOC	Wabash	new	1926	Manit	3,093	371 x 67	s	ss		
		Wabash	new	r1969	-	3,093	371 x 67	s	bg	-	
	MAPLEBRANCH See #063, CUBA										
	MARQUETTE (II) See #003, AGAWA (II)										

NUMBER	VESSEL	OWNER	ACQUIRED	BUILT	BUILDER	GROSS TONNAGE	LENGTH X BEAM	CONSTRUCTION	PROPULSION	DISPOSITION	NOTES
123	MARQUETTE & BESSEMER #1	US & OSNC	new	1903	BDDC	1,525	241 x 23	s	ss	S1937	43
124	MARQUETTE & BESSEMER #2 (I)	US & OSNC	new	1905	AmerC	3,514	338 x 54	s	ss	L1909	
125	MARQUETTE & BESSEMER #2 (II)	US & OSNC	new	1910	AmerC	2,583	338 x 56	s	ss	S1942	44
126	MATTAWAN	CPR	-	1876	P'mouth	22	50 x 10	w	ss	Xc1913	
	MAUDE See #023, AMERICA										
127	MICHIGAN	GWR1	new	1874	JenkW	1,465	265 x 38	w	sp	S1885	
128	MICHIGAN	CPR	new	1890	Wheeler	1,730	296 x 41	s	sp	S1924, W1942	45
129	MICHIGAN CENTRAL	CSR	new	1884	DDDCW	1,522	263 x 46	i	sp	S1913, L1926	46
	MICHIPICOTEN See #057, CITY OF WINDSOR										
130	MICHIPICOTEN	AC & HBR	-	-	-	12,000	569 x 56	s	ss	S?	
	MIDLAND CITY See #023, AMERICA										
131	MINNIE M.	AC & HBR	1900	1884	Oades	447	133 x 26	s	ss	S1910	
	MISSISSIPPI See #032, CANADA										
132	MISTY MAID	CPR DGL	new	1954	Turner	-	26 x ?	w	gs	B1954	
133	MISTY MIST	CPR DGL	new	1953	Turner?	-	25 x ?	w	gs	B1954	
	MODJESKA See #121, MANITOULIN										
134	MONARCH	NorNav	1899	1890	D & P	2,017	240 x 35	w	ss	W1906	
135	MONKSHAVEN	AC & HBR	1910	1892	Readh'd	2,097	249 x 36	s	ss	L1914	
	MONS MEG See #212, WILLIAM ARMSTRONG										
136	MONTGOMERY	-	-	1856	Bushn'l	925	204 x 34	w	ss	B1878	34
137	MORNING	NRC	1853	1849	Thomp	150	-	w	sp	X1862	
	MUSKEGON See #187, SHENANGO #2										
138	NEWONA	CATC	new?	1909	SH & WR	2,179	250 x 43	s	ss	S1927	
139	NIAGARA	-	-	1844?	-	-	-	w	sp	B1856	34
140	NIAGARA	GWR	new	1854	-	-	-	w	s-		
141	NIPIGONIAN	CPR DGL	new	1929	P'tang	10	40 x 9	w	gs	X1952	47
142	NORGOMA	OSTC	new	1950	CollS	1,477	188 x 38	s	ds	S1970s	
143	NORISLE	OSTC	new	1946	CollS	1,668	216 x 36	s	ss	S1970s	
144	NORMAC	OSTC	1931	1902	JSC	-	125 x 25	s	ss	S?	48
145	NORMAN	DNC	-	1872	OLake	153	98 x 24	w	ss	B1883	
146	NORONIC	NorNav	new	1913	WDDC	6,905	362 x 52	s	ss	B1949	
	NORSEMAN See #075, ENTERPRISE										
	NORTH See #031, CAMPANA										
147	NORTHUMBERLAND	NStC & TN	1920	1894	SH & WR	1,255	220 x 33	s	ss	B1949	
148	OGDENSBURG	CPC & PTC	new	1930	AmerL	1,389	290 x 45	s	bg	S1972	64
149	OGEMAH	W & PPR	1874	1852	-	-	-	w	bg	B1876	
	ONGIARA See #168, QUEEN CITY										
150	ONTARIO	CPR	new	1890	PolOS	1,615	297 x 41	s	sp	S1924, L1927	
151	ONTARIO #1	OCFC	new	1907	CanS	5,146	317 x 54	s	ss	X1951	
152	ONTARIO #2	OCFC	new	1915	PolT	5,568	308 x 54	s	ss	X1952	

NUMBER	VESSEL	OWNER	ACQUIRED	BUILT	BUILDER	GROSS TONNAGE	LENGTH X BEAM	CONSTRUCTION	PROPULSION	DISPOSITION	NOTES
153	ONTONAGON			1856	Banta	560	177 x 30	w	ss	B1883	34
154	OSSIFRAGE	AC & HBR	1900	1886	Wheeler	632	161 x 27	s	ss	S1910	
155	OTONABEE (I)	C & PR	1863	1853	-	84	-	w	sp	S1869, A1873	
156	OTONABEE (II)	C & PR	-	-	-	-	-	w	s-	-	
157	OTTAWA	CATC	new	1900	Toronto	2,431	256 x 43	s	ss	W1909	
158	OUTING	CPC & PTC	-	-	-	-	-	w	ss	-	
159	PALIKI	AC & HBR	1900	1889	Blumer	1,578	240 x 36	s	ss	S1924	
160	PEERLESS	Heron	new	1853	NiaDk	-	175 x 26	i	sp	S1861, L1861	49
161	PERE MARQUETTE	F & PMTC	new	1896	Wheeler		350 x 56	s	ss	-	
162	PERE MARQUETTE 10	LE & DRR	new	1945	Manit	2,769	386 x 53	s	ss	-	
163	PERE MARQUETTE 12	LE & DRR	new	1927	Manit	2,767	386 x 53	s	ss	-	
164	PERE MARQUETTE 14	LE & DRR	new	1904	DSBW	2,531	328 x 52	s	ss	X1957	
	PERE MARQUETTE 16 See #187, SHENANGO #2										
165	PERSEVERANCE	WR	new	1864	Shick	564	173 x 28	w	ss	B1868	
166	PILGRIM	DNC	-	-	-	-	-	w	s-	-	
	PITTSBURGH See #116, MANITOBA										
167	PRESCOTONT	CPC & PTC	new	1930	Davie	302	117 x 28	s	ds	S1971	64
168	QUEEN CITY	Doty	new	1885	Doty?	98	91 x 18	w	ss	S1888	
	ONGIARA ('88)	NiaNav	1888	1885	Doty?	98	91 x 18	w	ss	Xc1912	
169	QUINTE	DNC	1882	1871	Quebec	331	138 x 23	w	sp	B1889	50
170	R.G. CASSIDY	Wabash	1969	1953	-	439	-	s	ds	-	
171	REINDEER	DNC	-	-	-	-	-	w	ss	-	
172	RELIANCE	DNC	new	1881	Rathbun	221	121 x 24	w	ss	-	
		DNC	new	r1889	Rathbun	239	121 x 24	w	ss	Sc1910, X1920	51
173	RESCUE	DNC	-	-	-	-	-	w	ss	-	
174	RESOLUTE	DNC	new	1883	Rathbun	336	126 x 28	w	ss	-	
		DNC	new	r1887	Rathbun	372	137 x 38	w	ss	W1906	
	JOHN ROLPH	DNC	new	r1907	Rathbun	421	137 x 38	w	ss	Xc1925	
175	ROANOKE	Wabash	-	1930	Manit	3,074	382 x 57	s	ss		
		Wabash		r1969	-	3,074	382 x 57	s	bg	-	
176	ROCKET	-	-	1866	Smith	428	151 x 26	w	sp	-	
	BRITANNIC	-	-	r1892	-	428	151 x 26	w	sp	S1901	
		NorNav	1901	r1892	-	428	151 x 26	w	sp	S1908	
177	ROCKET	DNC	-	-	-	-	-	w	s-	-	
178	ROTHESAY CASTLE	-	-	1861	Renfrew	85	-	w	sp	-	
	SOUTHERN BELLE ('77)	-	-	r1880s	Rathbun	-	-	w	sp	X1906	
179	ROY A. JODREY	AC & HBR	new	1965	CanSC	22,000	641 x 72	s	ds	L1974	52
180	ROYAL EDWARD	CNoSS	1909	1907	F'field	11,117	526 x 60	s	ss	L1915	53
181	ROYAL GEORGE	CNoSS	1909	1907	F'field	11,146	526 x 60	s	ss	S1916, X1922	54
182	SAGINAW	GWR1	new	1873	PHDDC	365	142 x 26	w	ss	S1892, X1940	

NUMBER	VESSEL	OWNER	ACQUIRED	BUILT	BUILDER	GROSS TONNAGE	LENGTH X BEAM	CONSTRUCTION	PROPULSION	DISPOSITION	NOTES
183	ST. LAWRENCE	NRRNY	new	1863	Pearson	244	125 x 31	w	ss	A1873	
184	SAMUEL ZIMMERMAN	Macklem	new	1854	NiaDk	-	200 x 28	w	sp	B1863	
	SARONIC See #201, UNITED EMPIRE										
	SATURN See #096, J. FRATER TAYLOR										
185	SCOTIA II	CNR	1960s	1915	AW & C	1,858	300 x 50	s	ss		55
186	SHENANGO #1	US & OSNC	new	1895	CraigT	1,941	283 x 53	w	ss	B1904	
187	SHENANGO #2	US & OSNC	new	1895	CraigT	1,938	283 x 53	w	ss	S1898	
	MUSKEGON ('98)	DGR & WRR	1898	1895	CraigT	1,938	283 x 53	w	ss	S1900	
	PERE MARQUETTE 16 ('01)	F & PMTC	1900	1895	CraigT	1,938	283 x 53	w	ss	S1917, L1922	
188	SIR DENYS LOWSON	AC & HBR	new	1964	CanSC	17,000	605 x 62	s	ds	Sc1980	
189	SISKIWIT	CPR	1883	1879	Union	61	67 x 16	w	ss	S1894	
190	SOUTH EASTERN	LNC	new	1881	Cantin	395	182 x 30	w	ss	S1886	
		R & O	1886	1881	Cantin	395	182 x 30	w	ss	S1890	
		CPC & PTC	1890	1881	Cantin	395	182 x 30	w	ss	B1896	
	INTERNATIONAL ('96)	CPC & PTC	1890	r1896	-	395	182 x 30	w	ss	S1910, X1914	
	SOUTHERN BELLE See #178, ROTHESAY CASTLE										
191	TADOUSAC	-	-	1903	Bertram	2,359	260 x 43	s	ss	S1907	
	DORIC ('07)	NorNav	1907	1903	Bertram	2,359	260 x 43	s	ss	L1917	56
192	THEANO	AC & HBR	1900	1889	Smit	952	242 x 36	s	ss	L1906	
	THOMAS J. BARLUM See #016, ALGOSTEEL										
193	THOMAS J. DRUMMOND	AC & HBR	new	1910	McM & S	2,201	248 x 44	s	ss	S1917	57
194	TRANSFER (I)	CSR	new	1873	JenkW	1,222	242 x 43	w	sp	S1888, L1896	
195	TRANSFER (II)	CSR	new	1888	Cleve	1,511	265 x ?	s	ssp	S1912	58
196	TRANSIT (I)	GWR	new	1854	Newport	500	-	w	sp		
		GWR	new	r1869	Toronto	-	-	w	sp	-	
197	TRANSIT (II)	GWR1	new	1872	JenkW	1,057	168 x 39	w	ss	B1889	
198	TRANSIT	CPC & PTC	new	1874	D & W	141	108 x 21	w	ss	A1901	
199	TRANSPORT	CSR	new	1880	DDDCW	1,595	254 x 46	i	sp	S1912	
		Wabash	1912	1880	DDDCW	1,595	254 x 46	i	sp	S1929	
200	UNION	GWR1	new	1858	JenkW	1,190	163 x 33	w	sp	S1885	
201	UNITED EMPIRE	NWTC	new	1882	D & P	1,961	253 x 36	w	ss	S1899	
	SARONIC ('04)	NorNav	1899	r1904	Sarnia	1,961	253 x 36	w	ss	S1915	59
202	URANIA	LENC	1898	1875	Milw	899	180 x 27	w	sp	S1904	60
	URANUS See #206, W.C. FRANZ										
203	V.W. SCULLY	AC & HBR	1971	1965	Lauzon	17,563	730 x 75	s	sts	-	1
204	VARUNA	DNC	new	1880	Hepburn	134	94 x 17	w	ss	X1920	
205	VICTORIA	W & PPR	1874	1867	Lindsay	191	94 x 15	w	sp	-	61
206	W.C. FRANZ	AC & HBR	1913	1901	AmerL	3,429	346 x 48	s	ss	L1934	62
207	W.J. SPICER	GTR	new	1864	Stead	446	154 x 24	w	sp	S1875	
208	W.J. TAYLOR	StCTC	new	1883	JenkC	9	35 x 8	w	ss	-	

NUMBER	VESSEL	OWNER	ACQUIRED	BUILT	BUILDER	GROSS TONNAGE	LENGTH X BEAM	CONSTRUCTION	PROPULSION	DISPOSITION	NOTES
	W.L. KENNEDY See #201, UNITED EMPIRE										
	WARRENKO See #044, CHICORA										
209	WAUBIC	NorNav	new	1909	CollS	504	134 x 25	s	ss	-	
		NorNav	new	r1922	-	469	134 x 25	s	ss	S?	
		-	-	r1938	-	451	134 x 25	s	ds	B1959	
210	WESTERN WORLD	-	-	-	-	-	-	-	-	-	29
211	WHISTLE-WING	-	-	1871	P'boro	17	74 x 13	w	sp	-	
		-	-	r1874	-	71	74 x 13	w	sp	-	
212	WILLIAM ARMSTRONG	CPC & PTC	new	1876	Wood	181	100 x 30	w	ss	S1910, A1938	19, 63
	WILLIAM S. MACK See #086, HOME SMITH										
213	WINDSOR	Wabash	new	1930	Toledo	3,131	370 x 66	s	ss		
		Wabash	new	r1969		3,131	370 x 66	s	bg	-	
214	(no name)	CPR DGL	new	-	W'peg	-	20 x ?	wf	ogs	S1961	
215	(no name) barge	GTR	new	1854	Kingston	100	-	w	bg	Sc1857	
216	(no name) barge	GTR	new	1854	Kingston	100	-	w	bg	Sc1857	
217	(no name) barge	GTR	new	1854	Kingston	100	-	w	bg	Sc1857	
218	(no name) barge	GTR	new	1854	Kingston	100	-	w	bg	Sc1857	
219	(no name) barge	GTR	new	1854	Kingston	100	-	w	bg	Sc1857	
220	(no name) barge	GTR	new	1854	Kingston	100	-	w	bg	Sc1857	

BIBLIOGRAPHY

This bibliography lists most of the major sources of information consulted during the course of research, from which information ultimately found its way into this volume. Without doubt, there will probably be some oversights, but it is important to note that the references that follow are by no means the only sources available.

For those interested in further research, other sources of information worth investigating include manuscripts and material deposited within the Public Archives of Canada and the Archives of Ontario, not to mention many local archives, museums and libraries. Not to be overlooked are the numerous timetables, travel guides and brochures published by the railway and steamship companies. Periodicals published by the railway and steamship historical societies, of which there are many, as well as commercial magazines and newspapers are also important sources. These are only suggestions, but it should be remembered that even the most meagre and unusual sources can lead to a major discovery.

For ease of reference, the bibliography has been divided into categories such as "Shipping Histories" and "Railway Histories."

Lists of Shipping & Shipping Registers

Canada, *List of Shipping*, Department of Transport, Ottawa, issued annually.

Great Lakes Insurance Underwriters, *Great Lakes Insurance Register*, Great Lakes Insurance Underwriters, 1854, 1869, 1873 & 1874. (Ontario Archives microfilm reference Ms 401)

Manse, Thomas. *Know Your Ships — The Seaway Issue*, Thomas Manse, Sault Ste. Marie, Michigan, 1970.

Mills, John M., *Canadian Coastal and Inland Steam Vessels, 1809-1930*, Steamship Historical Society of America, Providence, Rhode Island, 1979.

United States, *Transportation Lines on the Great Lakes — 1949*, Corps of Engineers, Department of the Army, Washington, D.C., 1949. (Ontario Archives reference MU 3417, Merrilees Collection)

Shipping Histories

Barry, James P., *Ships of the Great Lakes*, Howell-North Books, Berkeley, California, 1973.

Beaton, Horace L. and Charles P. Beaton, *From the Wheelhouse*, The Boston Mills Press, Cheltenham, Ontario, 1979.

Charlebois, Dr. Peter, *Sternwheelers & Sidewheelers*, NC Press Limited, Toronto, 1978.

Croil, James, *Steam Navigation — 1898*, William Briggs, Toronto, 1898. Reprinted by Coles Publishing Company, Toronto, 1973.

Dunn, Lawrence, *A Source Book of Ships*, Ward Lock Limited, London (U.K.), 1970.

Greenwood, John Orville, *Namesakes 1930-1955*, Freshwater Press, Cleveland, Ohio, 1978.

__________, *Namesakes II*, Freshwater Press, Cleveland, Ohio, 1979.

Heisler, John P., *The Canals of Canada*, Department of Indian Affairs and Northern Development, Ottawa, 1973.

Heyl, Erik, *Early American Steamers* (various volumes), Erik Heyl, Buffalo, New York, (various dates).

Hilton, George W., *The Great Lakes Car Ferries*, Howell-North Books, Berkeley, California, 1962.

Mansfield, J.B., *History of the Great Lakes, Volume I*, J.H. Beers & Co., Chicago, 1899. Reprinted by Coles Publishing Company, Toronto, 1980, as three volumes: *Adventures of the Great Lakes; The Saga of the Great Lakes; Trading & Shipping on the Great Lakes.*

Musk, George, *Canadian Pacific — The Story of the Famous Shipping Line*, Holt, Rinehart and Winston of Canada Ltd., Toronto, 1981.

Plowden, David, *Farewell to Steam*, Burns and MacEachern, Limited, Toronto, 1966.

Pritchard, Jean, *The Welland Canal — Yesterday, Today, Tomorrow*, Jean Pritchard Publications, Port Robinson, Ontario, 1975.

Ransome-Wallis, P., *North Atlantic Panorama 1900-1976*, Wesleyan University Press, Middletown, Connecticut, 1977.

Tatley, Richard, *The Steamboat Era in the Muskokas, Vol. I & II*, The Boston Mills Press, Erin, Ontario, 1984.

____________, *Steamboating on the Trent-Severn*, Mika Publishing Company, Belleville, Ontario, 1978.

Turner, Robert D., *Sternwheelers and Steam Tugs: An Illustrated History of the Canadian Pacific Railway's British Columbia Lake and River Service*, Sono Nis Press, Victoria, B.C., 1984.

Young, Anna G., *Great Lakes Saga*, Richardson, Bond & Wright Limited, Toronto, 1965.

Railway Guides & Timetables

Canadian National Railways Timetables: 23 June 1929; June 1943; 25 November 1945.

Canadian Northern Railway Timetable: 14 February 1916.

Canadian Pacific Railway Timetables: 9 September 1884; 9 July 1888; 19 July 1892; 1 July 1912; 14 July 1918; 1 March 1930; 24 April 1955.

Grand Trunk Railway of Canada Timetables: May 1881; 22 September 1887; 20 May 1916.

National Railway Publications Company, *Travelers' Official Guide — June 1893*, National Railway Publications Company, New York, 1893/1972.

Rand McNally & Company, *Rand McNally Railway Guide — 1875*, Rand McNally & Company, Chicago, 1875.

Railway Histories

Andreae, C.A., *A Historical Railway Atlas of Southwestern Ontario*, C.A. Andreae, London, Ontario, 1972.

Beaumont, Ralph, *Steam Trains to the Bruce*, The Boston Mills Press, Erin, Ontario, 1977.

Berton, Pierre, *The Impossible Railway*, Alfred A. Knopf, New York, 1972.

Bowers, Peter, *Two Divisions to Bluewater: The Story of the C.N.R. to the Bruce*, The Boston Mills Press, Erin, Ontario, 1983.

Cooper, Charles, *Rails to the Lakes: The Story of the Hamilton & North Western Railway*, The Boston Mills Press, Erin, Ontario, 1980.

Curnoe, W. Glen, *The London & Port Stanley Railway, 1915-1965: A Pictorial History*, W. Glen Curnoe, London, Ontario, 1976.

Helm, Norman, *In the Shadow of Giants: The Story of the Toronto, Hamilton & Buffalo Railway*, The Boston Mills Press, Erin, Ontario, 1978.

Innis, Harold A., *A History of the Canadian Pacific Railway*, University of Toronto Press, Toronto, 1971.

Jackson, John N., and John Burtniak, *Railways in the Niagara Peninsula*, Mika Publishing Company, Belleville, Ontario, 1978.

Lamb, W. Kaye, *History of the Canadian Pacific Railway*, Collier MacMillan Canada Ltd., Toronto, 1977.

Lavallee, Omer S.A., *Van Horne's Road*, Railfare Enterprises Limited, Montreal, 1974.

Legget, Robert F., *Railways of Canada*, Douglas & McIntyre, Vancouver, 1980.

MacKay, Niall, *By Steam Boat and Steam Train: The Story of the Huntsville and Lake of Bays Railway and Navigation Companies*, The Boston Mills Press, Erin, Ontario, 1982.

__________, *Over the Hills to Georgian Bay: A Pictorial History of the Ottawa, Arnprior & Parry Sound Railway*, The Boston Mills Press, Erin, Ontario, 1981.
McIlwraith, Thomas F., *The Toronto, Grey & Bruce Railway, 1863-1884*, Upper Canada Railway Society, Toronto, 1963.
Middleton, William D., *When the Steam Railroads Electrified*, Kalmbach Publishing Company, Milwaukee, Wisconsin, 1974.
Mika, Nick & Helma, *Railways of Canada: A Pictorial History*, McGraw-Hill Ryerson Limited, Toronto, 1972.
Nock, O.S., *Algoma Central Railway*, Adam & Charles Black, London (U.K.), 1975.
Panko, Andrew, and Peter Bowen, *Niagara, St. Catharines & Toronto Electric Railway in Pictures*, Niagara Rail Publications Limited, Niagara-on-the-Lake, Ontario, 1984.
Phillips, Lance, *Yonder Comes the Train: The Story of the Iron Horse and Some of the Roads It Travelled*, A.S. Barnes & Co., New York, 1965.
Plomer, James, with Alan R. Capon, *Desperate Venture: Central Ontario Railway*, Mika Publishing Company, Belleville, Ontario, 1979.
Regehr, T.D., *The Canadian Northern Railway: Pioneer Road of the Northern Prairies, 1895-1918*, Macmillan Company of Canada Limited, Toronto, 1976.
Stevens, G.R., *Canadian National Railways (Volume 1): Sixty Years of Trial and Error, 1836-1896*, Clarke, Irwin & Company Limited, Toronto, 1960.
__________, *Canadian National Railways (Volume 2): Towards the Inevitable, 1896-1922*, Clarke, Irwin & Company Limited, Toronto, 1962.
Torrens, Leslie J., *The London and Port Stanley Railway, Volume One*, Les. Torrens, London, Ontario, 1984.
Trout, J.M. & Edw., *The Railways of Canada* for *1870-1*, Monetary Times, Toronto, 1871. Reprinted by Coles Publishing Company, Toronto, 1970.
Tucker, Albert, *Steam into Wilderness: Ontario Northland Railway, 1902-1962*, Fitzhenry & Whiteside, Toronto, 1978.
Walker, Frank N., *Four Whistles to Wood Up*, Upper Canada Railway Society, Toronto, 1953.
Wilgus, William J., *The Railway Interrelations of the United States and Canada*, Russel & Russel, New York, 1970. (first printed 1937)
Wilson, Dale, *Algoma Eastern Railway*, Nickel Belt Rails, Sudbury, Ontario, 1977.
__________, *Algoma Central Railway Story*, Nickel Belt Rails, Sudbury, Ontario, 1984.
__________, *From Abbey to Zorra via Bagdad*, Nickel Belt Rails, Sudbury, Ontario, 1980.
Wilson, Donald M., *Lost Horizons: The Story of the Rathbun Company and the Bay of Quinte Railway*, Mika Publishing Company, Belleville, Ontario, 1983.
__________, *The Ontario & Quebec Railway*, Mika Publishing Company, Belleville, Ontario, 1984.

Limited Circulation & In-house Publications

Algoma Central Railway, *Brief History and Date on the Algoma Central Railway*, Algoma Central Railway, Sault Ste. Marie, Ontario, February 1971.
Bush, Edward Forbes, *Manuscript Report Number 424: Overland Transport in the Rideau Region, 1800-1930*, Parks Canada, Ottawa, 1979.
Canada, *Our Transportation Services*, Canadian Citizenship Branch, Department of Citizenship & Immigration, Ottawa, 1954.
Canadian Pacific, *Early History of Canadian Pacific*, Canadian Pacific, Montreal, April 1971.

Local Histories

Adam, G. Mercer, *Toronto Old and New*, The Mail Printing Company, Toronto, 1891. Reprinted by Coles Publishing Company, Toronto, 1974.
Borg, Ronald (ed.), *Peterborough, Land of Shining Waters*, City & County of Peterborough, Peterborough, Ontario, 1967.
Croft, Melba Morris, *Fourth Entrance to Huronia — The History of Owen Sound*, Melba Morris Croft, Owen Sound, Ontario, 1980.

Guillet, Edwin G., *Pioneer Travel in Upper Canada*, University of Toronto Press, Toronto, 1966.
Mauro, Joseph M., *A History of Thunder Bay*, City of Thunder Bay, Thunder Bay, Ontario, 1981.
Spilsbury, John R. (ed.), *Cobourg: Early Days and Modern Times*, The Cobourg Book Committee, Cobourg, Ontario, 1981.

Periodicals

Dalby, Paul, "Metro — Niagara Cruises to be launched in June," *Toronto Star*, 31 March 1976.
Dowling, Edward J., "Car Ferries on the Detroit River," *Western Ontario Historical Notes*, volume 10, number 3, September 1952, pp. 97-102.
Dunn, Arthur D., P.Eng., "Historical Metallurgy Notes: In Search of History (1) — The Trent River Ore Cars," *CIM Bulletin*, The Metallurgical Society of CIM, Montreal, volume 74, number 829, May 1981, pp. 141-142.
Fleming, J.M., "Iron Ore Loading Dock at Port Arthur," *The Engineering Journal*, Montreal, January 1947.
The Globe (newspaper), Toronto, 1 July 1867, etc.
(Grain Dealers Journal), "Grand Trunk Pacific Elevator — Fort William, Ontario," *Grain Dealers Journal*, c.1908. (Ontario Archives reference: Pamphlet, n.d., "G", no. 13)
Lowe, Mick, "Wawa's 'dream' may thrive again," *Globe & Mail*, Toronto, 3 October 1983.
(Upper Canada Railway Society), "125 Years of the Great Western," *Rail & Transit*, Upper Canada Railway Society, Toronto, November-December 1978, pp. 18-23.
Walker, Dr. Frank N., "Buffalo, Brantford & Goderich Railway," *Newsletter*, Upper Canada Railway Society, Toronto, July-August 1975, pp. 10-15.
Winter, Brian, "The Port Whitby and Port Perry Railway," *Newsletter*, Upper Canada Railway Society, Toronto, December 1971, pp. 181-2.

REFERENCE TO PHOTO CREDITS:

Ontario Archives — OA
Public Archives of Canada — PAC
Metropolitan Toronto Library — MTL
University of Baltimore Library — UBL
Thunder Bay Historical Museum Society — TBHMS
St. Catharines Historical Museum — SCHM
Canadian National — CN
University of Western Ontario — UWO
Lennox & Addington County Museum — LACM
Canadian Pacific Corporate Archives — CPCA

INDEX

- A -

A.S. Glossbrenner 148
A. Watson French **172**
Africa 256
Agawa 135, 139, **140**, 142, 145
Agawa (II) (Glenshee, Howard M. Hanna Jr. I, Lionel Parsons, Marquette II) 148
Agawa Canyon 148
Alberta **227**, 237, **238**, 241-242, 246-250, **249**, 252-255
Alex, Nisick **149**
Alexander Leslie (H.A. Rock, J.T. Hutchinson) **201**
Alexandra see *Sunbeam*
Alexandria **187**
Algerian see *Kingston*
Algobay 148
Algocen (John J. Barlum) 145, 146
Algocen (II) 148
Algolake 148
Algoma (LSRML) *(City of Toronto, Racine)* **210**, 211
Algoma (CPR) **3**, **23**, **55**, 218, 237, **239**, 241-242, 244, 246
Algoma Central & Hudson Bay Railway 133-149, 169, **172**, 173
Algoma Eastern Railway 169, **175**
Algoma Mills, Ont. 22, 235
Algoma Steel Corporation 135, **137**, 142, 145-146
Algonquin **185**
Algoport 148
Algorail see *Home Smith*
Algorail (II) 148
Algosea 148
Algosoo see *J. Frater Taylor*
Algosoo (II) 148
Algosteel (Thomas J. Barlum) 145-148, **147**
Algoway 146, 148
Algoway (II) 148
Algowest 148
Algowood 148
Allandale, Ont. 25
Alliance 186
America (GWR) *(Coatzacoalocos)* 33-35, 37, 59
America (DNC) *(Maude, Midland City)*, 190, **191**
Amherstburg, Ont. 12, 21, 111, 113
Ann and Jane 61
Ann Arbor No. 6 see *Maitland No. 2*
Ann Arbor Railroad 161-162
Argyle see *Empress of India*
Armenia **188**, 190
Arthur C. see *Sunbeam*
Arthur K. Atkinson see *Maitland No. 2*
Arthur Orr 45-47, **47**, 50
Ashtabula, Ohio 158-161
Ashtabula 158-161, **160**, 164
Asia 213, **215**
Assiniboia 235, 250-256, **251**, 259-260
Atlantic (MCRR) 29
Atlantic (GNTC) see *Manitoulin* (NWTC)
Athabasca **227**, 237, **239**, 241-242, 246, 248, 250, 252-255
Aubrey Cosens V.C. 205

- B -

Bala, Ont. 25
Bala Park, Ont. 25, 177
Baltic see *Francis Smith*
Baltimore 29
Baltimore & Ohio Railroad 167-168
Barlum 139
Barrie, Ont. 25, **203**, **204**
Bavarian see *Kingston*
Bay of Quinte Railway 186-192, **187**
Beatty, Henry 213, 234, 237, 241
Beatty, James 213
Beauharnois see *Quinte*
Beaverton, Ont. 25
Belle Ewart, Ont. 25, 202
Belle of Temagami 206
Belleville, Ont. 19, 150
Ben Moreel 159
Bessemer & Lake Erie Railroad 154-155
Black Rock (Buffalo), New York 99-100
Blackwell, E.T. 37
Blairton, Ont. 129
Bobcaygeon, Ont. 25
Booth, John Rudolphus 43-46
Boston (NRR of NY) 89
Boston (GLTC) **36**
Bracebridge, Ont. 178
Bradford, Ont. 25, 202
Branch Line 226
Brantford & Buffalo Joint Stock Railroad 99-100
Britannic see *Rocket*
Brockville, Ont. 18, 52, 86, 91, 93-95, 177
Brockville & Ottawa Railway 52, 86, 91, 186
Brown & Company, A.P. 33
Buckeye State 29
Buffalo, New York 52, 99
Buffalo **30**
Buffalo & Lake Huron Railway 52, **53**, 99-100
Buffalo, Brantford & Goderich Railway 99-100
Buffalo, Rochester & Pittsburgh Railway 163-168
Burgess & Company 198
Burk's Falls, Ont. 25
Butcher's Boy 235, **236**
Butcher's Maid 235, **236**
Bytown & Prescott Railway 89

- C -

Cairo see *Royal Edward*
Calcutt, Henry 128, 131
Cambria see *Champion No. 2*
Campana (North) 213, **217**, 218, 242, **244**, 246
Canada (Mississippi) 33-35, **34**, 37, 59
Canada Atlantic Railway 43-52, 98-99, 169
Canada Atlantic Transfer **98**, 99
Canada Atlantic Transit Company 43-52, 170
Canada Central Railway 91
Canada Iron Furnace Company (see Canadian Furnace Company)
Canada Southern Railway 76, 79, 111-116, 159, 213
Canada Steamship Lines 84, 207, 209, 223, **224**, **225**
Canada Transit Company **215**, 242-243, 245-246
Canadian (GTR) 39, 104, 107
Canadian 211
Canadian Furnace Company 135, **138**
Canadian Gunner (Canatco) 50-51, **51**
Canadian Harvester (Dalwarnic) 50-51, **51**
Canadian National Railways 111, 142, 145, 148-149, 177-178 (see also Canada Atlantic Transit Company; Canadian Northern Railway; Grand Trunk Pacific Railway; Grand Trunk Railway of Canada; Incan Marine; Niagara, St. Catharines & Toronto Navigation Company; Northern Navigation Company; Onta-

rio Car Ferry Company)
Canadian Navigation Company 177
Canadian Northern Coal & Ore Dock Company 148, 169, **174**
Canadian Northern Railway 52, **57**, 69, 148, 169, **174**, 190, 196, 227
Canadian Northern Steamships Limited 196, **197**
Canadian Northern Terminal Elevators Company 52
Canadian Pacific Car & Passenger Transfer Company 90-98
Canadian Pacific Railway 52, **55-56**, **58**, 91-98, 116-118, 158-159, 168-169, **171-172**, **175**, 198, 206, **208**, 218, 234-261
Canadian Pacific Railway Railway - Devil's Gap Lodge 207, 209
Canadiana 209
Canals 13-18, 40, 61-62, 189
Canatco see *Canadian Gunner*
Cape Vincent, New York 87-88
Caribou (CPC & PTC) 90, 95
Caribou 135
Caribou (DTC) 207, **208**
Carmona see *Manitoba* (NWTC)
Carriella 205
Carrollton see *Marquette & Bessemer No. 1*
Caspian see *Passport*
Cayuga **70**, **83**, 84-85
Central Ontario Railway 148
Central Vermont Line 32
Central Vermont Railway 27, 90
Champion No. 2 (Cambria) 235, 242, **243**, 245-246
Charles Lyon 95, **96**, 97
Charlotte, New York 163-168
Chatham, Ont. 12
Chemong, Ont. 25
Chesapeake & Ohio Railroad 122
Chi-Cheemaun 207
Chicago, Illinois 39-40, 213, 255
Chicago, St. Paul, Minneapolis & Omaha Railroad 29
Chicora (Letter B., Warrenko) 79-80, **81**, 84, 211
Chief Commanda 205, **206**
Chief Commanda II 207
Chippawa, Ont. 19
Chippewa 79-80, **82**, 84
Chisholm, Captain H. 205
Cibola 79-80, **82**, 84
City of Belleville 90, 95
City of Buffalo 198
City of Collingwood 213, **214**, 218
City of Concord 66
City of London (L&PSR) 198, **199**
City of London **20**
City of London (NSNC) *(Kathleen)* 213
City of Midland 213
City of Parry Sound (Favourite) 213, 218
City of Toronto (1839) see *Algoma* (LSRML)
City of Toronto (1864) 76, **77**, 79
City of Toronto (NSNC) 213, 218, **220**, 222
City of Windsor (Michipicoten) 218
Clayton, New York 192
Clergue, Francis Hector 133, 135, 139
Cleveland, Ohio 14
Cleveland & Buffalo Transit Company 198, 200
Cleveland-Cliffs Iron Company 127, 269
Cleveland-Cliffs Steamship Company 127, 269
Clifton **74**, 75-76
Clyde see *Enterprise* (CP & MR & MC)
Clover Leaf Steamboat Line 27
Coal boats 151-168
Coal docks 142, 145, 147, 168-175
Coal trade 142, 145, 151-175, 189
Coatzacoalcos see *America* (GWR)
Cobourg, Ont. 19, 127-133, 150
Cobourg & Peterborough Railway 127-129
Cobourg, Peterborough & Marmora Railway & Mining Company 127-133, 150
Collingwood, Ont. 22, 39-42, 54, 211, 213, **217**, 222, **244**
Comet 190
Compagnie du Traverse du chemin de fer d'Hocchelaga à Longueauil 94
Conneaut, Ohio 151-158
Conners, W.J. 37
Cornwall see *Kingston*
Corona **83**, 84
Coteau Landing, Quebec 18, 52, 99
Counter, John 87-88
Courtright, Ont. 21, 111, 116
CPR No. 1 207
CPR No. 2 207
Cuba (Ionic, Maplebranch) 218, 223, **224**, 226
Cumberland **210**, 211
Cumberland, Barlow 210
Cumberland, Frederick 39-43, 202, 210
Cunard Line 196

- D -

Dalhousie 64, 66
Dalhousie City (Island King II) 69, **70-72**, 73
Dalwarnic see *Canadian Harvester*
Delaware, Lackawana & Western Railroad 27, 29, 218, 224
Delta Transportation Company 245
Deseronto, Ont. 18, 186-192, **187**
Deseronto 190
Deseronto Navigation Company 186-192
Depot Harbour, Ont. 22, 43-52, 169, **170**
Detroit, Michigan 12, 100-104, 107-111, 113-126
Detroit **115**, 116, 122-124
Detroit & Milwaukee Railway 33, 35, 102
Detroit, Grand Rapids & Western Railway 152
Detroit River Tunnel Company 113, 116, 118
Docks see Canadian Pacific Railway; Canadian Northern Railway; Coal docks; Deseronto Navigation Company; Grain elevators; Iron ore docks; Northern Navigation Company
Dolphin 235
Dominion Transportation Company 207-208
Doric see *Tadousac*
Doty Ferry Company 79, 81
Duluth, Minnesota 211, **215**, 228, 231, 233
Duluth & Iron Range Railroad 127
Duluth, South Shore & Atlantic Railway 245

- E -

E.B. Barber 148
Eastern Minneapolis Railroad 29
Eastern Minnesota Railroad 29
Ella Ross (Gypsy) **188**, 190
Emily 235
Emily May (Lady of the Lakes) 183, **203**, 205
Emma Munson 190
Empress **181**
Empress of Britain 250
Empress of India (Argyle, Frontier, Grimsby, Norseman) **65**, 66, **67**
Empress of Ireland 250
Engleman Transportation Company 35
Enterprise (WR) 64, 66
Enterprise (CP & MR & MC) 130-131
Enterprise (H & LBN) **204**, 205
Erie, Pennsylvania 151
Erieau, Ont. 21, 154-155, 158, 169
Erie & Ontario Railroad 62, 75
Erie & Ontario Railway 74-79
Erie & Niagara Railway 74-79
Erie & Western Transportation Company 27, 30
Erie Canal 14
Erie Railroad see New York, Lake Erie & Eastern Railroad
Essex Transit Company 111
Europa 33-34, **34**, 59

- F -

F.A. Johnson 124
F.H. Prince **32**
F.L. Danforth **55**
Favourite see *City of Parry Sound*
Ferries, railway car 87-126, 151-168
Ferries, swing 104
Ferries, transfer 102-104
Flint & Pere Marquette Railroad 27
Flint & Pere Marquette Transportation Company 27
Flora see *Urania*

Foote's Bay, Ont. 177
Forest City 29
Fort Erie, Ont. 21, 99-100
Fort Gratiot (Port Huron), Michigan 104, 107, 108
Fort William (Thunder Bay), Ont. 24, 52, 54, **56**, **57**, 169, **171-172**, **215**, **232**, 235 (see also Canadian Pacific Railway, Northern Navigation Company)
Francis Smith (Baltic) 211
Freight, package 45-46, 50, 218, 248
Freight, rates 39, 46, 63
Freight, traffic 50, 63, 95, 97, 107, 111, 116, 121-122, 132, 155, 158-159, 163, 167
Frontenac 11-13
Frontier see *Empress of India*

- G -
Gananoque, Ont. 18, 192
Garden City **17**, **68**, 69, **70**
George Orr 45-46, **47**
George Alexandre Lebel see *Incan St. Laurent*
Georgian 198, 235
Germanic 218, **220**, 223, 226, 229
Gildersleeve, Henry 87
Gladys see Northern Belle
Glenshee see Agawa (II)
Goderich, Ont. 22, 52, **53**, 213
Goderich Elevator & Transit Company 53
Goudreau 148
Grain elevators 23, 42, 44, 52-54, **249**, **251**
Grain trade 246, 248
Grand Haven, Michigan 35
Grand Junction Railway 150
Grand Trunk Pacific Railway 54, 218, 222
Grand Trunk Pacific Terminal Elevator Company 54, 57
Grand Trunk Railway of Canada 37-39, **53**, 54, 66, 89-90, 100, 104-111, 122, 131, 150, 152, 163-168, 177-178, 190, 192, **194**, 195, 213, 218, 222, 237, 240
Gravenhurst, Ont. 25, 178
Great Lakes Steamship Company 29
Great Lakes Transit Corporation 36-37
Great Northern Railway 27
Great Northern Transit Company 211-213, 244
Great Western **101**, 103-104, 108-111, **109**
Great Western Railway of Canada 33-37, 54, 100-104, 213, 224
Green Bay, Wisconsin 39-40
Griffin 11
Grimsby see *Empress of India*
Gringco **174**
Gypsy see *Ella Ross*

- H -
H.S. Rock see *Alexander Leslie*
Hagarty & Crangle Line 55
Haileybury, Ont. 26
Hamilton, Ont. 19, 54
Hamilton Steamboat Company 84, 207, **209**, 223
Hamonic 222-223, 226-228, **227**, 230-233, **232**
Harbours, railway 18-26 (see also by individual name)
Harlem **31**
Harriet B. see *Shenango No. 2*
Harwood, Ont. 24, 129-132, 150
Helliopolis see *Royal George*
Henry Plumb 90, 95
Heron, Andrew 74
Heron, Captain Dick 74
Home Smith (Algorail, William S. Mack) 142, 145-146, **147**, 148
Howard M. Hanna Jr. (I) see *Agawa* (II)
Hunter 40
Huntsville, Ont. 25, 178, **185**
Huntsville & Lake of Bays Navigation Company 25, 178, **185**
Huntsville & Lake of Bays Railway 178, **185**
Huron **106**,107-108, 111
Huronic 218, **221**, 222-228, 230-231, 234, 248

- I -
Ida Burton 205
Incan Marine 168
Incan St. Laurent (George Alexandre Lebel) 168
Incan Superior 168
Inchcape Group 168
International (I) (BB & GR) 99-100
International (II) (BB & GR) 100, **101**
International (GTR) **105**, 107, 118, **119**, 121
International (CPC & PTC) see *South Eastern*
International Bridge (Fort Erie) 100, 107
Ionic see *Cuba*
Iron ore docks 129-132, 133, 135, 142, 146, 148-150
Iron ore trade 127-150, 151-152, 269
Ironsides **35**
Iroquois **138**
Isaac Butts 130-131
Islander King II see *Dalhousie City*

- J -
J.C. Morrison 202, 205
J. Frater Taylor (Algosoo, Saturn) 139, 142, **143**, 145-146, 148
J.M. Osborn 241
J.T. Hutchinson see *Alexander Leslie*
Jackson's Point, Ont. 25
James P. Walsh **174**
James R. Elliott see *Normac*
John Counter 88, 100
John Counter & Company 87-88
John B. Aird 148
John J. Barlum see *Algocen*
John Rolph see *Resolute*
Juliette 235
Jumbo 90, 93, 95

- K -
Kathleen see *City of London* (NSNC)
Kawartha Lakes Navigation Company 177, 180
Kearsarge 45, **49**
Keewatin **6**, **232**, 235, 250, **252**, 252-257, 259-260
Kenora, Ont. 26, 207, 209
Key Harbour, Ont. 22, 148, 169
Kincardine, Ont. 22, 213
King Edward 135, 139, **141**, 142
Kingston, Ont. 18, 87-88
Kingston (Algerian, Bavarian, Cornwall) **38**, 38-39
Kingston (II) 177, **179**

- L -
Lackawana Transportation Company 27, 218, 224
Lady Elgin 40, **41**
Lady of the Lakes see *Emily May*
Lake Erie & Detroit River Railway 107, 108-122, 154, 169, 198, 200-201
Lake Erie Navigation Company 200-201
Lake Erie Transportation Company 27
Lake Joseph Wharf, Ont. 25, 78
Lake Ontario & Bay of Quinte Steamboat Company 177, **180**
Lake Superior & Ishpeming Railroad 127
Lake Superior Corporation 133, 135, 139, 142
Lake Superior Line (U.S.) 35, 39-40
Lake Superior Royal Mail Line 210-211, 237, 240
Lake Superior Transit Company 245
Lakefield, Ont. 25, 177, **181**
Lakes:
- Erie 21, 151-163, 169, 233-234
- Huron 22, 24, 169, 207-256
- Kawartha 24-25, 177, 180-182, 192-195
- Michigan 24, 151, 152, 155, 161
- Muskoka 25, 178, 183-185
- Nipissing 205-207
- Ontario 18-19, 163-169, 177, 186-192, 233-234
- Rice 24, 129-131
- Simcoe 25, 202-205
- Superior 24, 168-169, 210-256
- of the Woods 207-209

Lakeside **68**, 69
Lakeside Navigation Company 69
Lansdowne 108, **110**, 111
Leafield 135, **136**, 139
Lehigh Valley Railroad 27, 29
Lehigh Valley Transportation Company

27
Letter B. see *Chicora*
Lewiston, New York 76, 84
Lillian see *Marquette & Bessemer No. 2* (II)
Lindsay, Ont. 25, 192, 195
Little Current, Ont. 22, 169, **175**
Lionel Parsons see *Agawa* (II)
London & Port Stanley Railway 155, 196, 198-200, 235 (see also Lake Erie & Detroit River Railway)
Lottie 235
Louis Phillippe 226
Lyon, Captain David H. 91, 93, 95

- M -
Macassa **83**
Macklem, Oliver T. 74
Magdalena 235
Magnet 256
Maitland No. 1 159-163, **160**, **162**
Maitland No. 2 (Ann Arbor No. 6, Arthur K. Atkinson) 161, **162**
Maitland No. 3 161
Majestic 16, 211, 218, 223, **224**, **225**
Manita **181**
Manitoba (NWTC) *(Carmona, Pittsburgh)* 213, **215**, 242
Manitoba (CPR) **244**, 246, **247**, 248, 252-255, 257, 259
Manitou 135
Manitou (DTC) 207, **208**
Manitou Island II 207
Manitoulin (NWTC) *(Atlantic* 211, 217, **218**, 244
Manitoulin (OSTC) *(Modjeska)* 207, **209**
Manitowoc 122, **123**
Maplebranch see *Cuba*
Marmora Iron Company 129
Marquette (II) see *Agawa* (II)
Marquette & Bessemer Dock & Navigation Company 151-158
Marquette & Bessemer No. 1 (Carrollton) 155, **156**, 158
Marquette & Bessemer No. 2 (I) 155, **157**
Marquette & Bessemer No. 2 (II) (Lillian) 155, 158, 161
Mattawa, Ont. 26, 206
Mattawan 235
Maude see *America* (DNC)
May Flower 29
May Queen 29
Meaford, Ont. 22, 211
Medora **183**
Merrit, William Hamilton 62-63
Meteor **206**
Michigan (GWR) 104, 108
Michigan (CPR) 116, **117**, 118
Michigan Central 108, 113, **114**, 116, **262**
Michigan Central Line 27-29
Michigan Central Railroad 27, 80, 102-104, 111-116, 118, 159
Michigan Southern Line 27
Michigan Southern Railroad 27
Michipicoten (Harbour), Ont. 24, 133-149, 169, **173**
Michipicoten see *City of Windsor*
Michipicoten (AC & HBR) 148
Midland, Ont. 22, 54, **55**, 135, **220**
Midland City see *America* (DNC)
Midland Railway of Canada 54-55
Milloy, Captain D. 77, 79
Milwaukee, Wisconsin 35, 255
Minneapolis, St. Paul & Buffalo Steamship Company 29
Minneapolis, St. Paul & Sault Ste. Marie Railroad 29
Minneapolis, Sault Ste. Marie & Atlantic Railway 245
Minnesota Iron Company 127
Minnesota Steamship Company 127
Minnie M. 135, **138**, 139
Mississippi (MCRR) **28**, 29
Mississippi see *Canada* (GWR)
Misty Maid 209
Misty Mist 209
Modjeska see *Manitoulin* (OSTC)
Monarch 213, 218-219, **221**
Monkshaven 135, **136**, 139
Mons Meg see *William Armstrong*
Montgomery 40
Moosonee, Ont. 207
Morning **202**
Morristown, New York 91, 93-94
Muskegon see *Shenango No. 2*
Muskoka **183**
Muskoka & Georgian Bay Navigation Company 178
Muskoka & Nipissing Navigation Company 178
Muskoka Lakes Navigation & Hotel Company 178, 183-184
Muskoka Wharf, Ont. 25, 178

- N -
Neebing **138**
Newona 46, **48**, 50
New York Central & Hudson River Railroad 27, 76, 79, 84, 91, 97, 159, 161
New York & Lake Erie Line 27
New York, Lake Erie & Western Railroad 27, 31
Niagara-on-the-Lake, Ont. 19, 68, 74-85
Niagara 40
Niagara (GWR) 102-103
Niagara Navigation Company 79-85, 223
Niagara, St. Catharines & Toronto Navigation Company 69-73
Niagara, St. Catharines & Toronto Railway 69-73
Nipigonian 209
Nipissing **183**
Nipissing Navigation Company 205
Norfolk & Western Railway 124
Norgoma 207
Norisle 207
Normac (James R. Elliott) 207
Norman 190, 193
Noronic 223, 226, 228, 230-234, **232**
Norseman (LO & BQSC) see *North King*
Norseman see *Enterprise* (WR)
North see *Campana*
North Bay, Ont. 26, 205
North King (Norseman) 177, **180**
North Lake **36**
North Land **32**
North Shore Navigation Company 213-214
North West Transportation Company 213-218, 235, 237, 240, 242, 245
Northern Belle (Gladys) 211, **212**
Northern Navigation Company 213, 218-234
Northern Railroad of New York 88-90
Northern Railway of Canada 39-43, 54, 202-205, 211, 240, 244
Northern Steamship Company 27, 32
Northumberland 69, **71**, **72**, 73
Nova Scotia 111, 217

- O -
Ocean 29
Ogdensburg, New York 88-98
Ogdensburg 97
Ogdensburg Railroad 88-90
Ogdensburg & Lake Champlain Railroad 88-90
Ogema 192, **194**, 195
Ongiara see *Queen City*
Ontario (1817) 13
Ontario (NWTC) 213, **216**
Ontario (CPR) 116, **117**, 118
Ontario & Quebec Railway 116, 237, 240, 256
Ontario Car Ferry Company 163-168
Ontario No. 1 164-166, **165**, 168
Ontario No. 2 164-166, **165**, 168
Ontario Northland Railway 205
Ontario Northland Transportation Commission 205-207
Ontario, Simcoe & Huron Railway see Northern Railway of Canada
Ontario Transportation Company 29, 32
Ontonagon 40
Orillia, Ont. 25
Ossifrage 135, 139, **140**, 142
Oswego, New York 40, 189
Oswego & Syracuse Railroad 40
Otonabee (I) 129-130
Otonabee (II) 130-131
Ottawa, Ont. 24, 235
Ottawa **44**, 45-46, **48**, **170**
Ottawa & Prescott Railway 89-90
Outing 90
Owego **31**

Owen Sound, Ont. 22, 52, 54, **44**, 207, 211, 235, **239**, **244** (see also Canadian Pacific Railway; Toronto, Grey & Bruce Railway)
Owen Sound Steamship Company 235, 237, 240, 256
Owen Sound Transportation Company 205, 207-209

- P -
Pacific 211, **212**
Package freight see Freight, package
Paliki 135, **137**, 139, 142, 145
Parry Sound, Ont. 22
Passengers, fares 202, 237, 245, 248
Passengers, trains 66, 73, 75-76, 80, 84, 91, 93, 125-126, 131, 164, 222-223, 228-229, 231, 233, 256-261
Passport **86**, **176**
Peerless 66, **74**, 75-76
Penetanguishene, Ont. 22, 54
Pennsylvania-Ontario Transportation Company 158-160
Pennsylvania Railroad 27, 158-159
Pere Marquette Railway 118-122, 152, 154-158, 201 (see also Flint & Pere Marquette Railroad; Lake Erie & Detroit River Railroad)
Pere Marquette 155, **157**
Pere Marquette 10 **120**, 121-122
Pere Marquette 12 **8**, **120**, 121-122
Pere Marquette 14 **117**, **119**, 121-122
Pere Marquette 16 see *Shenango No. 2*
Perseverance 64, **66**
Peterborough, Ont. 25
Peterborough & Lake Chemong Railway 25
Peterborough & Lake Simcoe Navigation Company 177, **182**
Philadelphia **30**
Pilgrim 192
Pittsburgh see *Manitoba* (NWTC)
Pittsburgh, Shenango & Lake Erie Railroad 151-152, 154
Ploughboy **12**, **41**
Plymouth Rocck 29
Point Edward (Sarnia), Ont. 21, 54, 104, 107-108, 150, 222
Point au Baril, Ont. 22
Pontiac **269**
Port Arthur (Thunder Bay), Ont. 3, 23-24, 52, **57**, 148, **174**, **227**, 235 (see also Canadian Pacific Railway, Northern Navigation Company)
Port Arthur & Duluth Steam Packet Company 246
Port Burwell, Ont. 21, 158-159, **160**
Port Colborne, Ont. 21, 54, 60
Port Dalhousie, Ont. 17, 19, **32**, 54
Port Dalhousie & Thorold Railway 62-63
Port Dover, Ont. 21, 152-154, **153**
Port Hope, Ont. 19, 54, 127, 177
Port Hope, Lindsay & Beaverton Railway 127, 129
Port Huron, Michigan 103-104, 118, 121-122
Port Maitland, Ont. 16, 21, 159-163, 169
Port McNicoll, Ont. 22, 52, **58**, 250, 252 (see also Canadian Pacific Railway)
Port Perry, Ont. 25, 192, **194**, 195
Port Stanley, Ont. 21, 154-156, 169, 196, 198
Prescott, Ont. 18, 54, 88-98, **92**, 169, 177
Prescott & Ogdensburg Ferry Company 95
Prescotont **96**, 97
Prince Edward Island 69
Purkis, Isaac D. 90

- Q -
Quebec 213, **216**
Quebec, Montreal, Ottawa & Occidental Railway 94
Queen City (Ongiara) 79, **81**, 84
Quinte (Beauharnois) 192

- R -
R.G. Casidy 124
R.H. Boughton 61
Racine see *Algoma* (LSRML)
Rathburn Company 186-192
Reindeer 192
Reliance 192-193
Rescue 192
Resolute 192, **193**
Richelieu & Ontario Navigation Company 84, 86, **92**, 94, 177, **179**, **187**, 223
Rivers:
Detroit 21, 100-126
Niagara 19, 21, 99-100
Ottawa 24, 186, 235
St. Clair 21, 100-126
St. Lawrence 18-19, 87-99, 168, 234
St. Mary's 16, 24
Trent 24, 129-131
Roanoke 124
Rochester, New York 163-168, 177, 179
Rochester 226
Rocket (Britannic) 218, **219**, 222
Rocket (DNC) 192
Rome & Watertown Railroad 87-88
Rose Point, Ont. 22
Rosedale **55**
Rothesay Castle (Southern Belle) 76, **78**, 79
Roy A. Jodrey 148
Royal Canadian Navy see *King Edward*
Royal Edward (Cairo) 196, **197**
Royal George (Helliopolis) 196, **197**
Royal Mail Line 38-39, **176**, 177

- S -
Sagamo **184**
Saginaw 103, **105**, 108
St. Catharines & Niagara Central Railway 69
St. Clair, Michigan 111, 116
St. Clair Tunnel Company 21, 107-111
St. Lawrence 88-90
St. Lawrence & Ottawa Railway 54, 90
St. Paul & Duluth Railroad 29, 215
Samuel Zimmerman **74**, 75-76
Sand Point, Ont. 24, 186
Sandusky 100
Sarnia, Ont. 21, 54, 103-104, 118, 121-122, 213, 222, **224**, **225** (see also Northern Navigation Company)
Sarnia **119**
Sarnia Tunnel see St. Clair Tunnel Company
Saronic see *United Empire*
Saturn see *J. Frater Taylor*
Sault Ste. Marie, Michigan 16, 242, 245 (see also Canadian Pacific Railway)
Sault Ste. Marie, Ont. 16, 133, 135, **172**, 207, 211, 213 (see also Canadian Pacific Railway; Northern Navigation Company)
Scotia II 111
Seagwun 178
Shedden & Company 54
Shenango No. 1 152-155, **153**, 198
Shenango No. 2 (Harriet B., Muskegon, Pere Marquette 16) 152, **153**
Ships:
builders 264-266
owners 263-264, 267-269
sail 11, 15
steam 11-15
Sir Denys Lowson 148
Siskiwit **172**, 235
Slesta 139
Smith & Mitchell 235-236
Soo Line Railroad 245
South Eastern (International) 94-95
South Eastern Railway 94
Southampton, Ont. 22, 213
Southern Belle see *Rothesay Castle*
Southerner 29
Sovereign 213
Sparrow Lake, Ont. 25
Spartan 256
State of New York 198, 200
State of Ohio 198, **200**
Star 88
Stoney Creek **181**
Stoney Creek Navigation Company 177, **181**
Strathcona **140**
Sunbeam (Alexandra, Arthur C.) **180**

- T -
Tadousac (Doric) 218, 223, **225**, 226
Temagami, Ont. 26
Temagami Navigation Company 205-206
Temiskaming Navigation Company 206
Temiskaming & Northern Ontario Rail-

way 205
Theano 135, **137**, 139
Thomas J. Barlum see *Algosteel*
Thomas J. Drummond 139, 142, **144**
Thousand Islands Railway 186, 192
Thunder Bay, Ont. see Fort William, Ont.; Port Arthur, Ont.
Toledo, St. Louis & Kansas City Railroad 27
Toronto, Ont. 19, **53**, 54, 195, 234
Toronto **179**
Toronto & Nipissing Railway 25
Toronto, Grey & Bruce Railway 237, 240, 244, 256
Toronto, Hamilton & Buffalo Navigation Company 159-163
Toronto, Hamilton & Buffalo Railway 159-163, 169
Traffic see Freight traffic
Trains, passenger see Passengers, trains
Transfer (I) 111, 113
Transfer (II) 113, **114**, 122
Transit (I) (GWR) 102-103
Transit (II) (GWR) 103, 108
Transit (CPC & PTC) 90, 93-95
Transit trade 27-59, 100
Transport **112**, 113, 116, 122
Trent River Bridge, Ont. 24, 129-131, 150
Trent Valley Navigation Company 177, **181**
Trenton, Ont. 19
Troy 100
Turret Chief **23**, **140**

- U -

Union 102, 108
Union Steamboat Company 27, 31
Union Transit Company 29
United Empire (Saronic, W.L. Kennedy) 213, 218, **219**, 222-223
United States & Ontario Steam Navigation Company 151-158
Urania (Flora) 198, **200**
Uranus see *W.C. Franz*
Utica & Black River Railroad 90-91, 93

- V -

V.W. Scully 148
Van Horne, William C. 234, 241, 245
Vandalia 13
Varuna **191**, 192
Vermont Central Railroad 88-90
Vessels see Ships
Victoria 192-195, **193**, **194**

- W -

W.C. Franz (Uranus) 139, 142, **143**, 145
W. Grant Morden **58**
W.J. Crosby **173**
W.J. Spicer 104, 107
W.J. Taylor 107, **109**
W.L. Kennedy see *United Empire*
Wabash Railroad 116, 122-124
Walker, Hiram 118
Walk-in-the-Water 13
Warrenko see *Chicora*
Washington 11, 13
Waubic **222**, 226, 229-230
Waubuno 213, **214**
Welland Canal 14-17, 26, 61-66
Welland Railway 54, 62-68, 75
Weller's Bay, Ont. 19, 148
Wenonah II **184**
Western Transit Company 27, 30-31
Western World (GWR) 33
Western World 9MCRR) **28**, 29
Whistle-Wing **128**, 131
Whitby, Ont. 19, 54, 192, 195
Whitby & Port Perry Extension Railway 192-195
Whitby & Port Perry Railway 25, 54, 192-195
Whitby, Port Perry & Lindsay Railway 195
Wiarton, Ont. 22
William Armstrong (Mons Meg) 91, **92**, 93-95
William S. Mack see *Home Smith*
Windsor, Ont. 21, 100-104, 107-111, 113-126, 213, 228, 246
Windsor (D & MR) 102
Windsor (Wabash RR) 122, **124**
Wisconsin Central Railroad 29
Wolfe Island, Kingston & Toronto Railway 87
Wolfe Island Railway & Canal Company 87-88

- Y -

York, Town of, U.C. see Toronto, Ont.
York 11

This north-looking view of the Sarnia waterfront dates from the winter of 1915 or 1916. The small, three-chimnied, station house can be seen just above the freight-house roof at the centre of the picture while several Northern Navigation steamers, including the *Huronic*, are tied up for the winter at the upper left. The general state of the dock suggests that it had already been superceded by the Point Edward facilities. *— OA Acc. 9912-5-10*